CARL VON CLAUSEWITZ

ON WAR

EDITED WITH AN INTRODUCTION

BY ANATOL RAPOPORT

AEONIAN PRESS, INC.

MATTITUCK

Vom Kriege published 1832
This translation published 1908

Reprinted by Special Arrangement

To the Reader

It is our pleasure to keep available uncommon fiction and to this end, at the time of publication, we have used the best available sources. To aid catalogers and collectors, this title is printed in an edition limited to 300 copies. ——— **Enjoy!**

International Standard Book Number 0-89190-376-3

To order contact
AEONIAN PRESS, INC.
PO Box 1200
Mattituck, New York 11952

Manufactured in the United States of America

PREFACE BY MARIE von CLAUSEWITZ TO THE POSTHUMOUS EDITION OF HER HUSBAND'S WORKS, including *On War*

Readers will be rightly surprised that a woman should dare to write a preface for such a work as this. My friends will need no explanation; but I hope that a simple account of the circumstances that caused me to take this step will remove any impression of presumptuousness in the minds of those who do not know me.

The work which these lines precede occupied my inexpressively beloved husband almost completely for the last twelve years of his life. His fatherland and I unfortunately lost him far too early. To complete his work was his dearest wish, but it was not his intention to communicate it to the world during his lifetime. When I would try to dissuade him from this decision, he often responded, half jokingly, but perhaps also with a presentiment of his early death: "*You* shall publish it." These words (which in happier days often caused me tears, even though I scarcely took them seriously) oblige me in the view of my friends to introduce the posthumous works of my beloved husband with a few lines. Even though readers may have differing opinions on this point, they will surely not misinterpret the emotion that has caused me to overcome the timidity which makes it so difficult for a woman to appear before the reading public even in the most subordinate manner.

It goes without saying that I have no intentionn whatever of regarding myself as the true editor of a work that is far beyond my intellectual horizon. Only as a sympathetic companion do I want to help its entry into the world. I may claim this role since I was granted a similar function in the creation and development of the work. Those who knew of our happy marriage and knew that we shared *everything,* not only joy and pain but also every occupation, every concern of daily life, will realize that a task of this kind could not occupy my beloved husband without at the same time becoming thoroughly familiar to me. For the same reason no one can testify as well as I to the energy and love with which he dedicated himself to the task, the hopes he associated with it, and the manner and time of its creation. From early youth his richly endowed mind had felt the need for light and truth, and while he was broadly educated, his reflections were directed primarily toward military affairs, which are of such great importance to the well-being of nations and which constituted his profession. Scharnhorst first showed him the right course; his appointment as teacher at the General War College, as well as the simultaneous honor of being chosen to introduce His Royal Highness the Crown Prince to the study of war, gave him additional reasons for directing his research and efforts toward these matters, as well as to set down his findings in writing. An essay with which he concluded the instruction of His Royal Highness the Crown Prince in 1812 already contains the seeds of his later works. But it was not until 1816, in Coblenz, that he again took up his scholarly work and began to gather the fruit that had ripened in the course of his rich experiences during four significant years of warfare. To begin with he developed his views in brief essays only loosely connected with each other. The following undated note, which was among his papers, seems to belong to that early stage:

> The statements set down here deal with what in my opinion are the major elements of strategy. I regarded them as early drafts, and had more or less reached the point of fusing them into a single work.

These drafts did not follow any preliminary plan. My original intention was to set down my conclusions on the principal elements of this topic in short, precise, compact statements, without concern for system or formal connection. The manner in which Montesquieu dealt with his subject was vaguely in my mind. I thought that such concise, aphoristic chapters, which at the outset I simply wanted to call kernels, would attract the intelligent reader by what they suggested as much as by what they expressed; in other words, I had an intelligent reader in mind, who was already familiar with the subject. But my nature, which always drives me to develop and systematize, at last asserted itself here as well. From the studies I wrote on various topics in order to gain a clear and complete understanding of them, I managed for a time to lift only the most important conclusions and thus concentrate their essence in smaller compass. But eventually my tendency completely ran away with me; I elaborated as much as I could, and of course now had in mind a reader who was not yet acquainted with the subject.

The more I wrote and surrendered to the spirit of analysis, the more I reverted to a systematic approach, and so one chapter after another was added.

In the end I intended to revise it all again, strengthen the casual connections in the earlier essays, perhaps in the later ones draw together several analyses into a single conclusion, and thus produce a reasonable whole, which would form a small volume in octavo. But here too, I wanted at all costs to avoid every commonplace, everything obvious that has been stated a hundred times and is generally believed. It was my ambition to write a book that would not be forgotten after two or three years, and that possibly might be picked up more than once by those who are interested in the subject.

In Coblenz, where he had many duties, he could devote only a few hours now and then to his private studies. Not until 1818 when he was appointed Director of the General War College in Berlin did he acquire enough time to expand his work, and further enrich it with the historical interpretation of the more recent wars. This new leisure also reconciled him to his assignment, which in other respects could not quite satisfy him, since under the present arrangements of the college its educational program is not the Director's responsibility but is guided by a separate commission of studies. Free as he was of any petty vanity, of restless egotism and ambition, he nevertheless felt the need to be truly useful, and not let his God-given abilities go to waste. In his professional life he did not occupy a position that could satisfy this need, and he had little hope that he would ever reach such a position. Consequently, all his efforts were directed toward the realm of scientific understanding, and the benefits that he hoped would result from his work became his purpose in life. If in spite of this he was ever more determined not to have his work published until after his death, it must be the best proof that no vain desire for praise and recognition, no trace of egotistic motive, mingled with this noble urge for great and lasting influence.

He continued to work intensively until the spring of 1830, when he was transferred to the artillery. His energies were not taken up for a different purpose, and to such an extent that at least for the moment he had to renounce all literary work. He arranged his papers, sealed and labeled the individual packages, and sadly bade farewell to an activity that had come to mean so much to him. In August of that year he was transferred to Breslau, where he was assigned to head the 2d Artillery Inspection; but already in December he was recalled to Berlin and appointed chief of staff to Field Marshal Count Gneisnau (for the duration of the latter's command [in the East]). In March 1831 he accompanied his admired commander-in-chief to Posen. When he returned to Breslau in November, having suffered the most painful loss [in Gneisenau's death], he was cheered by the hope of resuming his work, and possibly completing it in the course of the winter. God decided otherwise. He returned to Breslau on 7 November, on the sixteenth he died, and the packages that his hand had sealed were not opened until after his death!

These literary remains are published in the following volumes, exactly as they were found, without one word being added or deleted. Nevertheless their publication called for a good deal of work, arranging of material, and consultation, and I am profoundly grateful to several loyal friends for their assistance in these tasks. Above all I must name Major O'Etzel, who was kind enough to read the proofs and to draw the maps that will accompany the historical sections of the edition. I also take the liberty of mentioning my beloved brother, my support in times of trial, who rendered so many different services in preparing the manuscripts for publciaton. Among others, in the course of careful checking and sorting the material he found the beginnings of the revision that my beloved husband mentions as a future project in the *Note of 1827*. The revisions have been inserted in those parts of Book I for which they were intended (they did not go further).

I want to thank many other friends for their advice and for ther sympathy and affection they have shown me; though I cannot name them all, they will surely not doubt my warmest gratitude. This gratitude is the greater since I am firmly convinced that everything they have done was done not only for me but also for the friend whom God took from them so prematurely.

For twenty-one years I was profoundly happy at the side of *such* a man. Treaured memories, hopes, the rich inheritance of sympathy and friendship that I owe to the beloved departed, and the elevating sense that his rare distinction is so generally and nobly recognized sustain this happiness despite my irreplaceable loss.

The trust that led a noble prince and princess to call me to their side is a new favor for which I thank God.[1] It has given me a new and valued task, to which I dedicate myself gladly. May this task be blessed, and may the cherished little prince, who is presently entrusted to my care, someday read this book, and be inspired by it to deeds similar to the deeds of his glorious ancestors!

Written in the Marble Palace at Potsdam, 30 June 1832.

Marie von Clausewitz
Born Countess Brühl

First Lady in Waiting of
Her Royal Highness
Princess Wilhelm

[1]Marie von Clausewitz had been appointed Governess of Prince Frederich Wilhelm, who later became the Emperor Frederick III.

CONTENTS

ON WAR

BOOK ONE
ON THE NATURE OF WAR

BOOK TWO
ON THE THEORY OF WAR

CONTENTS

BOOK THREE

OF STRATEGY IN GENERAL

BOOK FOUR

THE COMBAT

CONTENTS

PREFACE

THE present abridged version of Clausewitz's *magnum opus* follows the text of the New and Revised Edition (edited by Col. F. N. Maude) of Col. J. J. Graham's translation. This edition first appeared in 1908 and has been reprinted several times, most recently in 1966 (New York: Barnes & Noble; London, Routledge & Kegan Paul.)

Of the original three volumes, the present version includes all of Volume I (except for the last short chapter on night fighting) and six of the nine chapters of Book Eight of Volume III ('The Plan of War'). The selections were guided by an intention to offer to the contemporary general reader and to the student of international relations those portions of *On War* which relate most directly to our own time. Clausewitz was concerned both with the role of war in human affairs and with the conduct of military operations. His thoughts on the former subject are a lasting contribution to the treasury of ideas and a source of insight into the terrible problems now confronting humanity. His exposition of technical matters is of interest mostly to the military scholar. For this reason the sections dealing with the philosophical, social, psychological, and political aspects of war have been largely retained, and those dealing with strategic and tactical matters (to which Volume II is almost totally devoted) have been largely omitted. By way of exception, Chapter XXVI of Book Five in Volume II ('Arming the Nation'), though omitted, deals with the important idea of the 'People's War', developed in the context of defence, and Books Three and Four of Volume I (retained here) deal with strategy and tactics. The omission of the above-mentioned chapter is partly compensated by the fact that similar ideas are developed in the material included; the inclusion of Books Three and Four was for the purpose of illustrating how Clausewitz throughout the work intersperses military–technical considerations with political ones, faithful to his main thesis which asserts that politics and war form an indivisible whole.

The reader interested in the historical framework of Clausewitz's ideas is referred to the Sixteenth German Edition, based on the original text and richly annotated by Werner Hahlweg (Bonn: Fred. Dümmlers Verlag, 1952). The reader interested in the works of Clausewitz and about Clausewitz is referred to the bibliographical survey of Peter Paret (*World Politics*, Vol. 17, January 1965).

The foreword and the annotations of the present volume reflect the editor's emphasis on the relevance of Clausewitz's thought and influence to present-day international affairs. However, the notes of Col. Maude have been for the most part retained. Written on the eve of the First World War, these notes present an interesting historical perspective.

Clausewitz's notes are so designated. Col. Maude's notes are followed by his initials. Notes followed by initials A.R. or no initials are the editor's.

I am indebted to Professors Karl W. Deutsch and J. David Singer for many helpful comments, criticisms, and suggestions; to Mrs Claire Adler for valuable editorial help, and to Miss Dorothy Williams for the preparation of the manuscript.

Ann Arbor, Michigan A.R.
22 June 1967

INTRODUCTION BY ANATOL RAPOPORT

1. Three Philosophies of War

THE chapter on Clausewitz in Walter Goerlitz's *History of the German General Staff* is entitled 'The Philosopher of War', as if to say that there is 'a' philosophy of war, of which Clausewitz was the author or the discoverer, or, at least, the most important proponent. In the Middle Ages Aristotle was called simply The Philosopher, somewhat in the same spirit.

We now know that there are several philosophies and that Aristotle was the proponent of only one of them, albeit a very important one. Similarly, if we take stock of what has been written on war before and after Clausewitz, we see that several philosophies of war have emerged. Clausewitz was the proponent of one of them, a very important one.

The philosophy of war reflected in the present volume has had a profound influence on European military and political thought in the nineteenth century. Because of this influence, and because the philosophy was formulated with extraordinary clarity, *On War* is justly called a classic, along with other such works, each an exposition of an important philosophy. Examples are Francis Bacon's *Novum Organum* (a philosophy of science), Machiavelli's *The Prince* (a philosophy of politics), Hobbes's *Leviathan* (a philosophy of society), Hume's *Inquiry into Human Understanding* (a philosophy of knowledge), Adam Smith's *Wealth of Nations* (a philosophy of economics), Marx's *Capital* (a philosophy of both economics and society). In all these works the authors sought to impart not merely knowledge of what they thought to be the case, but also an understanding of what underlies it; that is, an understanding of a philosophy.

To understand a philosophy may mean two different things. In one sense, to understand a philosophy may mean to compare it with one's own view of the subject matter and, on the basis of such comparison, to accept or reject the philosophy in whole or in part. In another, deeper sense, to understand a philosophy means to see its logical structure, that is, the way its concepts and ideas relate to each other and how they are derived from other concepts or ideas. In order to understand a philosophy in the latter sense it is often necessary to compare it with other philosophies. A similar situation exists with regard to understanding a language. One can understand a language directly, that is, with reference to experience. A three-year-old child already understands his mother tongue in this sense. In another sense, to understand a language means to see how it is put together; that is the way a linguist perceives it. To understand the structure of a language it usually helps to compare it with other languages in order to see both the similarities and the differences among structures. With a view of emphasizing the deeper meaning of Clausewitz's philosophy, we shall compare it with other philosophies.

It is important to compare several philosophies of war for still another reason. The problem of war is universally recognized as one of the most awesome problems with which the human race is presently confronted. To deal with this problem we must understand the nature of war. If different philosophies give different answers to the question 'What is war?' we are faced with the problem of resolving the differences. One way is to accept one answer and reject the others. Another way, more sophisticated, is to conclude that war has many facets, and that the various philosophies of war merely reflect the fact that different thinkers have singled out different facets for attention.

There is still a third way of viewing these different conceptions of the nature of war: the nature of war is itself to a large extent determined by how man conceives of it. It is a common peculiarity of man-made phenomena that, unlike natural phenomena, they are influenced (sometimes very strongly) by what we think or say about them. Thus the answer to the all-important questions (no longer philosophical ones) of whether civilization will be destroyed by a global war, or whether war will persist as a chronic or recurring condition in human affairs, or whether war will be eradicated, may depend in no small measure on how people think, talk, and write about war, i.e. on which philosophies of war prevail. We would be well advised to inquire into the way the acceptance or rejection of a particular philosophy of war is likely to influence the role of war in human affairs and so profoundly affect our lives.

The three philosophies of war to be compared we shall call the *political*, the *eschatological*, and the *cataclysmic*. Clausewitz is an outstanding proponent of the political philosophy of war. (An earlier exposition was given by Machiavelli, and we shall be concerned also with its very recent 'Neo-Clausewitzian' version.)

*

Clausewitz views war as a rational instrument of national policy. The three words 'rational', 'instrument', and 'national' are the key concepts of his paradigm. In this view, the decision to wage war 'ought' to be rational, in the sense that it ought to be based on estimated costs and gains of the war. Next, war 'ought' to be instrumental, in the sense that it ought to be waged in order to achieve some goal, never for its own sake; and also in the sense that strategy and tactics ought to be directed towards just one end, namely towards victory. Finally, war 'ought' to be national, in the sense that its objective should be to advance the interests of a national state and that the entire effort of the nation ought to be mobilized in the service of the military objective.

We have paraphrased Clausewitz's philosophy in terms of what, according to its precepts, war *ought* to be. Actually, Clausewitz says what war *is*. At the same time he is well aware that actual decisions to wage war or to avoid it were often made without due considerations of relevant circumstances; that strategies and tactics were often determined by matters irrelevant to the objectives of war; and that, until his own time, wars had not been national wars. Thus the discrepancy between what Clausewitz says war is, and what many wars actually were, is not to be ascribed to ignorance of facts. Tradition, rooted in the ideas of the ancients and continuing throughout the centuries of European thought, ascribed to philosophy the task of discovering the essences of phenomena. Whether the essence was in the origin of the phenomenon in question (as Plato thought) or became manifest in the unfolding of the phenomenon (as Aristotle thought), *it* (the essence), rather than the accidental and variable realizations of the phenomenon, was traditionally assumed to be the proper subject of a philosophical investigation. Therefore, for Clausewitz, the difference between 'what is' and 'what ought to be' was not as sharp as it may appear in our more empirically oriented age. In depicting war as rational, instrumental, and national, Clausewitz thought that he was revealing the 'true nature' of war, stripped of non-essentials with which it may have been encumbered in particular historical contexts.

The explicit distinction between what war is and what it 'ought' to be is drawn by Clausewitz on another level of abstraction. His 'ought' must be understood at the outset in its logical, not its prescriptive sense.[1] Clausewitz starts out by defining war: *War is an act of violence intended to compel our opponent to fulfil our will.* From this definition it follows *logically* (according to Clausewitz) that every war ought to end in a complete victory of one side over the other, and also that 'moderation in war is an absurdity' since failure to utilize all the force at one's disposal defeats the purpose of war. War conceived in this way Clausewitz calls 'war in the abstract' or 'absolute war'. (Its relation to 'total war', of which we had a foretaste in our century, will be discussed below.)

Real wars differ from abstract war, says Clausewitz, because idealized conditions are never realized. Mobilization of forces is not instantaneous; events are governed not only by strict causality but also by chance; psychological factors are important determinants of decisions made by men, etc. Clausewitz subsumes all these perturbing circumstances under the concept of 'friction', an obvious allusion to the analogous concept in physics, which is invoked to explain the discrepancy between real and idealized mechanical processes.

It therefore seemed to Clausewitz that having taken 'friction' into account, he has grasped the 'true nature' of real war and so made the connexion between theory and experience. From the vantage point of a *comparative* philosophy of war, however, we can see that even Clausewitz's 'realistic' theory is only one of several possible idealized abstractions. It rests on a fundamental assumption, namely, that the *actor* in a real war is a perfectly defined entity called the State. This assumption is not made in other philosophies of war; consequently war appears in each of them in an entirely different light.

*

The eschatological philosophy of war comprises many variants. The common element in them is the idea that history, or at least some portion of history, will culminate in a 'final' war leading to the unfolding of some grand design – divine, natural, or human. Two main variants are to be noted. In one – the messianic – the agency destined to carry out the 'grand design' is presumed already to exist, frequently as a functioning military organization. For example, in this view, crusades and holy wars are seen as means of unifying the known world under a single faith or a single ruler. In recent times the American doctrine of Manifest Destiny and the Nazi doctrine of the Master Race were expressions of a messianic philosophy of war. In some versions the victors are assumed to be destined to carry out the mission of imposing a just peace on the world and so of eliminating war from future history. For example, most Americans believed that their entry into the First World War (and later the Second World War) would convert the war into a 'war to end war'.

In another, 'global', variant of eschatological philosophy the agency of the 'design' is presumed to arise from the chaos of the 'final war'. In Christian eschatology this agency is sometimes represented by the forces which will rally around Christ in the Second Coming; in Communist eschatology the 'world proletariat' is expected to convert the imperialist war into a class war and, after the victory over the bourgeoisie, to establish a world order in which wars will no longer occur. In a film made in the 1930s called *Things to Come*, based on the ideas of H. G. Wells, this role is given to a community of scientists who stop the 'final' world war by a tranquillizing gas and establish a temporary benevolent dictatorship which ushers in a rational and peaceful world order.

*

The cataclysmic view pictures war as a catastrophe that befalls some portion of humanity or the entire human race. The prophets, for example, who spoke of war as a scourge of God, subscribed to this view. Cataclysmic philosophy, like the eschatological, also appears in two variants, the ethnocentric and the global. In the ethnocentric version, war is something that is likely to happen to *us*, specifically something that *others* threaten to do to us. We see ourselves as deriving no benefit from war. Our own defensive measures appear to us not as means of pursuing goals but merely as means of forestalling disaster or alleviating its effects. (The necessity for contemporary civil defence measures – blast and fall-out shelters, etc. – is usually justified by its proponents on the basis of an ethnocentric–cataclysmic view of war.)

In the global version, on the other hand, war is a cataclysm which afflicts *humanity*. No one in particular is held to be responsible for war and no one is expected to gain from it. A philosophy of war of this sort is explicitly stated in the concluding chapter of Tolstoy's *War and Peace*. Tolstoy attributes wars to the action of hitherto unknown historical forces and declares the decisions of princes and the manoeuvres of generals to be irrelevant to either the outbreaks or the outcomes of wars. Tolstoy's philosophy of war is thus the polar opposite of Clausewitz's.

A cataclysmic philosophy of war underlies also some recent attempts to formulate scientific theories of war. In such theories war is usually regarded as related to certain dynamic properties of an 'international system' which, like physical systems, may persist at times in a relatively stable equilibrium and at other times 'break down' or 'explode', because the stresses and strains within the system have passed beyond certain critical limits.

To put it metaphorically, in political philosophy war is compared to a game of strategy (like chess); in eschatological philosophy, to a mission or the dénouement of a drama; in cataclysmic philosophy, to a fire or an epidemic.

These do not, of course, exhaust the views of war prevailing at different times and at different places. For example, war has at times been viewed as a pastime or an adventure, as the only proper occupation of a nobleman, as an affair of honour (e.g. in the days of chivalry), as a ceremony (e.g. among the Aztecs), as an outlet of aggressive instincts or a manifestation of a 'death wish', as nature's way of insuring the survival of the fittest, as an absurdity (e.g. among the Eskimos), as a tenacious custom, destined to die out like slavery, and as a crime.

2. *The Clausewitzian Century*

Vom Kriege first appeared in 1832, in the year following Clausewitz's death. Clausewitz entered military service in 1792 at the age of twelve. According to Maria von Clausewitz (the widow), who wrote the preface to the first edition, Clausewitz began work on *Vom Kriege* in 1816. Thus his entire life from the end of childhood to the beginning of work on his *magnum opus* coincided almost exactly with the era of Revolutionary and Napoleonic wars. The intellectual stature of Clausewitz is manifest in the clarity with which he saw this period as a transition between two historical epochs. On one side was the European international system of 1648–1789, which Clausewitz saw in a remarkably illuminating historical perspective. On the other side was the European international system of 1815–1914, of which Clausewitz became the prophet. Like Beethoven, Clausewitz stood astride two centuries. Building upon the fundamental concepts of the eighteenth, he laid the foundations of the conceptual edifice which dominated the nineteenth.

The actors in the Clausewitzian paradigm of international relations are, as has been said, sovereign states which for all practical purposes can be considered as persons. This paradigm (which today is recognized by many political scientists to be a highly abstract idealization) was a moderately realistic model of the international system which Clausewitz knew best, namely the European system prevailing in the century which ended with the French Revolution. Decisions to wage war and to conclude peace were made by sovereigns, whose staffs may have advised them on the expected costs and gains. These were estimated in terms of the *sovereign's* interests and ambitions;

and the latter were stated fairly simply in terms of territorial gains and losses, alliances honoured or broken, rises or falls in prestige, etc., all measured by standards which were rather uniform among the 'society' of sovereigns. In other words, the eighteenth-century sovereign had about as clear a notion of his 'interests' as an owner or a manager of a middle-sized business has nowadays about the interests of his firm.

The world, then, which Clausewitz saw through the prism of history, was a 'society' of sovereign states, say ten or twenty, each headed by a prince with a set of 'interests'. The prince pursued these interests by various methods which were by and large accepted by his peers as legitimate; for the peers, too, pursued their interests in a similar fashion. The eighteenth-century methods included bargaining and coalition formation (by means of intricate diplomacy and intrigue); marriage strategies (important because territories might go with dowries and could be enlarged by matrimonial mergers, and because the legitimacy of succession was based primarily on geneological lines); and war.

This international system had been functioning since 1648. The Treaty of Westphalia marked the end of the previous epoch dominated by the religious wars initiated by the Reformation. Central Europe had been devastated by the last (Thirty Years') war of that epoch, and the issue between the hegemony of the Roman Catholic Church in Central Europe and Protestant decentralization of religious authority remained unsettled. However, aside from the ambiguity of that outcome at the close of the Thirty Years' War, the idea of the sovereign state under secular authority was firmly established in European political thought. Concurrently, the notion of supra-national authority, which had dominated the Middle Ages, receded into obscurity. For a century and a half no one undertook to bring Europe or even any larger portion of it under a single authority, religious or secular. The princes circumscribed the horizons of their ambitions and looked only towards modest opportunistic objectives. If an occasion arose which promised an increase of holdings, influence, or prestige, they seized it. Otherwise they made the opportunities or waited for them to arise.

The wars of this period were limited in scope and were fought for limited objectives. Not the least important cause of this restraint was the character of the eighteenth-century army. Composed largely of highly trained professionals recruited for long periods of service, the eighteenth-century army was an expensive tool. If it were destroyed it could not be easily replaced. Understandably the princes were reluctant to risk large losses of personnel. The generals, too, had little to gain and much to lose from serious fighting. They were specialists with no internalized permanent loyalty to their sovereigns except to the extent that such loyalty was demanded by the ethics of their profession. Frequently generals left the service of one prince to join that of another, regardless of their nationalities, much in the manner of modern executives and attorneys who serve now one corporation, now another. Since all the generals were in that position, it is not unreasonable to suppose that a tacit understanding among them developed, so that campaigns were conducted with a view of minimizing dangers and even discomfort.[2]

Pitched battles were generally avoided in the pre-Napoleonic era. The object of the campaign frequently was to reach a situation (by proper manoeuvring) in which it could become clear that one's own side had a strategic or tactical advantage over the other. Because of a universal acceptance of strategic and tactical principles by the homogeneous military community, such situations were sufficiently clear to all concerned. Hence a 'decision' could be awarded to one side or the other, or the situation might be seen as a 'draw'. Capitulation was not a disgrace. A general could no more entertain the idea of 'fighting to the last man' than a good chess player would consider continuing to play an obviously lost game.

The 'art of war', as it was conceived in the eighteenth century, was largely an art of manoeuvre. It contained important elements of aesthetics and protocol. An army was judged by its appearance on the battlefield as much as by its skill and prowess. To be sure, some of the 'aesthetic' requirements could be defended on pragmatic grounds. The effectiveness of a fighting unit certainly depends on the coordination of its parts. This is especially true if the parts are to move in response to commands given by voice. Such commands can be effective only if the soldiers remain packed close together, whether they are standing or moving. Consequently, intensive training in close-order drill (which makes for attractive parade manoeuvres) also made sense as a preparation for the eighteenth-century battlefield. The one and only soldierly virtue demanded of the man in the ranks was obedience. Indeed, not much more could be demanded of him, since he had no stake in the outcome of the war, nor even any idea of the objectives of a campaign or of a battle.[3] His 'skill' was the ability to execute automatically each of a repertoire of movements in which he had been trained. The skill of an officer was like that of a conductor of an orchestra – to co-ordinate the movements of a unit of a specified size (depending on his rank), as required by the 'well-known' principles of tactics. The distinction between a well-executed battle and a well-executed parade (or, for that matter, a ballet) was not sharp in the eighteenth century.

This conception of war was challenged in the last decade of the century. In the wars of the French Revolution and in the Napoleonic wars armies took to the field and manoeuvred just as they did in the eighteenth century. But the meaning of these events changed. Failure to realize the change was costly to the opponents of France.

The revolutionary French Army was composed not of professionals, nor of conscripts who had neither a stake nor an understanding of the war they fought, but of 'patriots' – a new concept in European politics. These people believed t hat they were fighting *for* something. At first the wars were fought in defence of the Revolution against the onslaughts of the monarchical powers who sought to crush it. Soon the French passed over to the offensive. Many of them felt that they were carrying the Rights-of-Man on the points of their bayonets across Europe. Their spectacular successes kept their martial elan at a high pitch, and it eventually was carried over into the imperial Grand Armée. Revolutionary ardour was supplanted by the adoration of Napoleon Bonaparte. At any rate, whether the French fought for the Revolution or for France, for liberty or for an empire, the high-pitched morale of the French soldier was an entirely new factor in the war.

Napoleon understood the tremendous importance of this new factor. He nurtured and intensified the enthusiasm of the man in the ranks by dramatic speeches and by postures of solicitude. He was thus enabled to make use of tactics unthinkable in the context of eighteenth-century battle dispositions, in which the initiative of the individual soldier played no role. Having the entire economic and human resources of France behind him, he was not concerned with costs or personnel losses. He used murderous artillery fire. His objective in a battle was nor merely to outmanoeuvre but to annihilate the opposing force. Above all, he demolished the eighteenth-century tradition by destroying old *political* structures. He redrew the map of Europe to suit his ends and placed his relatives on thrones with no more thought to 'legitimacy' than if they were so many police commissioners. In this way, devoid of a shred of dynastic legitimacy himself, he made shambles of dynastic politics which had been the backbone of eighteenth-century international relations. At his coronation he symbolized the demise of both dynastic legitimacy and of the Holy Roman Empire by taking the crown from the hands of Pius VII and placing it on his own head.[4]

By deeds and words (Napoleon had an impressive gift of eloquence), Napoleon taught one great lesson: the universal currency of politics is power, and power resides in the ability to wreak physical destruction. Clausewitz embodied this lesson in unifying a philosophy of politics with a philosophy of war. What Napoleon expressed in cannonades and aphorisms, Clausewitz presented as a coherent system of thought, remarkably lucid and unencumbered by the ponderous metaphysical speculations which his professorial contemporaries took to be an essential mark of profundity and erudition.

Clausewitz was able to grasp the full significance of the lessons taught by Napoleon, because his was a military mind and an open one. A military mind is one which embraces war as an essential, productive, and inspiring component of human existence, quite in the same way as a scientific mind embraces science, an artistic mind embraces art, and a religious mind embraces religion. One is tempted to say that for a military mind war needs no justification (in terms of extraneous goals) any more than art or science need such justification for the artist or scientist. However, this is not always the case. Not every artist espouses 'art for art's sake' (though many do), and many outstanding scientists have derived inspiration from other than the purely cognitive functions of science. In his constant emphasis on war as an instrument of politics, Clausewitz expressly rejected the idea of 'war for war's sake'. However, if we examine Clausewitz's conception of politics, we find that it does not differ from his conception of war. His famous dictum stated in reverse would express his philosophy with equal accuracy: 'Peace is the continuation of struggle only by other means'.[5] Thus the rejection of 'war for war's sake' is no more than a recognition that war has two equally important components, the military and the political. In quite the same way a scientist dismisses 'theory for theory's sake' or 'experiment for experiment's sake'. Each must justify the other. Science is the fusion of the two.

In this extended sense, i.e. the combination of the military and political aspects, war (that is, a struggle for power) needed no further justification in Clausewitz's mind. He assumed it to be a fundamental condition of human existence. Incidentally, he also thought of war as a prerequisite of his personal happiness. In a letter to his fiancée, Countess von Brühl, we read:

> My fatherland needs the war and – frankly speaking – only war can bring me to the happy goal. In whichever way I might like to relate my life to the rest of the world, my way takes me always across a great battlefield; unless I enter upon it, no permanent happiness can be mine.[6]

Clausewitz's open mind was no less important in facilitating his acceptance of the lessons derived from the Napoleonic wars. Despite Clausewitz's modest disclaimers of competence in philosophy, he was actually a very able philosopher. He grasped the relationship of the idealized model to the reality it purports to represent; he understood the continual interaction between theory and practice in the development of a science, the vast complexity of causal relations in human affairs, the dilemma posed by the role of genius in the unfolding of the historical process. Above all, he despised dogmatism[7] and at the same time realized the importance for productive thought of abstract conceptual schemes. In short, Clausewitz thought like a philosopher–scientist in the broadest sense of this term: he sought simplicity and he distrusted it.

'Everything is very simple in war,' he wrote, 'but the simplest thing is difficult.'

When Napoleon broke the 'rules of civilized warfare', Clausewitz hailed him as a genius, not only because Napoleon exposed the sterility of eighteenth-century formalized military dogmas but also because he revealed (as Clausewitz thought) the *essential* principles of war and at the same time demonstrated the importance of intangibles (morale, intuitive grasp of the total situation, chance), so that war appeared as an amalgam of a science and an art. This is indeed how science as a whole (as distinguished from special sciences) appears to a scientist with a broad outlook: not as a code of standardized procedures but as a creative process.

A lesson is learned most firmly when the application of what has been learned turns failure into success. The failure, in Clausewitz's estimation, was the humiliating defeat suffered by Prussia in 1806. He attributes this failure to Prussia's adherence to eighteenth-century methods of warfare against an opponent emancipated from the limitations of those methods. The success, as Clausewitz saw it, was the resurgence of Prussia as a military power and the victory over Napoleon in 1813–15. Clausewitz attributes this resurgence to the replacement of the small professional (eighteenth-century model) army by a mass (citizen) army; that is, by recourse to the weapon with which France dominated Europe for almost two decades. In other words, Prussia achieved full nationhood by accepting the principle of the national war.

The power of Clausewitz's ideas derives (somewhat ironically, in view of their later social meaning) from their consistency with the new political climate engendered in Europe by the

French Revolution. In urging the replacement of cabinet wars by national wars, Clausewitz was saying in effect, 'Give the War to the People! The State is the People!' The task of completely 'democratizing' war was to be carried out a century later by the Nazis.

The change in outlook did not come easily. Opposition came from both military and political sources. Career soldiers often resist innovations, because innovations tend to make their special competence obsolete and to sharpen competition. Political opposition came from those who feared an armed citizenry more than they feared foreign invasions. A peasant with a gun may get ideas about his own place in society. In fact, the most energetic proponents of the mass army were the liberals who envisaged far-reaching social reforms as prerequisites of strengthening the nation. Such reforms were actually initiated in 1807 and continued until Napoleon's defeat.[8] The danger having passed, the reins of absolute rule were re-tightened. Nevertheless, the mass army came to stay and to dominate the European international system for the next hundred years.

Clausewitz himself was politically conservative and was probably aware of the potential danger which a mass army presented to absolutism. Nevertheless he favoured it, because foremost in his mind was the concept of the monolithic militarized national state, ready and willing at all times to exert its national will by a total mobilization of its destructive power.

As has been said, if Clausewitz's conception of the relation between war and politics is examined with reference to the ends and means of each, it appears that the two are interchangeable. The function of the military is to implement the will of the state; the will of the state is tacitly assumed to be directed towards continually increasing its power *vis-à-vis* other states, hence to seek and seize opportunities to gain strategic advantages for future struggles. In short, the interests of the state and of the army coincide in Clausewitz's conception of the state. Nevertheless, in his philosophy of war Clausewitz gives priority to civilian authority over the military. The military is supposed to serve the state, not vice versa. The reason for this distinction in Clausewitz's mind is his estimate of the perspectives open to the military and to the civilian leadership respectively. The military leader is a specialist. His horizon may not stretch beyond what appears as necessary for carrying out military tasks. The statesman (or monarch) encompasses the whole gamut of power relations, both political and military. In this way the statesman appears in Clausewitz's paradigm as a super-general who must possess the final authority over the general, in the same way as the general (who views the war as a whole) must possess supreme authority over his colonels and captains (who see only portions of the war).

In nineteenth-century Europe the relations between civilian and military authority were much more complex than the simple hierarchical structure envisaged by Clausewitz. However, the international system did gradually assume the form envisaged by him.

The nineteenth century was dominated by an unprecedented rise of science and technology and with it the emergence of a new dominant social class, the bourgeoisie, which derived its wealth, prestige, and eventually political power from being directly associated with the sciences and with technology and its by-products (industrialization, expanded trade, education, etc.). In the early nineteenth century the bourgeoisie was not primarily interested in war. It was not averse to wars, provided they did not cost too much and brought in profits (e.g. colonial conquests). But the bourgeoisie had no professional stake in war and did not relish the idea of donating their sons to fight for the glory of the state at a time when the nobility was still very much in evidence and largely in control of the military establishments. Consequently, in spite of the fact that the mass (conscripted) army remained as a fixture in Europe after the Napoleonic wars, the military profession continued as a special-interest group. The concerns of the military, like those of any professional group, were with promotions, social prestige, self-esteem, etc. Particularly in Prussia, the military remained the profession of the nobility. Hence professional and class interests coincided in that group.[9]

In the first decades after the Napoleonic wars the bourgeoisie, being engrossed in peaceful and profitable pursuits, was not favourably disposed towards the military. After the suppression of the revolutions of 1848–9, however, the military appeared to them in a more favourable light, namely as a bulwark against the ever growing threat of revolution.[10] At the same time the middle classes became more interested in commercial and political goals, such as national sea-ports, canals, trade privileges, and prestige, which could be attained and kept only with the help of the military.

Militarization of the national state progressed especially rapidly in Prussia, and with it the crystallization of the Clausewitzian model of the national state. Bismarck, the greatest of the Junkers, was keen enough to perceive that concessions to liberalism were one sure way to consolidate nationalist sentiments. The other sure way was to win easy military victories. These were reaped in the short decisive wars against Denmark (1864), Austria (1866), and France (1870). With the establishment of the German Empire in 1871 the Clausewitzian state almost became a reality in the shape of imperial Germany.

Of all Europeans, the Germans learned best the Clausewitzian prescripts (this time from victories), namely that boldness, an integrated diplo-military policy, a campaign strategy aimed directly towards the destruction of the opposing forces, an army based on mass conscription – that all of these spell power; and that the fruits of power used at the right moment against the right adversary bring more power.

France, too, learned – this time from her defeat. After crushing the short-lived Paris Commune and consolidating its political power, the French bourgeoisie, like the German, entered on the road to militarization. Defeated by a mass army, France staked her future on a mass army. The goal was *revanche*. About that time Clausewitz was discovered by the French military and was avidly read and quoted by the officers. It is interesting to note, however, that the French were most attracted to Clausewitz's emphasis on the 'spiritual' rather than the material components of military might. In view of France's inferiority in men and material *vis-à-vis* Germany, this was understandable. The offensive (pictured as an irresistible shock of a massed attack) became the French military dogma. We now know the price paid for this confidence, in the vast French losses in the battles of Verdun and at the river Somme in the First World War. It is difficult for us, who have seen the 'martial spirit' replaced by the mechanized juggernaut, to believe that even the famous red pantaloons of the French infantry were not discarded for something more modest and less conspicuous until the First World War was well under way.

The British, too, learned. As the showdown with Germany approached, the British military bemoaned what they thought was a naïve reliance on the efficacy of international law and the inhibitions placed on the military caste by certain notions of gentlemanly conduct. Paraphrasing Clausewitz's democratization of war in terms easily understood in a commercial culture, Col. F. N. Maude wrote in 1908:

> Most of our present-day politicians have made their money in business – a 'form of human competition greatly resembling war', to paraphrase Clausewitz. Did they, when in the throes of such competition, send formal notice to their rivals of their plans to get the better of them in commerce? Did Mr Carnegie, the archpriest of Peace at any price, when he built up the Steel Trust, notify his competitors when and how he proposed to strike the blows, which successively made him master of millions? Surely the Directors of a Great Nation may consider the interests of their shareholders – i.e. the people they govern – as sufficiently serious not to be endangered by the deliberate sacrifice of the preponderant position of readiness which generations of self-devotion, patriotism and wise forethought have won for them?[11]

*

The century 1815–1914 is conventionally (and at times nostalgically) pictured as a century of comparative peace, stability, and progress in Europe. Another way of seeing it, grimmer but perhaps more instructive, is as an incubation period. There have been other such periods. The pre-Napoleonic era (1648–1789), because of the comparatively limited magnitude of the wars, also appeared to be a stable period. But this era too was pregnant with the seed of its own destruction, which blossomed in the French Revolution. Several centuries earlier there was a quiescent era in Italy, when the wars between the mercantile city states (fought entirely by mercenaries) were almost totally bloodless. Machiavelli mentions, as an example, the battle of Zagonara (1424), a 'defeat renowned throughout all Italy [in which] there died only Lodovico degli Obizzi, with two of his men-at-arms, who falling from horseback, were smothered in the mire'.[12]

That era ended when the French invaded Italy in 1494 and made short work of the 'system', much in the same way as Napoleon did exactly three centuries later. A few years after the French invasion Machiavelli was expounding the same 'lessons' that Clausewitz was to expound three centuries later.[13] Machiavelli denounced the mercenaries, criticized harshly the hesitant and ineffectual methods of Italian warfare, and demanded the inoculation of the soldiers with the spirit of pugnacity, self-sacrifice, discipline, and loyalty to their land of birth.

A similar reaction followed the end of the League of Nations era, to which the Nazi *Blitzkrieg* put an end. Again the 'lesson' learned was put in an almost exact paraphrase of Clausewitz. Edward Mead Earle of the United States wrote in 1943:

> Strategy . . . is not merely a concept of wartime, but is an inherent element of statecraft at all times. . . . In the present day world, then, strategy is the art of controlling and utilizing the resources of a nation – or a coalition of nations – including its armed forces, to the end that its vital interests shall be effectively promoted and secured against enemies, actual, potential, or merely presumed. . . . The very existence of a nation depends upon its concept of the national interest and the means by which the national interest is promoted; therefore it is imperative that the citizens understand the fundamentals of strategy. We do not have and do not wish to have a military class to whom these matters will be delegated with plenary powers. Our armed forces, including our officer corps, are recruited on a democratic basis. This is as it should be, since there is only one safe repository of the national security of democratic state: the whole people.[14]

It is, of course, impossible to defend the thesis that Clausewitz set once and for all the direction to be followed by the diplo-military history of Europe. Clausewitz merely gave clarity to ideas and tendencies which were already shaping up.

In this respect Clausewitz was more a prophet than an innovator. In particular, Clausewitz's concept of 'absolute war' (the sort which, in his opinion, would be the rule if it were not for 'friction', i.e. limitations of time, space, chance, and human frailty) began to turn into reality in 1914. Battles then became massacres which transcended Napoleon's boldest dreams. The formidable bloodiness of the First World War can be ascribed to many causes: the murderous technology; the magnitude of the engagements; the replacement of the war of movement (in which disengagement was possible) by trench warfare, in which opposing masses were locked in a firm grip. Victory always seemed within grasp if only a sufficient mass could be hurled against the positions of the enemy to achieve a breakthrough, as for example, in the five-month battle of Verdun. Actually the decisive victories of the Germans on the Eastern Front in the first months of the First World War were the last such to occur in that war. Thereafter the war, although approaching the Clausewitzian 'absolute war', lost a vital ingredient of the Clausewitzian model – decisiveness. There was no decision. The nations were bled white.

3. A Temporary Eclipse of Clausewitzian Philosophy

In the paroxysms of the revolutions that followed the First World War the Clausewitzian conception of the state as the *ultima ratio*, the keystone of the political philosophy of war, suffered irreparable damage. Thereafter all war had to be justified by other than 'reasons of state'. As is known, such justifications were not lacking in the half-century to follow; but the conception of war as a *normal and perpetual* state of affairs (assuming all politics to be a variant of war) was never again to dominate political thought as completely as it did in Europe in the era 1648–1914, which spawned Clausewitz and learned from him.

After the First World War, the eschatological and the cataclysmic philosophies of war were in ascendance. Embittered public opinion was quick to ascribe the disaster of 1914 to the plottings in the chancelleries, to German militarism, to French revanchism, to British imperialism, to the munitions cartels, etc. There was a fundamental change of attitude towards war and towards the elites (the two were strongly linked in the minds of war-weary populations). In 1919 the slogan *Nie wieder Krieg* (no more war) found as much response in the German masses as *Gott strafe England* (God punish England) did in 1914. In Russia the Bolsheviks hammered away at the foundation of the old order with a quadruple slogan: *Doloi voinu! Zemlia krestianam! Fabriki rabochim! Vsia vlast' sovietam!* (Down with war; land to the peasants; factories to the workers; all power to the councils [of workers' peasants' and soldiers' deputies].) The Bolsheviks were successful in gaining a mass following precisely because their opponents, including socialist parties, still clung to the notion of 'carrying the war to a victorious finish' before deciding on Russia's political future. Indeed, whatever rationale the counter-revolution (led by the officers corps) could muster was only that of 'national interest'. The White Guardists insisted that they were not fighting for the restoration of the monarchy, nor even for any specific social order, but only for 'Russia'. They failed. Evidently, whatever 'national feeling' may have been mobilized at the start of the First World War had dissipated in the trenches. The image of the well-fed, well-dressed, well-mannered *burzhuy*, not of the German, became the principal target of mass hatred.

Similar but lesser shifts of mood occurred in Western Europe; but they were not sufficient to ignite social revolutions or, in the case of Germany, to carry the revolution to completion. The old German military establishment was badly wounded but not killed. It retired into temporary obscurity to recuperate.

In short, while many features of the old order survived in Europe, the 'Proud Tower'[15] collapsed. The international system would no longer be represented by a 'society' of sovereigns and function as a game of strategy played by chancelleries and general staffs. Revolutionary ideologies (of Right and Left), public opinion, internal political strife, unrest in the colonial world, and global concepts (embodied in the League of Nations, the World Court, the Locarno Treaty, the Briand Pact) muddied the classical Clausewitzian picture of international relations.

The rival philosophies of war, the eschatological and the cataclysmic, never attained the clarity of the Clausewitzian system. They appear mostly as ingredients of mixed philosophies. International institutions of conflict resolution reflected the view that war is something that *happens to* nations (i.e. an aggravation of conflict in the absence of conflict-reducing institutions) rather than something *used by* nations to attain goals not otherwise attainable. To be sure, since 'self-defence' was still recognized as an unalienable right of sovereign states and entrusted to their individual military establishments, these remained, flourished, and grew, augmented by the technologies developed during the First World War. Still the *rationale* in support of the military machines became almost exclusively defensive. In France this *rationale* permeated military strategy itself (the Maginot doctrine); in the Soviet Union it was reflected in the invariable portrayal of the next war as an attack on the U.S.S.R. by a coalition of capitalist states. We have subsumed these attitudes under the ethnocentric–cataclysmic philosophy of war. Later, when conquest once again became a frankly avowed instrument of policy (specifically of totalitarian states), it was rationalized in terms of ideologies with strong eschatological overtones; e.g. as a civilizing mission (the Japanese doctrine of the Greater East Asia Co-prosperity Sphere), as the renaissance of the Roman Empire (proclaimed by Mussolini), or as the prerogative of a Master Race (in Hitler's *Mein Kampf*).

Therefore, in pursuing our aim of comparing the political philosophy of war with other philosophies, we cannot match the classically 'pure' Clausewitzian system with other equally representative examples. The best we can do is select an example from each broad category, keeping in mind that eschatological and cataclysmic philosophies never found a soil as fertile as that which nurtured Clausewitzian thought from 1815 to 1914.

4. *An Eschatological Philosophy and Its Transformation*

In Lenin's paradigm of international relations the actors are no longer monolithic states whose wills are limited only by those of other states. The main seams of the power struggle are not along national boundaries but along chasms separating the interests of social classes. In each state there are two principal classes, the exploited and the exploiters. The latter control the state apparatus and use it to advance their class interests. Note the fundamental difference: in the Clausewitzian image, the state is an autonomous entity; *it* has interests. In the Leninist image, the classes have interests, and the ruling class *uses* 'it' (the state) to promote its own.

The dynamics of capitalist economy are such (according to Marx, in whose theories Lenin's philosophy of war is rooted) that the needs for new sources of materials, new markets, new supplies of cheap labour are constantly growing.[16] As the industrialization of Europe progressed, these supplies and markets were sought in the underdeveloped continents where the European powers staked out possessions and spheres of influence. There the several competing – or, as Lenin saw them, marauding – groups clashed. Already in the eighteenth century, England and France fought over the control of American territory and over India. Germany, having entered the race for colonies late, found England and France already in control of enormous colonial empires; and so the pressure of German expansion was directed to the Balkans and the Middle East. This pressure (*der Drang nach Osten*) was a threat to Russia's ambitions. Military alliances, linking France with Russia, Austria with Germany, and directed against each other, polarized the system. Thus when a clash was triggered by the assassination at Sarajevo, all the major powers were drawn into the struggle. This is the classical economic interpretation of the First World War, the prototype of an 'imperialist' war in Lenin's terminology. The main thrust of this interpretation was aimed at one of the pillars of Clausewitzian philosophy, namely that of 'national interest', conceived entirely in terms of an organically unified state. What was proclaimed as 'national interest' appears in Lenin's paradigm as only the interest of the ruling class and in no way the interest of the exploited class. Thus Lenin's philosophy depicts the 'true nature of war' in terms of concepts which do not occur in Clausewitz's framework of thought at all.

As has been said, the actors in Lenin's image of international war are the ruling (capitalist) classes of Europe. These actors must contend with their own populations, in particular the working classes, most of whom have everything to lose and nothing to gain from international wars.[17] Nevertheless, the actors are still identifiable; hence war is still conceived in instrumental terms, in the sense that it is instigated by the ruling classes in pursuit of economic gains or, at times, for the purpose of diverting the attention of the populations away from revolutionary tendencies. But war is no longer rational in Lenin's philosophy, for two reasons. First, the outbreak of any *particular* war is no longer *necessarily* a deliberate act of a clearly defined actor. Nations may be *impelled* towards war. That is to say there are forces acting on the *system* of class interests. These forces may set events in motion over which individual decision makers may have little or no control. Second, wars may have consequences completely unforeseen by the classes in whose interest the wars are presumably waged. For example, the First World War resulted in the dissolution of three empires. It set off revolutions throughout Europe, one of which 'went to completion', that is, resulted in the complete demise of the old elite. Certainly these events were not foreseen by the initiators of the First World War. Moreover, when it appeared that the war was deadlocked and was draining the life blood of the participant nations, none of the belligerents was able to stop it. Such a state of affairs had never been imagined by Clausewitz.

A philosophy, like a plant species, flourishes where the soil and the climate are right for it. We have seen how the conditions in nineteenth-century Europe were just right for the Clausewitzian philosophy of war. Lenin's eschatological philosophy had a much more limited habitat and a shorter life span. It found the most fertile soil in revolutionary Russia, where the concept of 'national interest' became meaningless to the vast majority of the people, if, indeed, it ever had any meaning. Bolshevik propaganda declared 'patriotism' to be a fraud perpetrated by the bourgeoisie in order to divert the masses from the pursuit of their own class interests, which were international in scope. The war-weary masses responded promptly. They overthrew Kerensky's Provincial Government (committed to 'war to a victorious finish') and voted against the war with their feet, as Lenin observed with grim humour. The army disintegrated; the front was opened to the Germans, and the new Soviet government immediately sued for peace. To Lenin's way of thinking the peace terms did not matter, for Lenin expected them to be annulled as soon as the proletarian revolution (which he believed to be inevitable) occurred in Germany.

Lenin was only partially right. The separate peace treaty (of Brest-Litovsk) was indeed annulled, but not by a victorious proletariat. It was annulled at Versailles by the victorious Allies, who promptly proceeded to build a *cordon sanitaire*, a chain of states hostile to Bolshevism, around the borders of Russia. The European patchwork of nation states was re-established and with it a semblance of stability. The situation was reminiscent of 1648 and 1815, but the basis of 'order' was no longer a 'balance of power'. It was now a system of 'collective security' embodied in the League of Nations, from which Russia was excluded. With the 'final imperialist war' and its sequel, the world proletarian revolution, the *dénouement* of Communist eschatology receded into an indefinite future. In the meantime Soviet power was to depend on its own resources. Since the nation state was the only known form of consolidated power, the Soviet State was established on that principle. Consequently threats to Soviet power were identified with threats to the Soviet State, and the only conceivable way to meet these threats (in the minds of the revolutionaries who became its rulers) was with military power. The imminence of a world social revolution may have remained as an article of faith, but it ceased to nurture the Leninist outlook on war.

Actually the Soviet leaders' outlook on war had already begun to undergo an essential change during the civil war of 1918–21. The realities of war demanded the creation of an organized war machine. The dilemma faced by the Soviet leaders was how to reconstruct an army after the old army had been deliberately destroyed by Bolshevik propaganda (pacifism, anti-patriotism, singling out the officers corps as the class enemy, etc.). In theory the problem seemed solvable. The army was to consist of workers and peasants; loyalty to tsar and country was to be replaced by loyalty to Soviet power and the world working class; discipline, formerly based on blind obedience, was to be replaced by the discipline of class consciousness; the hierarchical chain of command was to be replaced by a democratic organization. But events did not wait for the transformation to take place. Men had to be sent into battle at once, and they had to be led by men who knew something about tactics and the use of weapons. Nor was it practicable to make military decisions in open meetings.

The organization of the new (Red) army was entrusted to Leon Trotsky, who envisaged it as a complete rehabilitation of the armed forces of the Russian Republic. Trotsky saw no way of accomplishing this task other than by undoing the anti-military indoctrination which had destroyed the old army. This meant the restoration of stringent military discipline bordering on terror (death-penalty for failure), infusion of truly martial (not merely revolutionary) attitudes and, above all, the installation of former tsarist officers (almost the only available ones) in positions of leadership. To watch over the loyalty of these officers, Communist party members of unquestioned reliability were installed as commissars. The extent of militarization (in the established sense of the word) of the Red Army can be seen in Trotsky's reference to these commissars as 'a new Communist Order of Samurai – without caste privileges – who are able to die and to teach others to die for the cause of the working class'. [18]

There was violent opposition to Trotsky's policy of employing former tsarist officers. It may have stemmed partly from ideological shock. Guerrilla units operating deep in enemy territory, not a centralized army, an adjunct of a capitalist state, were the proper military arm of a revolution, Trotsky's opponents declared. There is no doubt, however, that the opposition to Trotsky's methods was also a reflection of a power struggle between Trotsky and his enemies, Stalin, Frunze, and Voroshilov.

The debate touched on all aspects of military doctrine – the relative merits of offensive and defensive operations, of a professional standing army versus a decentralized militia, etc.

As is well known, the political struggle ended in the consolidation of absolute power in the person of J. V. Stalin. However, Stalin, regardless of his military views during the civil war, eventually embarked on the task begun by Trotsky, namely that of building a war machine in many ways not different from the war machines of other militarized nation states, for that is what the Soviet Union became.

Along with the restoration of officers' ranks (with corresponding caste privileges), decorations, epaulettes, etc., came the resurgence of military–nationalist traditions. Kutuzov and Suvorov, who had fought Napoleon, were promoted the heroes of Russian History. The veneration of Suvorov was especially noteworthy, because one of his accomplishments was the crushing of the largest peasant revolt in pre-revolutionary Russia (the Pugachev Insurrection of 1773–5).

After the failure of Litvinov's attempt to weld an anti-Axis coalition, Stalin decided to rely exclusively on the military might of the Soviet Union in the pursuit of now frankly 'national interests'. The German–Soviet pact of 1939, the partition of Poland, the war against Finland, the annexation of Lithuania, Latvia, Esthonia, and Bessarabia were all 'seized opportunities' in the pure Clausewitzian tradition of 'continuing a national policy by other means'. This policy of seized opportunities was apparently resumed immediately after the end of the Second World War.

Those who see the Soviet Union as a military threat to the non-Communist world perceive Soviet foreign policy as a messianic eschatological one, tempered only by shrewd calculations of risks. In this view the world revolution has remained the ultimate goal of the Communist leaders, and they are expected to use military power whenever the proper opportunity arises in order to extend the Communist Empire. This view is usually supported by the fact that Communist regimes were established in Eastern Europe under the cover of Soviet military forces.

Those who tend to discount the importance of ideological determinants of international relations see the foreign policy of the Soviet Union in purely Clausewitzian terms. To them the

Soviet Union appears simply as a 'great power', intent on resisting encroachments on its sphere of influence by whatever means are available, and committed to augmenting this sphere by whatever means seem feasible.

This view finds strong support in the Soviet–German accord of 1939 and in the favourable allusions to Clausewitz in Soviet military writings. It must be noted that in all Soviet writings a theoretical or philosophical bent, evaluations of theories, of philosophies, and of individual thinkers must conform (or at least must appear to conform) with whatever had been said on the subject by the Founding Fathers (formerly four, now three) of Marxism–Leninism. Thus, since Marx repudiated Malthus, Malthusian ideas are either excluded or labelled differently in discussions of population dynamics. Ernst Mach remains the archvillain of 'bourgeois' philosophy of science, because Lenin so presented him.[19] Similarly Lenin's favourable references to Clausewitz find repeated echoes in Soviet military thought. For example, Marshal V. D. Sokolovsky writes:

> In describing the essence of war, Marxism–Leninism takes as its point of departure the premise that war is not an aim in itself, but rather a tool of politics.
>
> In his remarks on Clausewitz's *On War*, Lenin stressed that 'politics is the reason, and war is only the tool, not the other way around. Consequently, it remains only to subordinate the military point of view to the political.'[20]

We must also be aware that for the military mind the Clausewitzian outlook is the most comfortable one. The professional military man is preoccupied with the problem of using military power effectively. Such power is used most effectively (and moreover is sanctioned by tradition) when it is at the disposal of a politically stable nation state and directed against other states. This is the Clausewitzian paradigm of war. Thus the Soviet Military professional finds two mutually reinforcing sources of support in accepting the Clausewitzian view: his profession and the pronouncement of the Highest Authority.

As for Lenin's approval of Clausewitz, it probably stems from his obsession with the struggle for power. The whole Marxist conception of history is that of successive struggles for power, primarily between social classes. This was constantly applied by Lenin in a variety of contexts. Thus the entire history of philosophy appears in Lenin's writings as a vast struggle between 'idealism' and 'materialism'. The fate of the socialist movement was to be decided by a struggle between the revolutionists and the reformers. Clausewitz's acceptance of the struggle for power as the essence of international politics must have impressed Lenin as starkly realistic.[21]

However, Lenin did not project the Clausewitzian paradigm beyond the 'world proletarian revolution', which he believed to be imminent. Nor did he envisage the Soviet Union as a participant in a Clausewitzian system of very similar nation states. Nor did this come about. Instead the Soviet Union found itself first in a position of a pariah among the 'society of nations', then in that of a leader of an ideologically united bloc, then in that of a rival in the struggle for ideological leadership. None of these situations are envisaged in the Clausewitzian system.

The *avowed* foreign policy of the Soviet Union has remained from its incipience that of insuring world peace. In the light of the all-too-frequent discrepancies between proclaimed and actual aims of foreign policies, the avowal need not, of course, be taken seriously. It must, however, be taken into account in evaluating a *philosophy* of war.

The Clausewitzian state, in its heyday, did not insist that the aim of its foreign policy was to insure world peace. Nor did it indoctrinate its population with the idea that peace is the most precious condition and that all efforts must be directed towards its preservation. On the contrary, the Clausewitzian state held war in great esteem and the abhorrence of war in contempt. It goaded public opinion with standing grievances against specific enemy states, grievances which would some day be rectified by force of arms. Lost territories were to be recovered; new territories gained, etc. The legitimacy of war as an instrument of national policy, and its efficacy as a means of winning prestige and the respect of other states, is an essential feature of the Clausewitzian philosophy.

The disavowal of aggressive war as an instrument of policy

by the Soviet Union can perhaps be partly attributed to a change of climate in world public opinion: almost everyone is for peace. However, there is evidence that the disavowal represents a genuine orientation of the Soviet leadership, a reflection of the profound aversion to war of their population and of an intense standing commitment to build a great civilization on Communist principles. Actually, except for the brief period 1939–41 and possibly 1945–8, Soviet leaders did not subscribe to the Clausewitzian philosophy of international relations. Lenin's philosophy was, as has been noted, an eschatological one. When this conceptualization was dissipated (in the sense of ceasing to influence actual policy) it was supplanted by what was called above the ethnocentric–cataclysmic view of war. War was then seen as a disaster that threatened to *befall* the Soviet Union, and herculean efforts – economic, military, and diplomatic – were expended to meet this disaster. But with few exceptions – such as the attempt to build a system of collective security against the states which were openly planning or already actually engaged in aggressive wars (Germany, Italy, and Japan), and the short-lived 'non-Aggression Pact' of 1939–41 with Nazi Germany – the Soviet Union has not sought allies among capitalist states. The expectation of war was based on the polarization of the world into ideologically opposed camps, not at all on the way war was conceived in Clausewitzian philosophy, namely as an instrument for promoting the interests of a *single* state essentially an equal in a 'society' of states.

In summary, whatever the reason, whether the absence of martial inclinations in the Russian people, or the peculiar position of the Soviet Union in the international system, or the ideological underpinnings of Soviet foreign policy, or the preoccupation of the Soviet leaders with peaceful economic development, the Clausewitzian philosophy was never firmly established in the U.S.S.R. After a brief period of dominance the eschatological philosophy, in which the Soviet state was conceived, gave way to the ethnocentric–cataclysmic: now that the Communist state is stable and powerful, war is a disaster to be guarded *against*.[22]

The habitat of the genuine global eschatological philosophy

shifted to China, where it now has the status of an official doctrine.

5. Peace Research and Conflict Resolution

The global cataclysmic philosophy differs from the others in that it views war in relation to humanity as a whole, not in relation to an actor, be it a state, a class, or any other power-oriented system. In this perspective, war (especially the sort of war waged in our era) loses the rationales ascribed to it by other philosophies; for whatever advantage war may seem to confer on some, the total effect is certainly negative, if one perceives it from the point of view of humanity. In principle any arrangement resulting from a struggle could have been effected by agreement (if the results of the struggle could have been foreseen) without the losses incurred by the participants. Consequently the global philosophy places at the centre of attention not the possible uses to which war can be put, but the prevention of war. The emphasis is on uncovering the causes of war and on inventing institutionalized methods of conflict resolution.

This orientation leads to the idea of peace research, a programme of investigation aimed at understanding the conditions conducive to war and to peace. This tacit assumption which usually underlies such a programme is that, once these conditions are understood, war can be attacked as a problem similar to other global problems, such as disease, poverty, natural disasters, over-population, etc. We shall examine this assumption in the next section. For the moment we shall examine some approaches to peace research in which the global–cataclysmic view is reflected.

*

Peace research proceeds along two parallel lines. One is represented by the system–theoretic approach, the other by the empirical.

The system–theoretic approach begins with some postulated properties of a system, that is, a collection of entities having a structural and functional relation to each other. The *state* of a system is described by a set of instantaneous values of certain variable quantities, selected as being somehow fundamental for understanding the behaviour of the system. These variables are interdependent: changes in the values of some bring about changes in the values of others. The theoretical problem is to derive the behaviour of the system (as reflected in the states through which it passes) from the postulated interdependence of the variables.

A relatively simple example of a complete theory of this sort is the dynamic theory of the solar system. The state of this system is described by the instantaneous positions and velocities of all of its elements (the sun, the planets, the asteroids, and the satellites). These variables and their rates of change are in constant interaction (through mutual gravitational attraction). Taking this interaction into account, astronomers are able to chart the 'time course' of the system; that is, the positions and velocities of the planets at any specified time.[23] The accuracy of these predictions is very impressive. For example, eclipses of the sun and the moon can be predicted centuries in advance.

Some systems are so complex that the predictions of dynamic theory can be made only roughly. The atmosphere is an example. The variables of interest in this system are those which comprise the weather: velocities of air currents, gradients of temperature and humidity, quantities and time of precipitation, etc. All of these variables interact in ways which are well known, since the interactions are governed by established physical laws. Nevertheless weather prediction is difficult, simply because of the immense amounts of information that must be processed to 'read' the state of the system at a given time and to calculate the succeeding states.

Another example of a complex system is the economic system of a nation, a region, or the world. Here the problem of prediction is further complicated by the fact that the laws of interaction among the variables of interest (production rates, prices, demand, etc.) are known only very roughly and may themselves undergo changes, being influenced by events not comprised in the economic system, e.g. psychological or political factors.

The object of study in the system–theoretic approach to

peace research is the international system. Here the situation is still more difficult than in meteorology and economics, since the regularities or 'laws' governing the interaction of the variables are practically unknown (if indeed such laws exist). Such 'laws' can be postulated only hypothetically. Moreover, little is known about the relative importance of the different variables, nor of how they are to be reliably estimated.

The system-oriented peace researcher has only one recourse at the start: simply to guess or postulate both the relevant variables and the laws governing their interaction. Once this is done the hypothetico-deductive method of inquiry comes into play. For, having postulated some variables and their interactions, the system-theorist can deduce (mathematically) the *consequences of his assumptions*. If these consequences happen to correspond to observations made on the behaviour of the system or some aspect of it, to that extent the assumptions (the 'model', as this point of departure is called) are corroborated. A theory is then built by combining assumptions whose consequences have been corroborated by observation. The problem, then, is to select the variables which are significant indices of the behaviour of the system and to guess how they interact; and if several different sets of variables and relations (and hence different models) seem to be corroborated equally well – which ones to pursue first, and how to find discriminating tests between them.

Lewis F. Richardson, a British meteorologist, pioneered this method.[24] He began by postulating a hypothetical international system consisting of two nations (or blocs). He defined the state of this system by a pair of variables representing the attitudes of the nations towards each other. Positive values of these variables represented hostility (or fear), as reflected in the armament budgets of the nations or blocs, while negative values represented goodwill, as reflected in the trade volume between the rivals. Next, Richardson postulated the laws of the interaction as follows. The rate of growth of the armament budget of each nation he supposed to be stimulated in proportion to the already existing size of the rival's armament budget and inhibited in proportion to the nation's own armament budget.

A pair of constant terms were added to represent the effects on the rate of change of the budgets, independent of the existing levels. These assumptions are expressed mathematically by a pair of differential equations. The solutions of these equations give the time courses of the variables. A growth of the variables represents increasing armament budgets; a decrease represents disarmament or, in the negative region, increase in inter-bloc trade volume (cooperation). The constants of proportionality connecting the rates of change of the variables to the variables themselves constitute the system parameters, i.e. the properties of the system itself.

In order to compare the theory with observations it is necessary to select (*a*) a pair of rival blocs whose armament budgets and trade volumes are known in some time period, and (*b*) values of the system parameters. When these values and the initial values of the armament budgets (and/or trade volumes) are introduced into the equations, one can 'read out' the time course of the variables and so compare it with the observed time course of the armament budgets (and/or trade volumes). Richardson did this. He chose the Entente and the Central powers of pre-First World War Europe. For the initial year he chose 1908 (when the intense armament race began). For the system parameters he chose values which would fit the calculated to the observed initial increments in the armament budgets. The solved equations then predicted the time course of the continuing arms race to the outbreak of the war.

Next, Richardson examined the stability of his (highly simplified) system, given the chosen system parameters. He found that such a system was inherently unstable. That is to say, it could not exist in a state of equilibrium, interpreted, say, as a balance of power (stabilized arms budgets). Regardless of initial values, the system *had* to move away from the (theoretical) equilibrium, not towards it. *Which way* it would move depended on where it started from. From certain initial conditions it would have to move in the direction of an accelerating arms race. But from certain other initial conditions it would have to move in the opposite direction, towards disarmament and ever-increasing trade volumes. The situation in 1908 was such that the system was just barely on the arms-race side of the theoretical (unstable) equilibrium. Richardson remarks that if the combined armament budgets of the rival blocs had been just £5 million smaller (or, equivalently, the trade volume had been so much larger) the international system (or rather his model of it) would have moved towards a United Europe instead of towards a world war.

It must be stressed that the usefulness of the approach is not established by either the apparent agreement between the theoretical and the observed armament budgets or by the derived conclusion. The agreement may well have been spurious; the conclusion cannot at any rate be corroborated since we cannot 'replay' the pre-First World War system, starting with different initial conditions. Moreover, the model is altogether too primitive to serve as a basis of a theory of so complex a matter as international relations. Rather, the value of this approach is a heuristic one. It *illustrates* a method and so provides a starting point for further more extensive and more sophisticated investigations. Using the same paradigm, future investigators can turn their attention to other possibly more important variables, postulate other possibly more realistic interactions among them, make use of more powerful mathematical machinery (for example, computer simulation which was not available to Richardson), increase the number of actors, etc.

Above all, the value of the approach should be seen not in terms of the answers it provides but in terms of the questions it raises. For example, Richardson's model of the arms race raises the question of whether the system property of stability (or instability) is applicable to international systems. There is evidence that it does apply to economic systems. Economic systems seem to have some regulating mechanisms, which sometimes appear to fail, as in run-away inflations and self-aggravating crises. Can it be that some aspects of international relations also have 'built-in' dynamics and so are guided by an 'invisible hand', which traditionally was supposed to be operating in a market economy? If so, how do these 'blind forces' interact with supposedly rational decisions of statesmen, and to what extent are the latter merely rationalizations of the trends over which the decision-makers actually have no control? Can the behaviour of international, economic, ecological, and technological systems be studied by similar methods (for example the methods of cybernetics)? Does the understanding of the dynamics of an international system provide an opportunity of exercising a measure of control over it?

Clearly, the fruitfulness of the system–theoretic approach depends crucially on the recognition of the relevant variables. The search for these constitutes the other avenue of peace research – the empirical.

The empirical approach was pioneered also by Richardson and by his American contemporary Quincy Wright.[25] Both men devoted many years of toil to sifting mountainous masses of data pertaining to wars large and small, international and civil. Richardson extended the scope of his study to all 'deadly quarrels', as he called encounters involving violent deaths from single murders to world wars. A principal object of these investigations was to uncover *correlates* of war; that is, conditions regularly present at or immediately preceding the outbreak of wars, or those characterizing nations who were engaged in many wars or in protracted or severe wars; and, conversely, conditions which appeared to inhibit the state of war.

In a way Wright's and Richardson's findings seem inconclusive. No outstanding correlate of war was found. However, this only bespeaks the immense complexity of the phenomenon and the difficulty of ascribing operational meanings (in terms of data which can be collected and analysed) to the concepts which dominate our thinking about war, e.g. nationalism, hostility, power, rivalry, polarization, integration, severity of conflict, perception of national interest, and so on.

Work along the lines indicated by Wright and Richardson is progressing.[26] It involves problems of collecting 'hard data'; for example, compiling a catalogue of international wars, their magnitudes (as measured by several indices) and durations; problems of characterizing nation states by well-defined indices (demographic, political, industrial, military); problems of characterizing the state of the international system (with regard to trade, alliances, degree of polarization). The hope is that the incidence, magnitude, frequency, intensity, duration – in short, the epidemiological characteristics of wars – can be somehow related to other aspects of national and international life. The problem is conceived in a way similar to the way complex syndromes of disease (e.g. 'cancer', 'schizophrenia') are conceived in large-scale medical research.

The scientific investigations instigated by the global cataclysmic view of war are still in their infancy. The work goes on, largely through the efforts of individuals and small teams of researchers in universities where off-the-beaten-path investigations are encouraged or tolerated. Some of the groups have acquired the status of 'centres' or 'institutes'. The total effort (measured in allotted funds and personnel) is still infinitesimal compared with the research effort directed towards increasing the power and efficiency of weapons and the perfection of military tactics and strategy.

6. *Is a Synthesis Possible?*

We have described three views of war in their most representative variants, bringing out contrasts and differences for the purpose of clarity. Actually, however, the views are in many ways complementary rather than contradictory. For example, the events leading up to the First World War can be described in terms of concepts borrowed from all three views. In particular, Leninist and Clausewitzian as well as Richardsonian concepts can be utilized in describing the arms race of 1908–14. In listing the 'forces' which then drove Europe towards war, the virtual hegemony of the Clausewitzian view in the chancelleries and cabinets of Europe can certainly be included, and so can the appetite for markets on the part of the large industrial complexes.

But one must constantly keep in mind that, although the theories derived from the cataclysmic view are stated in quasi-physicalist terms (i.e. have a formal resemblance to physical theories), the strains and forces attributed to the international system are not physical strains and forces. Rather they are consequences of the way events are singled out for attention and interpreted by human minds. In accordance with these interpretations men make decisions and act. These decisions and acts are, in turn, events, which are singled out for attention, interpreted, and acted upon. Thus the key role attributed to calculations and decisions in the political (instrumental and rational) view of war is not necessarily simply the result of a misconception (as has been argued, for example, by Tolstoy in *War and Peace*). Moltke and Schlieffen designed the German military policy on the basis of Clausewitzian ideas.[27] The actual events in August 1914 were a realization of these ideas. They were consequences of specific orders given by specific individuals via a pre-designed system of ramified communication channels. The plan was realized (at first) because the orders were carried out; and they were carried out because millions of individuals had been pre-trained to understand and to obey the orders. Thus the vast German military machine, wheeling counter-clockwise across Luxembourg, Belgium, and France, was for a time a well-functioning 'instrument' put in motion by specifiable actors whose clearly defined goal was the destruction of the French war machine.

When, however, the German and French war machines clashed on the Marne, they could no longer be used as 'instruments' any more than an automobile stuck in a snow bank can be used as an instrument of location. Clausewitzian principles of strategy and tactics became useless. The military technology which had developed since 1870 made movement and manoeuvre impossible in 1914. From the time that the armies were immobilized the war ceased to serve the political aims of either side.

The fact that the stale-mated war continued on the Western Front for four years can no longer be interpreted in Clausewitzian terms. The now senseless slaughter must be ascribed to the systemic properties of the war itself rather than to the use of war as an instrument of policy. Similarly the rejection of the idea of the 'national war' by large portions of the European population in the 1920s and the post-war revolutions and near-revolutions in central and eastern Europe must be attributed at least in part to the penetration of the class-war concept into public consciousness.

It seems, therefore, that it is possible to develop a *descriptive* theory of war (at least in the period under consideration), which embodies all three views, their mutual interaction and their blending with one another.

It is a different matter when we consider the *prescriptive* implications of each type of theory. A prescriptive theory can be derived from a descriptive one if certain outcomes of action are singled out as more desirable than others. For example, physiology and pathology are descriptive sciences, since they only describe the processes going on in living organisms. Medicine, on the other hand, is largely a prescriptive science. A physician *prescribes* remedies; i.e. procedures which are known or thought to be effective in preventing or combating disease. Similarly there exist descriptive and prescriptive theories of grammar. The former are systematic descriptions of actually occurring patterns of speech; a prescriptive grammar is a set of rules which one is advised to follow if one wishes to produce speech patterns satisfying the standards of a particular speech community (usually a social elite). Political theories also can be descriptive and prescriptive. The former describe political institutions and practices actually occurring; the latter specify institutions or practices by means of which certain goals can presumably be achieved.

Each of the three views of war outlined in the foregoing contains an explicit or implicit prescriptive component. In Clausewitz's formulation the prescriptive component is quite explicit. Having defined war as a political instrument, Clausewitz proceeds to *instruct* a hypothetical client[28] on how this instrument is to be used in the pursuit of certain goals.

The Leninist view also has a prescriptive component. Having traced the sources of war to the clashes between rival groupings in competition for markets, etc., Lenin proceeds to instruct *his* client (the 'proletariat') on how to utilize the clashes of interest among the ruling groups in order to promote 'his' interests. We have placed 'proletariat' and 'his' in quotation marks to indicate that 'the proletariat' is a much more diffuse agent than a prince or a general (Clausewitz's clients). Consequently Lenin's prescriptive theory must (and does) contain specifications of actions without which it would be impossible for the proletariat to act as an agent – that is, in an organized way. Clearly these prescriptions have not been carried out on a world scale. In Russia it may be said that they have been carried out to a certain extent; namely, a numerically small but highly organized party was created which was able to seize the apparatus of state power, and to inspire the Russian masses to convert the war against Germany into a civil war and to destroy completely the power of the old elite. This party was identified in Bolshevik political theory as a sort of executive committee of the proletariat.

The prescriptive component of theories based on the cataclysmic philosophy of war is only implicit, and for the most part vague. The aims of such theories are mainly those of a descriptive theory: to discover the characteristics of the international system which propel it towards or away from war. The task has certainly not been completed (it has hardly begun). The relevance of whatever systemic 'causes of war' have been singled out for attention so far can be only conjectured. Also, aside from the lack of a descriptive theory acceptable by scientific standards (to which the proponents of the system–theoretic approach would like to adhere), the difficulty of deriving specific prescriptions from the cataclysmic philosophy lies in the absence of a well-defined client-actor. Presumably a prescriptive theory based on the cataclysmic paradigm would indicate ways in which wars could be prevented or stopped. Such prescriptions could be implemented only by institutions ready and able to put recommendations into effect. But such institutions for preventing war do not exist, at least not with effective power. Supranational bodies, like the United Nations, even though conceived as instruments for enforcing peace, typically find themselves unable to limit the actions of major powers 'pursuing their national interests', while the actions of individual states, even though some of them may be willing to carry out the prescriptions, are not sufficient if the prevention of war depends on the dynamic properties of the *entire system*. Thus it may be impossible to translate the knowledge of the systemic properties of the global system into actions aimed at preventing war, because there is no actor (a decision body) which can affect the global system to a sufficient extent, and with sufficient speed.

In summary, while it may be possible to integrate the three philosophies of war on the descriptive level, it is not possible to do so on the *prescriptive* level. The prescriptive components of the associated theories are addressed to different actors, some of which are only hypothetical. Moreover, while the theories themselves are not, the *prescriptions* of the various theories are incompatible with each other.

In a way the global problem of war (if war is so conceived) is no different from any other large-scale human problems. The solution of such problems depends not only on knowledge but also on the possibility of applying it. For example, the solution of the problem of eradicating typhoid fever depends in part on understanding the main source of the disease (e.g. a polluted water supply) but no less vitally also on the ability to install water-purifying plants (an engineering problem). A perfectly reliable, safe, and cheap contraceptive might or might not help to solve the problem of population control, depending on whether its use is accepted on a sufficiently wide scale. The problem of inducing acceptance is neither pharmacological nor physiological: it is a sociological and psychological problem.

Similarly, knowing the sources of war will not in itself help eradicate it. If there are groups who still subscribe to the Clausewitzian tenet that war can serve as a useful instrument in the pursuit of national interests, and if they are in a position to use the instrument, they are not likely to implement a programme which would make this instrument useless. It appears, then, that the identification of these groups and the development of means of dealing with them must form an integral part of any serious research programme.

7. The Contemporary International System

A cursory glance at the contemporary international system reveals that large portions of it are no longer Clausewitzian. In particular, the European system of nation states can no longer be viewed as a realization of the Clausewitzian model. Certain overlapping regions have been integrated into peacefully cooperating blocs without territorial and imperialistic ambitions (e.g. the Scandinavian states). Others have submerged their military policies in those of large blocs (such as NATO and the Warsaw Pact countries). Whatever territorial disputes smoulder in Europe are remnants of the Second World War (for example, the German–Polish border). Overseas empires have dissolved. There is reason to suppose that were it not for the continuing Cold War (whose poles lie *outside* of Western and Central Europe), the danger of a European war would be smaller today than it had ever been since the nation–state system came into being. War seems to have disappeared as a major item on the agenda of *European* politics. Europe seems to have unlearned the lessons taught by Machiavelli and Clausewitz.

Elsewhere, however, there are prominent danger spots, especially in the Middle East and potentially in Africa. The patchwork of states in those regions is still very new, and nationalism is still a vigorous, driving, political force. Inter-state wars can be therefore expected to occur in those regions. Machinery for extinguishing such war exists. Whether it is used or not depends on whether the major powers act in their individual interests (as traditionally conceived) – that is, in support of one or the other belligerents in the hope of thereby extending their own spheres of influence – or whether they act in their collective interest to maintain peace. In other words, whether wars occur among the newly emerging nation states, and whether they spread, depends on whether the political or the cataclysmic view of war prevails in the minds of the super-power leaders.

As for the danger of a war between the super-powers themselves, it has been maintained that the ability of each to destroy the other within a few hours has been an effective deterrent. To what extent the so-called balance of terror is actually a deterrent is not known, because the non-occurrence of a nuclear war is certainly no evidence of its impossibility. Nor can the so-called 'probability' of a nuclear war be meaningfully estimated. Probabilities of events are estimated from the frequencies of their occurrence. Thus it makes sense to speak of the probability of an air crash, a fire, a tornado, but not of a nuclear war, unless such wars become recurring events, which does not seem likely. On the other hand, as long as war does not break out between major powers there is no evidence that the balance of terror has *not* been a deterrent. We are therefore free to choose either assumption. Choosing, for the moment, the optimistic hypothesis, we have, in summary, the following image of the present international system, in particular of its susceptibility to war:

1. The super-powers may be deterred indefinitely from fighting each other by the balance of nuclear terror.
2. There are states which either have been integrated into co-operative sub-systems of the international system or cannot hope to compete for power in the international arena. Neither the leadership nor the populations of these states seriously think of war as a political instrument.
3. There are states whose diplo-military policies are dominated by the super-powers. Their policy makers are not in a *position* to think in Clausewitzian categories.
4. There are states which might well attempt to pursue their 'national interests' by war if necessary; but such wars can be easily extinguished by the super-powers unless the latter are ready and willing to fight each other.

The Israeli–Arab war of June 1967 comes readily to mind in this connexion. Whichever side instigated the war did so 'in the pursuit of national interests' as these have been traditionally understood. Whether this war was 'extinguished' by the super-powers (via the United Nations Security Council) or only temporarily halted remains to be seen. At any rate, the states of the Middle East are hardly likely to repeat the history of Clausewitzian Europe, where resort to war was held to be the normal procedure for settling international disputes. Further outbreaks of this sort are more likely to lead either to a settlement forced on the contestants from the outside, or to a world cataclysm.

In these contexts, then, war is not likely to be used *both deliberately and successfully* as an instrument of national policy, and the policy-makers concerned know this. In other words, the Clausewitzian conception of war has been rendered void *in these contexts*.

There remains, however, one context in which war can be

used deliberately and, as it appears to the actual or prospective participants, successfully. That is in the context of the revolutionary war. Revolutionary wars are not 'Clausewitzian' wars of sovereign states fighting each other for the usual objectives, these being increments of power or prestige within a matrix of comparable sovereign states. Revolutionary wars are not 'symmetrical'. Strategies and tactics used by one side are not those used by the other. Technical superiority invariably belongs to the side which seeks to suppress a revolution. The revolutionists, on the other hand, usually have the advantages of fighting on familiar territory, of greater tactical flexibility, and of support by the civilian population. Indeed, they often *are* the civilian populations in arms. Therefore in counter-revolutionary warfare the first principle of the prescriptive Clausewitzian theory of war usually cannot be carried out, the true objective of military action being to destroy the military forces of the adversary. The 'military forces' of the revolutionary adversary are diffuse. One is never sure whether one has destroyed them unless one is ready to destroy a large portion of the population, and this usually conflicts with the political aim of the war and hence also violates a fundamental Clausewitzian principle.

Following the Second World War, a number of European powers were engaged in the suppression of revolutions. The British were engaged in Greece and Malaya, the Dutch in Indonesia, the French in Algeria and Indo-China. Since 1960 only one great power has been actively engaged in suppressing revolutions outside its borders – indeed in accordance with an explicitly stated policy; namely, the United States. At the same time, the polarity of the international system shifted from the United States versus the Soviet Union to the United States versus China. China proclaimed herself to be the champion of 'wars of liberation'; the United States, of 'world order'. Both countries have committed themselves to theories of war, corresponding to their respective political positions: China to Mao Tze-Tung's theory of guerrilla warfare; the United States to counter-insurgency.[29] Neither theory bears any resemblance to Clausewitz's theory of war, either politically or militarily, being entirely outside the scope of the international military system envisaged by Clausewitz.

Yet the Clausewitzian philosophy of war now enjoys the greatest prestige in the military circles of the United States and among their advisory entourage. It is instructive to inquire into the reasons for this resurgence of Clausewitzian philosophy in a country which has had practically no experience as a participant in the Clausewitzian system.

8. The Resurgence of the Political Philosophy of War

The wars waged by the United States in the nineteenth century were punitive or exterminating actions against Indian tribes, an unsuccessful expedition against Canada in 1812, and easy wars of conquest against Mexico and the moribund Spanish empire. Neither of the two serious American war experiences before the Second World War (the Civil War and the First World War) were perceived by Americans as wars in the Clausewitzian sense to 'promote national interest'. On the contrary, the First World War (whatever may have been its actual underpinnings) was seen by most Americans as an ideological war, fought for principles, not for power. The entry of the United States into the Second World War appeared to Americans even more devoid of 'Clausewitzian' motives ('reasons of state'). It is this *perception*, rather than the actual determinants of the participation, which is relevant to the argument which follows.[30]

In view of the very real threat which Nazi Germany offered to whole populations, not just to states, the *moral* justification of the Second World War (irrelevant in the political philosophy of war) appeared unchallengeable. The crowning victory over the axis strengthened the Americans' conviction that the forces of righteousness triumphed over the forces of evil.

The experience of the Second World War was an exhilarating one for Americans because of the dramatic sequence of events: initial defeats, followed by a turning of the tide and rapidly accumulating victories. War became fixed in the American imagination as an extreme effort which one undertakes only when provoked, hence only when one is in the right. Such an effort, to Americans' way of thinking, was bound to be victorious. In other words, identification with the protagonists of good (as in mass-entertainment dramas) and a confident expectation of victory became the context in which the majority of Americans thought about war.

This thinking was carried over to the early post-war years. It turned out that the 'total threat' did not disappear with the defeat of the Axis. Instead it was supplanted by another 'total threat', namely the perceived (or imagined) threat of 'Communist domination of the world'. For the United States the response to this new threat was in terms of the same moralistic conception of war, in which America pictured herself as peaceful and passive yet ready for instant mobilization of her entire national energy to repel an attack – an ethnocentric cataclysmic view, a mirror image of the Soviet view. By this time an attack on any of the allies of the United States was regarded by the United States as an attack on itself. Simultaneously the concept of 'allies' was extended to 'The Free World', now defined as the entire world excepting the countries with well-entrenched Communist governments; and the concept of 'attack' was extended to any change of regime thought to have been instigated by Communists.

U.S. Secretary of State John Foster Dulles's doctrine of massive retaliation reflected the American perception of war in the early 1950s. The doctrine stated, in effect, that the United States would retaliate against any act which it defined as a threat to its security, on any scale of violence it deemed necessary, against any one whom it held responsible.

As is known, 'massive retaliation' was never applied, even though several events occurred in the late fifties and early sixties which were declared to be instances of 'Communist aggression'. Probably a major factor in the restraint exercised by the United States was the fact that the Soviet Union had acquired its own retaliatory weapon, in consequence of which retaliation for infringements on the 'Free World' became a risky matter.[31]

In the late fifties the doctrine of massive retaliation came under sharp criticism (Dulles died in 1959). The spearhead of the criticism was the argument that the effectiveness of a threat depends not only on the severity of the punishment threatened but also on its credibility. The credibility of a threat is impaired to the extent that the party who makes it also stands to suffer if the threat is carried out. Clearly a threat of a 'massive retaliation' is of this sort, if the retaliation is itself expected to incur a counter-retaliation. Once the weakness (insufficient credibility) of the massive retaliation posture became clear, the problem of making threats credible as well as terrible became prominent in the writings of the American strategists.

The psychological aspect of credibility is discussed extensively in the writings of Thomas C. Schelling and of Herman Kahn.[32] Both consider the possible utility of postures which would in effect convince the adversary that in a particular confrontation the United States is actually *unable to refrain* from carrying out the threat if the adversary transgresses a certain clearly defined boundary. If the adversary could be convinced of this, it is argued, the threat would act as a potent deterrent and would cancel whatever counter-threat the adversary was using. Schelling cites several examples of this tactic from actual military practice. The act of cutting off one's own retreat, or chaining a machine gunner to his weapon, may have their own tactical value in battle in the sense of utilizing to the utmost the resistance to an assault. The strategy of threat, however, gives these measures an added dimension. If the adversary *knows* that a unit cannot retreat even if it wanted to, he may raise the estimate of the costliness of the assault. The object of such stratagems, from this point of view, is not so much to inflict maximum damage on the adversary as to convince him that an attack will be costly.[33]

The ultimate version of this type of deterrence (perhaps meant as a caricature) is the so-called Doomsday Machine described by Kahn in *On Thermonuclear War* (p. 145 ff.). A Doomsday Machine is simply an accumulation of thermonuclear bombs set to go off if triggered by a pre-set signal. These bombs are massed on the territory of their possessors. Since they need not be air-lifted, there is no limit on the magnitude of the cache. It is therefore quite possible to accumulate enough of these devices so that the explosion, once set off, would destroy all life, for example, by blanketing the globe with radioactive fallout.

The signal which would trigger the explosion is under the control of the *adversary*. For example, the triggering mechanism of the Doomsday Machine bombs could be so programmed that a nuclear explosion anywhere within a given radius of the machine will set it off. This means that the adversary will set off the Doomsday Machine if he launches a nuclear attack against its possessor. Since the adversary would himself be destroyed in the ensuing holocaust, he is thereby deterred from initiating a nuclear attack. The Doomsday Machine differs from the ordinary counter-threat ('If you attack me, I shall attack you') in that it makes the *retraction* of the counter-threat impossible. This is accomplished by another triggering mechanism which sets off the explosion *if an attempt is made to dismantle the Doomsday Machine* (or to disconnect its main triggering mechanism). It follows that the adversary can neither use a nuclear threat against the possessor of a Doomsday Machine nor make use of a counter-threat to force its neutralization.

Whether the construction of the Doomsday Machine has ever been seriously considered does not concern us here. The idea is offered as an illustration of the way the 'credibility game' has become an essential part of the twilight zone between 'diplomacy' and war. This game, like the 'war game' proper, generates its own theories of offence and defence. The problem of offence is here essentially that of insuring that one's 'resolve' (i.e. intent to carry out threats or counter-threats) is received, understood, and, above all, believed by the adversary. The problem of defence is that of preventing the opponent from doing the same. As Schelling points out, a kidnapper who has no means of communicating to the family of the victim is helpless, because his threat is effective only to the extent that it is received and believed.

Investigations of this sort have remained largely on the speculative level, stimulated, as they were, largely by the situation resulting from the balance of terror. That is to say, there was no way of testing the theoretical conclusion without invoking unacceptable risks. Accordingly the attention of the strategists was attracted to another doctrine which *could* be put to a test, namely the doctrine of measured response, or limited war.[34]

The underlying idea of the doctrine is that the magnitude of the response should be just enough to checkmate the attempted 'aggression'.[35] The advantages to be derived from such a policy were the following:

1. By *actually* responding militarily, instead of merely threatening to respond to what the United States considered impermissible acts (e.g. the overthrow of the military junta by the Constitutionalists in the Dominican Republic in 1965), the United States could be *sure* of imposing its will throughout its sphere of influence, which, as we have seen, is now assumed to be the entire non-Communist world.
2. The real use of military action would make the threats of future military actions credible. It thus appears as a more effective deterrent than 'massive retaliation'.
3. Since the military resources of the United States are practically inexhaustible, enough counter-force could always be marshalled against any increase in the intensity of the 'aggressions' (the escalation principle).
4. There would be less danger of a mobilized public opinion, particularly abroad, against the use of force by the United States in the pursuit of its national interests. Whereas the threat of massive retaliation was difficult to reconcile with a defensive posture, by matching pressure with comparable counter-pressure the purely defensive posture of the United States (as a guardian of 'peace', i.e. of order) would be more convincing.

These considerations seem at this writing (1967) to underlie the strategy and tactics of the war which the United States is currently waging in South-east Asia. This policy has to be defended both against the opponents of the war and against those who insist on bringing into play sufficient force to gain a swift and decisive military victory.

Both oppositions are parried by an appeal to 'realism' and

'responsibility', i.e. to the principle of 'rational' use of force in the pursuit of national interests. A 'realistic' foreign policy, it is argued, is one which recognizes that force still plays a preponderant role in international affairs. At any rate, as long as there are adversaries who will not hesitate to use force to gain their ends, the United States, it is argued, must be prepared to do likewise. On the other hand, a 'realistic' approach to foreign policy also demands a sober appraisal of the costs and consequences of alternative courses of action. Ruthlessness is as risky in war as recklessness in business ventures, and besides it often defeats the political aims of the war.

This new military policy called for an extensive broadening of the military arsenal and of the repertoire of strategies and tactics. Clearly the reliance on nuclear capability, which had been consistent with the doctrine of massive retaliation, had to be abandoned. Emphasis was now given to the development of 'conventional' weapons and of techniques of using them. In short, the military establishment devoted itself with great energy to mastering the 'art of war' in its most diversified forms and to developing it further.

Nor was this intellectual effort confined to the military establishment. The military research industry in the United States now includes autonomous institutes financed by government contracts and extends deeply into the universities. Because of the traditional mobility of the American professional class, research talent moves easily from universities to military research institutes and back. Professors, free-lancers, managers and military officers attend the same conferences and share ideas related to basic and applied research, technology, strategy, and tactics. Early retirement age allows generals to move into lucrative executive positions in industry and so to 'make up' for the financial sacrifices entailed by the modest salary scales of the military career. The retired generals bring their outlook with them and help to cement the solidarity between the business and the military worlds. Recall that this solidarity developed in Germany on the basis of the revolutionary-suppressing potential of the military. In the United States this is not a necessary consideration; rather the solidarity is cemented by the common appetites of the business and military machines. Both thrive on unlimited growth. The two establishments nurture each other. In short, there has developed an immense scientific-technical-managerial adjunct to the military establishment, offering unprecedented career and business opportunities, social prestige, and considerable intellectual challenge.

The militarization of American society is thus proceeding in ways which are in harmony with the American social structure and cultural climate. A military caste has not emerged; there was no social or historical base for it. Instead a military *profession* arose which encompasses a range of expertise far beyond the traditional military specialities. The State did not become totalitarian. For support of its predominantly military foreign policy it relies on the passive acceptance of the policy by a population traditionally ignorant of foreign affairs, insensitive to global problems, and accustomed to viewing war as a job that has to be done (and always can be done) somewhere outside the United States. Both the messianic and the ethnocentric-cataclysmic views of war, which had been dominant in the United States, receded into the background. Instead a 'Neo-Clausewitzian' view became dominant, vigorously defended by the new American school of international relations.[36]

In details the Neo-Clausewitzian view differs from the classical Clausewitzian doctrine but agrees with it in essentials. The divergence stems from the radically different political and technological aspects of twentieth-century war. The Neo-Clausewitzians assume the stance of realism; hence they take into account the fundamental changes of the political and technological environment. The essential similarity between the modern and the classical forms of Clausewitzian philosophy of war is rooted in the basic conception of war as a political instrument and in the tacit assumption that the national interests of a state are clearly discernible and, in very large measure, identified with the power of a state *vis-à-vis* other states. Let us examine somewhat more closely these differences and similarities.

Although Clausewitz thought in terms of a general model of

international relations, it is clear that when he thought about the State and its destiny, he thought of Prussia. Similarly American diplo-military strategists orient themselves almost exclusively towards what they believe to be the national interest of the United States.

There is a difference, however, between Clausewitz's orientation and that of the American strategists. In spite of Clausewitz's strong identification with Prussia – conditioned, no doubt, by the powerful emergent nationalism in post-Napoleonic Europe – he could still envisage his prescriptive theory in general terms. He expected that his theories could and probably would be adopted by all 'civilized' states. Prussia was a state like other states. The United States, however, is not conceived by most American strategists as a state like other states. The problem of promoting American national interest, as most American strategists see it, is not that of preserving or extending the power of the United States *vis-à-vis* other *similar* states, which may at times be allies and at other times opponents. The problem is to preserve and increase the power of the United States (seen as the champion of the 'Free World') against encroachment by a permanent and implacable enemy who is *everywhere* and who challenges the United States, not only by virtue of possessing a comparable military machine, but also by corrupting populations; that is, inducing in them a desire for overthrowing the present world order. Since the strategists see the United States as the only effective defender of the world order (here the unique role of the United States is apparent), it follows that all social revolutions must be viewed as hostile to the United States. The problem then is not primarily to win specific clashes with specific rival states (as Clausewitz saw Prussia's problem), but how to stem the tide of world revolution.[87] The asymmetry of the present international system (contrasted with the symmetry of the Clausewitzian system) is well understood by the Neo-Clausewitzians.

The other departure from classical Clausewitzian philosophy is a consequence of taking into account the effect of total military effort in a clash between nuclear powers. Clausewitz took the supreme object of a war to be rendering the enemy incapable of resistance. In his day this meant the destruction of the enemy's military machine. This could easily be envisaged in the eighteenth century, when professional armies, once destroyed, could not be immediately replaced. With the appearance of mass ('citizens'') armies, the task of destroying a military machine became more difficult, because armies could continue to be replenished by mass conscription. (Recall that the almost total destruction of Napoleon's Army in the Russian campaign did not stop Napoleon from fighting for two more years.) Still, it was conceivable that a sufficiently *rapid* destruction of the opponent's field army would put him *hors de combat*, and would enable the victor to dictate the peace terms.

The large twentieth-century wars have not been fought on these terms. Total mobilization became a mobilization not only of soldiers but also of the entire industrial effort of a modern nation, hence of its labour force. To ensure victory, not only the immediate but also the potential military capacity of the opponent had to be destroyed, which meant attacking the centres of production and population. Aviation made this possible; and we have seen the application of this principle in Warsaw, Rotterdam, London, Dresden, Hamburg, Tokyo, and elsewhere.

It is important to examine here the difference between Clausewitz's conception of 'absolute war' and the twentieth-century notion of 'total war'. It is doubtful whether Clausewitz ever envisaged 'civilized' war as a slaughter of civilian populations. Even in his 'absolute war' he saw slaughter confined to the battlefield. However, regardless of how Clausewitz pictured war 'carried to its logical conclusion', in the present political and technological environment the actualization of Clausewitz's absolute war is total war, that is, genocide. The concept of the battlefield dissolved in twentieth-century war. The modern advocates of 'total war', e.g. the Nazis and some partisans of 'total victory' in the United States, explicitly included (and now include) civilian populations as military targets. For example, the United States Air Force ROTC manual, *Fundamentals of Aerospace Weapons Systems* defines a 'military target', as follows: 'Any person, thing, idea [*sic*], entity or location selected for destruction, inactivation, or rendering non-usable with weapons which will reduce or destroy the will or ability of the enemy to resist.'[38]

The differences between Clausewitz's conception and that of the Neo-Clausewitzians are largely due to the changed historical situation. The similarities between the two are more fundamental. One might say that the Neo-Clausewitzians have *adapted* the basic ideas of Clausewitz to our age. The acceptance of the Clausewitzian philosophy of war and the rejection of its twentieth-century consequences requires a revision of Clausewitz's logic. We shall see in a moment how the Neo-Clausewitzians have undertaken this task.

*

To recapitulate the basic tenets of Clausewitz's philosophy of international relations,

1. The State is conceived as a living entity, having well defined strivings and endowed with intelligence to seek and examine means to realize these strivings.
2. The State is sovereign, i.e. recognizes no authority above itself.
3. Since among the goals of all states is that of increasing their own power at the expense of that of other states, the interests of states, regardless of incidental and ephemeral coincidence, are always in conflict.
4. Clashes of interests between two states are typically resolved by the imposition of the will of one state upon that of another. Therefore war is a *normal* phase in the relations among states.

The personification of the State as an entity with a single will was a natural conception in the era of absolute monarchy, when the interests of political units were identified with the appetites of their princes. To be sure, in Clausewitz's time absolute monarchy had already dissolved in England and in France, and democratic ideas were becoming prominent in European thought. But to Clausewitz the demise of the despotic state by no means spelled the demise of the personified State. On the contrary, having identified the will of the *nation* with the will of the State, Clausewitz freed the State from whatever responsibility might be ascribed to rulers. A prince, being a person, could still be described as kind or cruel, honest or dishonest, etc. These qualities do not apply to the State, through which, in the estimation of the Prussian, Providence manifested its cosmic purpose.

In view of its subsequent culmination in the totalitarian regimes of our century, the monolithic State can no longer be glorified as the manifestation of the will of God. Nevertheless the idea of absolute sovereignty is still intact in the writings of the Neo-Clausewitzians. The idea is expressed mainly in the ubiquitous assumption that states *have* national interests which *will* be served, regardless of arrangements (e.g. supra-natural bodies which challenge absolute sovereignty).

The other essential ingredient of Clausewitzian thought which is preserved and nurtured by the Neo-Clausewitzians is the idea that war is, perhaps regrettably, a *normal* phase in the relations among states. This notion is much more difficult to defend than the notion of absolute sovereignty, even though it appears to be a logical consequence of the latter. This is because war has become an abomination to most of the inhabitants of this planet, and protestations of devotion to peace are on the lips of almost everyone who speaks publicly of international relations in a political context. Even in the United States, where less than 10 per cent of the population have ever had first-hand experience with war (and none on their own soil), the idea is still widespread that war is stupid and nasty, and that it is justifiable to fight wars only in order to prevent them.

It is primarily this affect-determined repugnance against war which is the main target of attack in the persuasive efforts of the Neo-Clausewitzians. The main thrust of their arguments is directed towards restoring the *legitimacy* of war. In the United States this implies the demolition of the eschatological idea of 'the war to end war' which dominated American public opinion from 1917 to 1945.

The arguments of the Neo-Clauswitzians proceed along three lines: (1) against the idea that the attempts to outlaw war and to establish a machinery of international law (e.g. the United

Nations, the World Court, disarmament agreements) can be significantly effective in the present or in the foreseeable future; (2) the identification of anti-Communism (i.e. the official United States ideology) with the 'defence of Western civilization', hence eventually of the interests of humanity; (3) the insistence that the magnitude and the intensity of war can be controlled, i.e. the refutation of the idea that in our day, war, even between the two super powers, must necessarily lead to the total holocaust.

Among the numerous tracts of the Neo-Clausewitzians the most ambitious, to my knowledge, is *Peace and War* by Raymond Aron. Aron presents himself as a *Westerner* concerned with the precious heritage of Western civilization, which unfortunately, in a world devoid of law, can be defended only by overwhelming military might. Now, defence in the age of global politics cannot be confined to a deterrence of overt attack and to the ability to repel it or to retaliate against the attacker. An essential component of the defence of the 'Free World' is resistance to 'subversion'. Since the United States is the only power which is willing and able to sustain such resistance, the global policy of the United States must, in Aron's view, have the support of those who cherish the values of Western civilization. Accordingly Aron equates the goals of United States foreign policy with the defence of Western values. Since he is French this posture absolves him from the charge of chauvinism, the component of the political philosophy of war which has fallen into disrepute.

In no other work, to my knowledge, is Clausewitzian philosophy in modern dress presented so clearly and ably as in Aron's *Peace and War*. It is a work of immense erudition; its tone is cool and reserved. Beginning, fittingly, with Clausewitz's definition of war ('War is an act of violence to compel our opponent to fulfil our will'), it encompasses not merely the political philosophy of war but also brings to bear upon it the history subsequent to the crystallization of the Clausewitzian system (including the demise of the social order of which the political philosophy of war was a natural expression) and all the modern ideas of social science. In this context the classical simplicity of Clausewitz's thesis disappears; but this is the price we moderns must pay for our sophistication. Everything now must be qualified. Concepts must be refined, broken up into subtly differentiated sub-concepts. Above all, the heterogeneity, the fluidity, and the asymmetry of the contemporary world must be constantly kept in mind. It is no longer possible to maintain, as Clausewitz did, that in war everything is simple and that only the execution of the simple principles is difficult. On the contrary, everything in Aron's description of modern international politics appears enormously complex, in peace even more than in war.[39] Nevertheless this 'world sociology' (for that is what the work purports to be) rests on the same Clausewitzian foundations: nations were born in violence, they relate to each other through violence, and will continue to do so in the foreseeable future. The counsel of those who will not accept this basic truth is useless or dangerous.

Aron's book provides a sophisticated, sociologically, psychologically, and historically oriented rationale for the revival of the political philosophy of war. Books of this style and scope serve to re-establish the respectability of this philosophy in academic circles. American strategists, on the other hand, by and large appeal more directly to the general public.

Herman Kahn's contribution, for example, was by way of diluting the dread of war nurtured by the image of the nuclear holocaust. His arguments are presented as an appeal to reason, and to the courage required to face calmly and realistically the dangers precipitated by the nuclear age. In spite of everyone's desire to avoid a nuclear exchange, Kahn argues, such events may nevertheless happen. To deny the possibility because it is too horrible to contemplate is to refuse to face reality. According to Kahn it behoves us as rational beings to combat this natural but crippling repugnance. Once we overcome it, and so acquire the freedom 'to think about the unthinkable', we shall be better equipped to deal with the dangers.

This stance seems to reflect the ethnocentric–cataclysmic philosophy rather than the political philosophy of war. As such it may serve the purpose of 'getting the foot in the door' in the task of breaking down the resistance *to the very idea* of nuclear war. The basic argument here is that refusing to think about evil does not help to eradicate evil, just as the refusal to think about syphilis or cancer can only hinder the struggle against these plagues. Man deals effectively with the formidable problems of life by applying his intellect; and the effective application of intellect requires the disengagement from sentiment, passion, and fear.[40]

Having thus presumably gained the right to be heard, Kahn proceeds to develop an essentially taxonomic description of the wars of the future. His primary interest is in nuclear war (the hitherto uncharted realm of military science). His orientation (aside from the opening ploy, in which war is pictured as a catastrophe to be guarded against) is more frankly Clausewitzian than that of most other strategists. In fact, the title of his *magnum opus*, *Thermonuclear War*, is an obvious bid for the mantle of Clausewitz. In a later book, *On Escalation*, Kahn extends the taxonomy of inter-nation conflict to a vast range, from 'Pre-crisis Manoeuvring' to the war of total nuclear destruction. Of the forty-four rungs of his 'escalation ladder', twenty-nine involve the use of nuclear weapons.

The main point of Kahn's analysis is that the dichotomies between war and peace and between conventional and nuclear war are a vast over-simplification, a result of primitive either–or thinking, which inhibits rational analysis, narrows the range of options, and so puts people who succumb to it at a disadvantage in the diplo-military game. And it is the ability to play this 'game' which separates the men from the boys in the international arena.[41]

The Neo-Clausewitzians have carried the political philosophy of war farther than Clausewitz; and Kahn has carried it farther than anyone. In Clausewitz's view, even though the inter-nation struggle for power forms a continuum with war as merely one of its phases, still a threshold between war and peace is recognized. Once war begins, *military* objectives become paramount. Moreover, in Clausewitz's view, the prime military objective is clear, simple, and compelling: to destroy the enemy's ability and will to resist. Thus, in spite of Clausewitz's insistence that political objectives are the primary goals and the military ones only means to achieve these goals, the *gross* principles of military strategy and tactics remain constant, however the specific military problems had been determined by the political objectives of the war. In Kahn's treatment of strategy, especially of nuclear strategy, this is no longer the case. The ideal of a quick, decisive war, the sort envisaged by Clausewitz, Moltke, and Schlieffen, and Hitler, and actually realized in 1864, 1866, 1870, and 1939–40, remains with Kahn only an ideal. Kahn's prescription for a 'realistic' appraisal of the potentialities of military strategy no longer permits a division of labour between the diplomat and the general. The *political* phase must now pervade the entire range of inter-nation conflict, including the war phase, even all the twenty-eight levels of nuclear war – all but the very last, the 'spasm war', i.e. total mutual annihilation. This 'political phase' is essentially a kind of bargaining which, in Kahn's estimation, can and ought to go on as the war is being waged. He notes that Americans are becoming used to the idea. To illustrate, he cites a question he sometimes asks of audiences who attend his public lectures (which he describes as 'college students, businessmen, members of the League of Women Voters, etc.') namely, 'what they think would happen if President Johnson were suddenly notified that a large [nuclear] bomb had just exploded over New York City.' Kahn goes on:

> Almost nobody in the audience now (as opposed to five years ago) will reply that Johnson would go ahead and launch a large all-out attack on the Soviet Union. The overwhelming majority always suggests only one bomb. Where are the others? . . . If the Soviet wanted to launch an exemplary attack, why had they not made some preliminary demands or sent us a message so that we could understand what was going on? . . .
>
> In order to pursue the example even further, I have suggested an elaborate scenario outlining why the Soviet had in fact launched the attack deliberately and so informed the U.S. . . . A large percentage of the audience now are very interested in the degree of vulnerability of the Soviet forces. . . . When I suggest that just for the sake of example, we assume that the Soviet forces are invulnerable and could destroy the United States totally . . . almost all agree that there should be retaliation but that it should

be limited. Most suggest that Moscow be destroyed, but many object to this on the grounds that this city is much more important to the Soviet Union than New York is to the United States. These usually suggest that the destruction of some smaller city, such as Leningrad or Kiev would be appropriate counter-escalation . . .

In the past five years, almost everyone in the U.S. who has any interest in these problems or is even modestly well informed has . . . learned that there are possibilities of control in such bizarre situations.[42]

*

Since the publication in 1947 of John von Neumann's and Oskar Morgenstern's *Theory of Games and Economic Behavior* the notion has become widespread, especially in the United States, that this theory could (perhaps in the future) serve as the foundation of scientific diplo-military strategy. A formal definition of the theory of games supports this notion. Game theory can be justifiably defined as a theory of rational decision in situations involving conflicts of interest among two or more independent actors. The notion finds further support in the circumstance that a well-developed theory of rational decision in situations involving *one* actor in an uncertain environment does exist. In situations involving risk, it is possible to calculate the 'expected gain' (or loss) associated with each of several alternative courses of action, so that the rational decision can be reasonably defined as one which maximizes this expected gain (or minimizes the expected loss). Insurance companies and gambling houses actually base their decisions on calculations of this sort. The principle applies to the management of any enterprise which must cope with statistically fluctuating environmental factors, e.g. the stock market, prices, supply, demand, weather.

In this theory (which could be called the theory of one-person games, or games against Nature) it is explicitly assumed that the fluctuations in the environment are affected by chance, i.e. an agency indifferent to the actors' preference for the outcomes. Game theory extends this method to situations where the environment is at least partially controlled by other actors who *do* have their own interests, i.e. conflicting preferences. Moreover, if 'our' actor is rational (i.e. if he calculates the possible outcomes of his various choices) so are the other actors. That is, in making *their* decisions they are able to take into account the possible courses of action of 'our' actor.

Game theory, then, treats specifically of *strategic* decisions, i.e. decisions contingent on the possible decisions of others, which, in turn, are assumed to be contingent on our possible decisions. The notion of strategy is, of course, not new. Strategic calculations constitute (or are thought to constitute) an integral part of military science. However, the development of *an abstract* mathematical theory of such calculations can be readily assumed to lay the foundations for a much farther-reaching development of strategic science than has been possible in context-bound situations. Abstract mathematical thinking 'emancipates' theory, as it were, and thereby gives it a powerful impetus for development. This has happened before, when geometry was severed from its applications to land measurement and architecture, when the theory of probability was developed apart from specific gambling context, etc.

Consequently the development of the abstract mathematical theory of games was seen in some quarters as the groundwork of a fruitful theory of rational decisions in conflict situations, i.e. of scientific strategic decision making.

So the outlook appears, on the basis of a formal definition of game theory and in the perspective of historical analogy. However, when we examine the actual contexts in which game theory could actually apply to decision making, we find that the application can be meaningful only if the following conditions are satisfied.

1. The relevant actors are named.
2. The strategies (options) available to each actor are precisely specified.
3. The outcomes, or at least the probabilities of the outcomes (if Chance also 'makes decisions'), are listed.
4. *At least* the preference order of all possible outcomes is given for each actor. In most situations, however, the specification of preference orders is not sufficient; a stronger 'utility scale' must be given on which it is possible to determine *also* the

relative magnitudes of the difference between the utilities of *pairs* of outcomes.

5. Possible coalitions are specified; whether, for example, the situation allows two or more actors to undertake joint decisions so as to ensure outcomes preferred by both (or all) to outcomes which would obtain if they acted independently.

6. A criterion of rationality is defined.

Those who deprecate the importance, the usefulness or the relevance of formal game theory to the conduct of international politics fall mostly into two categories. Some oppose the 'mechanization' of policy on moral grounds. The conceptualization of international politics as a game seems to imply that human beings are reduced to the status of pawns. Others dismiss game theory on the grounds that the conditions listed above are not realizable: the situations are too fluid and vague to yield to formal descriptions and calculations.

Both objections may be valid; but as they stand they are not decisive. Arguments based on moral repugnance elicit the pragmatic refutations cited above: not how we feel about the situation (so the refutations go) but what we do about it ought to be the proper object of ethical judgement. Besides, so the pragmatic argument goes, calculation of strategies is always relevant to a set of given preferences. Even if the objectives of nations were entirely humanitarian, it would still behove the leaders to make realistic appraisals of different courses of action with regard to their relative effectiveness, and these calculations would also necessitate the treatment of human beings as 'statistics'. Strategic thinking, it is argued, is morally neutral; it can be fitted to the implementation of any given goals, including ethically irreproachable ones.

Objections to game theory on the grounds of its inefficacy can also be partially answered. For one thing, the idealization and simplification of situations is a standard device in all scientific analysis. Therefore to reject a theory on the grounds that it fails to capture all the intricacies of the phenomena studied is to reject scientific analysis *in toto*. In view of the enormous successes of scientific analysis, precisely via the formulation of idealized and simplified models of physical systems, we cannot summarily reject the extension of this method to the analysis of behaving systems. True, the plasticity and complexity of human perceptions, motives, and reactions put obstacles in the way of developing a rational decision theory, but they do not render it impossible.

Actually a defence of game theory as a method relevant to the 'science' of international relations is not often resorted to by the diplo-military strategists of Neo-Clausewitzian persuasion. Those with sufficient mathematical background (a small minority) to understand formal game theory, realize that whatever heuristic value the theory may have, its *practical* value is extremely limited, being confined to the analysis of situations which satisfy the above-mentioned conditions. Those without specialized mathematical knowledge (e.g. political scientists, administrators, military men) tend to conceive of their expertise as that of the artist rather than of a scientist. Knowledge of the specifics of situations, conjectures based on long experience, political intuition, the awareness of details – in short, the power to discriminate rather than the readiness to generalize – is what men of affairs call expertise. Generally speaking, they have little patience with the abstract and often abstruse formulations of the mathematician. In this respect the Neo-Clausewitzians recapitulate Clausewitz: he also stressed the intuitive, 'artistic' aspects of strategic decisions, emphasized the crucial role of 'human factors' (including genius), and dismissed as sterile all pedantry and formalism in military science.

In my own polemic against the Neo-Clausewitzians[43] I discussed at great length the limitations of game theory as a theory of rational decision. This discussion was repeatedly interpreted as an implication that what I considered to be the errors of the American diplo-military strategists derived from hasty or illegitimate applications of game theory to the formulation of policy. To this presumed implication some replied that the accusation was irrelevant inasmuch as there were very few game theoreticians among the strategists. D. G. Brennan, for example, pointed out, referring to the output of the professional staff of the Hudson Institute,[44] that the '. . . number of individual pages on which there is any discussion of concepts from game theory could be counted on one hand'.[45]

It is true that some critics of present United States foreign policy[46] have pictured the diplo-military strategic community as being dominated by 'game theoreticians', an impression easily refuted by an examination of the backgrounds of the personnel comprising this community and of their methods of analysis. However, my discussion of game theory in the context of the polemic did not have the aim attributed to it. Rather it was aimed at pointing out the inadequacy of the political philosophy of war. This philosophy is embodied in the statement of the central problem of United States foreign policy by Robert Osgood: '... the problem is this: How can the United States utilize its military power as a rational and effective instrument of national policy?'[47] The key words are 'rational' and 'instrument'. They imply that the goals of 'national policy' are given, and are realizable by the use of military power. This puts the whole situation in the *context* of a game of strategy. Whatever be the inadequacies of game theory as a practical method, the *framework* of thought which underlies the method of game theory is taken by the Neo-Clausewitzians as the proper one for the conduct of national policy. It is against this *framework of thought* that I directed my polemic, not against the use of game theory as a practical method in arriving at rational decisions. Far from inveighing against game theory on that account I pointed out the insights to be gained from it. These insights in no way depend on the usefulness of game theory as a practical tool. They depend on the laying bare of the intricacies of certain kinds of conflict. One of the results of this analysis is the discovery of contexts in which the very notion of 'rational decision' dissolves into ambiguities and so loses the meaning ascribed to it in other contexts.

This 'dissolution of rationality' can be illustrated by exceedingly simple situations. Consider two opponents locked in combat, the outcome of which each knows can be only mutual annihilation. If only both could disengage *simultaneously*, both could avoid annihilation. But each knows that if he *tries* to disengage (e.g. turns his back on the enemy), then he alone will be annihilated. Assuming that mutual annihilation is preferred by each to only his own annihilation, what is the 'rational thing' for each combatant to do? 'Rationality' dictates against disengagement *whether* the other disengages or not, since, if the other tries to disengage, one can save oneself by annihilating the other with impunity; if one does not try to disengage, it is suicide for the other to do so. If, however, mutual disengagement is preferred by *both* combatants to the continuation of the combat, then the 'rational' choice by both actors *prevents* the outcome preferred by both. What, then, does 'rationality' mean in this context?[48]

Examples of this sort, formulated as games, fall into the category of so-called two-person non-zero-sum games, i.e. conflicts in which some outcomes are preferred to others by *both* players (although the actors still have conflicting interests). These games differ from the so-called zero-sum games, in which one player's gains are always equal to the other player's losses. In the case of zero-sum games (provided only the utilities of the outcomes can be specified), it is always possible (in principle) to find an optimal strategy (or strategy 'mixture') in the sense of getting the largest pay-off (or expected pay-off) which the conditions of the game allow (assuming that the opponent has chosen *his* optimal strategy or strategy mixture). Therefore the definition of rationality offers no difficulty in this case. The rational strategy of each player is the one which assures the greatest possible loss (or smallest possible gain) to the opponent. However, as we have seen, there exist 'games' (i.e. conflict situations) of the non-zero-sum type to which this definition of rationality does not apply. In such situations, if each actor tries to minimize his losses (or maximize his gains), the two may not get as much as they could get otherwise.

Clausewitz seems to have had no awareness of the non-zero-sum game situation. Stated in the terminology of game theory, his opening chapter defines war exclusively as a zero-sum game. 'Whatever is to the advantage of one side is to the disadvantage of the other' is assumed by Clausewitz to be a self-evident proposition.

The Neo-Clausewitzians, especially those with some knowledge of game theory, have transcended this view in their analyses of the logic of conflict. Especially T. E. Schelling[49] has gone to great lengths to explain the limitations of the zero-sum game as a paradigm of conflict, and to point out that even enemies have some common interests. Schelling advances the idea of 'cooperating with the enemy', a concept that Clausewitz would have declared to be a contradiction in terms. The claims sometimes made by strategic analysts that their work serves the cause of peace (as well as that of 'rational' war) is based on the fact that the 'common interests' of the super-powers (e.g. the avoidance of accidentally triggered nuclear war) are sometimes taken into account in the design of weapons systems.[50]

Nevertheless the core of Clausewitzian philosophy has remained imbedded in the Neo-Clausewitzian conception of international politics as a continuum of power struggle, and of 'rational policy' as a choice of a point on that continuum (determined by specific circumstances) which seems to confer the greatest strategic advantage to the chooser. Thus, while recognizing the troublesome paradoxes revealed by the paradigms of some non-zero-sum games, the Neo-Clausewitzians have never seriously questioned the meaning of rationality in the context of international conflict. This is all the more true because purely theoretical analysis is not really taken seriously by the wielders of power, in whose service the strategists work. Consequently the closer strategic analysis comes to actual strategic decisions, and the more concrete it becomes, the more it is forced into channels determined by the pressures of the moment. The strategic recommendations which are *used* are those dealing with the allocation of funds, personnel, and equipment; with weapons systems design, and with logistics. In these areas there are few, if any, opportunities 'to cooperate with the enemy'.

The pressure on decision-makers is to choose courses of action. To the extent that the concept of 'rational decision' enjoys prestige with the wielders of power, it must apply in the context of 'problem solving'. To solve a problem from the point of view of the power wielder is to answer the traditional question: 'How can I get the most for the least?' This is the fundamental question of technology, of competitive business, and of war. The very posing of the problem turns attention to those aspects of conflict which make concrete formulations possible. Efficacy of actions can be *measured* if it is expressed in dollars, fire power, investment rates, kill ratios, etc. That is, logistic calculations seem to shed the most light on the problem, as it is posed by the power wielders, because such calculations clarify and operationalize the meaning of 'efficacy'. Consequently, in a culture where science is practically identified with technology, success with virtue, and security with power, there is unrelenting pressure to translate vaguely stated political problems into clearly stated military ones.

To the extent that rational methods are employed to solve the problems so translated, they are developed in the framework of operations research (where the decisions are not contingent on those of a rational opponent) or, on the next level of sophistication, in the framework of a zero-sum game (where the interests of the opponent are always taken to be diametrically opposed to one's own). This is not surprising, since only in those contexts can 'rational decision' be unambiguously defined. Beyond these contexts is an intellectual barrier which cannot be breached without abandoning the notion that every decision problem has a rational solution in the sense of an optimal course of action chosen by an *individual* actor. This is what I have called elsewhere the zero-sum trap; the search for rational *individually* chosen strategies forces the perception of conflict into zero-sum paradigms.[51]

Once the zero-sum paradigm prevails, the 'logic of conflict' becomes simple. It reduces to the logic which underlies Clausewitz's philosophy of war. It makes shambles of the theory of 'limited war' as a form of 'cooperating with the enemy' which is one of the keystones of Neo-Clausewitzian diplo-military philosophy, and so introduces an inherent contradiction into it. American intervention in South-east Asia is publicized as a 'limited war'. It must be kept in mind that what appears to Americans as 'limited war' appears as total war to the people against whom it is waged. What appears as 'control' of the amount of pressure exerted on, say, the Vietnamese is only a delusion if, for reasons of prestige, the United States has no choice but to escalate the war if the 'pressure' fails to bring the Vietnamese to their knees. The Clausewitzian principle implies *logically* that military policy ought to be geared to political objectives. But *psychologically* the implication is read the other way: political objectives are determined by military capacity. This is what happened to Germany. This is what happened to every state which, encouraged by repeated military successes, has wedded policy to 'the rational use of force' in the pursuit of national interests.

*

Towards the close of Book Four of *On War*, Clausewitz utters what amounts to a prayer:

> May we succeed in lending a hand to those who in our dear native land are called upon to speak with authority on these matters, that we may be their guide into this field of inquiry, and excite them to make a candid examination of the subject.

Colonel F. N. Maude, editor of the 1908 English edition, remarks in a footnote:

'This prayer was abundantly granted – vidé the German victories of 1870.'

Here we may apply a principle, recognized by Clausewitz: the wisdom of a decision is relative to outcomes, immediate or remote. Writing here some sixty years after Col. Maude, we might add, '– vide also the fruits of 1914 and those of 1939'. As Kenneth Boulding once put it, nothing fails like success.

It is idle to speculate about what Clausewitz would have said had he been able to foresee the results of his teachings in Europe. Clausewitz was a man of his age; he stood on the threshold of an era when the nation state seemed to embody the answer to man's quest for immortality. Unlike the great mystical or cosmic religions (Christianity, Buddhism), which demand a dissolution of the self into a Godhead or the cosmos, state worship allows the *assertion* of the *self*; to be sure, also dissolved into the state, but nevertheless still differentiated from other selves (the enemy) and magnified in power many million fold. Thus state worship offers an outlet for boundless love and for boundless hate, both passions elevated to sacred duties.

Especially, for the Germans, state worship came easily in the nineteenth century, because until 1871 nationhood was for them not something to be taken for granted but something to be achieved on the basis of common language and a cultural heritage. In one of his poems, Clausewitz wrote:

> The full heart of the German
> Pours out in German tongue.
> In quips is French well spoken,
> And musical is the Italian's speech.
> But when the glance is turned heavenward,
> As when the three Swiss swore their Holy Pact,
> The German word sounds like the metal of their swords
> With which they smote the stranger's yoke.[52]

Indeed, language is the most concrete criterion of national identification. At the same time, love of one's native tongue is a mark of noble sensitivity, a passion entirely acceptable to the literate, the high-minded, and the gentle-mannered.

Thus in Clausewitz patriotism, liberty, and identification with the power of the State were all parts of a harmonious self. Clausewitz had no need to resort to sophistry or self-deception, nor to erect a barrier between his intellect and his humanity. Clausewitz was a *whole* man. He may have worshipped an evil deity, but he revered it with his whole being. In short, in retrospect we can see him as a sinister but noble figure in the unfolding of a tragedy.

It is difficult to forecast such a role for the contemporary disciples of Clausewitz. Much is known to them which could not be known to their master, including the fruits of European militarism, the illusory nature of security through power, and the obscene absurdities of total war. The underpinnings of military patriotism have been eroded away in our urbane, commercial–industrial age. Western nations no longer go to war to the sound of bugles. Gone are the regimental traditions, the Commander on his horse, the impeccably executed campaigns culminating in decisive battles. Gone are the virtually inviolate strategic and tactical principles to be taken seriously, like the classical chess openings. In fact there is almost nothing in the contemporary paroxysms of destruction which resembles in the least what Clausewitz pictured as war, whose 'true nature' he supposedly discovered. No head of state dares nowadays to justify starting a war 'in order to impose our will on our opponent'. All wars must pose as defensive wars (an absurdity according to Clausewitz, cf. p. 396); and at the highest pinnacles of state and military power war is solemnly declared to be a scourge of humanity.

Still, the Neo-Clausewitzians continue to assume the maxims of Clausewitz: the world is a collection of states, each a law unto itself. The object of international politics is power. Power is gained and maintained by violence.

To keep these assumptions intact, I suspect much must be suppressed, in particular some important questions. If the war-waging state has retained the appetites and the moral precepts of eighteenth-century princes, why should an enlightened twentieth-century man identify with such a state and serve it – in particular, advise it in the conduct of its predatory adventures? On the other hand, if the object of power is something besides power – for example, the defence of precious values, as some strategists maintain – then why do their descriptions of these values often reduce to banalities, which on both sides of the Cold War are mirror images of each other?[53]

It is difficult to believe that the dedication of the Neo-Clausewitzians to their professed ideologies is as genuine as was Clausewitz's dedication to the Prussian ideal of the State. The overriding dedication of the Neo-Clausewitzians resembles rather that of the eighteenth-century military men. It is dedication to their profession, the most strongly felt loyalty in our professionalized culture. The strategists must do what they do because they love it and take pride in it.[54] Clausewitz was, of course, also enormously proud of his work. There is, however, a vital difference. When Clausewitz glorified War, he knew what he was talking about. He sensed *all* the levels of war, from the plottings in the chancelleries to the screams of the dying. War was to Clausewitz an intense human experience; and when he wrote about the glorious future in store for the flowering Art of War (liberated from the shackles imposed on it by human frailty), he envisaged an intensification of that experience. He may appear to us to have been obsessed by a cruel passion, but he did not appear absurd.

Today speculations about 'progress in the art of war' are carried on in a surrealistic mode, as witnessed by the situation described by Herman Kahn as 'bizarre' (cf. p. 69). In fact, not only is the depicted situation bizarre but also the setting in which the discussion of it takes place: a group of 'college students, business men, members of the League of Woman Voters, etc.', arguing whether the 'elimination' of Moscow or of Leningrad plus Kiev is the more 'appropriate' response to the 'elimination' of New York. I suspect that these discussions are possible only if one seals off from one's consciousness every shred of identification with the human race. This is not hard to do, if one is spared, as are the strategists and their receptive audiences, direct contact with the realities behind the fantasies.

This is why the Neo-Clausewitzians cannot be seen as sinister figures but only as bizarre ones. In the name of realism they perpetuate an obsolete collective state of mind which has brought humanity to the brink of disaster. What is unfolding is not a tragedy but a ghastly farce.

Vom Kriege.

Hinterlassenes Werk

des

Generals Carl von Clausewitz.

Erster Theil.

Berlin,
bei Ferdinand Dümmler.

1832.

INTRODUCTION BY COL. F. N. MAUDE

THE Germans interpret their new national colours – black, red, and white – by the saying, 'Durch Nacht und Blut zur licht.' ('Through night and blood to light'), and no work yet written conveys to the thinker a clearer conception of all that the red streak in their flag stands for than this deep and philosophical analysis of 'War' by Clausewitz.

It reveals 'War', stripped of all accessories, as the exercise of force for the attainment of a political object, unrestrained by any law save that of expediency, and thus gives the key to the interpretation of German political aims, past, present, and future, which is unconditionally necessary for every student of the modern conditions of Europe. Step by step, every event since Waterloo follows with logical consistency from the teachings of Napoleon, formulated for the first time, some twenty years afterwards, by this remarkable thinker.

What Darwin accomplished for Biology generally Clausewitz did for the Life History of Nations nearly half a century before him, for both have proved the existence of the same law in each case, viz. 'The survival of the fittest' – the 'fittest', as Huxley long since pointed out, not being necessarily synonymous with the ethically 'best'. Neither of these thinkers was concerned with the ethics of the struggle which each studied so exhaustively, but to both men the phase or condition presented itself neither as moral nor immoral, any more than are famine, disease, or other natural phenomena, but as emanating from a force inherent in all living organisms which can only be mastered by understanding its nature. It is in that spirit that, one after the other, all the Nations of the Continent, taught by such drastic lessons as Koniggrätz and Sedan, have accepted the lesson, with the result that today Europe is an armed camp, and *peace is maintained by the equilibrium of forces, and will continue just as long as this equilibrium exists, and no longer*.

Whether this state of equilibrium is in itself a good or

desirable thing may be open to argument. I have discussed it at length in my 'War and the World's Life'; but I venture to suggest that to no one would a renewal of the era of warfare be a change for the better, as far as existing humanity is concerned. Meanwhile, however, with every year that elapses the forces at present in equilibrium are changing in magnitude – the pressure of populations which have to be fed is rising, and an explosion along the line of least resistance is, sooner or later, inevitable.

As I read the teaching of the recent Hague Conference, no responsible Government on the Continent is anxious to form in themselves that line of least resistance; *they* know only too well what War would mean; and we alone, absolutely unconscious of the trend of the dominant thought of Europe, are pulling down the dam which may at any moment let in on us the flood of invasion.

Now no responsible man in Europe, perhaps least of all in Germany, thanks us for this voluntary destruction of our defences, for all who are of any importance would very much rather end their days in peace than incur the burden of responsibility which War would entail. But they realize that the gradual dissemination of the principles taught by Clausewitz has created a condition of molecular tension in the minds of the Nations they govern analogous to the 'critical temperature of water heated above boiling-point under pressure', which may at any moment bring about an explosion which they will be powerless to control.

The case is identical with that of an ordinary steam boiler, delivering so and so many pounds of steam to its engines as long as the envelope can contain the pressure; but let a breach in its continuity arise – relieving the boiling water of all restraint – and in a moment the whole mass flashes into vapour, developing a power no work of man can oppose.

The ultimate consequences of defeat no man can foretell. The only way to avert them is to ensure victory; and, again following out the principles of Clausewitz, victory can only be ensured by the creation in peace of an organization which will bring every available man, horse, and gun (or ship and gun, if the war be on the sea) in the shortest possible time, and with the utmost possible momentum, upon the decisive field of action – which in turn leads to the final doctrine formulated by Von der Goltz in excuse for the action of the late President Kruger in 1899:

'The Statesman who, knowing his instrument to be ready, and seeing War inevitable, hesitates to strike first is guilty of a crime against his country.'

It is because this sequence of cause and effect is absolutely unknown to our Members of Parliament, elected by popular representation, that all our efforts to ensure a lasting peace by securing *efficiency with economy* in our National Defences have been rendered nugatory.

This estimate of the influence of Clausewitz's sentiments on contemporary thought in Continental Europe may appear exaggerated to those who have not familiarized themselves with M. Gustav de Bon's exposition of the laws governing the formation and conduct of crowds. I do not wish for one minute to be understood as asserting that Clausewitz has been conscientiously studied and understood in *any* Army, not even in the Prussian, but his work has been the ultimate foundation on which every drill regulation in Europe, except our own, has been reared. It is this ceaseless repetition of his fundamental ideas to which one-half of the male population of every Continental Nation has been subjected for two to three years of their lives, which has tuned their minds to vibrate in harmony with his precepts, and those who know and appreciate this fact at its true value have only to strike the necessary chords in order to evoke a response sufficient to overpower any other ethical conception which those who have not organized their forces beforehand can appeal to.

The recent set-back experienced by the Socialists in Germany is an illustration of my position. The Socialist leaders of that country are far behind the responsible Governors in their knowledge of the management of crowds. The latter had long before (in 1893, in fact) made their arrangements to prevent the spread of Socialistic propaganda beyond certain useful limits. As long as the Socialists only threatened capital they were not seriously interfered with, for the Government knew quite well that the undisputed sway of the employer was not for the ultimate good of the State. The standard of comfort must not be pitched too low if men are to be ready to die for their country. But the moment the Socialists began to interfere seriously with the discipline of the Army the word went round, and the Socialists lost heavily at the polls.

If this power of predetermined reaction to acquired ideas can be evoked successfully in a matter of internal interest only, in which the 'obvious interest' of the vast majority of the population is so clearly on the side of the Socialist, it must be evident how enormously greater it will prove when set in motion against an external enemy, where the 'obvious interest' of the people is, from the very nature of things, as manifestly on the side of the Government; and the Statesman who failed to take into account the force of the 'resultant thought wave' of a crowd of some seven million men, all trained to respond to their ruler's call, would be guilty of treachery as grave as one who failed to strike when he knew the Army to be ready for immediate action.

As already pointed out, it is to the spread of Clausewitz's ideas that the present state of more or less immediate readiness for war of all European Armies is due, and since the organization of these forces is uniform this 'more or less' of readiness exists in precise proportion to the sense of duty which animates the several Armies. Where the spirit of duty and self-sacrifice is low the troops are unready and inefficient; where, as in Prussia, these qualities, by the training of a whole century, have become instinctive, troops really are ready to the last button, and might be poured down upon any one of her neighbours with such rapidity that the very first collision must suffice to ensure ultimate success – a success by no means certain if the enemy, whoever he may be, is allowed breathing-time in which to set his house in order.

An example will make this clearer. In 1887 Germany was on the very verge of War with France and Russia. At that moment her superior efficiency, the consequence of this inborn sense of duty – surely one of the highest qualities of humanity – was so great that it is more than probable that less than six weeks would have sufficed to bring the French to their knees. Indeed, after the first fortnight it would have been possible to begin transferring troops from the Rhine to the Niemen; and the same case may arise again. But if France and Russia had been allowed even ten days' warning the German plan would have been completely defeated. France alone might then have claimed all the efforts that Germany could have put forth to defeat her.

Yet there are politicians in England so grossly ignorant of the German reading of the Napoleonic lessons that they expect that Nation to sacrifice the enormous advantage they have prepared by a whole century of self-sacrifice and practical patriotism by an appeal to a Court of Arbitration, and the further delays which must arise by going through the medieval formalities of recalling Ambassadors and exchanging ultimatums.

Most of our present-day politicians have made their money in business – a 'form of human competition greatly resembling War', to paraphrase Clausewitz. Did they, when in the throes of such competition, send formal notice to their rivals of their plans to get the better of them in commerce? Did Mr Carnegie, the archpriest of Peace at any price, when he built up the Steel Trust, notify his competitors when and how he proposed to strike the blows which successively made him master of millions? Surely the Directors of a Great Nation may consider the interests of their shareholders – i.e. the people they govern – as sufficiently serious not to be endangered by the deliberate sacrifice of the preponderant position of readiness which generations of self-devotion, patriotism and wise forethought have won for them?

As regards the strictly military side of this work, though the recent researches of the French General Staff into the records and documents of the Napoleonic period have shown conclusively that Clausewitz had never grasped the essential point of the Great Emperor's strategic method, yet it is admitted that he has completely fathomed the spirit which gave life to the form; and notwithstanding all the variations in application which have resulted from the progress of invention in every field of national activity (not in the technical improvements in armament alone), this spirit still remains the essential factor in the whole matter. Indeed, if anything, modern appliances have intensified its importance, for though, with equal armaments on both sides, the form of battles must always remain the same, the facility and certainty of combination which better methods of communicating orders and intelligence have conferred upon the Commanders has rendered the control of great masses immeasurably more certain than it was in the past.

Men kill each other at greater distances, it is true – but killing is a constant factor in all battles. The difference between 'now and then' lies in this, that, thanks to the enormous increase in range (the essential feature in modern armaments), it is possible to concentrate by surprise, on any chosen spot, a man-killing power fully twentyfold greater than was conceivable in the days of Waterloo; and whereas in Napoleon's time this concentration of man-killing power (which in his hands took the form of the great case-shot attack) depended almost entirely on the shape and condition of the ground, which might or might not be favourable, nowadays such concentration of fire-power is almost independent of the country altogether.

Thus, at Waterloo, Napoleon was compelled to wait till the ground became firm enough for his guns to gallop over; nowadays every gun at his disposal, and five times that number had he possessed them, might have opened on any point in the British position he had selected, as soon as it became light enough to see.

Or, to take a more modern instance, viz. the battle of St Privat-Gravelotte, August 18, 1870, where the Germans were able to concentrate on both wings batteries of two hundred guns and upwards, it would have been practically impossible, owing to the section of the slopes of the French position, to carry out the old-fashioned case-shot attack at all. Nowadays there would be no difficulty in turning on the fire of two thousand guns on any point of the position, and switching this fire up and down the line like water from a fire-engine hose, if the occasion demanded such concentration.

But these alterations in method make no difference in the truth of the picture of War which Clausewitz presents, with which every soldier, and above all every Leader, should be saturated.

Death, wounds, suffering, and privation remain the same,

whatever the weapons employed, and their reaction on the ultimate nature of man is the same now as in the struggle a century ago. It is this reaction that the Great Commander has to understand and prepare himself to control; and the task becomes ever greater as, fortunately for humanity, the opportunities for gathering experience become more rare.

In the end, and with every improvement in science, the result depends more and more on the character of the Leader and his power of resisting 'the sensuous impressions of the battlefield'. Finally, for those who would fit themselves in advance for such responsibility, I know of no more inspiring advice than that given by Krishna to Arjuna ages ago, when the latter trembled before the awful responsibility of launching his Army against the hosts of the Pandav's:

> This life within all living things, my Prince,
> Hides beyond harm. Scorn thou to suffer, then,
> For that which cannot suffer. Do thy part!
> Be mindful of thy name, and tremble not.
> Nought better can betide a martial soul
> Than lawful war. Happy the warrior
> To whom comes joy of battle. . . .
> . . . But if thou shunn'st
> This honourable field – a Kshittriya –
> If, knowing thy duty and thy task, thou bidd'st
> Duty and task go by – that shall be sin!
> And those to come shall speak thee infamy
> From age to age. But infamy is worse
> For men of noble blood to bear than death!
>
> . . . . .
>
> Therefore arise, thou Son of Kunti! Brace
> Thine arm for conflict; nerve thy heart to meet,
> As things alike to thee, pleasure or pain,
> Profit or ruin, victory or defeat.
> So minded, gird thee to the fight, for so
> Thou shalt not sin!

COL. F. N. MAUDE, C.B., *late* R.E.

INTRODUCTION OF THE AUTHOR

THAT the conception of the scientific does not consist alone, or chiefly, in system, and its finished theoretical constructions, requires nowadays no exposition. System in this treatise is not to be found on the surface, and instead of a finished building of theory, there are only materials.

The scientific form lies here in the endeavour to explore the nature of military phenomena to show their affinity with the nature of the things of which they are composed. Nowhere has the philosophical argument been evaded, but where it runs out into too thin a thread the Author has preferred to cut it short, and fall back upon the corresponding results of experience; for in the same way as many plants only bear fruit when they do not shoot too high, so in the practical arts the theoretical leaves and flowers must not be made to sprout too far, but kept near to experience, which is their proper soil.

Unquestionably it would be a mistake to try to discover from the chemical ingredients of a grain of corn the form of the ear of corn which it bears, as we have only to go to the field to see the ears ripe. Investigation and observation, philosophy and experience, must neither despise nor exclude one another; they mutually afford each other the rights of citizenship. Consequently, the propositions of this book, with their arch of inherent necessity, are supported either by experience or by the conception of War itself as external points, so that they are not without abutments.*

It is, perhaps, not impossible to write a systematic theory of War full of spirit and substance, but ours, hitherto, have been very much the reverse. To say nothing of their unscientific

* That this is not the case in the works of many military writers, especially of those who have aimed at treating of War itself in a scientific manner, is shown in many instances, in which by their reasoning, the *pro* and *contra* swallow each other up so effectually that there is no vestige of the tails even which were left in the case of the two lions.

spirit, in their striving after coherence and completeness of system, they overflow with commonplaces, truisms, and twaddle of every kind. If we want a striking picture of them we have only to read Lichtenberg's extract from a code of regulations in case of fire.

If a house takes fire, we must seek, above all things, to protect the right side of the house standing on the left, and, on the other hand, the left side of the house on the right; for if we, for example should protect the left side of the house on the left, then the right side of the house lies to the right of the left, and consequently as the fire lies to the right of this side, and of the right side (for we have assumed that the house is situated to the left of the fire), therefore the right side is situated nearer to the fire than the left, and the right side of the house might catch fire if it was not protected before it came to the left, which is protected. Consequently, something might be burnt that is not protected, and that sooner than something else would be burnt, even if it was not protected; consequently we must let alone the latter and protect the former. In order to impress the thing on one's mind, we have only to note if the house is situated to the right of the fire, then it is the left side, and if the house is to the left it is the right side.

In order not to frighten the intelligent reader by such commonplaces, and to make the little good that there is distasteful by pouring water upon it, the Author has preferred to give in small ingots of fine metal his impressions and convictions, the result of many years' reflection on War, of his intercourse with men of ability, and of much personal experience. Thus the seemingly weakly bound-together chapters of this book have arisen, but it is hoped they will not be found wanting in logical connexion. Perhaps soon a greater head may appear, and instead of these single grains, give the whole in a casting of pure metal without dross.

BRIEF MEMOIR OF GENERAL CLAUSEWITZ BY THE TRANSLATOR

THE Author of the work here translated, General Carl von Clausewitz, was born at Burg, near Magdeburg, in 1780, and entered the Prussian Army as Fahnenjunker (i.e. ensign) in 1792. He served in the campaigns of 1793-94 on the Rhine, after which he seems to have devoted some time to the study of the scientific branches of his profession. In 1801 he entered the Military School at Berlin, and remained there till 1803. During his residence there he attracted the notice of General Scharnhorst, then at the head of the establishment; and the patronage of this distinguished officer had immense influence on his future career, and we may gather from his writings that he ever afterwards continued to entertain a high esteem for Scharnhorst. In the campaign of 1806 he served as Aide-de-camp to Prince Augustus of Prussia; and being wounded and taken prisoner, he was sent into France until the close of that war. On his return, he was placed on General Scharnhorst's Staff, and employed in the work then going on for the reorganization of the Army. He was also at this time selected as military instructor to the late King of Prussia, then Crown Prince. In 1812 Clausewitz, with several other Prussian officers, having entered the Russian service, his first appointment was as Aide-de-camp to General Phul. Afterwards, while serving with Wittgenstein's army, he assisted in negotiating the famous convention of Tauroggen with York. Of the part he took in that affair he has left an interesting account in his work on the 'Russian Campaign'. It is there stated that, in order to bring the correspondence which had been carried on with York to a termination in one way or another, the Author was despatched to York's headquarters with two letters, one was from General d'Auvray, the Chief of the Staff of Wittgenstein's army, to General Diebitsch, showing the arrangements made to cut off York's corps from Macdonald (this was necessary in order to give York a plausible excuse for seceding from the French); the other was an intercepted letter from Macdonald to the Duke of Bassano. With regard to the former of these, the Author says, 'it would not have had weight with a man like York, but for a military justification, if the Prussian Court should require one as against the French, it was important.'

The second letter was calculated at the least to call up in General York's mind all the feelings of bitterness which perhaps for some days past had been diminished by the consciousness of his own behaviour towards the writer.

As the Author entered General York's chamber, the latter called out to him, 'Keep off from me; I will have nothing more to do with you; your d—d Cossacks have let a letter of Macdonald's pass through them, which brings me an order to march on Piktrepöhnen, in order there to effect our junction. All doubt is now at an end; your troops do not come up; you are too weak; march I must, and I must excuse myself from all further negotiation, which may cost me my head.' The Author said that he would make no opposition to all this, but begged for a candle, as he had letters to show the General, and, as the latter seemed still to hesitate, the Author added, 'Your Excellency will not surely place me in the embarrassment of departing without having executed my commission.' The General ordered candles, and called in Colonel von Roeder, the chief of his staff, from the ante-chamber. The letters were read. After a pause of an instant, the General said, 'Clausewitz, you are a Prussian, do you believe that the letter of General d'Auvray is sincere, and that Wittgenstein's troops will really be at the points he mentioned on the 31st?' The Author replied, 'I pledge myself for the sincerity of this letter upon the knowledge I have of General d'Auvray and the other men of Wittgenstein's headquarters; whether the dispositions he announces can be accomplished as he lays down I certainly cannot pledge myself; for your Excellency knows that in war we must often fall short of the line we have drawn for ourselves.' The General was silent for a few minutes of earnest reflection; then he held out his hand to the Author, and said,

'You have me. Tell General Diebitsch that we must confer early tomorrow at the mill of Poschenen, and that I am now firmly determined to separate myself from the French and their cause.' The hour was fixed for 8 a.m. After this was settled, the General added, 'But I will not do the thing by halves, I will get you Massenbach also.' He called in an officer who was of Massenbach's cavalry, and who had just left them. Much like Schiller's Wallenstein, he asked, walking up and down the room the while, 'What say your regiments?' The officer broke out with enthusiasm at the idea of a riddance from the French alliance, and said that every man of the troops in question felt the same.

'You young ones may talk; but my older head is shaking on my shoulders,' replied the General.*

After the close of the Russian campaign Clausewitz remained in the service of that country, but was attached as a Russian staff officer to Blucher's headquarters till the Armistice in 1813.

In 1814, he became Chief of the Staff of General Walmoden's Russo-German Corps, which formed part of the Army of the North under Bernadotte. His name is frequently mentioned with distinction in that campaign, particularly in connexion with the affair of Goehrde.

Clausewitz re-entered the Prussian service in 1815, and served as Chief of the Staff to Thielman's corps, which was engaged with Grouchy at Wavre, on the 18th of June.

After the Peace, he was employed in a command on the Rhine. In 1818, he became Major-General, and Director of the Military School at which he had been previously educated.

In 1830, he was appointed Inspector of Artillery at Breslau, but soon after nominated Chief of the Staff to the Army of Observation, under Marshal Gneisenau on the Polish frontier.

The latest notices of his life and services are probably to be found in the memoirs of General Brandt, who, from being on the staff of Gneisenau's army, was brought into daily intercourse with Clausewitz in matters of duty, and also frequently met him at the table of Marshal Gneisenau, at Posen.

* 'Campaign in Russia in 1812'; translated from the German of General Von Clausewitz (by Lord Ellesmere).

Amongst other anecdotes, General Brandt relates that, upon one occasion, the conversation at the Marshal's table turned upon a sermon preached by a priest, in which some great absurdities were introduced, and a discussion arose as to whether the Bishop should not be made responsible for what the priest had said. This led to the topic of theology in general, when General Brandt, speaking of himself, says, 'I expressed an opinion that theology is only to be regarded as an historical process, as a *moment* in the gradual development of the human race. This brought upon me an attack from all quarters, but more especially from Clausewitz, who ought to have been on my side, he having been an adherent and pupil of Kiesewetter's, who had indoctrinated him in the philosophy of Kant, certainly diluted – I might even say in homoeopathic doses.' This anecdote is only interesting as the mention of Kiesewetter points to a circumstance in the life of Clausewitz that may have had an influence in forming those habits of thought which distinguish his writings.

'The way,' says General Brandt, 'in which General Clausewitz judged of things, drew conclusions from movements and marches, calculated the times of the marches, and the points where decisions would take place, was extremely interesting. Fate has unfortunately denied him an opportunity of showing his talents in high command, but I have a firm persuasion that as a strategist he would have greatly distinguished himself. As a leader on the field of battle, on the other hand, he would not have been so much in his right place, from a *manque d'habitude du commandement*, he wanted the art *d'enlever les troupes*.'

After the Prussian Army of Observation was dissolved, Clausewitz returned to Breslau, and a few days after his arrival was seized with cholera, the seeds of which he must have brought with him from the army on the Polish frontier. His death took place in November 1831.

His writings are contained in nine volumes, published after his death, but his fame rests most upon the three volumes forming his treatise on 'War'. In the present attempt to render into English this portion of the works of Clausewitz, the translator is sensible of many deficiencies, but he hopes at all events to succeed in making this celebrated treatise better known in

England, believing, as he does, that so far as the work concerns the interests of this country, it has lost none of the importance it possessed at the time of its first publication.

J. J. GRAHAM (*Col.*)

BOOK ONE

ON THE NATURE OF WAR

CHAPTER I

WHAT IS WAR?

1. *Introduction*

WE propose to consider first the single elements of our subject, then each branch or part, and, last of all, the whole, in all its relations – therefore to advance from the simple to the complex. But it is necessary for us to commence with a glance at the nature of the whole, because it is particularly necessary that in the consideration of any of the parts their relation to the whole should be kept constantly in view.

2. *Definition*

We shall not enter into any of the abstruse definitions of War used by publicists. We shall keep to the element of the thing itself, to a duel. War is nothing but a duel on an extensive scale. If we would conceive as a unit the countless number of duels which make up a War, we shall do so best by supposing to ourselves two wrestlers. Each strives by physical force to compel the other to submit to his will: each endeavours to throw his adversary, and thus render him incapable of further resistance.

War therefore is an act of violence intended to compel our opponent to fulfil our will.

Violence arms itself with the inventions of Art and Science in order to contend against violence. Self-imposed restrictions, almost imperceptible and hardly worth mentioning, termed usages of International Law, accompany it without essentially impairing its power.[55] Violence, that is to say, physical force (for there is no moral force without the conception of States and Law), is therefore the *means*; the compulsory submission of the enemy to our will is the ultimate *object*. In order to attain this object fully, the enemy must be disarmed, and disarmament becomes therefore the immediate object of hostilities in theory. It takes the place of the final object, and puts it aside as something we can eliminate from our calculations.

3. Utmost use of force

Now, philanthropists may easily imagine there is a skilful method of disarming and overcoming an enemy without causing great bloodshed, and that this is the proper tendency of the Art of War. However plausible this may appear, still it is an error which must be extirpated; for in such dangerous things as War, the errors which proceed from a spirit of benevolence are the worst. As the use of physical power to the utmost extent by no means excludes the cooperation of the intelligence, it follows that he who uses force unsparingly, without reference to the bloodshed involved, must obtain a superiority if his adversary uses less vigour in its application. The former then dictates the law to the latter, and both proceed to extremities to which the only limitations are those imposed by the amount of counter-acting force on each side.

This is the way in which the matter must be viewed, and it is to no purpose, it is even against one's own interest, to turn away from the consideration of the real nature of the affair because the horror of its elements excites repugnance.

If the Wars of civilized people are less cruel and destructive than those of savages, the difference arises from the social condition both of States in themselves and in their relations to each other. Out of this social condition and its relations War arises, and by it War is subjected to conditions, is controlled and modified. But these things do not belong to War itself; they are only given conditions; and to introduce into the philosophy of War itself a principle of moderation would be an absurdity.

Two motives lead men to War: instinctive hostility and hostile intention. In our definition of War, we have chosen as its characteristic the latter of these elements, because it is the most general. It is impossible to conceive the passion of hatred of the wildest description, bordering on mere instinct, without combining with it the idea of a hostile intention. On the other hand, hostile intentions may often exist without being accompanied by any, or at all events by any extreme, hostility of feeling. Amongst savages views emanating from the feelings, amongst civilized nations those emanating from the understanding, have the predominance; but this difference arises from attendant circumstances, existing institutions, etc., and, therefore, is not to be found necessarily in all cases, although it prevails in the majority. In short, even the most civilized nations may burn with passionate hatred of each other.

We may see from this what a fallacy it would be to refer the War of a civilized nation entirely to an intelligent act on the part of the Government, and to imagine it as continually freeing itself more and more from all feeling of passion in such a way that at last the physical masses of combatants would no longer be required; in reality, their mere relations would suffice – a kind of algebraic action.

Theory was beginning to drift in this direction until the facts of the last War[56] taught it better. If War is an *act* of force, it belongs necessarily also to the feelings. If it does not originate in the feelings, it *reacts*, more or less, upon them, and the extent of this reaction depends not on the degree of civilization, but upon the importance and duration of the interests involved.

Therefore, if we find civilized nations do not put their prisoners to death, do not devastate towns and countries, this is because their intelligence exercises greater influence on their mode of carrying on War, and has taught them more effectual means of applying force than these rude acts of mere instinct. The invention of gunpowder, the constant progress of improvements in the construction of firearms, are sufficient proofs that the tendency to destroy the adversary which lies at the bottom of the conception of War is in no way changed or modified through the progress of civilization.

We therefore repeat our proposition, that War is an act of violence pushed to its utmost bounds; as one side dictates the law to the other, there arises a sort of reciprocal action, which logically must lead to an extreme. This is the first reciprocal action, and the first extreme with which we meet (*first reciprocal action*).

4. The aim is to disarm the enemy

We have already said that the aim of all action in War is to disarm the enemy, and we shall now show that this, theoretically at least, is indispensable.

If our opponent is to be made to comply with our will, we must place him in a situation which is more oppressive to him than the sacrifice which we demand; but the disadvantages of this position must naturally not be of a transitory nature, at least in appearance, otherwise the enemy, instead of yielding, will hold out, in the prospect of a change for the better. Every change in this position which is produced by a continuation of the War should therefore be a change for the worse. The worst condition in which a belligerent can be placed is that of being completely disarmed. If, therefore, the enemy is to be reduced to submission by an act of War, he must either be positively disarmed or placed in such a position that he is threatened with it. From this it follows that the disarming or overthrow of the enemy, whichever we call it, must always be the aim of Warfare. Now War is always the shock of two hostile bodies in collision, not the action of a living power upon an inanimate mass, because an absolute state of endurance would not be making War; therefore, what we have just said as to the aim of action in War applies to both parties. Here, then, is another case of reciprocal action. As long as the enemy is not defeated, he may defeat me; then I shall be no longer my own master; he will dictate the law to me as I did to him.[57] This is the second reciprocal action, and leads to a second extreme (*second reciprocal action*).

5. Utmost exertion of powers

If we desire to defeat the enemy, we must proportion our efforts to his powers of resistance. This is expressed by the product of two factors which cannot be separated, namely, *the sum of available means* and *the strength of the Will.* The sum of the available means may be estimated in a measure, as it depends (although not entirely) upon numbers; but the strength of volition is more difficult to determine, and can only be estimated to a certain extent by the strength of the motives. Granted we have obtained in this way an approximation to the strength of the power to be contended with, we can then take a review of our own means, and either increase them so as to obtain a preponderance, or, in case we have not the resources to effect this, then do our best by increasing our means as far as possible. But the adversary does the same; therefore, there is a new mutual enhancement, which, in pure conception, must create a fresh effort towards an extreme. This is the third case of reciprocal action, and a third extreme with which we meet (*third reciprocal action*).

6. *Modification in the reality*

Thus reasoning in the abstract, the mind cannot stop short of an extreme, because it has to deal with an extreme, with a conflict of forces left to themselves, and obeying no other but their own inner laws. If we should seek to deduce from the pure conception of War an absolute point for the aim which we shall propose and for the means which we shall apply, this constant reciprocal action would involve us in extremes, which would be nothing but a play of ideas produced by an almost invisible train of logical subtleties. If, adhering closely to the absolute, we try to avoid all difficulties by a stroke of the pen, and insist with logical strictness that in every case the extreme must be the object, and the utmost effort must be exerted in that direction, such a stroke of the pen would be a mere paper law, not by any means adapted to the real world.

Even supposing this extreme tension of forces was an absolute which could easily be ascertained, still we must admit that the human mind would hardly submit itself to this kind of logical chimera. There would be in many cases an unnecessary waste of power, which would be in opposition to other principles of statecraft; an effort of Will would be required disproportioned to the proposed object, which therefore it would be impossible to realize, for the human will does not derive its impulse from logical subtleties.

But everything takes a different shape when we pass from

abstractions to reality. In the former, everything must be subject to optimism, and we must imagine the one side as well as the other striving after perfection and even attaining it. Will this ever take place in reality? It will if,

(1). War becomes a completely isolated act, which arises suddenly, and is in no way connected with the previous history of the combatant States.

(2). If it is limited to a single solution, or to several simultaneous solutions.

(3). If it contains within itself the solution perfect and complete, free from any reaction upon it, through a calculation beforehand of the political situation which will follow from it.

7. *War is never an isolated act*

With regard to the first point, neither of the two opponents is an abstract person to the other, not even as regards that factor in the sum of resistance which does not depend on objective things, viz. the Will. This Will is not an entirely unknown quantity; it indicates what it will be tomorrow by what it is today. War does not spring up quite suddenly, it does not spread to the full in a moment; each of the two opponents can, therefore, form an opinion of the other, in a great measure, from what he is and what he does, instead of judging of him according to what he, strictly speaking, should be or should do. But, now, man with his incomplete organization is always below the line of absolute perfection, and thus these deficiencies, having an influence on both sides, become a modifying principle.

8. *War does not consist of a single instantaneous blow*

The second point gives rise to the following considerations:

If War ended in a single solution, or a number of simultaneous ones, then naturally all the preparations for the same would have a tendency to the extreme, for an omission could not in any way be repaired; the utmost, then, that the world of reality could furnish as a guide for us would be the preparations of the enemy, as far as they are known to us; all the rest would fall into the domain of the abstract. But if the result is made up from several successive acts, then naturally that which precedes with all its phases may be taken as a measure for that which will follow, and in this manner the world of reality again takes the place of the abstract, and thus modifies the effort towards the extreme.

Yet every War would necessarily resolve itself into a single solution, or a sum of simultaneous results, if all the means required for the struggle were raised at once, or could be at once raised; for as one adverse result necessarily diminishes the means, then if all the means have been applied in the first, a second cannot properly be supposed. All hostile acts which might follow would belong essentially to the first, and form in reality only its duration.

But we have already seen that even in the preparation for War the real world steps into the place of mere abstract conception – a material standard into the place of the hypotheses of an extreme: that therefore in that way both parties, by the influence of the mutual reaction, remain below the line of extreme effort, and therefore all forces are not at once brought forward.

It lies also in the nature of these forces and their application that they cannot all be brought into activity at the same time. These forces are *the armies actually on foot*, *the country*, with its superficial extent and its population, *and the allies*.

In point of fact, the country, with its superficial area and the population, besides being the source of all military force, constitutes in itself an integral part of the efficient quantities in War, providing either the theatre of war or exercising a considerable influence on the same.

Now, it is possible to bring all the movable military forces of a country into operation at once, but not all fortresses, rivers, mountains, people, etc. – in short, not the whole country, unless it is so small that it may be completely embraced by the first act of the War. Further, the cooperation of allies does not depend on the Will of the belligerents; and from the nature of the political relations of states to each other, this cooperation is frequently not afforded until after the War has commenced, or it may be increased to restore the balance of power.

That this part of the means of resistance, which cannot at once be brought into activity, in many cases, is a much greater part of the whole than might at first be supposed, and that it often restores the balance of power, seriously affected by the great force of the first decision, will be more fully shown hereafter. Here it is sufficient to show that a complete concentration of all available means in a moment of time is contradictory to the nature of War.

Now this, in itself, furnishes no ground for relaxing our efforts to accumulate strength to gain the first result, because an unfavourable issue is always a disadvantage to which no one would purposely expose himself, and also because the first decision, although not the only one, still will have the more influence on subsequent events, the greater it is in itself.

But the possibility of gaining a later result causes men to take refuge in that expectation, owing to the repugnance in the human mind to making excessive efforts; and therefore forces are not concentrated and measures are not taken for the first decision with that energy which would otherwise be used. Whatever one belligerent omits from weakness, becomes to the other a real objective ground for limiting his own efforts, and thus again, through this reciprocal action, extreme tendencies are brought down to efforts on a limited scale.[58]

9. The result in war is never absolute

Lastly, even the final decision of a whole War is not always to be regarded as absolute. The conquered State often sees in it only a passing evil, which may be repaired in after times by means of political combinations. How much this must modify the degree of tension, and the vigour of the efforts made, is evident in itself.

10. The probabilities of real life take the place of the conceptions of the extreme and the absolute

In this manner, the whole act of War is removed from the rigorous law of forces exerted to the utmost. If the extreme is no longer to be apprehended, and no longer to be sought for, it is left to the judgement to determine the limits for the efforts to be made in place of it, and this can only be done on the data furnished by the facts of the real world by the *laws of probability*. Once the belligerents are no longer mere conceptions, but individual States and Governments, once the War is no longer an ideal, but a definite substantial procedure, then the reality will furnish the data to compute the unknown quantities which are required to be found.

From the character, the measures, the situation of the adversary, and the relations with which he is surrounded, each side will draw conclusions by the law of probability as to the designs of the other, and act accordingly.

11. The political object now reappears

Here the question which we had laid aside forces itself again into consideration (*see* No. 2), viz. *the political object of the War*. The law of the extreme, the view to disarm the adversary, to overthrow him, has hitherto to a certain extent usurped the place of this end or object. Just as this law loses its force, the political object must again come forward. If the whole consideration is a calculation of probability based on definite persons and relations, then the political object, being the original motive, must be an essential factor in the product. The smaller the sacrifice we demand from our opponent, the smaller, it may be expected, will be the means of resistance which he will employ; but the smaller his preparation, the smaller will ours require to be. Further, the smaller our political object, the less value shall we set upon it, and the more easily shall we be induced to give it up altogether.[59]

Thus, therefore, the political object, as the original motive of the War, will be the standard for determining both the aim of the military force and also the amount of effort to be made. This it cannot be in itself, but it is so in relation to both the belligerent States, because we are concerned with realities, not with mere abstractions. One and the same political object may produce totally different effects upon different people, or even upon the same people at different times; we can, therefore, only admit the political object as the measure, by considering it in its effects upon those masses which it is to move, and consequently the nature of those masses also comes into consideration. It is easy to see that thus the result may be very different according as these masses are animated with a spirit which will infuse vigour into the action or otherwise. It is quite possible for such a state of feeling to exist between two States that a very trifling political motive for War may produce an effect quite disproportionate – in fact, a perfect explosion.

This applies to the efforts which the political object will call forth in the two States, and to the aim which the military action shall prescribe for itself. At times it may itself be that aim, as, for example, the conquest of a province. At other times the political object itself is not suitable for the aim of military action; then such a one must be chosen as will be an equivalent for it, and stand in its place as regards the conclusion of peace. But also, in this, due attention to the peculiar character of the States concerned is always supposed. There are circumstances in which the equivalent must be much greater than the political object, in order to secure the latter. The political object will be so much the more the standard of aim and effort, and have more influence in itself, the more the masses are indifferent, the less that any mutual feeling of hostility prevails in the two States from other causes, and therefore there are cases where the political object almost alone will be decisive.

If the aim of the military action is an equivalent for the political object, that action will in general diminish as the political object diminishes, and in a greater degree the more the political object dominates. Thus it is explained how, without any contradiction in itself, there may be Wars of all degrees of importance and energy, from a War of extermination down to the mere use of an army of observation. This, however, leads to a question of another kind which we have hereafter to develop and answer.

12. A suspension in the action of war unexplained by anything said as yet

However insignificant the political claims mutually advanced, however weak the means put forth, however small the aim to which military action is directed, can this action be suspended even for a moment? This is a question which penetrates deeply into the nature of the subject.

Every transaction requires for its accomplishment a certain time which we call its duration. This may be longer or shorter, according as the person acting throws more or less dispatch into his movements.

About this more or less we shall not trouble ourselves here. Each person acts in his own fashion; but the slow person does not protract the thing because he wishes to spend more time about it, but because by his nature he requires more time, and if he made more haste would not do the thing so well. This time, therefore, depends on subjective causes, and belongs to the length, so called, of the action.

If we allow now to every action in War this, its length, then we must assume, at first sight at least, that any expenditure of time beyond this length, that is, every suspension of hostile action, appears an absurdity; with respect to this it must not be forgotten that we now speak not of the progress of one or other of the two opponents, but of the general progress of the whole action of the War.

13. There is only one cause which can suspend the action, and this seems to be only possible on one side in any case

If two parties have armed themselves for strife, then a feeling of animosity must have moved them to it; as long now as they continue armed, that is, do not come to terms of peace, this feeling must exist; and it can only be brought to a standstill by either side by one single motive alone, which is, *that he waits for a more favourable moment for action.* Now, at first sight, it appears that this motive can never exist except on one side, because it, *eo ipso*, must be prejudicial to the other. If the one has an interest in acting, then the other must have an interest in waiting.

A complete equilibrium of forces can never produce a suspension of action, for during this suspension he who has the positive object (that is, the assailant) must continue progressing; for if we should imagine an equilibrium in this way, that he who has the positive object, therefore the strongest motive, can at the same time only command the lesser means, so that the equation is made up by the product of the motive and the power, then we must say, if no alteration in this condition of equilibrium is to be expected, the two parties must make peace; but if an alteration is to be expected, then it can only be favourable to one side, and therefore the other has a manifest interest to act without delay. We see that the conception of an equilibrium cannot explain a suspension of arms, but that it ends in the question of the *expectation of a more favourable moment.*[60]

Let us suppose, therefore, that one of two States has a positive object, as, for instance, the conquest of one of the enemy's provinces – which is to be utilized in the settlement of peace. After this conquest, his political object is accomplished, the necessity for action ceases, and for him a pause ensues. If the adversary is also contented with this solution, he will make peace, if not, he must act. Now, if we suppose that in four weeks he will be in a better condition to act, then he has sufficient grounds for putting off the time of action.

But from that moment the logical course for the enemy appears to be to act that he may not give the conquered party *the desired* time. Of course, in this mode of reasoning a complete insight into the state of circumstances on both sides is supposed.

14. Thus a continuance of action will ensue which will advance towards a climax

If this unbroken continuity of hostile operations really existed, the effect would be that everything would again be driven towards the extreme; for, irrespective of the effect of such incessant activity in inflaming the feelings, and infusing into the whole a greater degree of passion, a greater elementary force, there would also follow from this continuance of action a stricter continuity, a closer connexion between cause and effect, and thus every single action would become of more importance, and consequently more replete with danger.

But we know that the course of action in War has seldom or never this unbroken continuity, and that there have been many Wars in which action occupied by far the smallest portion of time employed, the whole of the rest being consumed in inaction. It is impossible that this should be always an anomaly; suspension of action in War must therefore be possible, that is no contradiction in itself. We now proceed to show how this is.

15. Here, therefore, the principle of polarity is brought into requisition

As we have supposed the interests of one Commander to be always antagonistic to those of the other, we have assumed a true *polarity*. We reserve a fuller explanation of this for another chapter, merely making the following observation on it at present.

The principle of polarity is only valid when it can be conceived in one and the same thing, where the positive and its opposite the negative completely destroy each other. In a battle both sides strive to conquer; that is true polarity, for the victory of the one side destroys that of the other. But when we speak of two different things which have a common relation external to themselves, then it is not the things but their relations which have the polarity.

16. Attack and defence are things differing in kind and of unequal force. Polarity is, therefore, not applicable to them

If there was only one form of War, to wit, the attack of the enemy, therefore no defence; or, in other words, if the attack was distinguished from the defence merely by the positive motive, which the one has and the other has not, but the methods of each were precisely one and the same: then in this sort of fight every advantage gained on the one side would be a corresponding disadvantage on the other, and true polarity would exist.

But action in War is divided into two forms, attack and

defence, which, as we shall hereafter explain more particularly, are very different and of unequal strength. Polarity therefore lies in that to which both bear a relation, in the decision, but not in the attack or defence itself.

If the one Commander wishes the solution put off, the other must wish to hasten it, but only by the same form of action. If it is A's interest not to attack his enemy at present, but four weeks hence, then it is B's interest to be attacked, not four weeks hence, but at the present moment. This is the direct antagonism of interests, but it by no means follows that it would be for B's interest to attack A at once. That is plainly something totally different.

17. The effect of polarity is often destroyed by the superiority of the defence over the attack, and thus the suspension of action in war is explained

If the form of defence is stronger than that of offence, as we shall hereafter show, the question arises, Is the advantage of a deferred decision as great on the one side as the advantage of the defensive form on the other? If it is not, then it cannot by its counter-weight overbalance the latter, and thus influence the progress of the action of the War. We see, therefore, that the impulsive force existing in the polarity of interests may be lost in the difference between the strength of the offensive and the defensive, and thereby become ineffectual.

If, therefore, that side for which the present is favourable, is too weak to be able to dispense with the advantage of the defensive, he must put up with the unfavourable prospects which the future holds out; for it may still be better to fight a defensive battle in the unpromising future than to assume the offensive or make peace at present. Now, being convinced that the superiority of the defensive (rightly understood) is very great, and much greater than may appear at first sight, we conceive that the greater number of those periods of inaction which occur in war are thus explained without involving any contradiction. The weaker the motives to action are, the more will those motives be absorbed and neutralized by this difference between attack and defence, the more frequently, therefore, will action in warfare be stopped, as indeed experience teaches.

18. A second ground consists in the imperfect knowledge of circumstances

But there is still another cause which may stop action in War, viz. an incomplete view of the situation. Each Commander can only fully know his own position; that of his opponent can only be known to him by reports, which are uncertain; he may, therefore, form a wrong judgement with respect to it upon data of this description, and, in consequence of that error, he may suppose that the power of taking the initiative rests with his adversary when it lies really with himself. This want of perfect insight might certainly just as often occasion an untimely action as untimely inaction, and hence it would in itself no more contribute to delay than to accelerate action in War. Still, it must always be regarded as one of the natural causes which may bring action in War to a standstill without involving a contradiction. But if we reflect how much more we are inclined and induced to estimate the power of our opponents too high than too low, because it lies in human nature to do so, we shall admit that our imperfect insight into facts in general must contribute very much to delay action in War, and to modify the application of the principles pending our conduct.

The possibility of a standstill brings into the action of War a new modification, inasmuch as it dilutes that action with the element of time, checks the influence or sense of danger in its course, and increases the means of reinstating a lost balance of force. The greater the tension of feelings from which the War springs, the greater therefore the energy with which it is carried on, so much the shorter will be the periods of inaction; on the other hand, the weaker the principle of warlike activity, the longer will be these periods: for powerful motives increase the force of the will, and this, as we know, is always a factor in the product of force.

19. Frequent periods of inaction in war remove it further from the absolute, and make it still more a calculation of probabilities

But the slower the action proceeds in War, the more frequent and longer the periods of inaction, so much the more easily can an error be repaired; therefore, so much the bolder a General will be in his calculations, so much the more readily will he keep them below the line of the absolute, and build everything upon probabilities and conjecture. Thus, according as the course of the War is more or less slow, more or less time will be allowed for that which the nature of a concrete case particularly requires, calculation of probability based on given circumstances.

20. Therefore, the element of chance only is wanting to make of war a game, and in that element it is least of all deficient

We see from the foregoing how much the objective nature of War makes it a calculation of probabilities; now there is only one single element still wanting to make it a game, and that element it certainly is not without: it is chance. There is no human affair which stands so constantly and so generally in close connexion with chance as War. But together with chance, the accidental, and along with it good luck, occupy a great place in War.

21. War is a game both objectively and subjectively[61]

If we now take a look at the *subjective nature* of War, that is to say, at those conditions under which it is carried on, it will appear to us still more like a game. Primarily the element in which the operations of War are carried on is danger; but which of all the moral qualities is the first in danger? *Courage.* Now certainly courage is quite compatible with prudent calculation, but still they are things of quite a different kind, essentially different qualities of the mind; on the other hand, daring reliance on good fortune, boldness, rashness, are only expressions of courage, and all these propensities of the mind look for the fortuitous (or accidental), because it is their element.

We see, therefore, how, from the commencement, the absolute, the mathematical as it is called, nowhere finds any sure basis in the calculations in the Art of War; and that from the outset there is a play of possibilities, probabilities, good and bad luck, which spreads about with all the coarse and fine threads of its web, and makes War of all branches of human activity the most like a gambling game.

22. How this accords best with the human mind in general

Although our intellect always feels itself urged towards clearness and certainty, still our mind often feels itself attracted by uncertainty. Instead of threading its way with the understanding along the narrow path of philosophical investigations and logical conclusions, in order, almost unconscious of itself, to arrive in spaces where it feels itself a stranger, and where it seems to part from all well-known objects, it prefers to remain with the imagination in the realms of chance and luck. Instead of living yonder on poor necessity, it revels here in the wealth of possibilities; animated thereby, courage then takes wings to itself, and daring and danger make the element into which it launches itself as a fearless swimmer plunges into the stream.

Shall theory leave it here, and move on, self-satisfied with absolute conclusions and rules? Then it is of no practical use. Theory must also take into account the human element; it must accord a place to courage, to boldness, even to rashness. The Art of War has to deal with living and with moral forces, the consequence of which is that it can never attain the absolute and positive. There is therefore everywhere a margin for the accidental, and just as much in the greatest things as in the smallest. As there is room for this accidental on the one hand, so on the other there must be courage and self-reliance in proportion to the room available. If these qualities are forthcoming in a high degree, the margin left may likewise be great. Courage and self-reliance are, therefore, principles quite essential to War; consequently, theory must only set up such rules as allow ample scope for all degrees and varieties of these necessary and noblest of military virtues. In daring there may still be wisdom, and prudence as well, only they are estimated by a different standard of value.[62]

23. War is always a serious means for a serious object. Its more particular definition

Such is War; such the Commander who conducts it; such the theory which rules it. But War is no pastime; no mere passion for venturing and winning; no work of a free enthusiasm: it is a serious means for a serious object. All that appearance which it wears from the varying hues of fortune, all that it assimilates into itself of the oscillations of passion, of courage, of imagination, of enthusiasm, are only particular properties of this means.

The War of a community – of whole Nations, and particularly of civilized Nations – always starts from a political condition, and is called forth by a political motive. It is, therefore, a political act. Now if it was a perfect, unrestrained, and absolute expression of force, as we had to deduce it from its mere conception, then the moment it is called forth by policy it would step into the place of policy, and as something quite independent of it would set it aside, and only follow its own laws, just as a mine at the moment of explosion cannot be guided into any other direction than that which has been given to it by preparatory arrangements. This is how the thing has really been viewed hitherto, whenever a want of harmony between policy and the conduct of a War has led to theoretical distinctions of the kind. But it is not so, and the idea is radically false. War in the real world, as we have already seen, is not an extreme thing which expends itself at one single discharge; it is the operation of powers which do not develop themselves completely in the same manner and in the same measure, but which at one time expand sufficiently to overcome the resistance opposed by inertia or friction, while at another they are too weak to produce an effect; it is therefore, in a certain measure, a pulsation of violent force more or less vehement, consequently making its discharges and exhausting its powers more or less quickly – in other words, conducting more or less quickly to the aim, but always lasting long enough to admit of influence being exerted on it in its course, so as to give it this or that direction, in short, to be subject to the will of a guiding intelligence. Now, if we reflect that War has its root in a political object, then naturally this original motive which called it into existence should also continue the first and highest consideration in its conduct. Still, the political object is no despotic lawgiver on that account; it must accommodate itself to the nature of the means, and though changes in these means may involve modification in the political objective, the latter always retains a prior right to consideration. Policy, therefore, is interwoven with the whole action of War, and must exercise a continuous influence upon it, as far as the nature of the forces liberated by it will permit.

24. *War is a mere continuation of policy by other means*

We see, therefore, that War is not merely a political act, but also a real political instrument, a continuation of political commerce, a carrying out of the same by other means. All beyond this which is strictly peculiar to War relates merely to the peculiar nature of the means which it uses. That the tendencies and views of policy shall not be incompatible with these means, the Art of War in general and the Commander in each particular case may demand, and this claim is truly not a trifling one. But however powerfully this may react on political views in particular cases, still it must always be regarded as only a modification of them; for the political view is the object, War is the means, and the means must always include the object in our conception.

25. *Diversity in the nature of wars*

The greater and the more powerful the motives of a War, the more it affects the whole existence of a people. The more violent the excitement which precedes the War, by so much the nearer will the War approach to its abstract form, so much the more will it be directed to the destruction of the enemy, so much the nearer will the military and political ends coincide, so much the more purely military and less political the War appears to be; but the weaker the motives and the tensions, so much the less will the natural direction of the military element – that is, force – be coincident with the direction which the political element indicates; so much the more must, therefore, the War become diverted from its natural direction, the political object diverge from the aim of an ideal War, and the War appear to become political.

But, that the reader may not form any false conceptions, we must here observe that by this natural tendency of War we only mean the philosophical, the strictly logical, and by no means the tendency of forces actually engaged in conflict, by which would be supposed to be included all the emotions and passions of the combatants. No doubt in some cases these also might be excited to such a degree as to be with difficulty restrained and confined to the political road; but in most cases such a contradiction will not arise, because by the existence of such strenuous exertions a great plan in harmony therewith would be implied. If the plan is directed only upon a small object, then the impulses of feeling amongst the masses will be also so weak that these masses will require to be stimulated rather than repressed.

26. *They may all be regarded as political acts*

Returning now to the main subject, although it is true that in one kind of War the political element seems almost to disappear, whilst in another kind it occupies a very prominent place, we may still affirm that the one is as political as the other; for if we regard the State policy as the intelligence of the personified State, then amongst all the constellations in the political sky whose movements it has to compute, those must be included which arise when the nature of its relations imposes the necessity of a great War. It is only if we understand by policy not a true appreciation of affairs in general, but the conventional conception of a cautious, subtle, also dishonest craftiness, averse from violence, that the latter kind of War may belong more to policy than the first.

27. Influence of this view on the right understanding of military history, and on the foundations of theory

We see, therefore, in the first place, that under all circumstances War is to be regarded not as an independent thing, but as a political instrument; and it is only by taking this point of view that we can avoid finding ourselves in opposition to all military history. This is the only means of unlocking the great book and making it intelligible. Secondly, this view shows us how Wars must differ in character according to the nature of the motives and circumstances from which they proceed.

Now, the first, the grandest, and most decisive act of judgement which the Statesman and General exercises is rightly to understand in this respect the War in which he engages, not to take it for something, or to wish to make of it something, which by the nature of its relations it is impossible for it to be. This is, therefore, the first, the most comprehensive, of all strategical questions. We shall enter into this more fully in treating of the plan of a War.

For the present we content ourselves with having brought the subject up to this point, and having thereby fixed the chief point of view from which War and its theory are to be studied.

28. Result for theory

War is, therefore, not only chameleon-like in character, because it changes its colour in some degree in each particular case, but it is also, as a whole, in relation to the predominant tendencies which are in it, a wonderful trinity, composed of the original violence of its elements, hatred and animosity, which may be looked upon as blind instinct; of the play of probabilities and chance, which make it a free activity of the soul; and of the subordinate nature of a political instrument, by which it belongs purely to the reason.[63]

The first of these three phases concerns more the people; the second, more the General and his Army; the third, more the Government. The passions which break forth in War must already have a latent existence in the peoples. The range which the display of courage and talents shall get in the realm of probabilities and of chance depends on the particular characteristics of the General and his Army, but the political objects belong to the Government alone.

These three tendencies, which appear like so many different law-givers, are deeply rooted in the nature of the subject, and at the same time variable in degree. A theory which would leave any one of them out of account, or set up any arbitrary relation between them, would immediately become involved in such a contradiction with the reality, that it might be regarded as destroyed at once by that alone.

The problem is, therefore, that theory shall keep itself poised in a manner between these three tendencies, as between three points of attraction.

The way in which alone this difficult problem can be solved we shall examine in the book on the 'Theory of War'. In every case the conception of War, as here defined, will be the first ray of light which shows us the true foundation of theory, and which first separates the great masses and allows us to distinguish them from one another.

CHAPTER II

END AND MEANS IN WAR

HAVING in the foregoing chapter ascertained the complicated and variable nature of War, we shall now occupy ourselves in examining into the influence which this nature has upon the end and means in War.

If we ask, first of all, for the object upon which the whole effort of War is to be directed, in order that it may suffice for the attainment of the political object, we shall find that it is just as variable as are the political object, and the particular circumstances of the War.

If, in the next place, we keep once more to the pure conception of War, then we must say that the political object properly lies out of its province, for if War is an act of violence to compel the enemy to fulfil our will, then in every case all depends on our overthrowing the enemy, that is, disarming him, and on that alone. This object, developed from abstract conceptions, but which is also the one aimed at in a great many cases in reality, we shall, in the first place, examine in this reality.

In connexion with the plan of a campaign we shall hereafter examine more closely into the meaning of disarming a nation, but here we must at once draw a distinction between three things, which, as three general objects, comprise everything else within them. They are the *military power*, *the country*, and *the will of the enemy*.

The *military power* must be destroyed, that is, reduced to such a state as not to be able to prosecute the War. This is the sense in which we wish to be understood hereafter, whenever we use the expression 'destruction of the enemy's military power'.

The *country* must be conquered, for out of the country a new military force may be formed.

But even when both these things are done, still the War, that is, the hostile feeling and action of hostile agencies, cannot be considered as at an end as long as the *will* of the enemy is not subdued also; that is, its Government and its Allies must be forced into signing a peace, or the people into submission; for whilst we are in full occupation of the country, the War may break out afresh, either in the interior or through assistance given by Allies. No doubt, this may also take place after a peace, but that shows nothing more than that every War does not carry in itself the elements for a complete decision and final settlement.

But even if this is the case, still with the conclusion of peace a number of sparks are always extinguished which would have smouldered on quietly, and the excitement of the passions abates, because all those whose minds are disposed to peace, of which in all nations and under all circumstances there is always a great number, turn themselves away completely from the road to resistance. Whatever may take place subsequently, we must always look upon the object as attained, and the business of War as ended, by a peace.

As protection of the country is the primary object for which the military force exists, therefore the natural order is, that first of all this force should be destroyed, then the country subdued; and through the effect of these two results, as well as the position we then hold, the enemy should be forced to make peace. Generally the destruction of the enemy's force is done by degrees, and in just the same measure the conquest of the country follows immediately. The two likewise usually react upon each other, because the loss of provinces occasions a diminution of military force. But this order is by no means necessary, and on that account it also does not always take place. The enemy's Army, before it is sensibly weakened, may retreat to the opposite side of the country, or even quite outside of it. In this case, therefore, the greater part or the whole of the country is conquered.

But this object of War in the abstract, this final means of attaining the political object in which all others are combined, the *disarming the enemy*, is rarely attained in practice and is not a condition necessary to peace. Therefore it can in no wise be set up in theory as a law. There are innumerable instances of treaties in which peace has been settled before either party could be looked upon as disarmed; indeed, even before the balance of power had undergone any sensible alteration. Nay, further, if we look at the case in the concrete, then we must say that in a whole class of cases, the idea of a complete defeat of the enemy would be a mere imaginative flight, especially when the enemy is considerably superior.

The reason why the object deduced from the conception of War is not adapted in general to real War lies in the difference between the two, which is discussed in the preceding chapter. If it was as pure theory gives it, then a War between two States of very unequal military strength would appear an absurdity; therefore impossible. At most, the inequality between the physical forces might be such that it could be balanced by the moral forces, and that would not go far with our present social condition in Europe. Therefore, if we have seen Wars take place between States of very unequal power, that has been the case because there is a wide difference between War in reality and its original conception.

There are two considerations which as motives may practically take the place of inability to continue the contest. The first is the improbability, the second is the excessive price, of success.

According to what we have seen in the foregoing chapter, War must always set itself free from the strict law of logical necessity, and seek aid from the calculation of probabilities; and as this is so much the more the case, the more the War has a bias that way, from the circumstances out of which it has arisen – the smaller its motives are, and the excitement it has raised – so it is also conceivable how out of this calculation of probabilities even motives to peace may arise. War does not, therefore, always require to be fought out until one party is overthrown; and we may suppose that, when the motives and passions are slight, a weak probability will suffice to move that side to which it is unfavourable to give way. Now, were the other side convinced of this beforehand, it is natural that he would strive for this probability only, instead of first wasting time and effort in the attempt to achieve the total destruction of the enemy's Army.

Still more general in its influence on the resolution to peace is the consideration of the expenditure of force already made, and further required. As War is no act of blind passion, but is dominated by the political object, therefore the value of that object determines the measure of the sacrifices by which it is to be purchased. This will be the case, not only as regards extent, but also as regards duration. As soon, therefore, as the required outlay becomes so great that the political object is no longer equal in value, the object must be given up, and peace will be the result.

We see, therefore, that in Wars where one side cannot completely disarm the other, the motives to peace on both sides will rise or fall on each side according to the probability of future success and the required outlay. If these motives were equally strong on both sides, they would meet in the centre of their political difference.[64] Where they are strong on one side, they might be weak on the other. If their amount is only sufficient, peace will follow, but naturally to the advantage of that side which has the weakest motive for its conclusion. We purposely pass over here the difference which the *positive* and *negative* character of the political end must necessarily produce practically; for although that is, as we shall hereafter show, of the highest importance, still we are obliged to keep here to a more general point of view, because the original political views in the course of the War change very much, and at last may become totally different, *just because they are determined by results and probable events.*

Now comes the question how to influence the probability of success. In the first place, naturally by the same means which we use when the object is the subjugation of the enemy, by the destruction of his military force and the conquest of his provinces; but these two means are not exactly of the same import here as they would be in reference to that object. If we attack the enemy's Army, it is a very different thing whether we intend to follow up the first blow with a succession of others, until the whole force is destroyed, or whether we mean to content ourselves with a victory to shake the enemy's feeling of security, to convince him of our superiority, and to instil into him a feeling of apprehension about the future. If this is our object, we only go so far in the destruction of his forces as is sufficient. In like manner, the conquest of the enemy's provinces is quite a different measure if the object is not the destruction of the enemy's Army. In the latter case the destruction of the Army is the real effectual action, and the taking of the provinces only a consequence of it; to take them before the Army had been defeated would always be looked upon only as a necessary evil. On the other hand, if our views are not directed upon the complete destruction of the enemy's force, and if we are sure that the enemy does not seek but fears to bring matters to a bloody decision, the taking possession of a weak or defenceless province is an advantage in itself, and if this advantage is of sufficient importance to make the enemy apprehensive about the general result, then it may also be regarded as a shorter road to peace.

But now we come upon a peculiar means of influencing the probability of the result without destroying the enemy's Army, namely, upon the expeditions which have a direct connexion with political views. If there are any enterprises which are particularly likely to break up the enemy's alliances or make them inoperative, to gain new alliances for ourselves, to raise political powers in our own favour, etc., etc., then it is easy to conceive how much these may increase the probability of success, and become a shorter way towards our object than the routing of the enemy's forces.

The second question is how to act upon the enemy's expenditure in strength, that is, to raise the price of success.

The enemy's outlay in strength lies in the *wear and tear* of his forces, consequently in the *destruction* of them on our part, and in the *loss* of *provinces*, consequently the *conquest* of them by us.

Here, again, on account of the various significations of these means, so likewise it will be found that neither of them will be identical in its signification in all cases if the objects are different. The smallness in general of this difference must not cause us perplexity, for in reality the weakest motives, the finest shades of difference, often decide in favour of this or that method of applying force. Our only business here is to show that, certain conditions being supposed, the possibility of attaining our purpose in different ways is no contradiction, absurdity, nor even error.

Besides these two means, there are three other peculiar ways of directly increasing the waste of the enemy's force. The first is *invasion*, that is *the occupation of the enemy's territory, not with a view to keeping it*, but in order to levy contributions upon it, or to devastate it.

The immediate object here is neither the conquest of the enemy's territory nor the defeat of his armed force, but merely to *do him damage in a general way*. The second way is to select for the object of our enterprises those points at which we can do the enemy most harm. Nothing is easier to conceive than two different directions in which our force may be employed, the first of which is to be preferred if our object is to defeat the enemy's Army, while the other is more advantageous if the defeat of the enemy is out of the question. According to the usual mode of speaking, we should say that the first is primarily military, the other more political. But if we take our view from the highest point, both are equally military, and neither the one nor the other can be eligible unless it suits the circumstances of the case. The third, by far the most important, from the great number of cases which it embraces, is the *wearing out* of the enemy. We choose this expression not only to explain our meaning in few words, but because it represents the thing exactly, and is not so figurative as may at first appear. The idea of wearing out in a struggle amounts in practice to *a gradual exhaustion of the physical powers and of the will by the long continuance of exertion.*

Now, if we want to overcome the enemy by the duration of the contest, we must content ourselves with as small objects as possible, for it is in the nature of the thing that a great end requires a greater expenditure of force than a small one; but the smallest object that we can propose to ourselves is simple passive resistance, that is a combat without any positive view. In this way, therefore, our means attain their greatest relative value, and therefore the result is best secured. How far now can this negative mode of proceeding be carried? Plainly not to absolute passivity, for mere endurance would not be fighting; and the defensive is an activity by which so much of the enemy's power must be destroyed that he must give up his object. That alone is what we aim at in each single act, and therein consists the negative nature of our object.

No doubt this negative object in its single act is not so effective as the positive object in the same direction would be, supposing it successful; but there is this difference in its favour, that it succeeds more easily than the positive, and therefore it holds out greater certainty of success; what is wanting in the efficacy of its single act must be gained through time, that is, through the duration of the contest, and therefore this negative intention, which constitutes the principle of the pure defensive, is also the natural means of overcoming the enemy by the duration of the combat, that is of wearing him out.

Here lies the origin of that difference of *Offensive* and *Defensive*, the influence of which prevails throughout the whole province of War. We cannot at present pursue this subject further than to observe that from this negative intention are to be deduced all the advantages and all the stronger forms of combat which are on the side of the *Defensive*, and in which that philosophical-dynamic law which exists between the greatness and the certainty of success is realized. We shall resume the consideration of all this hereafter.

If then the negative purpose, that is the concentration of all the means into a state of pure resistance, affords a superiority in the contest, and if this advantage is sufficient to *balance* whatever superiority in numbers the adversary may have, then the mere *duration* of the contest will suffice gradually to bring the loss of force on the part of the adversary to a point at which the political object can no longer be an equivalent, a point at which, therefore, he must give up the contest. We see then that this class of means, the wearing out of the enemy, includes the great number of cases in which the weaker resists the stronger.

Frederick the Great, during the Seven Years' War, was never strong enough to overthrow the Austrian monarchy; and if he had tried to do so after the fashion of Charles the Twelfth, he would inevitably have had to succumb himself. But after his skilful application of the system of husbanding his resources had shown the powers allied against him, through a seven years' struggle, that the actual expenditure of strength far exceeded what they had at first anticipated, they made peace.

We see then that there are many ways to one's object in War; that the complete subjugation of the enemy is not essential in every case; that the destruction of the enemy's military force, the conquest of the enemy's provinces, the mere occupation of them, the mere invasion of them – enterprises which are aimed directly at political objects – lastly, a passive expectation of the enemy's blow, are all means which, each in itself, may be used to force the enemy's will according as the peculiar circumstances of the case lead us to expect more from the one or the other. We could still add to these a whole category of shorter methods of gaining the end, which might be called arguments *ad hominem*. What branch of human affairs is there in which these sparks of individual spirit have not made their appearance, surmounting all formal considerations? And least of all can they fail to appear in War, where the personal character of the combatants plays such an important part, both in the cabinet and in the field. We limit ourselves to pointing this out, as it would be pedantry to attempt to reduce such influences into classes.

Including these, we may say that the number of possible ways of reaching the object rises to infinity.

To avoid underestimating these different short roads to one's purpose, either estimating them only as rare exceptions, or holding the difference which they cause in the conduct of War as insignificant, we must bear in mind the diversity of political objects which may cause a War – measure at a glance the distance which there is between a death struggle for political existence and a War which a forced or tottering alliance makes a matter of disagreeable duty. Between the two innumerable gradations occur in practice. If we reject one of these gradations in theory, we might with equal right reject the whole, which would be tantamount to shutting the real world completely out of sight.

These are the circumstances in general connected with the aim which we have to pursue in War; let us now turn to the means.

There is only one single means, it is the *Fight*. However diversified this may be in form, however widely it may differ from a rough vent of hatred and animosity in a hand-to-hand encounter, whatever number of things may introduce themselves which are not actual fighting, still it is always implied in the conception of War that all the effects manifested have their roots in the combat.

That this must always be so in the greatest diversity and complication of the reality is proved in a very simple manner. All that takes place in War takes place through armed forces, but where the forces of War, i.e. armed men, are applied, there the idea of fighting must of necessity be at the foundation.

All, therefore, that relates to forces of War – all that is connected with their creation, maintenance, and application – belongs to military activity.

Creation and maintenance are obviously only the means, whilst application is the object.

The contest in War is not a contest of individual against individual, but an organized whole, consisting of manifold parts; in this great whole we may distinguish units of two kinds, the one determined by the subject, the other by the object. In an Army the mass of combatants ranges itself always into an order of new units, which again form members of a higher order. The combat of each of these members forms, therefore, also a more or less distinct unit. Further, the motive of the fight; therefore its object forms its unit.

Now, to each of these units which we distinguish in the contest we attach the name of combat.

If the idea of combat lies at the foundation of every application of armed power, then also the application of armed force in general is nothing more than the determining and arranging a certain number of combats.

Every activity in War, therefore, necessarily relates to the combat either directly or indirectly. The soldier is levied, clothed, armed, exercised, he sleeps, eats, drinks, and marches, all *merely to fight at the right time and place.*

If, therefore, all the threads of military activity terminate in the combat, we shall grasp them all when we settle the order of the combats. Only from this order and its execution proceed the effects, never directly from the conditions preceding them. Now, in the combat all the action is directed to the *destruction* of the enemy, or rather of *his fighting powers*, for this lies in the conception of combat. The destruction of the enemy's fighting power is, therefore, always the means to attain the object of the combat.

This object may likewise be the mere destruction of the enemy's armed force; but that is not by any means necessary, and it may be something quite different. Whenever, for instance, as we have shown, the defeat of the enemy is not the only means to attain the political object, whenever there are other objects which may be pursued as the aim in a War, then it follows of itself that such other objects may become the object of particular acts of Warfare, and therefore also the object of combats.

But even those combats which, as subordinate acts, are in the strict sense devoted to the destruction of the enemy's fighting force need not have that destruction itself as their first object.

If we think of the manifold parts of a great armed force, of the number of circumstances which come into activity when it is employed, then it is clear that the combat of such a force must also require a manifold organization, a subordinating of parts and formation. There may and must naturally arise for particular parts a number of objects which are not themselves the destruction of the enemy's armed force, and which, while they certainly contribute to increase that destruction, do so only in an indirect manner. If a battalion is ordered to drive the enemy from a rising ground, or a bridge, etc., then properly the occupation of any such locality is the real object, the destruction of the enemy's armed force which takes place only the means or secondary matter. If the enemy can be driven away merely by a demonstration, the object is attained all the same; but this hill or bridge is, in point of fact, only required as a means of increasing the gross amount of loss inflicted on the enemy's armed force. If this is the case on the field of battle, much more must it be so on the whole theatre of war, where not only one Army is opposed to another, but one State, one Nation, one whole country to another. Here the number of possible relations, and consequently possible combinations, is much greater, the diversity of measures increased, and by the gradation of objects, each subordinate to another the first means employed is further apart from the ultimate object.

It is therefore for many reasons possible that the object of a combat is not the destruction of the enemy's force, that is, of the force immediately opposed to us, but that this only appears as a means. But in all such cases it is no longer a question of complete destruction, for the combat is here nothing else but a measure of strength – has in itself no value except only that of the present result, that is, of its decision.

But a measuring of strength may be effected in cases where the opposing sides are very unequal by a mere comparative estimate. In such cases no fighting will take place, and the weaker will immediately give way.

If the object of a combat is not always the destruction of the enemy's forces therein engaged – and if its object can often be attained as well without the combat taking place at all, by merely making a resolve to fight, and by the circumstances to which this resolution gives rise – then that explains how a whole campaign may be carried on with great activity without the actual combat playing any notable part in it.

That this may be so military history proves by a hundred

examples. How many of those cases can be justified, that is, without involving a contradiction, and whether some of the celebrities who rose out of them would stand criticism, we shall leave undecided, for all we have to do with the matter is to show the possibility of such a course of events in War.

We have only one means in War – the battle; but this means, by the infinite variety of paths in which it may be applied, leads us into all the different ways which the multiplicity of objects allows of, so that we seem to have gained nothing; but that is not the case, for from this unity of means proceeds a thread which assists the study of the subject, as it runs through the whole web of military activity and holds it together.

But we have considered the destruction of the enemy's force as one of the objects which may be pursued in War, and left undecided what relative importance should be given to it amongst other objects. In certain cases it will depend on circumstances, and as a general question we have left its value undetermined. We are once more brought back upon it, and we shall be able to get an insight into the value which must necessarily be accorded to it.

The combat is the single activity in War; in the combat the destruction of the enemy opposed to us is the means to the end; it is so even when the combat does not actually take place, because in that case there lies at the root of the decision the supposition at all events that this destruction is to be regarded as beyond doubt. It follows, therefore, that the destruction of the enemy's military force is the foundation-stone of all action in War, the great support of all combinations, which rest upon it like the arch on its abutments. All action, therefore, takes place on the supposition that if the solution by force of arms which lies at its foundation should be realized, it will be a favourable one. The decision by arms is, for all operations in War, great and small, what cash payment is in bill transactions. However remote from each other these relations, however seldom the realization may take place, still it can never entirely fail to occur.

If the decision by arms lies at the foundation of all combinations, then it follows that the enemy can defeat each of them by gaining a victory on the field, not merely in the one on which our combination directly depends, but also in any other encounter, if it is only important enough; for every important decision by arms – that is, destruction of the enemy's forces – reacts upon all preceding it, because, like a liquid element, they tend to bring themselves to a level.

Thus, the destruction of the enemy's armed force appears, therefore, always as the superior and more effectual means, to which all others must give way.

It is, however, only when there is a supposed equality in all other conditions that we can ascribe to the destruction of the enemy's armed force the greater efficacy. It would, therefore, be a great mistake to draw the conclusion that a blind dash must always gain the victory over skill and caution. An unskilful attack would lead to the destruction of our own and not of the enemy's force, and therefore is not what is here meant. The superior efficacy belongs not to the *means* but to the *end*, and we are only comparing the effect of one realized purpose with the other.

If we speak of the destruction of the enemy's armed force, we must expressly point out that nothing obliges us to confine this idea to the mere physical force; on the contrary, the moral is necessarily implied as well, because both in fact are interwoven with each other, even in the most minute details, and therefore cannot be separated. But it is just in connexion with the inevitable effect which has been referred to, of a great act of destruction (a great victory) upon all other decisions by arms, that this moral element is most fluid, if we may use that expression, and therefore distributes itself the most easily through all the parts.

Against the far superior worth which the destruction of the enemy's armed force has over all other means stands the expense and risk of this means, and it is only to avoid these that any other means are taken. That these must be costly stands to reason, for the waste of our own military forces must, *ceteris paribus*, always be greater the more our aim is directed upon the destruction of the enemy's power..

The danger lies in this, that the greater efficacy which we seek recoils on ourselves, and therefore has worse consequences in case we fail of success.

Other methods are, therefore, less costly when they succeed, less dangerous when they fail; but in this is necessarily lodged the condition that they are only opposed to similar ones, that is, that the enemy acts on the same principle; for if the enemy should choose the way of a great decision by arms, *our means must on that account be changed against our will, in order to correspond with his.* Then all depends on the issue of the act of destruction; but of course it is evident that, *ceteris paribus*, in this act we must be at a disadvantage in all respects because our views and our means had been directed in part upon other objects, which is not the case with the enemy. Two different objects of which one is not part of the other exclude each other, and therefore a force which may be applicable for the one may not serve for the other. If, therefore, one of two belligerents is determined to seek the great decision by arms, then he has a high probability of success, as soon as he is certain his opponent will not take that way, but follows a different object; and every one who sets before himself any such other aim only does so in a reasonable manner, provided he acts on the supposition that his adversary has as little intention as he has of resorting to the great decision by arms.

But what we have here said of another direction of views and forces relates only to other *positive objects*, which we may propose to ourselves in War, besides the destruction of the enemy's force, not by any means to the pure defensive, which may be adopted with a view thereby to exhaust the enemy's forces. In the pure defensive the positive object is wanting, and therefore, while on the defensive, our forces cannot at the same time be directed on other objects; they can only be employed to defeat the intentions of the enemy.

We have now to consider the opposite of the destruction of the enemy's armed force, that is to say, the preservation of our own. These two efforts always go together, as they mutually act and react on each other; they are integral parts of one and the same view, and we have only to ascertain what effect is produced when one or the other has the predominance. The endeavour to destroy the enemy's force has a positive object, and leads to positive results, of which the final aim is the conquest of the enemy. The preservation of our own forces has a negative object, leads therefore to the defeat of the enemy's intentions, that is to pure resistance, of which the final aim can be nothing more than to prolong the duration of the contest, so that the enemy shall exhaust himself in it.

The effort with a positive object calls into existence the act of destruction; the effort with the negative object awaits it.

How far this state of expectation should and may be carried we shall enter into more particularly in the theory of attack and defence, at the origin of which we again find ourselves. Here we shall content ourselves with saying that the awaiting must be no absolute endurance, and that in the action bound up with it the destruction of the enemy's armed force engaged in this conflict may be the aim just as well as anything else. It would therefore be a great error in the fundamental idea to suppose that the consequence of the negative course is that we are precluded from choosing the destruction of the enemy's military force as our object, and must prefer a bloodless solution. The advantage which the negative effort gives may certainly lead to that, but only at the risk of its not being the most advisable method, as that question is dependent on totally different conditions, resting not with ourselves but with our opponents. This other bloodless way cannot, therefore, be looked upon at all as the natural means of satisfying our great anxiety to spare our forces; on the contrary, when circumstances are not favourable, it would be the means of completely ruining them. Very many Generals have fallen into this error, and been ruined by it. The only necessary effect resulting from the superiority of the negative effort is the delay of the decision, so that the party acting takes refuge in that way, as it were, in the expectation of the decisive moment. The consequence of that is generally *the postponement of the action* as much as possible in time, and also in space, in so far as space is in connexion with it. If the moment has arrived in which this can no longer be done without ruinous disadvantage, then the advantage of the negative must be considered as exhausted, and then comes forward unchanged the effort for the destruction of the enemy's force, which was kept back by a counterpoise, but never discarded.

We have seen, therefore, in the foregoing reflections, that

there are many ways to the aim, that is, to the attainment of the political object; but that the only means is the combat, and that consequently everything is subject to a supreme law: which is the *decision by arms*; that where this is really demanded by one, it is a redress which cannot be refused by the other; that, therefore, a belligerent who takes any other way must make sure that his opponent will not take this means of redress, or his cause may be lost in that supreme court; hence therefore the destruction of the enemy's armed foıce, amongst all the objects which can be pursued in War, appears always as the one which overrules all others.

What may be achieved by combinations of another kind in War we shall only learn in the sequel, and naturally only by degrees. We content ourselves here with acknowledging in general their possibility, as something pointing to the difference between the reality and the conception, and to the influence of particular circumstances. But we could not avoid showing at once that the *bloody solution of the crisis*, the effort for the destruction of the enemy's force, is the firstborn son of War. If when political objects are unimportant, motives weak, the excitement of forces small, a cautious commander tries in all kinds of ways, without great crises and bloody solutions, to twist himself skilfully into a peace through the characteristic weaknesses of his enemy in the field and in the Cabinet, we have no right to find fault with him, if the premises on which he acts are well founded and justified by success; still we must require him to remember that he only travels on forbidden tracks, where the God of War may surprise him; that he ought always to keep his eye on the enemy, in order that he may not have to defend himself with a dress rapier if the enemy takes up a sharp sword.

The consequences of the nature of War, how ends and means act in it, how in the modifications of reality it deviates sometimes more, sometimes less, from its strict original conception, fluctuating backwards and forwards, yet always remaining under that strict conception as under a supreme law: all this we must retain before us, and bear constantly in mind in the consideration of each of the succeeding subjects, if we would rightly comprehend their true relations and proper importance, and not become involved incessantly in the most glaring contradictions with the reality, and at last with our own selves.

CHAPTER III

THE GENIUS FOR WAR

EVERY special calling in life, if it is to be followed with success, requires peculiar qualifications of understanding and soul. Where these are of a high order, and manifest themselves by extraordinary achievements, the mind to which they belong is termed *genius*.

We know very well that this word is used in many significations which are very different both in extent and nature, and that with many of these significations it is a very difficult task to define the essence of Genius; but as we neither profess to be philosopher nor grammarian, we must be allowed to keep to the meaning usual in ordinary language, and to understand by 'genius' a very high mental capacity for certain employments.

We wish to stop for a moment over this faculty and dignity of the mind, in order to vindicate its title, and to explain more fully the meaning of the conception. But we shall not dwell on that (genius) which has obtained its title through a very great talent, on genius properly so called, that is a conception which has no defined limits. What we have to do is to bring under consideration every common tendency of the powers of the mind and soul towards the business of War, the whole of which common tendencies we may look upon as the *essence of military genius*. We say 'common', for just therein consists military genius, that it is not one single quality bearing upon War, as, for instance, courage, while other qualities of mind and soul are wanting or have a direction which is unserviceable for War, but that it is *an harmonious association of powers*, in which one or other may predominate, but none must be in opposition.

If every combatant required to be more or less endowed with military genius, then our armies would be very weak; for as it implies a peculiar bent of the intelligent powers, therefore it can only rarely be found where the mental powers of a people are called into requisition and trained in many different ways. The fewer the employments followed by a Nation, the more that of arms predominates, so much the more prevalent will military genius also be found. But this merely applies to its prevalence, by no means to its degree, for that depends on the general state of intellectual culture in the country. If we look at a wild, warlike race, then we find a warlike spirit in individuals much more common than in a civilized people; for in the former almost every warrior possesses it, whilst in the civilized whole, masses are only carried away by it from necessity, never by inclination. But amongst uncivilized people we never find a really great General, and very seldom what we can properly call a military genius, because that requires a development of the intelligent powers which cannot be found in an uncivilized State. That a civilized people may also have a warlike tendency and development is a matter of course; and the more this is general, the more frequently also will military spirit be found in individuals in their armies. Now as this coincides in such case with the higher degree of civilization, therefore from such nations have issued forth the most brilliant military exploits, as the Romans and the French have exemplified. The greatest names in these and in all other nations that have been renowned in War belong strictly to epochs of higher culture.

From this we may infer how great a share the intelligent powers have in superior military genius. We shall now look more closely into this point.

War is the province of danger, and therefore courage above all things is the first quality of a warrior.

Courage is of two kinds: first, physical courage, or courage in presence of danger to the person; and next, moral courage, or courage before responsibility, whether it be before the judgement-seat of external authority, or of the inner power, the conscience. We only speak here of the first.

Courage before danger to the person, again, is of two kinds. First, it may be indifference to danger, whether proceeding from the organism of the individual, contempt of death, or habit: in any of these cases it is to be regarded as a permanent condition.

Secondly, courage may proceed from positive motives, such as personal pride, patriotism, enthusiasm of any kind. In this case courage is not so much a normal condition as an impulse.

We may conceive that the two kinds act differently. The first kind is more certain, because it has become a second nature, never forsakes the man; the second often leads him farther. In the first there is more of firmness, in the second, of boldness. The first leaves the judgement cooler, the second raises its power at times, but often bewilders it. The two combined make up the most perfect kind of courage.

War is the province of physical exertion and suffering. In order not to be completely overcome by them, a certain strength of body and mind is required, which, either natural or acquired, produces indifference to them. With these qualifications, under the guidance of simply a sound understanding, a man is at once a proper instrument for War; and these are the qualifications so generally to be met with amongst wild and half-civilized tribes. If we go further in the demands which War makes on its votaries, then we find the powers of the understanding predominating. War is the province of uncertainty: three-fourths of those things upon which action in War must be calculated, are hidden more or less in the clouds of great uncertainty. Here, then, above all a fine and penetrating mind is called for, to search out the truth by the tact of its judgement.

An average intellect may, at one time, perhaps hit upon this truth by accident; an extraordinary courage, at another, may compensate for the want of this tact; but in the majority of cases the average result will always bring to light the deficient understanding.

War is the province of chance. In no sphere of human activity is such a margin to be left for this intruder, because none is so much in constant contact with him on all sides. He increases the uncertainty of every circumstance, and deranges the course of events.

From this uncertainty of all intelligence and suppositions, this continual interposition of chance, the actor in War constantly finds things different from his expectations; and this cannot fail to have an influence on his plans, or at least on the presumptions connected with these plans. If this influence is so great as to render the predetermined plan completely nugatory, then, as a rule, a new one must be substituted in its place; but at the moment the necessary data are often wanting for this, because in the course of action circumstances press for immediate decision, and allow no time to look about for fresh data, often not enough for mature consideration.

But it more often happens that the correction of one premise, and the knowledge of chance events which have arisen, are not sufficient to overthrow our plans completely, but only suffice to produce hesitation. Our knowledge of circumstances has increased, but our uncertainty, instead of having diminished, has only increased. The reason of this is, that we do not gain all our experience at once, but by degrees; thus our determinations continue to be assailed incessantly by fresh experience; and the mind, if we may use the expression, must always be 'under arms'.

Now, if it is to get safely through this perpetual conflict with the unexpected, two qualities are indispensable: in the first place an intellect which, even in the midst of this intense obscurity, is not without some traces of inner light, which lead to the truth, and then the courage to follow this faint light. The first is figuratively expressed by the French phrase *coup d'œil*. The other is *resolution*. As the battle is the feature in War to which attention was originally chiefly directed, and as time and space are important elements in it, more particularly when cavalry with their rapid decisions were the chief arm, the idea of rapid and correct decision related in the first instance to the estimation of these two elements, and to denote the idea an expression was adopted which actually only points to a correct judgement by eye. Many teachers of the Art of War then gave this limited signification as the definition of *coup d'œil*. But it is undeniable that all able decisions formed in the moment of action soon came to be understood by the expression, as, for instance, the hitting upon the right point of attack, etc. It is, therefore, not only the physical, but more frequently the mental eye which is meant in *coup d'œil*. Naturally, the expression, like the thing, is always more in its place in the field of tactics: still, it must not be wanting in strategy, inasmuch as in it rapid decisions are often necessary. If we strip this conception of that which the expression has given it of the over-figurative and restricted, then it amounts simply to the rapid discovery of a truth which to the ordinary mind is either not visible at all or only becomes so after long examination and reflection.

Resolution is an act of courage in single instances,[65] and if it becomes a characteristic trait, it is a habit of the mind. But here we do not mean courage in face of bodily danger, but in face of responsibility, therefore to a certain extent against moral danger. This has been often called *courage d'esprit*, on the ground that it springs from the understanding; nevertheless, it is no act of the understanding on that account; it is an act of feeling. Mere intelligence is still not courage, for we often see the cleverest people devoid of resolution. The mind must, therefore, first awaken the feeling of courage, and then be guided and supported by it, because in momentary emergencies the man is swayed more by his feelings than his thoughts.

We have assigned to resolution the office of removing the torments of doubt, and the dangers of delay, when there are no sufficient motives for guidance. Through the unscrupulous use of language which is prevalent, this term is often applied to the mere propensity to daring, to bravery, boldness, or temerity. But, when there are *sufficient motives* in the man, let them be objective or subjective, true or false, we have no right to speak of his resolution; for, when we do so, we put ourselves in his place, and we throw into the scale doubts which did not exist with him.

Here there is no question of anything but of strength and weakness. We are not pedantic enough to dispute with the use of language about this little misapplication, our observation is only intended to remove wrong objections.

This resolution now, which overcomes the state of doubting, can only be called forth by the intellect, and, in fact, by a peculiar tendency of the same. We maintain that the mere union of a superior understanding and the necessary feelings are not sufficient to make up resolution. There are persons who possess the keenest perception for the most difficult problems, who are also not fearful of responsibility, and yet in cases of difficulty cannot come to a resolution. Their courage and their sagacity operate independently of each other, do not give each other a hand, and on that account do not produce resolution as a result. The forerunner of resolution is an act of the mind making evident the necessity of venturing and thus influencing the will. This quite peculiar direction of the mind, which conquers every other fear in man by the fear of wavering or doubting, is what makes up resolution in strong minds; therefore, in our opinion, men who have little intelligence can never be resolute. They may act without hesitation under perplexing circumstances, but then they act without reflection. Now, of course, when a man acts without reflection he cannot be at variance with himself by doubts, and such a mode of action may now and then lead to the right point; but we say now as before, it is the average result which indicates the existence of military genius. Should our assertion appear extraordinary to any one, because he knows many a resolute hussar officer who is no deep thinker, we must remind him that the question here is about a peculiar direction of the mind, and not about great thinking powers.

We believe, therefore, that resolution is indebted to a special direction of the mind for its existence, a direction which belongs to a strong head rather than to a brilliant one. In corroboration of this genealogy of resolution we may add that there have been many instances of men who have shown the greatest resolution in an inferior rank, and have lost it in a higher position. While, on the one hand, they are obliged to resolve, on the other they see the dangers of a wrong decision, and as they are surrounded with things new to them, their understanding loses its original force, and they become only the more timid the more they become aware of the danger of the irresolution into which they have fallen, and the more they have formerly been in the habit of acting on the spur of the moment.

From the *coup d'œil* and resolution we are naturally led to speak of its kindred quality, *presence of mind*, which in a region of the unexpected like War must act a great part, for it is indeed nothing but a great conquest over the unexpected. As we admire presence of mind in a pithy answer to anything said unexpectedly, so we admire it in a ready expedient on sudden danger. Neither the answer nor the expedient need be in themselves extraordinary, if they only hit the point; for that which as the result of mature reflection would be nothing unusual, therefore insignificant in its impression on us, may as an instantaneous act of the mind produce a pleasing impression. The expression 'presence of mind' certainly denotes very fitly the readiness and rapidity of the help rendered by the mind.

Whether this noble quality of a man is to be ascribed more to the peculiarity of his mind or to the equanimity of his feelings, depends on the nature of the case, although neither of the two can be entirely wanting. A telling repartee bespeaks rather a ready wit, a ready expedient on sudden danger implies more particularly a well-balanced mind.

If we take a general view of the four elements composing the atmosphere in which War moves, of *danger*, *physical effort*, *uncertainty*, and *chance*, it is easy to conceive that a great force of mind and understanding is requisite to be able to make way with safety and success amongst such opposing elements, a force which, according to the different modifications arising out of circumstances, we find termed by military writers and annalists as *energy*, *firmness*, *staunchness*, *strength of mind and character*. All these manifestations of the heroic nature might be regarded as one and the same power of volition, modified according to circumstances; but nearly related as these things are to each other, still they are not one and the same, and it is desirable for us to distinguish here a little more closely at least the action of the powers of the soul in relation to them.

In the first place, to make the conception clear, it is essential to observe that the weight, burden, resistance, or whatever it may be called, by which that force of the soul in the General is brought to light, is only in a very small measure the enemy's activity, the enemy's resistance, the enemy's action directly. The enemy's activity only affects the General directly in the first place in relation to his person, without disturbing his action as Commander. If the enemy, instead of two hours, resists for four, the Commander instead of two hours is four hours in danger; this is a quantity which plainly diminishes the higher the rank of the Commander. What is it for one in the post of Commander-in-Chief? It is nothing.

Secondly, although the opposition offered by the enemy has a direct effect on the Commander through the loss of means arising from prolonged resistance, and the responsibility connected with that loss, and his force of will is first tested and called forth by these anxious considerations, still we maintain that this is not the heaviest burden by far which he has to bear, because he has only himself to settle with. All the other effects of the enemy's resistance act directly upon the combatants under his command, and through them react upon him.

As long as his men full of good courage fight with zeal and spirit, it is seldom necessary for the Chief to show great energy of purpose in the pursuit of his object. But as soon as difficulties arise – and that must always happen when great results are at stake – then things no longer move on of themselves like a well-oiled machine, the machine itself then begins to offer resistance, and to overcome this the Commander must have a great force of will. By this resistance we must not exactly suppose disobedience and murmurs, although these are frequent enough with particular individuals; it is the whole feeling of the dissolution of all physical and moral power, it is the heartrending sight of the bloody sacrifice which the Commander has to contend with in himself, and then in all others who directly or indirectly transfer to him their impressions, feelings, anxieties, and desires. As the forces in one individual after another become prostrated, and can no longer be excited and supported by an effort of his own will, the whole inertia of the mass gradually rests its weight on the Will of the Commander: by the spark in his breast, by the light of his spirit, the spark of purpose, the light of hope, must be kindled afresh in others: in so far only as he is equal to this, he stands above the masses and continues to be their master; whenever that influence ceases, and his own spirit is no longer strong enough to revive the spirit of all others, the masses drawing him down with them sink into the lower region of animal nature, which shrinks from danger and knows not shame. These are the weights which the courage and intelligent faculties of the military Commander have to overcome if he is to make his name illustrious. They increase with the masses and therefore, if the forces in question are to continue equal to the burden, they must rise in proportion to the height of the station.[66]

Energy in action expresses the strength of the motive through which the action is excited, let the motive have its origin in a conviction of the understanding, or in an impulse. But the latter can hardly ever be wanting where great force is to show itself.

Of all the noble feelings which fill the human heart in the exciting tumult of battle, none, we must admit, are so powerful and constant as the soul's thirst for honour and renown, which the German language treats so unfairly and tends to depreciate by the unworthy associations in the words *Ehrgeiz* (greed of honour) and *Ruhmsucht* (hankering after glory). No doubt it is just in War that the abuse of these proud aspirations of the soul must bring upon the human race the most shocking outrages, but by their origin they are certainly to be counted amongst the noblest feelings which belong to human nature, and in War they are the vivifying principle which gives the enormous body a spirit. Although other feelings may be more general in their influence, and many of them – such as love of country, fanaticism, revenge, enthusiasm of every kind – may seem to stand higher, the thirst for honour and renown still remains indispensable. Those other feelings may rouse the great masses in general and excite them more powerfully, but they do not give the Leader a desire to will more than others, which is an essential requisite in his position if he is to make himself distinguished in it. They do not, like a thirst for honour, make the military act specially the property of the Leader, which he strives to turn to the best account; where he ploughs with toil, sows with care, that he may reap plentifully. It is through these aspirations we have been speaking of in Commanders, from the highest to the lowest, this sort of energy, this spirit of emulation, these incentives, that the action of armies is chiefly animated and made successful. And now as to that which specially concerns the head of all, we ask, Has there ever been a great Commander destitute of the love of honour, or is such a character even conceivable?

Firmness denotes the resistance of the will in relation to the force of a single blow, *staunchness* in relation to a continuance of blows. Close as is the analogy between the two, and often as the one is used in place of the other, still there is a notable difference between them which cannot be mistaken, inasmuch as firmness against a single powerful impression may have its root in the mere strength of a feeling, but staunchness must be supported rather by the understanding, for the greater the duration of an action the more systematic deliberation is connected with it, and from this staunchness partly derives its power.

If we now turn to *strength of mind or soul,* then the first question is, What are we to understand thereby?

Plainly it is not vehement expressions of feeling, nor easily excited passions, for that would be contrary to all the usage of language, but the power of listening to reason in the midst of the most intense excitement, in the storm of the most violent passions. Should this power depend on strength of understanding alone? We doubt it. The fact that there are men of the greatest intellect who cannot command themselves certainly proves nothing to the contrary, for we might say that it perhaps requires an understanding of a powerful rather than of a comprehensive nature; but we believe we shall be nearer the truth if we assume that the power of submitting oneself to the control of the understanding, even in moments of the most violent excitement of the feelings, that power which we call *self-command*, has its root in the heart itself. It is, in point of fact, another feeling, which in strong minds balances the excited passions without destroying them; and it is only through this equilibrium that the mastery of the understanding is secured. This counterpoise is nothing but a sense of the dignity of man, that noblest pride, that deeply-seated desire of the soul always to act as a being endued with understanding and reason. We may therefore say that a strong mind is one which does not lose its balance even under the most violent excitement.

If we cast a glance at the variety to be observed in the human character in respect to feeling, we find, first, some people who have very little excitability, who are called phlegmatic or indolent.

Secondly, some very excitable, but whose feelings still never overstep certain limits, and who are therefore known as men full of feeling, but sober-minded.

Thirdly, those who are very easily roused, whose feelings blaze up quickly and violently like gunpowder, but do not last.

Fourthly, and lastly, those who cannot be moved by slight causes, and who generally are not to be roused suddenly, but only gradually; but whose feelings become very powerful and are much more lasting. These are men with strong passions, lying deep and latent.

This difference of character lies probably close on the confines of the physical powers which move the human organism, and belongs to that amphibious organization which we call the nervous system, which appears to be partly material, partly spiritual. With our weak philosophy, we shall not proceed further in this mysterious field. But it is important for us to spend a moment over the effects which these different natures have on action in War, and to see how far a great strength of mind is to be expected from them.

Indolent men cannot easily be thrown out of their equanimity, but we cannot certainly say there is strength of mind where there is a want of all manifestation of power.

At the same time, it is not to be denied that such men have a certain peculiar aptitude for War, on account of their constant equanimity. They often want the positive motive to action, impulse, and consequently activity, but they are not apt to throw things into disorder.

The peculiarity of the second class is that they are easily excited to act on trifling grounds, but in great matters they are easily overwhelmed. Men of this kind show great activity in helping an unfortunate individual, but by the distress of a whole Nation they are only inclined to despond, not roused to action.

Such people are not deficient in either activity or equanimity in War; but they will never accomplish anything great unless a great intellectual force furnishes the motive, and it is very seldom that a strong, independent mind is combined with such a character.

Excitable, inflammable feelings are in themselves little suited for practical life, and therefore they are not very fit for War. They have certainly the advantage of strong impulses, but that cannot long sustain them. At the same time, if the excitability in such men takes the direction of courage, or a sense of honour, they may often be very useful in inferior positions in War, because the action in War over which commanders in inferior positions have control is generally of shorter duration. Here one courageous resolution, one effervescence of the forces of the soul, will often suffice. A brave attack, a soul-stirring hurrah, is the work of a few moments, whilst a brave contest on the battle-field is the work of a day, and a campaign the work of a year.[67]

Owing to the rapid movement of their feelings, it is doubly difficult for men of this description to preserve equilibrium of the mind; therefore they frequently lose head, and that is the worst phase in their nature as respects the conduct of War. But it would be contrary to experience to maintain that very excitable spirits can never preserve a steady equilibrium – that is to say, that they cannot do so even under the strongest excitement. Why should they not have the sentiment of self-respect, for, as a rule, they are men of a noble nature? This feeling is seldom wanting in them, but it has not time to produce an effect. After an outburst they suffer most from a feeling of inward humiliation. If through education, self-observance, and experience of life, they have learned, sooner or later, the means of being on their guard, so that at the moment of powerful excitement they are conscious betimes of the counteracting force within their own breasts, then even such men may have great strength of mind.

Lastly, those who are difficult to move, but on that account susceptible of very deep feelings, men who stand in the same relation to the preceding as red heat to a flame, are the best adapted by means of their Titanic strength to roll away the enormous masses by which we may figuratively represent the difficulties which beset command in War. The effect of their feelings is like the movement of a great body, slower, but more irresistible.

Although such men are not so likely to be suddenly surprised by their feelings and carried away so as to be afterwards ashamed of themselves, like the preceding, still it would be contrary to experience to believe that they can never lose their equanimity, or be overcome by blind passion; on the contrary, this must always happen whenever the noble pride of self-control is wanting, or as often as it has not sufficient weight. We see examples of this most frequently in men of noble minds belonging to savage nations, where the low degree of mental cultivation favours always the dominance of the passions. But even amongst the most civilized classes in civilized States, life is full of examples of this kind – of men carried away by the violence of their passions, like the poacher of old chained to the stag in the forest.

We therefore say once more a strong mind is not one that is merely susceptible of strong excitement, but one which can maintain its serenity under the most powerful excitement, so that, in spite of the storm in the breast, the perception and judgement can act with perfect freedom, like the needle of the compass in the storm-tossed ship.

By the term *strength of character*, or simply *character*, is denoted tenacity of conviction, let it be the result of our own or of others' views, and whether they are principles, opinions, momentary inspirations, or any kind of emanations of the understanding; but this kind of firmness certainly cannot manifest itself if the views themselves are subject to frequent change. This frequent change need not be the consequence of external influences; it may proceed from the continuous activity of our own mind, in which case it indicates a characteristic unsteadiness of mind. Evidently we should not say of a man who changes his views every moment, however much the motives of change may originate with himself, that he has character. Only those men, therefore, can be said to have this quality whose conviction is very constant, either because it is deeply rooted and clear in itself, little liable to alteration, or because, as in the case of indolent men, there is a want of mental activity, and therefore a want of motives to change; or lastly, because an explicit act of the will, derived from an imperative maxim of the understanding, refuses any change of opinion up to a certain point.

Now in War, owing to the many and powerful impressions to which the mind is exposed, and in the uncertainty of all knowledge and of all science, more things occur to distract a man from the road he has entered upon, to make him doubt himself and others, than in any other human activity.

The harrowing sight of danger and suffering easily leads to the feelings gaining ascendancy over the conviction of the understanding; and in the twilight which surrounds everything a deep clear view is so difficult that a change of opinion is more conceivable and more pardonable. It is, at all times, only conjecture or guesses at truth which we have to act upon. This is why differences of opinion are nowhere so great as in War, and the stream of impressions acting counter to one's own convictions never ceases to flow. Even the greatest impassibility of mind is hardly proof against them, because the impressions are powerful in their nature, and always act at the same time upon the feelings.

When the discernment is clear and deep, none but general principles and views of action from a high standpoint can be the result; and on these principles the opinion in each particular case immediately under consideration lies, as it were, at anchor. But to keep to these results of bygone reflection, in opposition to the stream of opinions and phenomena which the present brings with it, is just the difficulty. Between the particular case and the principle there is often a wide space which cannot always be traversed on a visible chain of conclusions, and where a certain faith in self is necessary and a certain amount of scepticism is serviceable. Here often nothing else will help us but an imperative maxim which, independent of reflection, at once controls it: that maxim is, in all doubtful cases to adhere to the first opinion, and not to give it up until a clear conviction forces us to do so. We must firmly believe in the superior authority of well-tried maxims, and under the dazzling influence of momentary events not forget that their value is of an inferior stamp. By this preference which in doubtful cases we give to first convictions, by adherence to the same our actions acquire that stability and consistency which make up what is called character.

It is easy to see how essential a well-balanced mind is to strength of character; therefore men of strong minds generally have a great deal of character.

Force of character leads us to a spurious variety of it – *obstinacy*.

It is often very difficult in concrete cases to say where the one ends and the other begins; on the other hand, it does not seem difficult to determine the difference in idea.

Obstinacy is no fault of the understanding; we use the term as denoting a resistance against our better judgement, and it would be inconsistent to charge that to the understanding, as the understanding is the power of judgement. Obstinacy is *a fault of the feelings* or heart. This inflexibility of will, this impatience of contradiction, have their origin only in a particular kind of egotism, which sets above every other pleasure that of governing both self and others by its own mind alone. We should call it a kind of vanity, were it not decidedly something better. Vanity is satisfied with mere show, but obstinacy rests upon the enjoyment of the thing.

We say, therefore, force of character degenerates into obstinacy whenever the resistance to opposing judgements proceeds not from better convictions or a reliance upon a more trustworthy maxim, but from a feeling of opposition. If this definition, as we have already admitted, is of little assistance practically, still it will prevent obstinacy from being considered merely force of character intensified, whilst it is something essentially different – something which certainly lies close to it and is cognate to it, but is at the same time so little an intensification of it that there are very obstinate men who from want of understanding have very little force of character.

Having in these high attributes of a great military Commander made ourselves acquainted with those qualities in which heart and head cooperate, we now come to a speciality of military activity which perhaps may be looked upon as the most marked if it is not the most important, and which only makes a demand on the power of the mind without regard to the forces of feelings. It is the connexion which exists between War and country or ground.

This connexion is, in the first place, a permanent condition of War, for it is impossible to imagine our organized Armies effecting any operation otherwise than in some given space; it is, secondly, of the most decisive importance, because it modifies, at times completely alters, the action of all forces; thirdly, while on the one hand it often concerns the most minute features of locality, on the other it may apply to immense tracts of country.

In this manner a great peculiarity is given to the effect of this connexion of War with country and ground. If we think of other occupations of man which have a relation to these objects, on horticulture, agriculture, on building houses and hydraulic works, on mining, on the chase, and forestry, they are all confined within very limited spaces which may be soon explored with sufficient exactness. But the Commander in War must commit the business he has in hand to a corresponding space which his eye cannot survey, which the keenest zeal cannot always explore, and with which, owing to the constant changes taking place, he can also seldom become properly acquainted. Certainly the enemy generally is in the same situation; still, in the first place, the difficulty, although common to both, is not the less a difficulty, and he who by talent and practice overcomes it will have a great advantage on his side; secondly, this equality of the difficulty on both sides is merely an abstract supposition which is rarely realized in the particular case, as one of the two opponents (the defensive) usually knows much more of the locality than his adversary.

This very peculiar difficulty must be overcome by a natural mental gift of a special kind which is known by the – too restricted – term of (*Ortsinn*) sense of locality. It is the power of quickly forming a correct geometrical idea of any portion of country, and consequently of being able to find one's place in it exactly at any time. This is plainly an act of the imagination. The perception no doubt is formed partly by means of the physical eye, partly by the mind, which fills up what is wanting with ideas derived from knowledge and experience, and out of the fragments visible to the physical eye forms a whole; but that this whole should present itself vividly to the reason, should become a picture, a mentally drawn map, that this picture should be fixed, that the details should never again separate themselves – all that can only be effected by the mental faculty which we call imagination. If some great poet or painter should feel hurt that we require from his goddess such an office; if he shrugs his shoulders at the notion that a sharp gamekeeper must necessarily excel in imagination, we readily grant that we only speak here of imagination in a limited sense, of its service in a really menial capacity. But, however slight this service, still it must be the work of that natural gift, for if that gift is wanting, it would be difficult to imagine things plainly in all the completeness of the visible. That a good memory is a great assistance we freely allow, but whether memory is to be considered as an independent faculty of the mind in this case, or whether it is just that power of imagination which here fixes these things better on the memory, we leave undecided, as in many respects it seems difficult upon the whole to conceive these two mental powers apart from each other.

That practice and mental acuteness have much to do with it is not to be denied. Puysegur, the celebrated Quartermaster-General of the famous Luxemburg, used to say that he had very little confidence in himself in this respect at first, because if he had to fetch the *parole* from a distance he always lost his way.

It is natural that scope for the exercise of this talent should increase along with rank. If the hussar and rifleman in command of a patrol must know well all the highways and byways, and if for that a few marks, a few limited powers of observation, are sufficient, the Chief of an Army must make himself familiar with the general geographical features of a province and of a country; must always have vividly before his eyes the direction of the roads, rivers, and hills, without at the same time being able to dispense with the narrower 'sense of locality' (*Ortsinn*). No doubt, information of various kinds as to objects in general, maps, books, memoirs, and for details the assistance of his Staff, are a great help to him; but it is nevertheless certain that if he has himself a talent for forming an ideal picture of a country quickly and distinctively, it lends to his action an easier and firmer step, saves him from a certain mental helplessness, and makes him less dependent on others.

If this talent then is to be ascribed to imagination, it is also almost the only service which military activity requires from that erratic goddess, whose influence is more hurtful than useful in other respects.

We think we have now passed in review those manifestations

of the powers of mind and soul which military activity requires from human nature. Everywhere intellect appears as an essential cooperative force; and thus we can understand how the work of War, although so plain and simple in its effects, can never be conducted with distinguished success by people without distinguished powers of the understanding.

When we have reached this view, then we need no longer look upon such a natural idea as the turning an enemy's position, which has been done a thousand times, and a hundred other similar conceptions, as the result of a great effort of genius.

Certainly one is accustomed to regard the plain honest soldier as the very opposite of the man of reflection, full of inventions and ideas, or of the brilliant spirit shining in the ornaments of refined education of every kind. This antithesis is also by no means devoid of truth; but it does not show that the efficiency of the soldier consists only in his courage, and that there is no particular energy and capacity of the brain required in addition to make a man merely what is called a true soldier. We must again repeat that there is nothing more common than to hear of men losing their energy on being raised to a higher position, to which they do not feel themselves equal; but we must also remind our readers that we are speaking of pre-eminent services, of such as give renown in the branch of activity to which they belong. Each grade of command in War therefore forms its own stratum of requisite capacity of fame and honour.

An immense space lies between a General – that is, one at the head of a whole War, or of a theatre of War – and his Second in Command, for the simple reason that the latter is in more immediate subordination to a superior authority and supervision, consequently is restricted to a more limited sphere of independent thought. This is why common opinion sees no room for the exercise of high talent except in high places, and looks upon an ordinary capacity as sufficient for all beneath: this is why people are rather inclined to look upon a subordinate General grown grey in the service, and in whom constant discharge of routine duties has produced a decided poverty of mind, as a man of failing intellect, and, with all respect for his bravery, to laugh at his simplicity. It is not our object to gain for these brave men a better lot – that would contribute nothing to their efficiency, and little to their happiness; we only wish to represent things as they are, and to expose the error of believing that a mere bravo without intellect can make himself distinguished in War.

As we consider distinguished talents requisite for those who are to attain distinction, even in inferior positions, it naturally follows that we think highly of those who fill with renown the place of Second in Command of an Army; and their seeming simplicity of character as compared with a polyhistor, with ready men of business, or with councillors of state, must not lead us astray as to the superior nature of their intellectual activity. It happens sometimes that men import the fame gained in an inferior position into a higher one, without in reality deserving it in the new position; and then if they are not much employed, and therefore not much exposed to the risk of showing their weak points, the judgement does not distinguish very exactly what degree of fame is really due to them; and thus such men are often the occasion of too low an estimate being formed of the characteristics required to shine in certain situations.

For each station, from the lowest upwards, to render distinguished services in War, there must be a particular genius. But the title of genius, history and the judgement of posterity only confer, in general, on those minds which have shone in the highest rank, that of Commanders-in-Chief. The reason is that here, in point of fact, the demand on the reasoning and intellectual powers generally is much greater.

To conduct a whole War, or its great acts, which we call campaigns, to a successful termination, there must be an intimate knowledge of State policy in its higher relations. The conduct of the War and the policy of the State here coincide, and the General becomes at the same time the Statesman.

We do not give Charles XII the name of a great genius, because he could not make the power of his sword subservient to a higher judgement and philosophy – could not attain by it to a glorious object. We do not give that title to Henry IV (of France) because he did not live long enough to set at rest the relations of different States by his military activity, and to occupy himself in that higher field where noble feelings and a chivalrous disposition have less to do in mastering the enemy than in overcoming internal dissension.

In order that the reader may appreciate all that must be comprehended and judged of correctly at a glance by a General, we refer to the first chapter. We say the General becomes a Statesman, but he must not cease to be the General. He takes into view all the relations of the State on the one hand; on the other, he must know exactly what he can do with the means at his disposal.[68]

As the diversity, and undefined limits, of all the circumstances bring a great number of factors into consideration in War, as the most of these factors can only be estimated according to probability, therefore, if the Chief of an Army does not bring to bear upon them a mind with an intuitive perception of the truth, a confusion of ideas and views must take place, in the midst of which the judgement will become bewildered. In this sense, Buonaparte was right when he said that many of the questions which come before a General for decision would make problems for a mathematical calculation not unworthy of the powers of Newton or Euler.

What is here required from the higher powers of the mind is a sense of unity, and a judgement raised to such a compass as to give the mind an extraordinary faculty of vision which in its range allays and sets aside a thousand dim notions which an ordinary understanding could only bring to light with great effort, and over which it would exhaust itself. But this higher activity of the mind, this glance of genius, would still not become matter of history if the qualities of temperament and character of which we have treated did not give it their support.

Truth alone is but a weak motive of action with men, and hence there is always a great difference between knowing and action, between science and art. The man receives the strongest impulse to action through the feelings, and the most powerful succour, if we may use the expression, through those faculties of heart and mind which we have considered under the terms of resolution, firmness, perseverance, and force of character.

If, however, this elevated condition of heart and mind in the

General did not manifest itself in the general effects resulting from it, and could only be accepted on trust and faith, then it would rarely become matter of history.

All that becomes known of the course of events in War is usually very simple, and has a great sameness in appearance;[69] no one on the mere relation of such events perceives the difficulties connected with them which had to be overcome. It is only now and again, in the memoirs of Generals or of those in their confidence, or by reason of some special historical inquiry directed to a particular circumstance, that a portion of the many threads composing the whole web is brought to light. The reflections, mental doubts, and conflicts which precede the execution of great acts are purposely concealed because they affect political interests, or the recollection of them is accidentally lost because they have been looked upon as mere scaffolding which had to be removed on the completion of the building.

If, now, in conclusion, without venturing upon a closer definition of the higher powers of the soul, we should admit a distinction in the intelligent faculties themselves according to the common ideas established by language, and ask ourselves what kind of mind comes closest to military genius, then a look at the subject as well as at experience will tell us that searching rather than inventive minds, comprehensive minds rather than such as have a special bent, cool rather than fiery heads, are those to which in time of War we should prefer to trust the welfare of our women and children, the honour and the safety of our fatherland.

CHAPTER IV

OF DANGER IN WAR

USUALLY before we have learnt what danger really is, we form an idea of it which is rather attractive than repulsive. In the intoxication of enthusiasm, to fall upon the enemy at the charge – who cares then about bullets and men falling? To throw oneself, blinded by excitement for a moment, against cold death, uncertain whether we or another shall escape him, and all this close to the golden gate of victory, close to the rich fruit which ambition thirsts for – can this be difficult? It will not be difficult, and still less will it appear so. But such moments which, however, are not the work of a single pulse-beat, as is supposed, but rather like doctors' draughts, must be taken diluted and spoilt by mixture with time – such moments, we say, are but few.

Let us accompany the novice to the battlefield. As we approach, the thunder of the cannon becoming plainer and plainer is soon followed by the howling of shot, which attracts the attention of the inexperienced. Balls begin to strike the ground close to us, before and behind. We hasten to the hill where stands the General and his numerous Staff. Here the close striking of the cannon balls and the bursting of shells is so frequent that the seriousness of life makes itself visible through the youthful picture of imagination. Suddenly some one known to us falls – a shell strikes amongst the crowd and causes some involuntary movements: we begin to feel that we are no longer perfectly at ease and collected; even the bravest is at least to some degree confused. Now, a step farther into the battle which is raging before us like a scene in a theatre, we get to the nearest General of Division; here ball follows ball, and the noise of our own guns increases the confusion. From the General of Division to the Brigadier. He, a man of acknowledged bravery, keeps carefully behind a rising ground, a house, or a tree – a sure sign of increasing danger. Grape rattles on the roofs of the houses and in the fields; cannon balls howl over us, and plough the air in all directions, and soon there is a frequent whistling of musket balls. A step farther towards the troops, to that sturdy infantry which for hours has maintained its firmness under this heavy fire; here the air is filled with the hissing of balls which announce their proximity by a short sharp noise as they pass within an inch of the ear, the head, or the breast.

To add to all this, compassion strikes the beating heart with pity at the sight of the maimed and fallen. The young soldier cannot reach any of these different strata of danger without feeling that the light of reason does not move here in the same medium, that it is not refracted in the same manner as in speculative contemplation. Indeed, he must be a very extraordinary man who, under these impressions for the first time, does not lose the power of making any instantaneous decisions. It is true that habit soon blunts such impressions; in half an hour we begin to be more or less indifferent to all that is going on around us: but an ordinary character never attains to complete coolness and the natural elasticity of mind; and so we perceive that here again ordinary qualities will not suffice – a thing which gains truth, the wider the sphere of activity which is to be filled. Enthusiastic, stoical, natural bravery, great ambition, or also long familiarity with danger – much of all this there must be if all the effects produced in this resistant medium are not to fall far short of that which in the student's chamber may appear only the ordinary standard.

Danger in War belongs to its friction; a correct idea of its influence is necessary for truth of perception, and therefore it is brought under notice here.

CHAPTER V

OF BODILY EXERTION IN WAR

IF no one were allowed to pass an opinion on the events of War, except at a moment when he is benumbed by frost, sinking from heat and thirst, or dying with hunger and fatigue, we should certainly have fewer judgements correct *objectively*; but they would be so, *subjectively*, at least; that is, they would contain in themselves the exact relation between the person giving the judgement and the object. We can perceive this by observing how modestly subdued, even spiritless and desponding, is the opinion passed upon the results of untoward events by those who have been eye-witnesses, but especially if they have been parties concerned. This is, according to our view, a criterion of the influence which bodily fatigue exercises, and of the allowance to be made for it in matters of opinion.

Amongst the many things in War for which no tariff can be fixed, bodily effort may be specially reckoned. Provided there is no waste, it is a coefficient of all the forces, and no one can tell exactly to what extent it may be carried. But what is remarkable is, that just as only a strong arm enables the archer to stretch the bowstring to the utmost extent, so also in War it is only by means of a great directing spirit that we can expect the full power latent in the troops to be developed. For it is one thing if an Army, in consequence of great misfortunes, surrounded with danger, falls all to pieces like a wall that has been thrown down, and can only find safety in the utmost exertion of its bodily strength; it is another thing entirely when a victorious Army, drawn on by proud feelings only, is conducted at the will of its Chief. The same effort which in the one case might at most excite our pity must in the other call forth our admiration, because it is much more difficult to sustain.

By this comes to light for the inexperienced eye one of those things which put fetters in the dark, as it were, on the action of the mind, and wear out in secret the powers of the soul.

Although here the question is strictly only respecting the extreme effort required by a Commander from his Army, by a leader from his followers, therefore of the spirit to demand it and of the art of getting it, still the personal physical exertion of Generals and of the Chief Commander must not be overlooked. Having brought the analysis of War conscientiously up to this point, we could not but take account also of the weight of this small remaining residue.

We have spoken here of bodily effort, chiefly because, like danger, it belongs to the fundamental causes of friction, and because its indefinite quantity makes it like an elastic body, the friction of which is well known to be difficult to calculate.

To check the abuse of these considerations, of such a survey of things which aggravate the difficulties of War, nature has given our judgement a guide in our sensibilities. Just as an individual cannot with advantage refer to his personal deficiencies if he is insulted and ill-treated, but may well do so if he has successfully repelled the affront, or has fully revenged it, so no Commander or Army will lessen the impression of a disgraceful defeat by depicting the danger, the distress, the exertions, things which would immensely enhance the glory of a victory. Thus our feeling, which after all is only a higher kind of judgement, forbids us to do what seems an act of justice to which our judgement would be inclined.

CHAPTER VI

INFORMATION IN WAR

BY the word 'information' we denote all the knowledge which we have of the enemy and his country; therefore, in fact, the foundation of all our ideas and actions. Let us just consider the nature of this foundation, its want of trustworthiness, its changefulness, and we shall soon feel what a dangerous edifice War is, how easily it may fall to pieces and bury us in its ruins. For although it is a maxim in all books that we should trust only certain information, that we must be always suspicious, that is only a miserable book comfort, belonging to that description of knowledge in which writers of systems and compendiums take refuge for want of anything better to say.

Great part of the information obtained in War is contradictory, a still greater part is false, and by far the greatest part is of a doubtful character. What is required of an officer is a certain power of discrimination, which only knowledge of men and things and good judgement can give. The law of probability must be his guide. This is not a trifling difficulty even in respect of the first plans, which can be formed in the chamber outside the real sphere of War, but it is enormously increased when in the thick of War itself one report follows hard upon the heels of another; it is then fortunate if these reports in contradicting each other show a certain balance of probability, and thus themselves call forth a scrutiny. It is much worse for the inexperienced when accident does not render him this service, but one report supports another, confirms it, magnifies it, finishes off the picture with fresh touches of colour, until necessity in urgent haste forces from us a resolution which will soon be discovered to be folly, all those reports having been lies, exaggerations, errors, etc., etc. In a few words, most reports are false, and the timidity of men acts as a multiplier of lies and untruths. As a general rule, every one is more inclined to lend credence to the bad than the good. Every one is inclined to magnify the bad in some measure, and although the alarms which are thus propagated like the waves of the sea subside into themselves, still, like them, without any apparent cause they rise again. Firm in reliance on his own better convictions, the Chief must stand like a rock against which the sea breaks its fury in vain. The role is not easy; he who is not by nature of a buoyant disposition, or trained by experience in War, and matured in judgement, may let it be his rule to do violence to his own natural conviction by inclining from the side of fear to that of hope; only by that means will he be able to preserve his balance. This difficulty of seeing things correctly, which is one of the greatest sources of friction in War, makes things appear quite different from what was expected. The impression of the senses is stronger than the force of the ideas resulting from methodical reflection, and this goes so far that no important undertaking was ever yet carried out without the Commander having to subdue new doubts in himself at the time of commencing the execution of his work. Ordinary men who follow the suggestions of others become, therefore, generally undecided on the spot; they think that they have found circumstances different from what they had expected, and this view gains strength by their again yielding to the suggestions of others. But even the man who has made his own plans, when he comes to see things with his own eyes will often think he has done wrong. Firm reliance on self must make him proof against the seeming pressure of the moment; his first conviction will in the end prove true, when the foreground scenery which fate has pushed on to the stage of War, with its accompaniments of terrific objects, is drawn aside and the horizon extended. This is one of the great chasms which separate *conception* from *execution*.

CHAPTER VII

FRICTION IN WAR

As long as we have no personal knowledge of War, we cannot conceive where these difficulties lie of which so much is said, and what that genius and those extraordinary mental powers required in a General have really to do. All appears so simple, all the requisite branches of knowledge appear so plain, all the combinations so unimportant, that in comparison with them the easiest problem in higher mathematics impresses us with a certain scientific dignity. But if we have seen War, all becomes intelligible; and still, after all, it is extremely difficult to describe what it is which brings about this change, to specify this invisible and completely efficient factor.

Everything is very simple in War, but the simplest thing is difficult. These difficulties accumulate and produce a friction which no man can imagine exactly who has not seen War. Suppose now a traveller, who towards evening expects to accomplish the two stages at the end of his day's journey, four or five leagues, with post-horses, on the high road – it is nothing. He arrives now at the last station but one, finds no horses, or very bad ones; then a hilly country, bad roads; it is a dark night, and he is glad when, after a great deal of trouble, he reaches the next station, and finds there some miserable accommodation. So in War, through the influence of an infinity of petty circumstances, which cannot properly be described on paper, things disappoint us, and we fall short of the mark. A powerful iron will overcomes this friction; it crushes the obstacles, but certainly the machine along with them. We shall often meet with this result. Like an obelisk towards which the principal streets of a town converge, the strong will of a proud spirit stands prominent and commanding in the middle of the Art of War.

Friction is the only conception which in a general way corresponds to that which distinguishes real War from War on paper. The military machine, the Army and all belonging to it, is in fact simple, and appears on this account easy to manage. But let us reflect that no part of it is in one piece, that it is composed entirely of individuals, each of which keeps up its own friction in all directions. Theoretically all sounds very well: the commander of a battalion is responsible for the execution of the order given; and as the battalion by its discipline is glued together into one piece, and the chief must be a man of acknowledged zeal, the beam turns on an iron pin with little friction. But it is not so in reality, and all that is exaggerated and false in such a conception manifests itself at once in War. The battalion always remains composed of a number of men, of whom, if chance so wills, the most insignificant is able to occasion delay and even irregularity. The danger which War brings with it, the bodily exertions which it requires, augment this evil so much that they may be regarded as the greatest causes of it.

This enormous friction, which is not concentrated, as in mechanics, at a few points, is therefore everywhere brought into contact with chance, and thus incidents take place upon which it was impossible to calculate, their chief origin being chance. As an instance of one such chance take the weather. Here the fog prevents the enemy from being discovered in time, a battery from firing at the right moment, a report from reaching the General; there the rain prevents a battalion from arriving at the right time, because instead of for three it had to march perhaps eight hours; the cavalry from charging effectively because it is stuck fast in heavy ground.

These are only a few incidents of detail by way of elucidation, that the reader may be able to follow the author, for whole volumes might be written on these difficulties. To avoid this, and still to give a clear conception of the host of small difficulties to be contended with in War, we might go on heaping up illustrations, if we were not afraid of being tiresome. But those who have already comprehended us will permit us to add a few more.

Activity in War is movement in a resistant medium. Just as a man immersed in water is unable to perform with ease and regularity the most natural and simplest movement, that of walking, so in War, with ordinary powers, one cannot keep even the line of mediocrity. This is the reason that the correct theorist is like a swimming master, who teaches on dry land movements which are required in the water, which must appear grotesque and ludicrous to those who forget about the water. This is also why theorists, who have never plunged in themselves, or who cannot deduce any generalities from their experience, are unpractical and even absurd, because they only teach what every one knows – how to walk.

Further, every War is rich in particular facts, while at the same time each is an unexplored sea, full of rocks which the General may have a suspicion of, but which he has never seen with his eye, and round which, moreover, he must steer in the night. If a contrary wind also springs up, that is, if any great accidental event declares itself adverse to him, then the most consummate skill, presence of mind, and energy are required, whilst to those who only look on from a distance all seems to proceed with the utmost ease. The knowledge of this friction is a chief part of that so often talked of, experience in War, which is required in a good General. Certainly he is not the best General in whose mind it assumes the greatest dimensions, who is the most over-awed by it (this includes that class of over-anxious Generals, of whom there are so many amongst the experienced); but a General must be aware of it that he may overcome it, where that is possible, and that he may not expect a degree of precision in results which is impossible on account of this very friction. Besides, it can never be learnt theoretically; and if it could, there would still be wanting that experience of judgement which is called tact, and which is always more necessary in a field full of innumerable small and diversified objects than in great and decisive cases, when one's own judgement may be aided by consultation with others. Just as the man of the world, through tact of judgement which has become habit, speaks, acts, and moves only as suits the occasion, so the officer experienced in War will always, in great and small matters, at every pulsation of War as we may say, decide and determine suitably to the occasion. Through this experience and practice the idea comes to his mind of itself that so and so will not suit. And thus he will not easily place himself in a position by which he is compromised, which, if it often occurs in War, shakes all the foundations of confidence and becomes extremely dangerous.

It is therefore this friction, or what is so termed here, which makes that which appears easy in War difficult in reality. As we proceed, we shall often meet with this subject again, and it will hereafter become plain that besides experience and a strong will, there are still many other rare qualities of the mind required to make a man a consummate General.

CHAPTER VIII

CONCLUDING REMARKS

THOSE things which as elements meet together in the atmosphere of War and make it a resistant medium for every activity we have designated under the terms danger, bodily effort (exertion), information, and friction. In their impediment effects they may therefore be comprehended again in the collective notion of a general friction. Now is there, then, no kind of oil which is capable of diminishing this friction? Only one, and that one is not always available at the will of the Commander or his Army. It is the habituation of an Army to War.

Habit gives strength to the body in great exertion, to the mind in great danger, to the judgement against first impressions. By it a valuable circumspection is generally gained throughout every rank, from the hussar and rifleman up to the General of Division, which facilitates the work of the Chief Commander.

As the human eye in a dark room dilates its pupil, draws in the little light that there is, partially distinguishes objects by degrees, and at last knows them quite well, so it is in War with the experienced soldier, whilst the novice is only met by pitch dark night.

Habituation to War no General can give his Army at once, and the camps of manoeuvre (peace exercises) furnish but a weak substitute for it, weak in comparison with real experience in War, but not weak in relation to other Armies in which the training is limited to mere mechanical exercises of routine. So to regulate the exercises in peace time as to include some of these causes of friction, that the judgement, circumspection, even resolution of the separate leaders may be brought into exercise, is of much greater consequence than those believe who do not know the thing by experience. It is of immense importance that the soldier, high or low, whatever rank he has, should not have to encounter in War those things which, when seen for the first time, set him in astonishment and perplexity; if he has only met with them one single time before, even by that he is half acquainted with them. This relates even to bodily fatigues. They should be practised less to accustom the body to them than the mind. In War the young soldier is very apt to regard unusual fatigues as the consequence of faults, mistakes, and embarrassment in the conduct of the whole, and to become distressed and despondent as a consequence. This would not happen if he had been prepared for this beforehand by exercises in peace.

Another less comprehensive but still very important means of gaining habituation to War in time of peace is to invite into the service officers of foreign armies who have had experience in War. Peace seldom reigns over all Europe, and never in all quarters of the world. A State which has been long at peace should, therefore, always seek to procure some officers who have done good service at the different scenes of Warfare, or to send there some of its own, that they may get a lesson in War.

However small the number of officers of this description may appear in proportion to the mass, still their influence is very sensibly felt.[70] Their experience, the bent of their genius, the stamp of their character, influence their subordinates and comrades; and besides that, if they cannot be placed in positions of superior command, they may always be regarded as men acquainted with the country, who may be questioned on many special occasions.

BOOK TWO

ON THE THEORY OF WAR

CHAPTER I

BRANCHES OF THE ART OF WAR

WAR in its literal meaning is fighting, for fighting alone is the efficient principle in the manifold activity which in a wide sense is called War. But fighting is a trial of strength of the moral and physical forces by means of the latter. That the moral cannot be omitted is evident of itself, for the condition of the mind has always the most decisive influence on the forces employed in War.

The necessity of fighting very soon led men to special inventions to turn the advantage in it in their own favour: in consequence of these the mode of fighting has undergone great alterations; but in whatever way it is conducted its conception remains unaltered, and fighting is that which constitutes War.

The inventions have been from the first weapons and equipments for the individual combatants. These have to be provided and the use of them learnt before the War begins. They are made suitable to the nature of the fighting, consequently are ruled by it; but plainly the activity engaged in these appliances is a different thing from the fight itself; it is only the preparation for the combat, not the conduct of the same. That arming and equipping are not essential to the conception of fighting is plain, because mere wrestling is also fighting.

Fighting has determined everything appertaining to arms and equipment, and these in turn modify the mode of fighting; there is, therefore, a reciprocity of action between the two.

Nevertheless, the fight itself remains still an entirely special activity, more particularly because it moves in an entirely special element, namely, in the element of danger.

If, then, there is anywhere a necessity for drawing a line between two different activities, it is here; and in order to see clearly the importance of this idea, we need only just to call to mind how often eminent personal fitness in one field has turned out nothing but the most useless pedantry in the other.

It is also in no way difficult to separate in idea the one activity from the other, if we look at the combatant forces fully armed and equipped as a given means, the profitable use of which requires nothing more than a knowledge of their general results.

The Art of War is therefore, in its proper sense, the art of making use of the given means in fighting, and we cannot give it a better name than the '*Conduct of War*'. On the other hand, in a wider sense all activities which have their existence on account of War, therefore the whole creation of troops, that is levying them, arming, equipping, and exercising them, belong to the Art of War.

To make a sound theory it is most essential to separate these two activities, for it is easy to see that if every act of War is to begin with the preparation of military forces, and to presuppose forces so organized as a primary condition for conducting War, that theory will only be applicable in the few cases to which the force available happens to be exactly suited. If, on the other hand, we wish to have a theory which shall suit most cases, and will not be wholly useless in any case, it must be founded on those means which are in most general use, and in respect to these only on the actual results springing from them.

The conduct of War is, therefore, the formation and conduct of the fighting. If this fighting was a single act, there would be no necessity for any further subdivision, but the fight is composed of a greater or less number of single acts, complete in themselves, which we call combats, as we have shown in the first chapter of the first book, and which form new units. From this arises the totally different activities, that of the *formation* and *conduct* of these single combats in themselves, and the *combination* of them with one another, with a view to the ultimate object of the War. The first is called *tactics*, the other *strategy*.

This division into tactics and strategy is now in almost general use, and every one knows tolerably well under which head to place any single fact, without knowing very distinctly the grounds on which the classification is founded. But when such divisions are blindly adhered to in practice, they must have some deep root. We have searched for this root, and we might say that it is just the usage of the majority which has brought us to it. On the other hand, we look upon the arbitrary, unnatural definitions of these conceptions sought to be established by some writers as not in accordance with the general usage of the terms.

According to our classification, therefore, tactics *is the theory of the use of military forces in combat*. Strategy *is the theory of the use of combats for the object of the War*.[71]

The way in which the conception of a single, or independent combat, is more closely determined, the conditions to which this unit is attached, we shall only be able to explain clearly when we consider the combat; we must content ourselves for the present with saying that in relation to space, therefore in combats taking place at the same time, the unit reaches just as far as *personal command* reaches; but in regard to time, and therefore in relation to combats which follow each other in close succession, it reaches to the moment when the crisis which takes place in every combat is entirely passed.

That doubtful cases may occur, cases, for instance, in which several combats may perhaps be regarded also as a single one, will not overthrow the ground of distinction we have adopted, for the same is the case with all grounds of distinction of real things which are differentiated by a gradually diminishing scale. There may, therefore, certainly be acts of activity in War which, without any alteration in the point of view, may just as well be counted strategic as tactical; for example, very extended positions resembling a chain of posts, the preparations for the passage of a river at several points, etc.

Our classification reaches and covers only the *use of the military force*. But now there are in War a number of activities which are subservient to it, and still are quite different from it; sometimes closely allied, sometimes less near in their affinity. All these activities relate to the *maintenance of the military force*.[72] In the same way as its creation and training precede its use, so its maintenance is always a necessary condition. But, strictly viewed, all activities thus connected with it are always to be regarded only as preparations for fighting; they are certainly nothing more than activities which are very close to the action, so that they run through the hostile act alternate in importance with the use of the forces. We have therefore a right to exclude them as well as the other preparatory activities from the Art of War in its restricted sense, from the conduct of War properly so called; and we are obliged to do so if we would comply with the first principle of all theory, the elimination of all heterogeneous elements. Who would include in the real 'conduct of War' the whole litany of subsistence and administration, because it is admitted to stand in constant reciprocal action with the use of the troops, but is something essentially different from it?

We have said, in the third chapter of our first book, that as the fight or combat is the only directly effective activity, therefore the threads of all others, as they end in it, are included in it. By this we meant to say that to all others an object was thereby appointed which, in accordance with the laws peculiar to themselves, they must seek to attain. Here we must go a little closer into this subject.

The subjects which constitute the activities outside of the combat are of various kinds.

The one part belongs, in one respect, to the combat itself, is identical with it, whilst it serves in another respect for the maintenance of the military force. The other part belongs purely to the subsistence, and has only, in consequence of the reciprocal action, a limited influence on the combats by its results. The subjects which in one respect belong to the fighting itself are *marches*, *camps*, and *cantonments*, for they suppose so many different situations of troops, and where troops are supposed there the idea of the combat must always be present.

The other subjects, which only belong to the maintenance, are *subsistence*, *care of the sick*, the *supply and repair of arms and equipment*.

Marches are quite identical with the use of the troops. The act of marching in the *combat*, generally called manoeuvring, certainly does not necessarily include the use of weapons, but it is so completely and necessarily combined with it that it forms an integral part of that which we call a combat. But the march outside the combat is nothing but the execution of a strategic measure. By the strategic plan is settled *when, where, and with what forces* a battle is to be delivered – and to carry that into execution the march is the only means.

The march outside of the combat is therefore an instrument of strategy, but not on that account exclusively a subject of strategy, for as the armed force which executes it may be involved in a possible combat at any moment, therefore its execution stands also under tactical as well as strategic rules. If we prescribe to a column its route on a particular side of a river or of a branch of a mountain, then that is a strategic measure, for it contains the intention of fighting on that particular side of the hill or river in preference to the other, in case a combat should be necessary during the march.

But if a column, instead of following the road through a valley, marches along the parallel ridge of heights, or for the convenience of marching divides itself into several columns, then these are tactical arrangements, for they relate to the manner in which we shall use the troops in the anticipated combat.

The particular order of march is in constant relation with readiness for combat, is therefore tactical in its nature, for it is nothing more than the first or preliminary disposition for the battle which may possibly take place.

As the march is the instrument by which strategy apportions its active elements, the combats, but these last often only appear by their results and not in the details of their real course, it could not fail to happen that in theory the instrument has often been substituted for the efficient principle. Thus we hear of a decisive skilful march, allusion being thereby made to those combat-combinations to which these marches led. This substitution of ideas is too natural and conciseness of expression too desirable to call for alteration, but still it is only a condensed chain of ideas in regard to which we must never omit to bear in mind the full meaning, if we would avoid falling into error.

We fall into an error of this description if we attribute to strategical combinations a power independent of tactical results. We read of marches and manoeuvres combined, the object attained, and at the same time not a word about combat, from which the conclusion is drawn that there are means in War of conquering an enemy without fighting. The prolific nature of this error we cannot show until hereafter.

But although a march can be regarded absolutely as an integral part of the combat, still there are in it certain relations which do not belong to the combat, and therefore are neither tactical nor strategic. To these belong all arrangements which concern only the accommodation of the troops, the construction of bridges, roads, etc. These are only conditions; under many circumstances they are in very close connexion, and may almost identify themselves with the troops, as in building a bridge in presence of the enemy; but in themselves they are always extraneous activities, the theory of which does not form part of the theory of the conduct of War.

Camps, by which we mean every disposition of troops in concentrated, therefore in battle order, in contra-distinction to cantonments or quarters, are a state of rest, therefore of restoration; but they are at the same time also the strategic appointment of a battle on the spot chosen; and by the manner in which they are taken up they contain the fundamental lines of the battle, a condition from which every defensive battle starts; they are therefore essential parts of both strategy and tactics.

Cantonments take the place of camps for the better refreshment of the troops. They are therefore, like camps, strategic subjects as regards position and extent; tactical subjects as regards internal organization, with a view to readiness to fight.

The occupation of camps and cantonments no doubt usually combines with the recuperation of the troops another object also, for example, the covering a district of country, the holding a position; but it can very well be only the first. We remind our readers that strategy may follow a great diversity of objects, for everything which appears an advantage may be the object of a combat, and the preservation of the instrument with which War is made must necessarily very often become the object of its partial combinations.

If, therefore, in such a case strategy ministers only to the maintenance of the troops, we are not on that account out of the field of strategy, for we are still engaged with the use of the military force, because every disposition of that force upon any point whatever of the theatre of War is such a use.

But if the maintenance of the troops in camp or quarters calls forth activities which are no employment of the armed force, such as the construction of huts, pitching of tents, subsistence and sanitary services in camps or quarters, then such belong neither to strategy nor tactics.

Even entrenchments, the site and preparation of which are plainly part of the order of battle, therefore tactical subjects, do not belong to the theory of the conduct of War so far as respects the *execution of their construction*, the knowledge and skill required for such work being, in point of fact, qualities inherent in the nature of an organized Army; the theory of the combat takes them for granted.

Amongst the subjects which belong to the mere keeping up of an armed force, because none of the parts are identified with the combat, the victualling of the troops themselves comes first, as it must be done almost daily and for each individual. Thus it is that it completely permeates military action in the parts constituting strategy – we say parts constituting strategy, because during a battle the subsistence of troops will rarely have any influence in modifying the plan, although the thing is conceivable enough. The care for the subsistence of the troops comes therefore into reciprocal action chiefly with strategy, and there is nothing more common than for the leading strategic features of a campaign and War to be traced out in connexion with a view to this supply. But however frequent and however important these views of supply may be, the subsistence of the troops always remains a completely different activity from the use of the troops, and the former has only an influence on the latter by its results.

The other branches of administrative activity which we have mentioned stand much farther apart from the use of the troops. The care of sick and wounded, highly important as it is for the good of an Army, directly affects it only in a small portion of the individuals composing it, and therefore has only a weak and indirect influence upon the use of the rest. The completing and replacing articles of arms and equipment, except so far as by the organism of the forces it constitutes a continuous activity inherent in them – takes place only periodically, and therefore seldom affects strategic plans.

We must, however, here guard ourselves against a mistake.

In certain cases these subjects may be really of decisive importance. The distance of hospitals and depots of munitions may very easily be imagined as the sole cause of very important strategic decisions. We do not wish either to contest that point or to throw it into the shade. But we are at present occupied not with the particular facts of a concrete case, but with abstract theory; and our assertion therefore is that such an influence is too rare to give the theory of sanitary measures and the supply of munitions and arms an importance in the theory of the conduct of War such as to make it worth while to include in the theory of the conduct of War the consideration of the different ways and systems which the above theories may furnish, in the same way as is certainly necessary in regard to victualling troops.

If we have clearly understood the results of our reflections, then the activities belonging to War divide themselves into two principal classes, into such as are only '*preparations for War*' and into the '*War itself*'. This division must therefore also be made in theory.

The knowledge and applications of skill in the preparations for War are engaged in the creation, discipline, and maintenance of all the military forces; what general names should be given to them we do not enter into, but we see that artillery, fortification, elementary tactics, as they are called, the whole organization and administration of the various armed forces, and all such things are included. But the theory of War itself occupies itself with the use of these prepared means for the object of the war. It needs of the first only the results, that is, the knowledge of the principal properties of the means taken in hand for use. This we call 'The Art of War' in a limited sense, or 'Theory of the Conduct of War', or 'Theory of the Employment of Armed Forces', all of them denoting for us the same thing.

The present theory will therefore treat the combat as the real contest, marches, camps, and cantonments as circumstances which are more or less identical with it. The subsistence of the troops will only come into consideration like *other given instances* in respect of its results, not as an activity belonging to the combat.

The Art of War thus viewed in its limited sense divides itself again into tactics and strategy. The former occupies itself with the form of the separate combat, the latter with its use. Both connect themselves with the circumstances of marches, camps, cantonments only through the combat, and these circumstances are tactical or strategic according as they relate to the form or to the signification of the battle.

No doubt there will be many readers who will consider superfluous this careful separation of two things lying so close together as tactics and strategy, because it has no direct effect on the conduct itself of War. We admit, certainly that it would be pedantry to look for direct effects on the field of battle from a theoretical distinction.

But the first business of every theory is to clear up conceptions and ideas which have been jumbled together, and, we may say, entangled and confused; and only when a right understanding is established, as to names and conceptions, can we hope to progress with clearness and facility, and be certain that author and reader will always see things from the same point of view. Tactics and strategy are two activities mutually permeating each other in time and space, at the same time essentially different activities, the inner laws and mutual relations of which cannot be intelligible at all to the mind until a clear conception of the nature of each activity is established.

He to whom all this is nothing, must either repudiate all theoretical consideration, *or his understanding has not as yet been pained* by the confused and perplexing ideas resting on no fixed point of view, leading to no satisfactory result, sometimes dull, sometimes fantastic, sometimes floating in vague generalities, which we are often obliged to hear and read on the conduct of War, owing to the spirit of scientific investigation having hitherto been little directed to these subjects.

CHAPTER II

ON THE THEORY OF WAR

1. The first conception of the 'Art of War' was merely the preparation of the armed forces

FORMERLY by the term 'Art of War', or 'Science of War', nothing was understood but the totality of those branches of knowledge and those appliances of skill occupied with material things. The pattern and preparation and the mode of using arms, the construction of fortifications and entrenchments, the organism of an army and the mechanism of its movements, were the subject of these branches of knowledge and skill above referred to, and the end and aim of them all was the establishment of an armed force fit for use in War. All this concerned merely things belonging to the material world and a one-sided activity only, and it was in fact nothing but an activity advancing by gradations from the lower occupations to a finer kind of mechanical art. The relation of all this to War itself was very much the same as the relation of the art of the sword cutler to the art of using the sword. The employment in the moment of danger and in a state of constant reciprocal action of the particular energies of mind and spirit in the direction proposed to them was not yet even mooted.

2. True war first appears in the art of sieges

In the art of sieges we first perceive a certain degree of guidance of the combat, something of the action of the intellectual faculties upon the material forces placed under their control, but generally only so far that it very soon embodied itself again in new material forms, such as approaches, trenches, counter-approaches, batteries, etc., and every step which this action of the higher faculties took was marked by some such result; it was only the thread that was required on which to string these material inventions in order. As the intellect can hardly manifest itself in this kind of War, except in such things, so therefore nearly all that was necessary was done in that way.

3. Then tactics tried to find its way in the same direction

Afterwards tactics attempted to give to the mechanism of its joints the character of a general disposition, built upon the peculiar properties of the instrument, which character leads indeed to the battlefield, but instead of leading to the free activity of mind, leads to an Army made like an automaton by its rigid formations and orders of battle, which, movable only by the word of command, is intended to unwind its activities like a piece of clockwork.[73]

4. The real conduct of war only made its appearance incidentally and incognito

The conduct of War properly so called, that is, a use of the prepared means adapted to the most special requirements, was not considered as any suitable subject for theory, but one which should be left to natural talents alone. By degrees, as War passed from the hand-to-hand encounters of the middle ages into a more regular and systematic form, stray reflections on this point also forced themselves into men's minds, but they mostly appeared only incidentally in memoirs and narratives, and in a certain measure incognito.

5. Reflections on military events brought about the want of a theory

As contemplation on War continually increased, and its history every day assumed more of a critical character, the urgent want appeared of the support of fixed maxims and rules, in order that in the controversies naturally arising about military events the war of opinions might be brought to some one point. This whirl of opinions, which neither revolved on any central pivot nor according to any appreciable laws, could not but be very distasteful to people's minds.

6. Endeavours to establish a positive theory

There arose, therefore, an endeavour to establish maxims, rules, and even systems for the conduct of War. By this the attainment of a positive object was proposed, without taking into view the endless difficulties which the conduct of War presents in that respect. The conduct of War, as we have shown, has no definite limits in any direction, while every system has the circumscribing nature of a synthesis, from which results an irreconcileable opposition between such a theory and practice.

7. Limitation to material objects

Writers on theory felt the difficulty of the subject soon enough, and thought themselves entitled to get rid of it by directing their maxims and systems only upon material things and a one-sided activity. Their aim was to reach results, as in the science for the preparation for War, entirely certain and positive, and therefore only to take into consideration that which could be made matter of calculation.

8. Superiority of numbers

The superiority in numbers being a material condition, it was chosen from amongst all the factors required to produce victory, because it could be brought under mathematical laws through combinations of time and space. It was thought possible to leave out of sight all other circumstances, by supposing them to be equal on each side, and therefore to neutralize one another. This would have been very well if it had been done to gain a preliminary knowledge of this one factor, according to its relations, but to make it a rule for ever to consider superiority of numbers as the sole law; to see the whole secret of the Art of War in the formula, *in a certain time, at a certain point, to bring up superior masses* – was a restriction overruled by the force of realities.

9. Victualling of troops

By one theoretical school an attempt was made to systematize another material element also, by making the subsistence of troops, according to a previously established organism of the Army, the supreme legislator in the higher conduct of War. In this way certainly they arrived at definite figures, but at figures which rested on a number of arbitrary calculations, and which therefore could not stand the test of practical application.[74]

10. Base

An ingenious author tried to concentrate in a single conception, that of a *Base*, a whole host of objects, amongst which sundry relations even with immaterial forces found their way in as well. The list comprised the subsistence of the troops, the keeping them complete in numbers and equipment, the security of communications with the home country, lastly, the security of retreat in case it became necessary; and, first of all, he proposed to substitute this conception of a base for all these things; then for the base itself to substitute its own length (extent); and, last of all, to substitute the angle formed by the army with this base: all this was done merely to obtain a pure geometrical result utterly useless. This last is, in fact, unavoidable, if we reflect that none of these substitutions could be made without violating truth and leaving out some of the things contained in the original conception. The idea of a base is a real necessity for strategy, and to have conceived it is meritorious; but to make such a use of it as we have depicted is completely inadmissible, and could not but lead to partial conclusions which have forced these theorists into a direction opposed to common sense, namely, to a belief in the decisive effect of the enveloping form of attack.

11. Interior Lines

As a reaction against this false direction, another geometrical principle, that of the so-called interior lines, was then elevated to the throne. Although this principle rests on a sound foundation, on the truth that the combat is the only effectual means in War, still it is, just on account of its purely geometrical nature, nothing but another case of one-sided theory which can never gain ascendancy in the real world.

12. All these attempts are open to objection

All these attempts at theory are only to be considered in their analytical part as progress in the province of truth, but in their synthetical part, in their precepts and rules, they are quite unserviceable.

They strive after determinate quantities, whilst in War all is undetermined, and the calculation has always to be made with varying quantities.

They direct the attention only upon material forces, while the whole military action is penetrated throughout by intelligent forces and their effects.

They only pay regard to activity on one side, whilst War is a constant state of reciprocal action, the effects of which are mutual.

13. As a rule they exclude genius

All that was not attainable by such miserable philosophy, the offspring of partial views, lay outside the precincts of science – and was the field of genius, which *raises itself above rules*.

Pity the warrior who is contented to crawl about in this beggardom of rules, which are too bad for genius, over which it can set itself superior, over which it can perchance make merry! What genius does must be the best of all rules, and theory cannot do better than to show how and why it is so.

Pity the theory which sets itself in opposition to the mind! It cannot repair this contradiction by any humility, and the humbler it is so much the sooner will ridicule and contempt drive it out of real life.

14. The difficulty of theory as soon as moral quantities come into consideration

Every theory becomes infinitely more difficult from the moment that it touches on the province of moral quantities. Architecture and painting know quite well what they are about as long as they have only to do with matter; there is no dispute about mechanical or optical construction. But as soon as the moral activities begin their work, as soon as moral impressions and feelings are produced, the whole set of rules dissolves into vague ideas.

The science of medicine is chiefly engaged with bodily phenomena only; its business is with the animal organism, which, liable to perpetual change, is never exactly the same for two moments. This makes its practice very difficult, and places the judgement of the physician above his science; but how much more difficult is the case if a moral effect is added, and how much higher must we place the physician of the mind?

15. The moral quantities must not be excluded in war

But now the activity in War is never directed solely against matter; it is always at the same time directed against the intelligent force which gives life to this matter, and to separate the two from each other is impossible.

But the intelligent forces are only visible to the inner eye, and this is different in each person, and often different in the same person at different times.

As danger is the general element in which everything moves in War, it is also chiefly by courage, the feeling of one's own power, that the judgement is differently influenced. It is to a certain extent the crystalline lens through which all appearances pass before reaching the understanding.

And yet we cannot doubt that these things acquire a certain objective value simply through experience.

Every one knows the moral effect of a surprise, of an attack in flank or rear. Every one thinks less of the enemy's courage as soon as he turns his back, and ventures much more in pursuit than when pursued. Every one judges of the enemy's General by his reputed talents, by his age and experience, and shapes his course accordingly. Every one casts a scrutinizing glance at the spirit and feeling of his own and the enemy's troops. All these and similar effects in the province of the moral nature of man have established themselves by experience, are perpetually recurring, and therefore warrant our reckoning them as real quantities of their kind. What could we do with any theory which should leave them out of consideration?

Certainly experience is an indispensable title for these truths. With psychological and philosophical sophistries no theory, no General, should meddle.

16. Principal difficulty of a theory for the conduct of war

In order to comprehend clearly the difficulty of the proposition which is contained in a theory for the conduct of War, and thence to deduce the necessary characteristics of such a theory, we must take a closer view of the chief particulars which make up the nature of activity in War.

17. First speciality – moral forces and their effects (Hostile feeling)

The first of these specialities consists in the moral forces and effects.

The combat is, in its origin, the expression of *hostile feeling*, but in our great combats, which we call Wars, the hostile feeling frequently resolves itself into merely a hostile *view*, and there is usually no innate hostile feeling residing in individual against individual. Nevertheless, the combat never passes off without such feelings being brought into activity. National hatred, which is seldom wanting in our Wars, is a substitute for personal hostility in the breast of individual opposed to individual. But where this also is wanting, and at first no animosity of feeling subsists, a hostile feeling is kindled by the combat itself; for an act of violence which any one commits upon us by order of his superior, will excite in us a desire to retaliate and be revenged on him, sooner than on the superior power at whose command the act was done. This is human, or animal if we will; still it is so. We are very apt to regard the combat in theory as an abstract trial of strength, without any participation on the part of the feelings, and that is one of the thousand errors which theorists deliberately commit, because they do not see its consequences.

Besides that excitation of feelings naturally arising from the combat itself, there are others also which do not essentially belong to it, but which, on account of their relationship, easily unite with it – ambition, love of power, enthusiasm of every kind, etc., etc.

18. The impressions of danger (Courage)

Finally, the combat begets the element of danger, in which all the activities of War must live and move, like the bird in the air or the fish in the water. But the influences of danger all pass into the feelings, either directly – that is, instinctively – or through the medium of the understanding. The effect in the first case would be a desire to escape from the danger, and, if that cannot be done, fright and anxiety. If this effect does not take place, then it is *courage*, which is a counterpoise to that instinct. Courage is, however, by no means an act of the understanding, but likewise a feeling, like fear; the latter looks to the physical preservation, courage to the moral preservation. Courage, then, is a nobler instinct. But because it is so, it will not allow itself to be used as a lifeless instrument, which produces its effects exactly according to prescribed measure. Courage is therefore no mere counterpoise to danger in order to neutralize the latter in its effects, but a peculiar power in itself.

19. Extent of the influence of danger

But to estimate exactly the influence of danger upon the principal actors in War, we must not limit its sphere to the physical danger of the moment. It dominates over the actor, not only by threatening him, but also by threatening all entrusted to him, not only at the moment in which it is actually present, but also through the imagination at all other moments, which have a connexion with the present; lastly, not only directly by itself, but also indirectly by the responsibility which makes it bear with tenfold weight on the mind of the chief actor. Who could advise, or resolve upon a great battle, without feeling his mind more or less wrought up, or perplexed by, the danger and responsibility which such a great act of decision carries in itself? We may say that action in War, in so far as it is real action, not a mere condition, is never out of the sphere of danger.

20. *Other powers of feeling*

If we look upon these affections which are excited by hostility and danger as peculiarly belonging to War, we do not, therefore, exclude from it all others accompanying man in his life's journey. They will also find room here frequently enough. Certainly we may say that many a petty action of the passions is silenced in this serious business of life; but that holds good only in respect to those acting in a lower sphere, who, hurried on from one state of danger and exertion to another, lose sight of the rest of the things of life, *become unused to deceit*, because it is of no avail with death, and so attain to that soldierly simplicity of character which has always been the best representative of the military profession. In higher regions it is otherwise, for the higher a man's rank, the more he must look around him; then arise interests on every side, and a manifold activity of the passions of good and bad. Envy and generosity, pride and humility, fierceness and tenderness, all may appear as active powers in this great drama.

21. *Peculiarity of mind*

The peculiar characteristics of mind in the chief actor have, as well as those of the feelings, a high importance. From an imaginative, flighty, inexperienced head, and from a calm, sagacious understanding, different things are to be expected.

22. *From the diversity in mental individualities arises the diversity of ways leading to the end*

It is this great diversity in mental individuality, the influence of which is to be supposed as chiefly felt in the higher ranks, because it increases as we progress upwards, which chiefly produces the diversity of ways leading to the end noticed by us in the first book, and which gives, to the play of probabilities and chance, such an unequal share in determining the course of events.

23. Second peculiarity – living reaction

The second peculiarity in War is the living reaction, and the reciprocal action resulting therefrom. We do not here speak of the difficulty of estimating that reaction, for that is included in the difficulty before mentioned, of treating the moral powers as quantities; but of this, that reciprocal action, by its nature, opposes anything like a regular plan. The effect which any measure produces upon the enemy is the most distinct of all the data which action affords; but every theory must keep to classes (or groups) of phenomena, and can never take up the really individual case in itself: that must everywhere be left to judgement and talent. It is therefore natural that in a business such as War, which in its plan – built upon general circumstances – is so often thwarted by unexpected and singular accidents, more must generally be left to talent; and less use can be made of a *theoretical guide* than in any other.

24. Third peculiarity – uncertainty of all data

Lastly, the great uncertainty of all data in War is a peculiar difficulty, because all action must, to a certain extent, be planned in a mere twilight, which in addition not unfrequently – like the effect of a fog or moonshine – gives to things exaggerated dimensions and an unnatural appearance.

What this feeble light leaves indistinct to the sight talent must discover, or must be left to chance. It is therefore again talent, or the favour of fortune, on which reliance must be placed, for want of objective knowledge.

25. Positive theory is impossible

With materials of this kind we can only say to ourselves that it is a sheer impossibility to construct for the Art of War a theory which, like a scaffolding, shall ensure to the chief actor an external support on all sides. In all those cases in which he is thrown upon his talent he would find himself away from this scaffolding of theory and in opposition to it, and, however many-sided it might be framed, the same result would ensue of which we spoke when we said that talent and genius act beyond the law, and theory is in opposition to reality.

26. *Means left by which a theory is possible (The difficulties are not everywhere equally great)*

Two means present themselves of getting out of this difficulty. In the first place, what we have said of the nature of military action in general does not apply in the same manner to the action of every one, whatever may be his standing. In the lower ranks the spirit of self-sacrifice is called more into request, but the difficulties which the understanding and judgement meet with are infinitely less. The field of occurrences is more confined. Ends and means are fewer in number. Data more distinct; mostly also contained in the actually visible. But the higher we ascend the more the difficulties increase, until in the Commander-in-Chief they reach their climax, so that with him almost everything must be left to genius.

Further, according to a division of the subject in *agreement with its nature*, the difficulties are not everywhere the same, but diminish the more results manifest themselves in the material world, and increase the more they pass into the moral, and become motives which influence the will. Therefore it is easier to determine, by theoretical rules, the order and conduct of a battle, than the use to be made of the battle itself. Yonder physical weapons clash with each other, and although mind is not wanting therein, matter must have its rights. But in the effects to be produced by battles when the material results become motives, we have only to do with the moral nature. In a word, it is easier to make a theory for *tactics* than for *strategy*.

27. *Theory must be of the nature of observation, not of doctrine*

The second opening for the possibility of a theory lies in the point of view that it does not necessarily require to be a *direction* for action. As a general rule, whenever an *activity* is for the most part occupied with the same objects over and over again, with the same ends and means, although there may be trifling alterations and a corresponding number of varieties of combination, such things are capable of becoming a subject of study for the reasoning faculties. But such study is just the most essential part of every *theory*, and has a peculiar title to that name. It is an analytical investigation of the subject that leads to an exact knowledge; and if brought to bear on the results of experience, which in our case would be military history, to a thorough familiarity with it. The nearer theory attains the latter object, so much the more it passes over from the objective form of knowledge into the subjective one of skill in action; and so much the more, therefore, it will prove itself effective when circumstances allow of no other decision but that of personal talents; it will show its effects in that talent itself. If theory investigates the subjects which constitute War; if it separates more distinctly that which at first sight seems amalgamated; if it explains fully the properties of the means; if it shows their probable effects; if it makes evident the nature of objects; if it brings to bear all over the field of War the light of essentially critical investigation – then it has fulfilled the chief duties of its province. It becomes then a guide to him who wishes to make himself acquainted with War from books; it lights up the whole road for him, facilitates his progress, educates his judgement, and shields him from error.

If a man of expertness spends half his life in the endeavour to clear up an obscure subject thoroughly, he will probably know more about it than a person who seeks to master it in a short time. Theory is instituted that each person in succession may not have to go through the same labour of clearing the ground and toiling through his subject, but may find the thing in order, and light admitted on it. It should educate the mind of the future leader in War, or rather guide him in his self-instruction, but not accompany him to the field of battle; just as a sensible tutor forms and enlightens the opening mind of a youth without, therefore, keeping him in leading strings all through his life.

If maxims and rules result of themselves from the considerations which theory institutes, if the truth accretes itself into that form of crystal, then theory will not oppose this natural law of the mind; it will rather, if the arch ends in such a keystone, bring it prominently out; but so does this, only in order to satisfy the philosophical law of reason, in order to show distinctly the point to which the lines all converge, not in order to form out of it an algebraical formula for use upon the battlefield; for even these maxims and rules serve more to determine in the reflecting mind the leading outline of its habitual movements than as landmarks indicating to it the way in the act of execution.

28. By this point of view theory becomes possible, and ceases to be in contradiction to practice

Taking this point of view, there is a possibility afforded of a satisfactory, that is, of a useful, theory of the conduct of War, never coming into opposition with the reality, and it will only depend on rational treatment to bring it so far into harmony with action that between theory and practice there shall no longer be that absurd difference which an unreasonable theory, in defiance of common sense, has often produced, but which, just as often, narrow-mindedness and ignorance have used as a pretext for giving way to their natural incapacity.

29. Theory therefore considers the nature of ends and means – ends and means in tactics

Theory has therefore to consider the nature of the means and ends.

In tactics the means are the disciplined armed forces which are to carry on the contest. The object is victory. The precise definition of this conception can be better explained hereafter in the consideration of the combat. Here we content ourselves by denoting the retirement of the enemy from the field of battle as the sign of victory. By means of this victory strategy gains the object for which it appointed the combat, and which constitutes its special signification. This signification has certainly some influence on the nature of the victory. A victory which is intended to weaken the enemy's armed forces is a different thing from one which is designed only to put us in possession of a position. The signification of a combat may therefore have a sensible influence on the preparation and conduct of it, consequently will be also a subject of consideration in tactics.

30. Circumstances which always attend the application of the means

As there are certain circumstances which attend the combat throughout, and have more or less influence upon its result, therefore these must be taken into consideration in the application of the armed forces.

These circumstances are the locality of the combat (ground), the time of day, and the weather.

31. Locality

The locality, which we prefer leaving for solution, under the head of 'Country and Ground', might, strictly speaking, be without any influence at all if the combat took place on a completely level and uncultivated plain.

In a country of steppes such a case may occur, but in the cultivated countries of Europe it is almost an imaginary idea. Therefore a combat between civilized nations, in which country and ground have no influence, is hardly conceivable.

32. Time of day

The time of day influences the combat by the difference between day and night; but the influence naturally extends further than merely to the limits of these divisions, as every combat has a certain duration, and great battles last for several hours. In the preparations for a great battle, it makes an essential difference whether it begins in the morning or the evening. At the same time, certainly many battles may be fought in which the question of the time of day is quite immaterial, and in the generality of cases its influence is only trifling.

33. Weather

Still more rarely has the weather any decisive influence, and it is mostly only by fogs that it plays a part.

34. End and means in strategy

Strategy has in the first instance only the victory, that is, the tactical result, as a means to its object, and ultimately those things which lead directly to peace. The application of its means to this object is at the same time attended by circumstances which have an influence thereon more or less.

35. Circumstances which attend the application of the means of strategy

These circumstances are country and ground, the former including the territory and inhabitants of the whole theatre of war; next the time of the day, and the time of the year as well; lastly, the weather, particularly any unusual state of the same, severe frost, etc.

36. These form new means

By bringing these things into combination with the results of a combat, strategy gives this result – and therefore the combat – a special signification, places before it a particular object. But when this object is not that which leads directly to peace, therefore a subordinate one, it is only to be looked upon as a means; and therefore in strategy we may look upon the results of combats or victories, in all their different significations, as means. The conquest of a position is such a result of a combat applied to ground. But not only are the different combats with special objects to be considered as means, but also every higher aim which we may have in view in the combination of battles directed on a common object is to be regarded as a means. A winter campaign is a combination of this kind applied to the season.

There remain, therefore, as objects, only those things which may be supposed as leading *directly* to peace. Theory investigates all these ends and means according to the nature of their effects and their mutual relations.

37. Strategy deduces only from experience the ends and means to be examined

The first question is, How does strategy arrive at a complete list of these things? If there is to be a philosophical inquiry leading to an absolute result, it would become entangled in all those difficulties which the logical necessity of the conduct of War and its theory exclude. It therefore turns to experience, and directs its attention on those combinations which military history can furnish. In this manner, no doubt, nothing more than a limited theory can be obtained, which only suits circumstances such as are presented in history. But this incompleteness is unavoidable, because in any case theory must either have deduced from, or have compared with, history what it advances with respect to things. Besides, this incompleteness in every case is more theoretical than real.

One great advantage of this method is that theory cannot lose itself in abstruse disquisitions, subtleties, and chimeras, but must always remain practical.[75]

38. How far the analysis of the means should be carried

Another question is, How far should theory go in its analysis of the means? Evidently only so far as the elements in a separate form present themselves for consideration in practice. The range and effect of different weapons is very important to tactics; their construction, although these effects result from it, is a matter of indifference; for the conduct of War is not making powder and cannon out of a given quantity of charcoal, sulphur, and saltpetre, of copper and tin: the given quantities for the conduct of War are arms in a finished state and their effects. Strategy makes use of maps without troubling itself about triangulations; it does not inquire how the country is subdivided into departments and provinces, and how the people are educated and governed, in order to attain the best military results; but it takes things as it finds them in the community of European States, and observes where very different conditions have a notable influence on War.

39. Great simplification of the knowledge required

That in this manner the number of subjects for theory is much simplified, and the knowledge requisite for the conduct of War much reduced, is easy to perceive. The very great mass of knowledge and appliances of skill which minister to the action of War in general, and which are necessary before an army fully equipped can take the field, unite in a few great results before they are able to reach, in actual War, the final goal of their activity; just as the streams of a country unite themselves in rivers before they fall into the sea. Only those activities emptying themselves directly into the sea of War have to be studied by him who is to conduct its operations.

40. This explains the rapid growth of great generals, and why a general is not a man of learning

This result of our considerations is in fact so necessary, that any other would have made us distrustful of their accuracy. Only thus is explained how so often men have made their appearance with great success in War, and indeed in the higher ranks even in supreme Command, whose pursuits had been previously of a totally different nature; indeed how, as a rule, the most distinguished Generals have never risen from the very learned or really erudite class of officers, but have been mostly men who, from the circumstances of their position, could not have attained to any great amount of knowledge. On that account those who have considered it necessary or even beneficial to commence the education of a future General by instruction in all details have always been ridiculed as absurd pedants. It would be easy to show the injurious tendency of such a course, because the human mind is trained by the knowledge imparted to it and the direction given to its ideas. Only what is great can make it great; the little can only make it little, if the mind itself does not reject it as something repugnant.

41. Former contradictions

Because this simplicity of knowledge requisite in War was not attended to, but that knowledge was always jumbled up with the whole impedimenta of subordinate sciences and arts, therefore the palpable opposition to the events of real life which resulted could not be solved otherwise than by ascribing it all to genius, which requires no theory and for which no theory could be prescribed.

42. On this account all use of knowledge was denied, and everything ascribed to natural talents

People with whom common sense had the upper hand felt sensible of the immense distance remaining to be filled up between a genius of the highest order and a learned pedant; and they became in a manner free-thinkers, rejected all belief in theory, and affirmed the conduct of War to be a natural function of man, which he performs more or less well according as he has brought with him into the world more or less talent in that direction. It cannot be denied that these were nearer to the truth than those who placed a value on false knowledge; at the same time it may easily be seen that such a view is itself but an exaggeration. No activity of the human understanding is possible without a certain stock of ideas; but these are, for the greater part at least, not innate but acquired, and constitute his knowledge. The only question therefore is, of what kind should these ideas be; and we think we have answered it if we say that they should be directed on those things which man has directly to deal with in War.

43. The knowledge must be made suitable to the position

Inside this field of military activity, the knowledge required must be different according to the station of the Commander.

It will be directed on smaller and more circumscribed objects if he holds an inferior, upon greater and more comprehensive ones if he holds a higher situation. There are Field Marshals who would not have shone at the head of a cavalry regiment, and vice versa.

44. The knowledge in war is very simple, but not, at the same time, very easy

But although the knowledge in War is simple, that is to say directed to so few subjects, and taking up those only in their final results, the art of execution is not, on that account, easy. Of the difficulties to which activity in War is subject generally, we have already spoken in the first book; we here omit those things which can only be overcome by courage, and maintain also that the activity of mind, is only simple and easy in inferior stations, but increases in difficulty with increase of rank, and in the highest position, in that of Commander-in-Chief, is to be reckoned among the most difficult which there is for the human mind.

45. Of the nature of this knowledge

The Commander of an Army neither requires to be a learned explorer of history nor a publicist, but he must be well versed in the higher affairs of State; he must know and be able to judge correctly of traditional tendencies, interests at stake, the immediate questions at issue, and the characters of leading persons; he need not be a close observer of men, a sharp dissector of human character, but he must know the character, the feelings, the habits, the peculiar faults and inclinations of those whom he is to command. He need not understand anything about the make of a carriage, or the harness of a battery horse, but he must know how to calculate exactly the march of a column, under different circumstances, according to the time it requires. These are matters the knowledge of which cannot be forced out by an apparatus of scientific formula and machinery: they are only to be gained by the exercise of an accurate judgement in the observation of things and of men, aided by a special talent for the apprehension of both.

The necessary knowledge for a high position in military action is therefore distinguished by this, that by observation, therefore by study and reflection, it is only to be attained through a special talent which as an intellectual instinct understands how to extract from the phenomena of life only the essence or spirit, as bees do the honey from the flowers; and that it is also to be gained by experience of life as well as by study and reflection. Life will never bring forth a Newton or an Euler by its rich teachings, but it may bring forth great calculators in War, such as Condé or Frederick.

It is therefore not necessary that, in order to vindicate the intellectual dignity of military activity, we should resort to untruth and silly pedantry. There never has been a great and distinguished Commander of contracted mind, but very numerous are the instances of men who, after serving with the greatest distinction in inferior positions, remained below mediocrity in the highest, from insufficiency of intellectual capacity. That even amongst those holding the post of Commander-in-Chief there may be a difference according to the degree of their plenitude of power is a matter of course.

46. Science must become art

Now we have yet to consider one condition which is more necessary for the knowledge of the conduct of War than for any other, which is, that it must pass completely into the mind and almost completely cease to be something objective. In almost all other arts and occupations of life the active agent can make use of truths which he has only learnt once, and in the spirit and sense of which he no longer lives, and which he extracts from dusty books. Even truths which he has in hand and uses daily may continue something external to himself. If the architect takes up a pen to settle the strength of a pier by a complicated calculation, the truth found as a result is no emanation from his own mind. He had first to find the data with labour, and then to submit these to an operation of the mind, the rule for which he did not discover, the necessity of which he is perhaps at the moment only partly conscious of, but which he applies, for the most part, as if by mechanical dexterity. But it is never so in War. The moral reaction, the ever-changeful form of things, makes it necessary for the chief actor to carry in himself the whole mental apparatus of his knowledge, that anywhere and at every pulse-beat he may be capable of giving the requisite decision from himself. Knowledge must, by this complete assimilation with his own mind and life, be converted into real power. This is the reason why everything seems so easy with men distinguished in War, and why everything is ascribed to natural talent. We say natural talent, in order thereby to distinguish it from that which is formed and matured by observation and study.

We think that by these reflections we have explained the problem of a theory of the conduct of War, and pointed out the way to its solution.

Of the two fields into which we have divided the conduct of War, tactics and strategy, the theory of the latter contains unquestionably, as before observed, the greatest difficulties, because the first is almost limited to a circumscribed field of objects, but the latter, in the direction of objects leading directly to peace, opens to itself an unlimited field of possibilities. Since for the most part the Commander-in-Chief has only to keep these objects steadily in view, therefore the part of strategy in which he moves is also that which is particularly subject to this difficulty.

Theory, therefore, especially where it comprehends the highest services, will stop much sooner in strategy than in tactics at the simple consideration of things, and content itself to assist the Commander to that insight into things which, blended with his whole thought, makes his course easier and surer, never forces him into opposition with himself in order to obey an objective truth.

CHAPTER III

ART OR SCIENCE OF WAR

1. Usage still unsettled
(Power and knowledge. Science when mere knowing; Art, when doing, is the object)

THE choice between these terms seems to be still unsettled, and no one seems to know rightly on what grounds it should be decided, and yet the thing is simple. We have already said elsewhere that 'knowing' is something different from 'doing'. The two are so different that they should not easily be mistaken the one for the other. The 'doing' cannot properly stand in any book, and therefore also Art should never be the title of a book. But because we have once accustomed ourselves to combine in conception, under the name of theory of Art, or simply Art, the branches of knowledge (which may be separately pure sciences) necessary for the practice of an Art, therefore it is consistent to continue this ground of distinction, and to call everything Art when the object is to carry out the 'doing' (being able), as for example, Art of building; Science, when merely knowledge is the object; as Science of mathematics, of astronomy. That in every Art certain complete sciences may be included is intelligible of itself, and should not perplex us. But still it is worth observing that there is also no science without a mixture of Art. In mathematics, for instance, the use of figures and of algebra is an Art, but that is only one amongst many instances. The reason is, that however plain and palpable the difference is between knowledge and power in the composite results of human knowledge, yet it is difficult to trace out their line of separation in man himself.

2. Difficulty of separating perception from judgement
(Art of war)

All thinking is indeed Art. Where the logician draws the line, where the premises stop which are the result of cognition –

where judgement begins, there Art begins. But more than this: even the perception of the mind is judgement again, and consequently Art; and at last, even the perception by the senses as well. In a word, if it is impossible to imagine a human being possessing merely the faculty of cognition, devoid of judgement or the reverse, so also Art and Science can never be completely separated from each other.[76] The more these subtle elements of light embody themselves in the outward forms of the world, so much the more separate appear their domains; and now once more, where the object is creation and production, there is the province of Art; where the object is investigation and knowledge Science holds sway. After all this it results of itself that it is more fitting to say Art of War than Science of War.

So much for this, because we cannot do without these conceptions. But now we come forward with the assertion that War is neither an Art nor a Science in the real signification, and that it is just the setting out from that starting-point of ideas which has led to a wrong direction being taken, which has caused War to be put on a par with other arts and sciences, and has led to a number of erroneous analogies.

This has indeed been felt before now, and on that account it was maintained that War is a handicraft; but there was more lost than gained by that, for a handicraft is only an inferior art, and as such is also subject to definite and rigid laws. In reality the Art of War did go on for some time in the spirit of a handicraft – we allude to the times of the Condottieri[77] – but then it received that direction, not from intrinsic but from external causes; and military history shows how little it was at that time in accordance with the nature of the thing.

3. War is part of the intercourse of the human race

We say therefore War belongs not to the province of Arts and Sciences, but to the province of social life. It is a conflict of great interests which is settled by bloodshed, and only in that is it different from others. It would be better, instead of comparing it with any Art, to liken it to business competition, which is also a conflict of human interests and activities; and it is still more like State policy, which again, on its part, may be looked upon as a kind of business competition on a great scale. Besides, State policy is the womb in which War is developed, in which its outlines lie hidden in a rudimentary state, like the qualities of living creatures in their germs.[78]

4. Difference

The essential difference consists in this, that War is no activity of the will, which exerts itself upon inanimate matter like the mechanical Arts; or upon a living but still passive and yielding subject, like the human mind and the human feelings in the ideal Arts, but against a living and reacting force. How little the categories of Arts and Sciences are applicable to such an activity strikes us at once; and we can understand at the same time how that constant seeking and striving after laws like those which may be developed out of the dead material world could not but lead to constant errors. And yet it is just the mechanical Arts that some people would imitate in the Art of War. The imitation of the ideal Arts was quite out of the question, because these themselves dispense too much with laws and rules, and those hitherto tried, always acknowledged as insufficient and one-sided, are perpetually undermined and washed away by the current of opinions, feelings, and customs.

Whether such a conflict of the living, as takes place and is settled in War, is subject to general laws, and whether these are capable of indicating a useful line of action, will be partly investigated in this book; but so much is evident in itself, that this, like every other subject which does not surpass our powers of understanding, may be lighted up, and be made more or less plain in its inner relations by an inquiring mind, and that alone is sufficient to realize the idea of a *theory*.

CHAPTER IV

METHODICISM

IN order to explain ourselves clearly as to the conception of method, and method of action, which play such an important part in War, we must be allowed to cast a hasty glance at the logical hierarchy through which, as through regularly constituted official functionaries, the world of action is governed.

Law, in the widest sense strictly applying to perception as well as action, has plainly something subjective and arbitrary in its literal meaning, and expresses just that on which we and those things external to us are dependent. As a subject of cognition, *Law* is the relation of things and their effects to one another; as a subject of the will, it is a motive of action, and is then equivalent to *command* or *prohibition*.

Principle is likewise such a law for action, except that it has not the formal definite meaning, but is only the spirit and sense of law in order to leave the judgement more freedom of application when the diversity of the real world cannot be laid hold of under the definite form of a law. As the judgement must of itself suggest the cases in which the principle is not applicable, the latter therefore becomes in that way a real aid or guiding star for the person acting.

Principle is *objective* when it is the result of objective truth, and consequently of equal value for all men; it is *subjective*, and then generally called *Maxim* if there are subjective relations in it, and if it therefore has a certain value only for the person himself who makes it.

Rule is frequently taken in the sense of *Law*, and then means the same as *Principle*, for we say 'no rule without exceptions', but we do not say 'no law without exceptions', a sign that with *Rule* we retain to ourselves more freedom of application.

In another meaning *Rule* is the means used of discerning a recondite truth in a particular sign lying close at hand, in order to attach to this particular sign the law of action directed upon the whole truth. Of this kind are all the rules of games of play, all abridged processes in mathematics, etc.

Directions and *instructions* are determinations of action which have an influence upon a number of minor circumstances too numerous and unimportant for general laws.

Lastly, *Method, mode of acting*, is an always recurring proceeding selected out of several possible ones; and *Methodicism* (METHODISMUS) is that which is determined by method instead of by general principles or particular prescriptions. By this the cases which are placed under such methods must necessarily be supposed alike in their essential parts. As they cannot all be this, then the point is that at least as many as possible should be; in other words, that Method should be calculated on the most probable cases. Methodicism is therefore not founded on determined particular premises, but on the average probability of cases one with another; and its ultimate tendency is to set up an average truth, the constant and uniform application of which soon acquires something of the nature of a mechanical appliance, which in the end does that which is right almost unwittingly.

The conception of law in relation to perception is not necessary for the conduct of War, because the complex phenomena of War are not so regular, and the regular are not so complex, that we should gain anything more by this conception than by the simple truth. And where a simple conception and language is sufficient, to resort to the complex becomes affected and pedantic. The conception of law in relation to action cannot be used in the theory of the conduct of War, because owing to the variableness and diversity of the phenomena there is in it no determination of such a general nature as to deserve the name of law.

But principles, rules, prescriptions, and methods are conceptions indispensable to a theory of the conduct of War, in so far as that theory leads to positive doctrines, because in doctrines the truth can only crystallize itself in such forms.

As tactics is the branch of the conduct of War in which theory can attain the nearest to positive doctrine, therefore these conceptions will appear in it most frequently.

Not to use cavalry against unbroken infantry except in some

case of special emergency, only to use firearms within effective range in the combat, to spare the forces as much as possible for the final struggle – these are tactical principles. None of them can be applied absolutely in every case, but they must always be present to the mind of the Chief, in order that the benefit of the truth contained in them may not be lost in cases where that truth can be of advantage.

If from the unusual cooking by an enemy's camp his movement is inferred, if the intentional exposure of troops in a combat indicates a false attack, then this way of discerning the truth is called rule, because from a single visible circumstance that conclusion is drawn which corresponds with the same.

If it is a rule to attack the enemy with renewed vigour, as soon as he begins to limber up his artillery in the combat, then on this particular fact depends a course of action which is aimed at the general situation of the enemy as inferred from the above fact, namely, that he is about to give up the fight, that he is commencing to draw off his troops, and is neither capable of making a serious stand while thus drawing off nor of making his retreat gradually in good order.

Regulations and *methods* bring preparatory theories into the conduct of War, in so far as disciplined troops are inoculated with them as active principles. The whole body of instructions for formations, drill, and field service are regulations and methods: in the drill instructions the first predominate, in the field service instructions the latter. To these things the real conduct of War attaches itself; it takes them over, therefore, as given modes of proceeding, and as such they must appear in the theory of the conduct of War.

But for those activities retaining freedom in the employment of these forces there cannot be regulations, that is, definite instructions, because they would do away with freedom of action. Methods, on the other hand, as a general way of executing duties as they arise, calculated as we have said, on an average of probability, or as a dominating influence of principles and rules carried through to application, may certainly appear in the theory of the conduct of War, provided only they are not represented as something different from what they are, not as the absolute and necessary modes of action (systems), but as the best of general forms which may be used as shorter ways in place of a particular disposition for the occasion, at discretion.

But the frequent application of methods will be seen to be most essential and unavoidable in the conduct of War, if we reflect how much action proceeds on mere conjecture, or in complete uncertainty, because one side is prevented from learning all the circumstances which influence the dispositions of the other, or because, even if these circumstances which influence the decisions of the one were really known, there is not, owing to their extent and the dispositions they would entail, sufficient time for the other to carry out all necessary counteracting measures – that therefore measures in War must always be calculated on a certain number of possibilities; if we reflect how numberless are the trifling things belonging to any single event, and which therefore should be taken into account along with it, and that therefore there is no other means to suppose the one counteracted by the other, and to base our arrangements only upon what is of a general nature and probable; if we reflect lastly that, owing to the increasing number of officers as we descend the scale of rank, less must be left to the true discernment and ripe judgement of individuals the lower the sphere of action, and that when we reach those ranks where we can look for no other notions but those which the regulations of the service and experience afford, we must help them with the methodic forms bordering on those regulations. This will serve both as a support to their judgement and a barrier against those extravagant and erroneous views which are so especially to be dreaded in a sphere where experience is so costly.

Besides this absolute need of method in action, we must also acknowledge that it has a positive advantage, which is that, through the constant repetition of a formal exercise, a readiness, precision, and firmness is attained in the movement of troops which diminishes the natural friction, and makes the machine move easier.

Method will therefore be the more generally used, become the more indispensable, the farther down the scale of rank the position of the active agent; and on the other hand, its use will diminish upwards, until in the highest position it quite disappears. For this reason it is more in its place in tactics than in strategy.

War in its highest aspects consists not of an infinite number of little events, the diversities in which compensate each other, and which therefore by a better or worse method are better or worse governed, but of separate great decisive events which must be dealt with separately. It is not like a field of stalks, which, without any regard to the particular form of each stalk, will be mowed better or worse, according as the mowing instrument is good or bad, but rather as a group of large trees, to which the axe must be laid with judgement, according to the particular form and inclination of each separate trunk.

How high up in military activity the admissibility of method in action reaches naturally determines itself, not according to actual rank, but according to things; and it affects the highest positions in a less degree, only because these positions have the most comprehensive subjects of activity. A constant order of battle, a constant formation of advance guards and outposts, are methods by which a General ties not only his subordinates' hands, but also his own in certain cases. Certainly they may have been devised by himself, and may be applied by him according to circumstances, but they may also be a subject of theory, in so far as they are based on the general properties of troops and weapons. On the other hand, any method by which definite plans for wars or campaigns are to be given out all ready made as if from a machine are absolutely worthless.

As long as there exists no theory which can be sustained, that is, no enlightened treatise on the conduct of War, method in action cannot but encroach beyond its proper limits in high places, for men employed in these spheres of activity have not always had the opportunity of educating themselves, through study and through contact with the higher interests. In the impracticable and inconsistent disquisitions of theorists and critics they cannot find their way, their sound common sense rejects them, and as they bring with them no knowledge but that derived from experience, therefore in those cases which admit of, and require, a free individual treatment they readily make use of the means which experience gives them – that is, an imitation of the particular methods practised by great Generals, by which a method of action then arises of itself. If we see Frederick the Great's Generals always making their appearance in the so-called oblique order of battle, the Generals of the French Revolution always using turning movements with a long extended line of battle,[79] and Buonaparte's lieutenants rushing to the attack with the bloody energy of concentrated masses, then we recognize in the recurrence of the mode of proceeding evidently an adopted method, and see therefore that method of action can reach up to regions bordering on the highest. Should an improved theory facilitate the study of the conduct of War, form the mind and judgement of men who are rising to the highest commands, then also method in action will no longer reach so far, and so much of it as is to be considered indispensable will then at least be formed from theory itself, and not take place out of mere imitation. However pre-eminently a great Commander does things, there is always something subjective in the way he does them; and if he has a certain manner, a large share of his individuality is contained in it which does not always accord with the individuality of the person who copies his manner.

At the same time, it would neither be possible nor right to banish subjective methodicism or manner completely from the conduct of War: it is rather to be regarded as a manifestation of that influence which the general character of a War has upon its separate events, and to which satisfaction can only be done in that way if theory is not able to foresee this general character and include it in its considerations. What is more natural than that the War of the French Revolution had its own way of doing things? and what theory could ever have included that peculiar method?[80] The evil is only that such a manner originating in a special case easily outlives itself, because it continues whilst circumstances imperceptibly change. This is what theory should prevent by lucid and rational criticism. When in the year 1806 the Prussian Generals, Prince Louis at Saalfeld, Tauentzien on the Dornberg near Jena, Grawert before and Rüchel behind Kappellendorf, all threw themselves into the open jaws of destruction in the oblique order of Frederick the Great and managed to ruin Hohenlohe's Army in a way that no Army was ever ruined, even on the field of battle, all this was done through a manner which had outlived its day, together with the most downright stupidity to which methodicism ever led.

CHAPTER V

CRITICISM

THE influence of theoretical principles upon real life is produced more through criticism than through doctrine, for as criticism is an application of abstract truth to real events, therefore it not only brings truth of this description nearer to life, but also accustoms the understanding more to such truths by the constant repetition of their application. We therefore think it necessary to fix the point of view for criticism next to that for theory.

From the simple narration of an historical occurrence which places events in chronological order, or at most only touches on their more immediate causes, we separate the *critical.*

In this *critical* three different operations of the mind may be observed.

First, the historical investigation and determining of doubtful facts. This is properly historical research, and has nothing in common with theory.

Secondly, the tracing of effects to causes. This is the *real critical inquiry*; it is indispensable to theory, for everything which in theory is to be established, supported, or even merely explained, by experience can only be settled in this way.

Thirdly, the testing of the means employed. This is *criticism, properly speaking*, in which praise and censure is contained. This is where theory helps history, or rather, the teaching to be derived from it.

In these two last strictly critical parts of historical study, all depends on tracing things to their primary elements, that is to say, up to undoubted truths, and not, as is so often done, resting half-way, that is, on some arbitrary assumption or supposition.

As respects the tracing of effect to cause, that is often attended with the insuperable difficulty that the real causes are not known. In none of the relations of life does this so frequently happen as in War, where events are seldom fully known, and still less motives, as the latter have been, perhaps purposely, concealed by the chief actor, or have been of such a transient and accidental character that they have been lost for history. For this reason critical narration must generally proceed hand in hand with historical investigation, and still such a want of connexion between cause and effect will often present itself, that it does not seem justifiable to consider effects as the necessary results of known causes. Here, therefore, voids must occur, that is, historical results which cannot be made use of for teaching. All that theory can demand is that the investigation should be rigidly conducted up to that point, and there leave off without drawing conclusions. A real evil springs up only if the known is made perforce to suffice as an explanation of effects, and thus a false importance is ascribed to it.

Besides this difficulty, critical inquiry also meets with another great and intrinsic one, which is that the progress of events in War seldom proceeds from one simple cause, but from several in common, and that it therefore is not sufficient to follow up a series of events to their origin in a candid and impartial spirit, but that it is then also necessary to apportion to each contributing cause its due weight. This leads, therefore, to a closer investigation of their nature, and thus a critical investigation may lead into what is the proper field of theory.

The critical *consideration*, that is, the testing of the means, leads to the question, Which are the effects peculiar to the means applied, and whether these effects were comprehended in the plans of the person directing?

The effects peculiar to the means lead to the investigation of their nature, and thus again into the field of theory.

We have already seen that in criticism all depends upon attaining to positive truth; therefore, that we must not stop at arbitrary propositions which are not allowed by others, and to which other perhaps equally arbitrary assertions may again be opposed, so that there is no end to *pros* and *cons*; the whole is without result, and therefore without instruction.

We have seen that both the search for causes and the examination of means lead into the field of theory; that is, into the field of universal truth, which does not proceed solely from the case immediately under examination. If there is a theory which can be used, then the critical consideration will appeal to the proofs there afforded, and the examination may there stop. But where no such theoretical truth is to be found, the inquiry must be pushed up to the original elements. If this necessity occurs often, it must lead the historian (according to a common expression) into a labyrinth of details. He then has his hands full, and it is impossible for him to stop to give the requisite attention everywhere; the consequence is, that in order to set bounds to his investigation, he adopts some arbitrary assumptions which, if they do not appear so to him, do so to others, as they are not evident in themselves or capable of proof.

A sound theory is therefore an essential foundation for criticism, and it is impossible for it, without the assistance of a sensible theory, to attain to that point at which it commences chiefly to be instructive, that is, where it becomes demonstration, both convincing and *sans réplique*.

But it would be a visionary hope to believe in the possibility of a theory applicable to every abstract truth, leaving nothing for criticism to do but to place the case under its appropriate law: it would be ridiculous pedantry to lay down as a rule for criticism that it must always halt and turn round on reaching the boundaries of sacred theory. The same spirit of analytical inquiry which is the origin of theory must also guide the critic in his work; and it can and must therefore happen that he strays beyond the boundaries of the province of theory and elucidates those points with which he is more particularly concerned. It is more likely, on the contrary, that criticism would completely fail in its object if it degenerated into a mechanical application of theory. All positive results of theoretical inquiry, all principles, rules, and methods, are the more wanting in generality and positive truth the more they become positive doctrine. They exist to offer themselves for use as required, and it must always be left for judgement to decide whether they are suitable or not. Such results of theory must never be used in criticism as rules or norms for a standard, but in the same way as the person acting should use them, that is, merely as aids to judgement. If it is an acknowledged principle in tactics that in the usual order of battle cavalry should be placed behind infantry, not in line with it, still it would be folly on this account to condemn every deviation from this principle. Criticism must investigate the grounds of the deviation, and it is only in case these are insufficient that it has a right to appeal to principles laid down in theory. If it is further established in theory that a divided attack diminishes the probability of success, still it would be just as unreasonable, whenever there is a divided attack and an unsuccessful issue, to regard the latter as the result of the former, without further investigation into the connexion between the two, as where a divided attack is successful to infer from it the fallacy of that theoretical principle. The spirit of investigation which belongs to criticism cannot allow either. Criticism therefore supports itself chiefly on the results of the analytical investigation of theory; what has been made out and determined by theory does not require to be demonstrated over again by criticism, and it is so determined by theory that criticism may find it ready demonstrated.

This office of criticism, of examining the effect produced by certain causes, and whether a means applied has answered its object, will be easy enough if cause and effect, means and end, are all near together.

If an Army is surprised, and therefore cannot make a regular and intelligent use of its powers and resources, then the effect of the surprise is not doubtful. If theory has determined that in a battle the convergent form of attack is calculated to produce greater but less certain results, then the question is whether he who employs that convergent form had in view chiefly that greatness of result as his object; if so, the proper means were chosen. But if by this form he intended to make the result more certain, and that expectation was founded not on some exceptional circumstances (in this case), but on the general nature of the convergent form, as has happened a hundred times, then he mistook the nature of the means and committed an error.

Here the work of military investigation and criticism is easy, and it will always be so when confined to the immediate effects and objects. This can be done quite at option, if we abstract the connexion of the parts with the whole, and only look at things in that relation.

But in War, as generally in the world, there is a connexion between everything which belongs to a whole; and therefore, however small a cause may be in itself, its effects reach to the end of the act of warfare, and modify or influence the final result in some degree, let that degree be ever so small. In the same manner every means must be felt up to the ultimate object.

We can therefore trace the effects of a cause as long as events are worth noticing, and in the same way we must not stop at the testing of a means for the immediate object, but test also this object as a means to a higher one, and thus ascend the series of facts in succession, until we come to one so absolutely necessary in its nature as to require no examination or proof. In many cases, particularly in what concerns great and decisive measures, the investigation must be carried to the final aim, to that which leads immediately to peace.

It is evident that in thus ascending, at every new station which we reach a new point of view for the judgement is attained, so that the same means which appeared advisable at one station, when looked at from the next above it may have to be rejected.

The search for the causes of events and the comparison of means with ends must always go hand in hand in the critical review of an act, for the investigation of causes leads us first to the discovery of those things which are worth examining

This following of the clue up and down is attended with considerable difficulty, for the farther from an event the cause lies which we are looking for, the greater must be the number of other causes which must at the same time be kept in view and allowed for in reference to the share which they have in the course of events, and then eliminated, because the higher the importance of a fact the greater will be the number of separate forces and circumstances by which it is conditioned. If we have unravelled the causes of a battle being lost, we have certainly also ascertained a part of the causes of the consequences which this defeat has upon the whole War, but only a part, because the effects of other causes, more or less according to circumstances, will flow into the final result.

The same multiplicity of circumstances is presented also in the examination of the means the higher our point of view, for the higher the object is situated, the greater must be the number of means employed to reach it. The ultimate object of the War is the object aimed at by all the Armies simultaneously, and it is therefore necessary that the consideration should embrace all that each has done or could have done.

It is obvious that this may sometimes lead to a wide field of inquiry, in which it is easy to wander and lose the way, and in which this difficulty prevails – that a number of assumptions or suppositions must be made about a variety of things which do not actually appear, but which in all probability did take place, and therefore cannot possibly be left out of consideration.

When Buonaparte, in 1797,[81] at the head of the Army of Italy, advanced from the Tagliamento against the Archduke Charles, he did so with a view to force that General to a decisive action before the reinforcements expected from the Rhine had reached him. If we look only at the immediate object, the means were well chosen and justified by the result, for the Archduke was so inferior in numbers that he only made a show of resistance on the Tagliamento, and when he saw his adversary so strong and resolute, yielded ground, and left open the passages of the Norican Alps. Now to what use could Buonaparte turn this fortunate event? To penetrate into the heart of the Austrian empire itself, to facilitate the advance of the Rhine Armies under Moreau and Hoche, and open communication with them? This was the view taken by Buonaparte, and from this point of view he was right. But now, if criticism places itself at a higher point of view – namely, that of the French Directory, which body could see and know that the Armies on the Rhine could not commence the campaign for six weeks, then the advance of Buonaparte over the Norican Alps can only be regarded as an extremely hazardous measure; for if the Austrians had drawn largely on their Rhine Armies to reinforce their Army in Styria, so as to enable the Archduke to fall upon the Army of Italy, not only would that Army have been routed, but the whole campaign lost. This consideration, which attracted the serious attention of Buonaparte at Villach, no doubt induced him to sign the armistice of Leoben with so much readiness.

If criticism takes a still higher position, and if it knows that the Austrians had no reserves between the Army of the Archduke Charles and Vienna, then we see that Vienna became threatened by the advance of the Army of Italy.

Supposing that Buonaparte knew that the capital was thus uncovered, and knew that he still retained the same superiority in numbers over the Archduke as he had in Styria, then his advance against the heart of the Austrian States was no longer without purpose, and its value depended on the value which the Austrians might place on preserving their capital. If that was so great that, rather than lose it, they would accept the conditions of peace which Buonaparte was ready to offer them, it became an object of the first importance to threaten Vienna. If Buonaparte had any reason to know this, then criticism may stop there, but if this point was only problematical, then criticism must take a still higher position, and ask what would have followed if the Austrians had resolved to abandon Vienna and retire farther into the vast dominions still left to them. But it is easy to see that this question cannot be answered without bringing into the consideration the probable movements of the Rhine Armies on both sides. Through the decided superiority of numbers on the side of the French – 130,000 to 80,000 – there could be little doubt of the result; but then next arises the question, What use would the Directory make of a victory; whether they would follow up their success to the opposite frontiers of the Austrian monarchy, therefore to the complete breaking up or overthrow of that power, or whether they would be satisfied with the conquest of a considerable portion to serve as a security for peace? The probable result in each case must be estimated, in order to come to a conclusion as to the probable determination of the Directory. Supposing the result of these considerations to be that the French forces were much too weak for the complete subjugation of the Austrian monarchy, so that the attempt might completely reverse the respective positions of the contending Armies, and that even the conquest and occupation of a considerable district of country would place the French Army in strategic relations to which they were not equal, then that result must naturally influence the estimate of the position of the Army of Italy, and compel it to lower its expectations. And this it was no doubt which influenced Buonaparte, although fully aware of the helpless condition of the Archduke, still to sign the peace of Campo Formio, which imposed no greater sacrifices on the Austrians than the loss of provinces which, even if the campaign took the most favourable turn for them, they could not have reconquered. But the French could not have reckoned on even the moderate treaty of Campo Formio, and therefore it could not have been their object in making their bold advance if two considerations had not presented themselves to their view, the first of which consisted in the question, what degree of value the Austrians would attach to each of the above-mentioned results; whether, notwithstanding the probability of a satisfactory result in either of these cases, would it be worth while to make the sacrifices inseparable from a continuance of the War, when they could be spared those sacrifices by a peace on terms not too humiliating? The second consideration is the question whether the Austrian Government, instead of seriously weighing the possible results of a resistance pushed to extremities, would not prove completely disheartened by the impression of their present reverses.

The consideration which forms the subject of the first is no idle piece of subtle argument, but a consideration of such decidedly practical importance that it comes up whenever the plan of pushing War to the utmost extremity is mooted, and by its weight in most cases restrains the execution of such plans.

The second consideration is of equal importance, for we do not make War with an abstraction but with a reality, which we must always keep in view, and we may be sure that it was not overlooked by the bold Buonaparte – that is, that he was keenly alive to the terror which the appearance of his sword inspired. It was reliance on that which led him to Moscow. There it led him into a scrape. The terror of him had been weakened by the gigantic struggles in which he had been engaged; in the year 1797 it was still fresh, and the secret of a resistance pushed to extremities had not been discovered; nevertheless even in 1797 his boldness might have led to a negative result if, as already said, he had not with a sort of presentiment avoided it by signing the moderate peace of Campo Formio.

We must now bring these considerations to a close – they will suffice to show the wide sphere, the diversity and embarrassing nature of the subjects embraced in a critical examination carried to the fullest extent, that is, to those measures of a great and decisive class which must necessarily be included. It follows from them that besides a theoretical acquaintance with the subject, natural talent must also have a great influence on the value of critical examinations, for it rests chiefly with the latter to throw the requisite light on the interrelations of things, and to distinguish from amongst the endless connexions of events those which are really essential.[82]

But talent is also called into requisition in another way. Critical examination is not merely the appreciation of those means which have been actually employed, but also of all possible means, which therefore must be suggested in the first place – that is, must be discovered; and the use of any particular means is not fairly open to censure until a better is pointed out. Now, however small the number of possible combinations may be in most cases, still it must be admitted that to point out those which have not been used is not a mere analysis of actual things, but a spontaneous creation which cannot be prescribed, and depends on the fertility of genius.

We are far from seeing a field for great genius in a case which admits only of the application of a few simple combinations, and we think it exceedingly ridiculous to hold up, as is often done, the turning of a position as an invention showing the highest genius; still nevertheless this creative self-activity on the part of the critic is necessary, and it is one of the points which essentially determine the value of critical examination.

When Buonaparte on 30 July 1796,[83] determined to raise the siege of Mantua, in order to march with his whole force against the enemy, advancing in separate columns to the relief of the place, and to beat them in detail, this appeared the surest way to the attainment of brilliant victories. These victories actually followed, and were afterwards again repeated on a still more brilliant scale on the attempt to relieve the fortress being again renewed. We hear only one opinion on these achievements, that of unmixed admiration.

At the same time, Buonaparte could not have adopted this course on 30 July without quite giving up the idea of the siege of Mantua, because it was impossible to save the siege train, and it could not be replaced by another in this campaign. In fact, the siege was converted into a blockade, and the town, which if the siege had continued must have very shortly fallen, held out for six months in spite of Buonaparte's victories in the open field.

Criticism has generally regarded this as an evil that was unavoidable, because critics have not been able to suggest any better course. Resistance to a relieving Army within lines of circumvallation had fallen into such disrepute and contempt that it appears to have entirely escaped consideration as a means. And yet in the reign of Louis XIV that measure was so often used with success that we can only attribute to the force of fashion the fact that a hundred years later it never occurred to anyone even to propose such a measure. If the practicability of such a plan had ever been entertained for a moment, a closer consideration of circumstances would have shown that 40,000 of the best infantry in the world under Buonaparte, behind strong lines of circumvallation round Mantua, had so little to fear from the 50,000 men coming to the relief under Wurmser, that it was very unlikely that any attempt even would be made upon their lines. We shall not seek here to establish this point, but we believe enough has been said to show that this means was one which had a right to a share of consideration. Whether Buonaparte himself ever thought of such a plan we leave undecided; neither in his memoirs nor in other sources is there any trace to be found of his having done so; in no critical works has it been touched upon, the measure being one which the mind had lost sight of. The merit of resuscitating the idea of this means is not great, for it suggests itself at once to any one who breaks loose from the trammels of fashion. Still it is necessary that it should suggest itself for us to bring it into consideration and compare it with the means which Buonaparte employed. Whatever may be the result of the comparison, it is one which should not be omitted by criticism.

When Buonaparte, in February 1814,[84] after gaining the battles at Etoges, Champ-Aubert, and Montmirail, left Blücher's Army, and turning upon Schwartzenberg, beat his troops at Montereau and Mormant, every one was filled with admiration, because Buonaparte, by thus throwing his concentrated force first upon one opponent, then upon another, made a brilliant use of the mistakes which his adversaries had committed in dividing their forces. If these brilliant strokes in different directions failed to save him, it was generally considered to be no fault of his, at least. No one has yet asked the question; What would have been the result if, instead of turning from Blücher upon Schwartzenberg, he had tried another blow at Blücher, and pursued him to the Rhine? We are convinced that it would have completely changed the course of the campaign, and that the Army of the Allies, instead of marching to Paris, would have retired behind the Rhine. We do not ask others to share our conviction, but no one who understands the thing will doubt, at the mere mention of this alternative course, that it is one which should not be overlooked in criticism.

In this case the means of comparison lie much more on the surface than in the foregoing, but they have been equally overlooked, because one-sided views have prevailed, and there has been no freedom of judgement.

From the necessity of pointing out a better means which might have been used in place of those which are condemned has arisen the form of criticism almost exclusively in use, which contents itself with pointing out the better means without demonstrating in what the superiority consists. The consequence is that some are not convinced, that others start up and do the same thing, and that thus discussion arises which is without any fixed basis for the argument. Military literature abounds with matter of this sort.

The demonstration we require is always necessary when the superiority of the means propounded is not so evident as to leave no room for doubt, and it consists in the examination of each of the means on its own merits, and then of its comparison with the object desired. When once the thing is traced back to a simple truth, controversy must cease, or at all events a new result is obtained, whilst by the other plan the *pros* and *cons* go on for ever consuming each other.

Should we, for example, not rest content with assertion in the case before mentioned, and wish to prove that the persistent pursuit of Blücher would have been more advantageous than the turning on Schwartzenberg, we should support the arguments on the following simple truths:

1. In general it is more advantageous to continue our blows in one and the same direction, because there is a loss of time in striking in different directions; and at a point where the moral power is already shaken by considerable losses there is the more reason to expect fresh successes, therefore in that way no part of the preponderance already gained is left idle.

2. Because Blücher, although weaker than Schwartzenberg, was, on account of his enterprising spirit, the more important adversary; in him, therefore, lay the centre of attraction which drew the others along in the same direction.

3. Because the losses which Blücher had sustained almost amounted to a defeat, which gave Buonaparte such a preponderance over him as to make his retreat to the Rhine almost certain, and at the same time no reserves of any consequence awaited him there.

4. Because there was no other result which would be so terrific in its aspects, would appear to the imagination in such gigantic proportions, an immense advantage in dealing with a Staff so weak and irresolute as that of Schwartzenberg notoriously was at this time. What had happened to the Crown Prince of Würtemberg at Montereau, and to Count Wittgenstein at Mormant, Prince Schwartzenberg must have known well enough; but all the untoward events on Blücher's distant and separate line from the Marne to the Rhine would only reach him by the avalanche of rumour. The desperate movements which Buonaparte made

upon Vitry at the end of March, to see what the Allies would do if he threatened to turn them strategically, were evidently done on the principle of working on their fears; but it was done under far different circumstances, in consequence of his defeat at Laon and Arcis, and because Blücher, with 100,000 men, was then in communication with Schwartzenberg.

There are people, no doubt, who will not be convinced on these arguments, but at all events they cannot retort by saying, that 'whilst Buonaparte threatened Schwartzenberg's base by advancing to the Rhine, Schwartzenberg at the same time threatened Buonaparte's communications with Paris', because we have shown by the reasons above given that Schwartzenberg would never have thought of marching on Paris.

With respect to the example quoted by us from the campaign of 1796, we should say: Buonaparte looked upon the plan he adopted as the surest means of beating the Austrians; but admitting that it was so, still the object to be attained was only an empty victory, which could have hardly any sensible influence on the fall of Mantua. The way which we should have chosen would, in our opinion, have been much more certain to prevent the relief of Mantua; but even if we place ourselves in the position of the French General and assume that it was not so, and look upon the certainty of success to have been less, the question then amounts to a choice between a more certain but less useful, and therefore less important, victory on the one hand, and a somewhat less probable but far more decisive and important victory on the other hand.[85] Presented in this form, boldness must have declared for the second solution, which is the reverse of what took place, when the thing was only superficially viewed. Buonaparte certainly was anything but deficient in boldness, and we may be sure that he did not see the whole case and its consequences as fully and clearly as we can at the present time.

Naturally the critic, in treating of the means, must often appeal to military history, as experience is of more value in the Art of War than all philosophical truth. But this exemplification from history is subject to certain conditions, of which we shall treat in a special chapter, and unfortunately these conditions are so seldom regarded that reference to history generally only serves to increase the confusion of ideas.

We have still a most important subject to consider, which is, How far criticism in passing judgements on particular events is permitted, or in duty bound, to make use of its wider view of things, and therefore also of that which is shown by results; or when and where it should leave out of sight these things in order to place itself, as far as possible, in the exact position of the chief actor?

If criticism dispenses praise or censure, it should seek to place itself as nearly as possible at the same point of view as the person acting, that is to say, to collect all he knew and all the motives on which he acted, and, on the other hand, to leave out of the consideration all that the person acting could not or did not know, and above all, the result. But this is only an object to aim at, which can never be reached because the state of circumstances from which an event proceeded can never be placed before the eye of the critic exactly as it lay before the eye of the person acting. A number of inferior circumstances, which must have influenced the result, are completely lost to sight, and many a subjective motive has never come to light.

The latter can only be learnt from the memoirs of the chief actor, or from his intimate friends; and in such memoirs things of this kind are often treated of in a very desultory manner, or purposely misrepresented. Criticism must, therefore, always forgo much which was present in the minds of those whose acts are criticized.

On the other hand, it is much more difficult to leave out of sight that which criticism knows in excess. This is only easy as regards accidental circumstances, that is, circumstances which have been mixed up, but are in no way necessarily related. But it is very difficult, and, in fact, can never be completely done with regard to things really essential.

Let us take first, the result. If it has not proceeded from accidental circumstances, it is almost impossible that the knowledge of it should not have an effect on the judgement passed on events which have preceded it, for we see these things in the light of this result, and it is to a certain extent by it that we first become acquainted with them and appreciate them. Military history, with all its events, is a source of instruction for criticism itself, and it is only natural that criticism should throw that light on things which it has itself obtained from the consideration of the whole. If therefore it might wish in some cases to leave the result out of the consideration, it would be impossible to do so completely.

But it is not only in relation to the result, that is, with what takes place at the last, that this embarrassment arises; the same occurs in relation to preceding events, therefore with the data which furnished the motives to action. Criticism has before it, in most cases, more information on this point than the principal in the transaction. Now it may seem easy to dismiss from the consideration everything of this nature, but it is not so easy as we may think. The knowledge of preceding and concurrent events is founded not only on certain information, but on a number of conjectures and suppositions; indeed, there is hardly any of the information respecting things not purely accidental which has not been preceded by suppositions or conjectures destined to take the place of certain information in case such should never be supplied. Now is it conceivable that criticism in after times, which has before it as facts all the preceding and concurrent circumstances, should not allow itself to be thereby influenced when it asks itself the question: What portion of the circumstances, which at the moment of action were unknown, would it have held to be probable? We maintain that in this case, as in the case of the results, and for the same reason, it is impossible to disregard all these things completely.

If therefore the critic wishes to bestow praise or blame upon any single act, he can only succeed to a certain degree in placing himself in the position of the person whose act he has under review. In many cases he can do so sufficiently near for any practical purpose, but in many instances it is the very reverse, and this fact should never be overlooked.

But it is neither necessary nor desirable that criticism should completely identify itself with the person acting. In War, as in all matters of skill, there is a certain natural aptitude required which is called talent. This may be great or small. In the first case it may easily be superior to that of the critic, for what critic can pretend to the skill of a Frederick or a Buonaparte? Therefore, if criticism is not to abstain altogether from offering an opinion where eminent talent is concerned, it must be allowed to make use of the advantage which its enlarged horizon affords. Criticism must not, therefore, treat the solution of a problem by a great General like a sum in arithmetic; it is only through the results and through the exact coincidences of events that it can recognize with admiration how much is due to the exercise of genius, and that it first learns the essential combination which the glance of that genius devised.

But for every, even the smallest, act of genius it is necessary that criticism should take a higher point of view, so that, having at command many objective grounds of decision, it may be as little subjective as possible, and that the critic may not take the limited scope of his own mind as a standard.

This elevated position of criticism, its praise and blame pronounced with a full knowledge of all the circumstances, has in itself nothing which hurts our feelings; it only does so if the critic pushes himself forward, and speaks in a tone as if all the wisdom which he has obtained by an exhaustive examination of the event under consideration were really his own talent. Palpable as is this deception, it is one which people may easily fall into through vanity, and one which is naturally distasteful to others. It very often happens that although the critic has no such arrogant pretensions, they are imputed to him by the reader because he has not expressly disclaimed them, and then follows immediately a charge of a want of the power of critical judgement.

If therefore a critic points out an error made by a Frederick or a Buonaparte, that does not mean that he who makes the criticism would not have committed the same error; he may even be ready to grant that had he been in the place of these great Generals he might have made much greater mistakes; he merely sees this error from the chain of events, and he thinks that it should not have escaped the sagacity of the General.

This is, therefore, an opinion formed through the connexion of events, and therefore through the *result*. But there is another quite different effect of the result itself upon the judgement, that is if it is used quite alone as an example for or against the soundness of a measure. This may be called *judgement according to the result*. Such a judgement appears at first sight inadmissible and yet it is not.

When Buonaparte marched to Moscow in 1812, all depended upon whether the taking of the capital, and the events which preceded the capture, would force the Emperor Alexander to make peace, as he had been compelled to do after the battle of Friedland in 1807, and the Emperor Francis in 1805 and 1809 after Austerlitz and Wagram; for if Buonaparte did not obtain a peace at Moscow, there was no alternative but to return – that is, there was nothing for him but a strategic defeat. We shall leave out of the question what he did to get to Moscow, and whether in his advance he did not miss many opportunities of bringing the Emperor Alexander to peace; we shall also exclude all consideration of the disastrous circumstances which attended his retreat, and which perhaps had their origin in the general conduct of the campaign. Still the question remains the same, for however much more brilliant the course of the campaign up to Moscow might have been, still there was always an uncertainty whether the Emperor Alexander would be intimidated into making peace; and then, even if a retreat did not contain in itself the seeds of such disasters as did in fact occur, still it could never be anything else than a great strategic defeat. If the Emperor Alexander agreed to a peace which was disadvantageous to him, the campaign of 1812 would have ranked with those of Austerlitz, Friedland, and Wagram. But these campaigns also, if they had not led to peace, would in all probability have ended in similar catastrophes. Whatever, therefore, of genius, skill, and energy the Conqueror of the World applied to the task, this last question addressed to fate[86] remained always the same. Shall we then discard the campaigns of 1805, 1807, 1809, and say on account of the campaign of 1812 that they were acts of imprudence; that the results were against the nature of things, and that in 1812 strategic justice at last found vent for itself in opposition to blind chance? That would be an unwarrantable conclusion, a most arbitrary judgement, a case only half proved, because no human eye can trace the thread of the necessary connexion of events up to the determination of the conquered Princes.

Still less can we say the campaign of 1812 merited the same success as the others, and that the reason why it turned out otherwise lies in something unnatural, for we cannot regard the firmness of Alexander as something unpredictable.

What can be more natural than to say that in the years 1805, 1807, 1809, Buonaparte judged his opponents correctly, and that in 1812 he erred in that point? On the former occasions, therefore, he was right, in the latter wrong, and in both cases we judge by the *result*.

All action in War, as we have already said, is directed on probable, not on certain, results. Whatever is wanting in certainty must always be left to fate, or chance, call it which you will. We may demand that what is so left should be as little as possible, but only in relation to the particular case – that is, as little as is possible in this one case, but not that the case in which the least is left to chance is always to be preferred. That would be an enormous error, as follows from all our theoretical views. There are cases in which the greatest daring is the greatest wisdom.

Now in everything which is left to chance by the chief actor, his personal merit, and therefore his responsibility as well, seems to be completely set aside; nevertheless we cannot suppress an inward feeling of satisfaction whenever expectation realizes itself, and if it disappoints us our mind is dissatisfied; and more than this of right and wrong should not be meant by the judgement which we form from the mere result, or rather that we find there.

Nevertheless, it cannot be denied that the satisfaction which our mind experiences at success, the pain caused by failure, proceed from a sort of mysterious feeling; we suppose between that success ascribed to good fortune and the genius of the chief a fine connecting thread, invisible to the mind's eye, and the supposition gives pleasure. What tends to confirm this idea is that our sympathy increases, becomes more decided, if the successes and defeats of the principal actor are often repeated. Thus it becomes intelligible how good luck in War assumes a much nobler nature than good luck at play. In general, when a fortunate warrior does not otherwise lessen our interest in his behalf, we have a pleasure in accompanying him in his career.

Criticism, therefore, after having weighed all that comes within the sphere of human reason and conviction, will let the result speak for that part where the deep mysterious relations are not disclosed in any visible form, and will protect this silent sentence of a higher authority from the noise of crude opinions on the one hand, while on the other it prevents the gross abuse which might be made of this last tribunal.

This verdict of the result must therefore always bring forth that which human sagacity cannot discover; and it will be chiefly as regards the intellectual powers and operations that it will be called into requisition, partly because they can be estimated with the least certainty, partly because their close connexion with the will is favourable to their exercising over it an important influence. When fear or bravery precipitates the decision, there is nothing objective intervening between them for our consideration, and consequently nothing by which sagacity and calculation might have met the probable result.

We must now be allowed to make a few observations on the instrument of criticism, that is, the language which it uses, because that is to a certain extent connected with the action in War; for the critical examination is nothing more than the deliberation which should precede action in War. We therefore think it very essential that the language used in criticism should have the same character as that which deliberation in War must have, for otherwise it would cease to be practical, and criticism could gain no admittance in actual life.

We have said in our observations on the theory of the conduct of War that it should educate the mind of the Commander for War, or that its teaching should guide his education; also that it is not intended to furnish him with positive doctrines and systems which he can use like mental appliances. But if the construction of scientific formulae is never required, or even allowable, in War to aid the decision on the case presented, if truth does not appear there in a systematic shape, if it is not found in an indirect way, but directly by the natural perception of the mind, then it must be the same also in a critical review.

It is true as we have seen that, wherever complete demonstration of the nature of things would be too tedious, criticism must support itself on those truths which theory has established on the point. But, just as in War the actor obeys these theoretical truths rather because his mind is imbued with them than because he regards them as objective inflexible laws, so criticism must also make use of them, not as an external law or an algebraic formula, of which fresh proof is not required each time they are applied, but it must always throw a light on this proof itself, leaving only to theory the more minute and circumstantial proof. Thus it avoids a mysterious, unintelligible phraseology, and makes its progress in plain language, that is, with a clear and always visible chain of ideas.

Certainly this cannot always be completely attained, but it must always be the aim in critical expositions. Such expositions must use complicated forms of science as sparingly as possible, and never resort to the construction of scientific aids as of a truth apparatus of its own, but always be guided by the natural and unbiased impressions of the mind.

But this pious endeavour, if we may use the expression, has unfortunately seldom hitherto presided over critical examinations: the most of them have rather been emanations of a species of vanity – a wish to make a display of ideas.

The first evil which we constantly stumble upon is a lame, totally inadmissible application of certain one-sided systems as of a formal code of laws. But it is never difficult to show the one-sidedness of such systems, and this only requires to be done once to throw discredit for ever on critical judgements which are based on them. We have here to deal with a definite subject, and as the number of possible systems after all can be but small, therefore also they are themselves the lesser evil.

Much greater is the evil which lies in the pompous retinue of technical terms – scientific expressions and metaphors, which these systems carry in their train, and which like a rabble – like the baggage of an Army broken away from its Chief – hang about in all directions. Any critic who has not adopted a system, either because he has not found one to please him, or because he has not yet been able to make himself master of one, will at least occasionally make use of a piece of one, as one would use a ruler, to show the blunders committed by a General. The most of them are incapable of reasoning without using as a help here and there some shreds of scientific military theory. The smallest of these fragments, consisting in mere scientific words and metaphors, are often nothing more than ornamental flourishes of critical narration. Now it is in the nature of things that all technical and scientific expressions which belong to a system lose their propriety, if they ever had any, as soon as they are distorted, and used as general axioms, or as small crystalline talismans, which have more power of demonstration than simple speech.

Thus it has come to pass that our theoretical and critical books, instead of being straightforward, intelligible dissertations, in which the author always knows at least what he says and the reader what he reads, are brimful of these technical terms, which form dark points of interference where author and reader part company. But frequently they are something worse, being nothing but hollow shells without any kernel. The author himself has no clear perception of what he means, contents himself with vague ideas, which if expressed in plain language would be unsatisfactory even to himself.

A third fault in criticism is the *misuse* of *historical examples*, and a display of great reading or learning. What the history of the Art of War is we have already said, and we shall further explain our views on examples and on military history in general in special chapters. One fact merely touched upon in a very cursory manner may be used to support the most opposite views, and three or four such facts of the most heterogeneous description, brought together out of the most distant lands and remote times and heaped up, generally distract and bewilder the judgement and understanding without demonstrating anything; for when exposed to the light they turn out to be only trumpery rubbish, made use of to show off the author's learning.

But what can be gained for practical life by such obscure, partly false, confused arbitrary conceptions? So little is gained that theory on account of them has always been a true antithesis of practice, and frequently a subject of ridicule to those whose soldierly qualities in the field are above question.

But it is impossible that this could have been the case, if theory in simple language, and by natural treatment of those things which constitute the Art of making War, had merely sought to establish just so much as admits of being established; if, avoiding all false pretensions and irrelevant display of scientific forms and historical parallels, it had kept close to the subject, and gone hand in hand with those who must conduct affairs in the field by their own natural genius.

CHAPTER VI

ON EXAMPLES

EXAMPLES from history make everything clear, and furnish the best description of proof in the empirical sciences. This applies with more force to the Art of War than to any other. General Scharnhorst, whose handbook is the best ever written on actual War, pronounces historical examples to be of the first importance, and makes an admirable use of them himself. Had he survived the War in which he fell, the fourth part of his revised treatise on artillery would have given a still greater proof of the observing and enlightened spirit in which he sifted matters of experience.

But such use of historical examples is rarely made by theoretical writers; the way in which they more commonly make use of them is rather calculated to leave the mind unsatisfied, as well as to offend the understanding. We therefore think it important to bring specially into view the use and abuse of historical examples.

Unquestionably the branches of knowledge which lie at the foundation of the Art of War come under the denomination of empirical sciences; for although they are derived in a great measure from the nature of things, still we can only learn this very nature itself for the most part from experience; and besides that, the practical application is modified by so many circumstances that the effects can never be completely learnt from the mere nature of the means.

The effects of gunpowder, that great agent in our military activity, were only learnt by experience, and up to this hour experiments are continually in progress in order to investigate them more fully. That an iron ball to which powder has given a velocity of 1,000 feet in a second, smashes every living thing which it touches in its course is intelligible in itself; experience is not required to tell us that; but in producing this effect how many hundred circumstances are concerned, some of which can only be learnt by experience! And the physical is not the only effect which we have to study, it is the moral which we are in search of, and that can only be ascertained by experience; and there is no other way of learning and appreciating it but by experience. In the middle ages, when firearms were first invented, their effect, owing to their rude make, was materially but trifling compared to what it now is, but their effect morally was much greater. One must have witnessed the firmness of one of those masses taught and led by Buonaparte, under the heaviest and most unintermittent cannonade, in order to understand what troops, hardened by long practice in the field of danger, can do, when by a career of victory they have reached the noble principle of demanding from themselves their utmost efforts. In pure conception no one would believe it.[87] On the other hand, it is well known that there are troops in the service of European Powers at the present moment who would easily be dispersed by a few cannon shots.

But no empirical science, consequently also no theory of the Art of War, can always corroborate its truths by historical proof; it would also be, in some measure, difficult to support experience by single facts. If any means is once found efficacious in War, it is repeated; one nation copies another, the thing becomes the fashion, and in this manner it comes into use, supported by experience, and takes its place in theory, which contents itself with appealing to experience in general in order to show its origin, but not as a verification of its truth.

But it is quite otherwise if experience is to be used in order to overthrow some means in use, to confirm what is doubtful, or introduce something new; then particular examples from history must be quoted as proofs.

Now, if we consider closely the use of historical proofs, four points of view readily present themselves for the purpose.

First, they may be used merely as an *explanation* of an idea. In every abstract consideration it is very easy to be misunderstood, or not to be intelligible at all: when an author is afraid of this, an exemplification from history serves to throw the light which is wanted on his idea, and to ensure his being intelligible to his reader.

Secondly, it may serve as an *application* of an idea, because by means of an example there is an opportunity of showing the action of those minor circumstances which cannot all be comprehended and explained in any general expression of an idea; for in that consists, indeed, the difference between theory and experience. Both these cases belong to examples properly speaking, the two following belong to historical proofs.

Thirdly, a historical fact may be referred to particularly, in order to support what one has advanced. This is in all cases sufficient, if we have *only* to prove the *possibility* of a fact or effect.[88]

Lastly, in the fourth place, from the circumstantial detail of a historical event, and by collecting together several of them, we may deduce some theory, which therefore has its true *proof* in this testimony itself.

For the first of these purposes all that is generally required is a cursory notice of the case, as it is only used partially. Historical correctness is a secondary consideration; a case invented might also serve the purpose as well, only historical ones are always to be preferred, because they bring the idea which they illustrate nearer to practical life.

The second use supposes a more circumstantial relation of events, but historical authenticity is again of secondary importance, and in respect to this point the same is to be said as in the first case.

For the third purpose the mere quotation of an undoubted

fact is generally sufficient. If it is asserted that fortified positions may fulfil their object under certain conditions, it is only necessary to mention the position of Bunzelwitz in support of the assertion.

But if, through the narrative of a case in history, an abstract truth is to be demonstrated, then everything in the case bearing on the demonstration must be analysed in the most searching and complete manner; it must, to a certain extent, develop itself carefully before the eyes of the reader. The less effectually this is done the weaker will be the proof, and the more necessary it will be to supply the demonstrative proof which is wanting in the single case by a number of cases, because we have a right to suppose that the more minute details which we are unable to give neutralize each other in the effects in a certain number of cases.

If we want to show by example derived from experience that cavalry are better placed behind than in a line with infantry; that it is very hazardous without a decided preponderance of numbers to attempt an enveloping movement, with widely separated columns, either on a field of battle or in the theatre of war – that is, either tactically or strategically – then in the first of these cases it would not be sufficient to specify some lost battles in which the cavalry was on the flanks and some gained in which the cavalry was in rear of the infantry; and in the latter of these cases it is not sufficient to refer to the battles of Rivoli and Wagram, to the attack of the Austrians on the theatre of war in Italy, in 1796, or of the French upon the German theatre of war in the same year. The way in which these orders of battle or plans of attack essentially contributed to disastrous issues in those particular cases must be shown by closely tracing out circumstances and occurrences. Then it will appear how far such forms or measures are to be condemned, a point which it is very necessary to show, for a total condemnation would be inconsistent with truth.

It has been already said that when a circumstantial detail of facts is impossible, the demonstrative power which is deficient may to a certain extent be supplied by the number of cases quoted; but this is a very dangerous method of getting out of the difficulty, and one which has been much abused. Instead of one well-explained example, three or four are just touched upon, and thus a show is made of strong evidence. But there are matters where a whole dozen of cases brought forward would prove nothing, if, for instance, they are facts of frequent occurrence, and therefore a dozen other cases with an opposite result might just as easily be brought forward. If any one will instance a dozen lost battles in which the side beaten attacked in separate converging columns, we can instance a dozen that have been gained in which the same order was adopted. It is evident that in this way no result is to be obtained.

Upon carefully considering these different points, it will be seen how easily examples may be misapplied.

An occurrence which, instead of being carefully analysed in all its parts, is superficially noticed, is like an object seen at a great distance, presenting the same appearance on each side, and in which the details of its parts cannot be distinguished. Such examples have, in reality, served to support the most contradictory opinions. To some Daun's campaigns are models of prudence and skill. To others, they are nothing but examples of timidity and want of resolution. Buonaparte's passage across the Noric Alps in 1797 may be made to appear the noblest resolution, but also as an act of sheer temerity. His strategic defeat in 1812 may be represented as the consequence either of an excess, or of a deficiency, of energy. All these opinions have been broached, and it is easy to see that they might very well arise, because each person takes a different view of the connexion of events. At the same time these antagonistic opinions cannot be reconciled with each other, and therefore one of the two must be wrong.

Much as we are obliged to the worthy Feuquières for the numerous examples introduced in his memoirs – partly because a number of historical incidents have thus been preserved which might otherwise have been lost, and partly because he was one of the first to bring theoretical, that is, abstract, ideas into connexion with the practical in war, in so far that the cases brought forward may be regarded as intended to exemplify and confirm what is theoretically asserted – yet, in the opinion of an impartial reader, he will hardly be allowed to have attained the object he proposed to himself, that of proving theoretical principles by historical examples. For although he sometimes relates occurrences with great minuteness, still he falls short very often of showing that the deductions drawn necessarily proceed from the inner relations of these events.

Another evil which comes from the superficial notice of historical events, is that some readers are either wholly ignorant of the events, or cannot call them to remembrance sufficiently to be able to grasp the author's meaning, so that there is no alternative between either accepting blindly what is said, or remaining unconvinced.

It is extremely difficult to put together or unfold historical events before the eyes of a reader in such a way as is necessary, in order to be able to use them as proofs; for the writer very often wants the means, and can neither afford the time nor the requisite space; but we maintain that, when the object is to establish a new or doubtful opinion, one single example, thoroughly analysed, is far more instructive than ten which are superficially treated. The great mischief of these superficial representations is not that the writer puts his story forward as a proof when it has only a false title, but that he has not made himself properly acquainted with the subject, and that from this sort of slovenly, shallow treatment of history, a hundred false views and attempts at the construction of theories arise, which would never have made their appearance if the writer had looked upon it as his duty to deduce from the strict connexion of events everything new which he brought to market, and sought to prove from history.

When we are convinced of these difficulties in the use of historical examples, and at the same time of the necessity (of making use of such examples), then we shall also come to the conclusion that the latest military history is naturally the best field from which to draw them, inasmuch as it alone is sufficiently authentic and detailed.

In ancient times, circumstances connected with War, as well as the method of carrying it on, were different; therefore its events are of less use to us either theoretically or practically; in addition to which, military history, like every other, naturally loses in the course of time a number of small traits and lineaments originally to be seen, loses in colour and life, like a worn-out or darkened picture; so that perhaps at last only the large masses and leading features remain, which thus acquire undue proportions.

If we look at the present state of warfare, we should say that the Wars since that of the Austrian succession are almost the only ones which, at least as far as armament, have still a considerable similarity to the present, and which, notwithstanding the many important changes which have taken place both great and small, are still capable of affording much instruction. It is quite otherwise with the War of the Spanish succession, as the use of firearms had not then so far advanced towards perfection, and cavalry still continued the most important arm. The farther we go back, the less useful becomes military history, as it gets so much the more meagre and barren of detail. The most useless of all is that of the old world.

But this usefulness is not altogether absolute, it relates only to those subjects which depend on a knowledge of minute details, or on those things in which the method of conducting war has changed. Although we know very little about the tactics in the battles between the Swiss and the Austrians, the Burgundians and French, still we find in them unmistakable evidence that they were the first in which the superiority of a good infantry over the best cavalry was displayed.[89] A general glance at the time of the Condottieri teaches us how the whole method of conducting War is dependent on the instrument used; for at no period have the forces used in War had so much the characteristics of a special instrument, and been a class so totally distinct from the rest of the national community. The memorable way in which the Romans in the second Punic War attacked the Carthaginian possessions in Spain and Africa, while Hannibal still maintained himself in Italy, is a most instructive subject to study, as the general relations of the States and Armies concerned in the indirect act of defence are sufficiently well known.

But the more things descend into particulars and deviate in character from the most general relations, the less we can look for examples and lessons of experience from very remote periods for we have neither the means of judging properly of corresponding events, nor can we apply them to our completely different method of War.

Unfortunately, however, it has always been the fashion with historical writers to talk about ancient times. We shall not say how far vanity and charlatanism may have had a share in this, but in general we fail to discover any honest intention and earnest endeavour to instruct and convince, and we can therefore only look upon such quotations and references as embellishments to fill up gaps and hide defects.

It would be an immense service to teach the Art of War entirely by historical examples, as Feuquières proposed to do; but it would be full work for the whole life of a man, if we reflect that he who undertakes it must first qualify himself for the task by a long personal experience in actual War.

Whoever, stirred by ambition, undertakes such a task, let him prepare himself for his pious undertaking as for a long pilgrimage; let him give up his time, spare no sacrifice, fear no temporal rank or power, and rise above all feelings of personal vanity, of false shame, in order, according to the French code, to speak *the Truth, the whole Truth, and nothing but the Truth.*

BOOK THREE

OF STRATEGY IN GENERAL

CHAPTER I

STRATEGY

IN the second chapter of the second book, Strategy has been defined as '*the employment of the battle as the means towards the attainment of the object of the War*'. Properly speaking it has to do with nothing but the battle, but its theory must include in this consideration the instrument of this real activity – the armed force – in itself and in its principal relations, for the battle is fought by it, and shows its effects upon it in turn. It must be well acquainted with the battle itself as far as relates to its possible results, and those mental and moral powers which are the most important in the use of the same.

Strategy is the employment of the battle to gain the end of the War; it must therefore give an aim to the whole military action, which must be in accordance with the object of the War; in other words, Strategy forms the plan of the War; and to this end it links together the series of acts which are to lead to the final decision, that is to say, it makes the plans for the separate campaigns and regulates the combats to be fought in each. As these are all things which to a great extent can only be determined on conjectures some of which turn out incorrect, while a number of other arrangements pertaining to details cannot be made at all beforehand, it follows, as a matter of course, that Strategy must go with the Army to the field in order to arrange particulars on the spot, and to make the modifications in the general plan which incessantly become necessary in War. Strategy can therefore never take its hand from the work for a moment.

That this, however, has not always been the view taken is evident from the former custom of keeping Strategy in the cabinet and not with the Army, a thing only allowable if the cabinet is so near to the Army that it can be taken for the chief headquarters of the Army.

Theory will therefore attend on Strategy in the determination of its plans, or, as we may more properly say, it will throw a light on things in themselves, and on their relations to each other, and bring out prominently the little that there is of principle or rule.

If we recall to mind from the first chapter how many things of the highest importance War touches upon, we may conceive that a consideration of all requires a rare grasp of mind.

A Prince or General who knows exactly how to organize his War according to his object and means, who does neither too little nor too much, gives by that the greatest proof of his genius. But the effects of this talent are exhibited not so much by the invention of new modes of action, which might strike the eye immediately, as in the successful final result of the whole. It is the exact fulfilment of silent suppositions, it is the noiseless harmony of the whole action which we should admire, and which only makes itself known in the total result.

The inquirer who, tracing back from the final result, does not perceive the signs of that harmony is one who is apt to seek for genius where it is not, and where it cannot be found.

The means and forms which Strategy uses are in fact so extremely simple, so well known by their constant repetition, that it only appears ridiculous to sound common sense when it hears critics so frequently speaking of them with high-flown emphasis. Turning a flank, which has been done a thousand times, is regarded here as a proof of the most brilliant genius, there as a proof of the most profound penetration, indeed even of the most comprehensive knowledge. Can there be in the book-world more absurd productions?[90]

It is still more ridiculous if, in addition to this, we reflect that the same critic, in accordance with prevalent opinion, excludes all moral forces from theory, and will not allow it to be concerned with anything but the material forces, so that all must be confined to a few mathematical relations of equilibrium and preponderance, of time and space, and a few lines and angles. If it were nothing more than this, then out of such a miserable business there would not be a scientific problem for even a schoolboy.

But let us admit: there is no question here about scientific formulas and problems; the relations of material things are all very simple; the right comprehension of the moral forces which come into play is more difficult. Still, even in respect to them, it is only in the highest branches of Strategy that moral complications and a great diversity of quantities and relations are to be looked for, only at that point where Strategy borders on political science, or rather where the two become one, and there, as we have before observed, they have more influence on the 'how much' and 'how little' is to be done than on the form of execution. Where the latter is the principal question, as in the single acts both great and small in War, the moral quantities are already reduced to a very small number.

Thus, then, in Strategy everything is very simple, but not on that account very easy. Once it is determined from the relations of the State what should and may be done by War, then the way to it is easy to find; but to follow that way straightforward, to carry out the plan without being obliged to deviate from it a thousand times by a thousand varying influences, requires, besides great strength of character, great clearness and steadiness of mind, and out of a thousand men who are remarkable, some for mind, others for penetration, others again for boldness or strength of will, perhaps not one will combine in himself all those qualities which are required to raise a man above mediocrity in the career of a general.

It may sound strange, but for all who know War in this respect it is a fact beyond doubt, that much more strength of will is required to make an important decision in Strategy than in tactics. In the latter we are hurried on with the moment; a Commander feels himself borne along in a strong current, against which he durst not contend without the most destructive consequences, he suppresses the rising fears, and boldly ventures farther. In Strategy, where all goes on at a slower rate, there is more room allowed for our own apprehensions and those of others, for objections and remonstrances, consequently also for unseasonable regrets; and as we do not see things in Strategy as we do at least half of them in tactics, with the living eye, but everything must be conjectured and assumed, the convictions produced are less powerful. The consequence is that most Generals, when they should act, remain stuck fast in bewildering doubts.

Now let us cast a glance at history – upon Frederick the Great's campaign of 1760, celebrated for its fine marches and manoeuvres: a perfect masterpiece of Strategic skill as critics tell us. Is there really anything to drive us out of our wits with admiration in the King's first trying to turn Daun's right flank, then his left, then again his right, etc.? Are we to see profound wisdom in this? No, that we cannot, if we are to decide naturally and without affectation. What we rather admire above all is the sagacity of the King in this respect, that while pursuing a great object with very limited means, he undertook nothing beyond his powers, and *just enough* to gain his object. This sagacity of the General is visible not only in this campaign, but throughout all the three Wars of the Great King!

To bring Silesia into the safe harbour of a well-guaranteed peace was his object.

At the head of a small State, which was like other States in most things, and only ahead of them in some branches of administration; he could not be an Alexander, and, as Charles XII, he would only, like him, have broken his head. We find, therefore, in the whole of his conduct of War, a controlled power, always well balanced, and never wanting in energy, which in the most critical moments rises to astonishing deeds, and the next moment oscillates quietly on again in subordination to the play of the most subtil political influences. Neither vanity, thirst for glory, nor vengeance could make him deviate from his course, and this course alone it is which brought him to a fortunate termination of the contest.

These few words do but scant justice to this phase of the genius of the great General; the eyes must be fixed carefully on the extraordinary issue of the struggle, and the causes which brought about that issue must be traced out, in order thoroughly to understand that nothing but the King's penetrating eye brought him safely out of all his dangers.

This is one feature in this great Commander which we admire in the campaign of 1760 – and in all others, but in this especially – because in none did he keep the balance even against such a superior hostile force, with such a small sacrifice.

Another feature relates to the difficulty of execution. Marches to turn a flank, right or left, are easily combined; the idea of keeping a small force always well concentrated to be able to meet the enemy on equal terms at any point, to multiply a force by rapid movement, is as easily conceived as expressed; the mere contrivance in these points, therefore, cannot excite our admiration, and with respect to such simple things, there is nothing further than to admit that they are simple.

But let a General try to do these things like Frederick the Great. Long afterwards authors, who were eye-witnesses, have spoken of the danger, indeed of the imprudence, of the King's camps, and doubtless, at the time he pitched them, the danger appeared three times as great as afterwards.

It was the same with his marches, under the eyes, nay, often under the cannon of the enemy's Army; these camps were taken up, these marches made, not from want of prudence, but because in Daun's system, in his mode of drawing up his Army, in the responsibility which pressed upon him, and in his character, Frederick found that security which justified his camps and marches. But it required the King's boldness, determination, and strength of will to see things in this light, and not to be led astray and intimidated by the danger of which thirty years after people still wrote and spoke. Few Generals in this situation would have believed these simple strategic means to be practicable.

Again, another difficulty in execution lay in this, that the King's Army in this campaign was constantly in motion. Twice it marched by wretched cross-roads, from the Elbe into Silesia, in rear of Daun and pursued by Lascy (beginning of July, beginning of August). It required to be always ready for battle, and its marches had to be organized with a degree of skill which necessarily called forth a proportionate amount of exertion. Although attended and delayed by thousands of waggons, still its subsistence was extremely difficult. In Silesia, for eight days before the battle of Leignitz, it had constantly to march, defiling alternately right and left in front of the enemy: this costs great fatigue, and entails great privations.

Is it to be supposed that all this could have been done without producing great friction in this machine? Can the mind of a

Commander elaborate such movements with the same ease as the hand of a land surveyor uses the astrolabe? Does not the sight of the sufferings of their hungry, thirsty comrades pierce the hearts of the Commander and his Generals a thousand times? Must not the murmurs and doubts which these cause reach his ear? Has an ordinary man the courage to demand such sacrifices, and would not such efforts most certainly demoralize the Army, break up the bands of discipline, and, in short, undermine its military virtue, if firm reliance on the greatness and infallibility of the Commander did not compensate for all? Here, therefore, it is that we should pay respect; it is these miracles of execution which we should admire. But it is impossible to realize all this in its full force without a foretaste of it by experience. He who only knows War from books or the drill-ground cannot realize the whole effect of this counterpoise in action; *we beg him, therefore, to accept from us on faith and trust all that he is unable to supply from any personal experience of his own.*

This illustration is intended to give more clearness to the course of our ideas, and in closing this chapter we will only briefly observe that in our exposition of Strategy we shall describe those separate subjects which appear to us the most important, whether of a moral or material nature; then proceed from the simple to the complex, and conclude with the inner connexion of the whole act of War, in other words, with the plan for a War or campaign.

OBSERVATION

In an earlier manuscript of the second book are the following passages endorsed by the author himself to be used for the first Chapter of the second Book*: the projected revision of that chapter not having been made, the passages referred to are introduced here in full.*

By the mere assemblage of armed forces at a particular point, a battle there becomes possible, but does not always take place. Is that possibility now to be regarded as a reality and therefore an effective thing? Certainly, it is so by its results, and these effects, whatever they may be, can never fail.

1. *Possible combats are on account of their results to be looked upon as real ones.*

If a detachment is sent away to cut off the retreat of a flying enemy, and the enemy surrenders in consequence without further resistance, still it is through the combat which is offered to him by this detachment sent after him that he is brought to his decision.

If a part of our Army occupies an enemy's province which was undefended, and thus deprives the enemy of very considerable means of keeping up the strength of his Army, it is entirely through the battle which our detached body gives the enemy to expect, in case he seeks to recover the lost province, that we remain in possession of the same.

In both cases, therefore, the mere possibility of a battle has produced results, and is therefore to be classed amongst actual events. Suppose that in these cases the enemy has opposed our troops with others superior in force, and thus forced ours to give up their object without a combat, then certainly our plan has failed, but the battle which we offered at (either of) these points has not on that account been without effect, for it attracted the enemy's forces to that point. And in case our whole undertaking has done us harm, it cannot be said that these positions, these possible battles, have been attended with no results; their effects, then, are similar to those of a lost battle.

In this manner we see that the destruction of the enemy's military forces, the overthrow of the enemy's power, is only to be done through the effect of a battle, whether it be that it actually takes place, or that it is merely offered, and not accepted.

2. *Twofold object of the combat*

But these effects are of two kinds, direct and indirect; they are of the latter, if other things intrude themselves and become the object of the combat – things which cannot be regarded as the destruction of enemy's force, but only leading up to it, certainly by a circuitous road, but with so much the greater effect. The possession of provinces, towns, fortresses, roads, bridges, magazines, etc., may be the *immediate* object of a battle, but never the ultimate one. Things of this description can never be looked upon otherwise than as means of gaining greater superiority, so as at last to offer battle to the enemy in such a way that it will be impossible for him to accept it. Therefore all these things must only be regarded as intermediate links, steps, as it were, leading up to the effectual principle, but never as that principle itself.

3. Examples

In 1814, by the capture of Buonaparte's capital the object of the War was attained. The political divisions which had their roots in Paris came into active operation, and an enormous split left the power of the Emperor to collapse of itself. Nevertheless the point of view from which we must look at all this is, that through these causes the forces and defensive means of Buonaparte were suddenly very much diminished, the superiority of the Allies, therefore, just in the same measure increased, and any further resistance then became *impossible*. It was this impossibility which produced the peace with France. If we suppose the forces of the Allies at that moment diminished to a like extent through external causes; if the superiority vanishes, then at the same time vanishes also all the effect and importance of the taking of Paris.

We have gone through this chain of argument in order to show that this is the natural and only true view of the thing from which it derives its importance. It leads always back to the question, What at any given moment of the War or campaign will be the probable result of the great or small combats which the two sides might offer to each other? In the consideration of a plan for a campaign, this question only is decisive as to the measures which are to be taken all through from the very commencement.

4. When this view is not taken, then a false value is given to other things.

If we do not accustom ourselves to look upon War, and the single campaigns in a War, as a chain which is all composed of battles strung together, one of which always brings on another; if we adopt the idea that the taking of a certain geographical point, the occupation of an undefended province, is in itself anything; then we are very likely to regard it as an acquisition which we may retain; and if we look at it so, and not as a term in the whole series of events, we do not ask ourselves whether this possession may not lead to greater disadvantages hereafter. How often we find this mistake recurring in military history.

We might say that, just as in commerce the merchant cannot set apart and place in security gains from one single transaction by itself, so in War a single advantage cannot be separated from the result of the whole. Just as the former must always operate with the whole bulk of his means, just so in War, only the sum total will decide on the advantage or disadvantage of each item.

If the mind's eye is always directed upon the series of combats, so far as they can be seen beforehand, then it is always looking in the right direction, and thereby the motion of the force acquires that rapidity, that is to say, willing and doing acquire that energy which is suitable to the matter, and which is not to be thwarted or turned aside by extraneous influences.[91]

CHAPTER II

ELEMENTS OF STRATEGY

THE causes which condition the use of the combat in Strategy may be easily divided into elements of different kinds, such as the moral, physical, mathematical, geographical, and statistical elements.

The first class includes all that can be called forth by moral qualities and effects; to the second belong the whole mass of the military force, its organization, the proportion of the three arms, etc., etc.; to the third, the angle of the lines of operation, the concentric and eccentric movements in as far as their geometrical nature has any value in the calculation; to the fourth, the influences of country, such as commanding points, hills, rivers, woods, roads, etc., etc.; lastly, to the fifth, all the means of supply. The separation of these things once for all in the mind does good in giving clearness and helping us to estimate at once, at a higher or lower value, the different classes as we pass onwards. For, in considering them separately, many lose of themselves their borrowed importance; one feels, for instance, quite plainly that the value of a base of operations, even if we look at nothing in it but its relative position to the line of operations, depends much less in that simple form on the geometrical element of the angle which they form with one another, than on the nature of the roads and the country through which they pass.

But to treat upon Strategy according to these elements would be the most unfortunate idea that could be conceived, for these elements are generally manifold, and intimately connected with each other in every single operation of War. We should lose ourselves in the most soulless analysis, and as if in a horrid dream, we should be for ever trying in vain to build up an arch to connect this base of abstractions with facts belonging to the real world. Heaven preserve every theorist from such an undertaking! We shall keep to the world of things in their totality, and not pursue our analysis further than is necessary from time to time to give distinctness to the idea which we wish to impart, and which has come to us, not by a speculative investigation, but through the impression made by the realities of War in their entirety.

CHAPTER III

MORAL FORCES

We must return again to this subject, which is touched upon in the third chapter of the second book (p. 201), because the moral forces are amongst the most important subjects in War. They form the spirit which permeates the whole being of War. These forces fasten themselves soonest and with the greatest affinity on to the Will which puts in motion and guides the whole mass of powers, uniting with it as it were in one stream, because this is a moral force itself. Unfortunately they will escape from all book-analysis, for they will neither be brought into numbers nor into classes, and require to be both seen and felt.

The spirit and other moral qualities which animate an Army, a General, or Governments, public opinion in provinces in which a War is raging, the moral effect of a victory or of a defeat are things which in themselves vary very much in their nature, and which also, according as they stand with regard to our object and our relations, may have an influence in different ways.

Although little or nothing can be said about these things in books, still they belong to the theory of the Art of War, as much as everything else which constitutes War. For I must here once more repeat that it is a miserable philosophy if, according to the old plan, we establish rules and principles wholly regardless of all moral forces, and then, as soon as these forces make their appearance, we begin to count exceptions which we thereby establish as it were theoretically, that is, make into rules; or if we resort to an appeal to genius, which is above all rules, thus giving out by implication, not only that rules were only made for fools, but also that they themselves are no better than folly.

Even if the theory of the Art of War does no more in reality than recall these things to remembrance, showing the necessity of allowing to the moral forces their full value, and of always taking them into consideration, by so doing it extends its borders over the region of immaterial forces, and by establishing that point of view, condemns beforehand every one who would endeavour to justify himself before its judgement seat by the mere physical relations of forces.

Further out of regard to all other so-called rules, theory cannot banish the moral forces beyond its frontier, because the effects of the physical forces and the moral are completely fused, and are not to be decomposed like a metal alloy by a chemical process. In every rule relating to the physical forces, theory must present to the mind at the same time the share which the moral powers will have in it, if it would not be led to categorical propositions, at one time too timid and contracted, at another too dogmatical and wide. Even the most matter-of-fact theories have, without knowing it, strayed over into this moral kingdom; for, as an example, the effects of a victory cannot in any way be explained without taking into consideration the moral impressions. And therefore the most of the subjects which we shall go through in this book are composed half of physical, half of moral causes and effects, and we might say the physical are almost no more than the wooden handle, whilst the moral are the noble metal, the real bright-polished weapon.

The value of the moral powers, and their frequently incredible influence, are best exemplified by history, and this is the most generous and the purest nourishment which the mind of the General can extract from it. At the same time it is to be observed, that it is less demonstrations, critical examinations, and learned treatises, than sentiments, general impressions, and single flashing sparks of truth, which yield the seeds of knowledge that are to fertilize the mind.

We might go through the most important moral phenomena in War, and with all the care of a diligent professor try what we could impart about each, either good or bad. But as in such a method one slides too much into the commonplace and trite, whilst real mind quickly makes its escape in analysis, the end is that one gets imperceptibly to the relation of things which everybody knows. We prefer, therefore, to remain here more than usually incomplete and rhapsodical, content to have drawn attention to the importance of the subject in a general way, and to have pointed out the spirit in which the views given in this book have been conceived.

CHAPTER IV

THE CHIEF MORAL POWERS

THESE are *The Talents of the Commander*; *The Military Virtue of the Army*; *Its National feeling*. Which of these is the most important no one can tell in a general way, for it is very difficult to say anything in general of their strength, and still more difficult to compare the strength of one with that of another. The best plan is not to undervalue any of them, a fault which human judgement is prone to, sometimes on one side, sometimes on another, in its whimsical oscillations. It is better to satisfy ourselves of the undeniable efficacy of these three things by sufficient evidence from history.

It is true, however, that in modern times the Armies of European states have arrived very much at a par as regards discipline and fitness for service, and that the conduct of War has – as philosophers would say – naturally developed itself, thereby become a method, common as it were to all Armies, so that even from Commanders there is nothing further to be expected in the way of application of special means of Art, in the limited sense (such as Frederick the Second's oblique order). Hence it cannot be denied that, as matters now stand, greater scope is afforded for the influence of National spirit and habituation of an army to War. A long peace may again alter all this.[92]

The national spirit of an Army (enthusiasm, fanatical zeal, faith, opinion) displays itself most in mountain warfare, where every one down to the common soldier is left to himself. On this account, a mountainous country is the best campaigning ground for popular levies.

Expertness of an Army through training, and that well-tempered courage which holds the ranks together as if they had been cast in a mould, show their superiority in an open country.

The talent of a General has most room to display itself in a closely intersected, undulating country. In mountains he has too little command over the separate parts, and the direction of all is beyond his powers; in open plains it is simple and does not exceed those powers.

According to these undeniable elective affinities, plans should be regulated.

CHAPTER V

MILITARY VIRTUE OF AN ARMY

THIS is distinguished from mere bravery, and still more from enthusiasm for the business of War. The first is certainly a necessary constituent part of it, but in the same way as bravery, which is a natural gift in some men, may arise in a soldier as a part of an Army from habit and custom, so with him it must also have a different direction from that which it has with others. It must lose that impulse to unbridled activity and exercise of force which is its characteristic in the individual, and submit itself to demands of a higher kind, to obedience, order, rule, and method. Enthusiasm for the profession gives life and greater fire to the military virtue of an Army, but does not necessarily constitute a part of it.

War is a special business, and however general its relations may be, and even if all the male population of a country, capable of bearing arms, exercise this calling, still it always continues to be different and separate from the other pursuits which occupy the life of man. To be imbued with a sense of the spirit and nature of this business, to make use of, to rouse, to assimilate into the system the powers which should be active in it, to penetrate completely into the nature of the business with the understanding, through exercise to gain confidence and expertness in it, to be completely given up to it, to pass out of the man into the part which it is assigned to us to play in War, that is the military virtue of an Army in the individual.

However much pains may be taken to combine the soldier and the citizen in one and the same individual, whatever may be done to nationalize Wars, and however much we may imagine times have changed since the days of the old Condottieri, never will it be possible to do away with the individuality of the business; and if that cannot be done, then those who belong to it, as long as they belong to it, will always look upon themselves as a kind of guild, in the regulations, laws and customs in which the 'Spirit of War' by preference finds its expression. And so it is in fact. Even with the most decided inclination to look at War from the highest point of view, it would be very wrong to look down upon this corporate spirit (*esprit de corps*) which may and should exist more or less in every Army. This corporate spirit forms the bond of union between the natural forces which are active in that which we have called military virtue. The crystals of military virtue have a greater affinity for the spirit of a corporate body than for anything else.

An Army which preserves its usual formations under the heaviest fire, which is never shaken by imaginary fears, and in the face of real danger disputes the ground inch by inch, which, proud in the feeling of its victories, never loses its sense of obedience, its respect for and confidence in its leaders, even under the depressing effects of defeat; an Army with all its physical powers, inured to privations and fatigue by exercise, like the muscles of an athlete; an Army which looks upon all its toils as the means to victory, not as a curse which hovers over its standards, and which is always reminded of its duties and virtues by the short catechism of one idea, namely the *honour of its arms*; Such an Army is imbued with the true military spirit.

Soldiers may fight bravely like the Vendéans, and do great things like the Swiss, the Americans, or Spaniards, without displaying this military virtue. A Commander may also be successful at the head of standing Armies, like Eugene and Marlborough, without enjoying the benefit of its assistance; we must not, therefore, say that a successful War without it cannot be imagined; and we draw especial attention to that point, in order the more to individualize the conception which is here brought forward, that the idea may not dissolve into a generalization, and that it may not be thought that military virtue is in the end everything. It is not so. Military virtue in an Army is a definite moral power which may be supposed wanting, and the influence of which may therefore be estimated – like any instrument the power of which may be calculated.

Having thus characterized it, we proceed to consider what can be predicated of its influence, and what are the means of gaining its assistance.

Military virtue is for the parts, what the genius of the Commander is for the whole. The General can only guide the whole, not each separate part, and where he cannot guide the part, there military virtue must be its leader. A General is chosen by the reputation of his superior talents, the chief leaders of large masses after careful probation; but this probation diminishes as we descend the scale of rank, and in just the same measure we may reckon less and less upon individual talents; but what is wanting in this respect military virtue should supply. The natural qualities of a warlike people play just this part: *bravery, aptitude, powers of endurance and enthusiasm.*

These properties may therefore supply the place of military virtue, and vice versa, from which the following may be deduced:

1. Military virtue is a quality of standing Armies only, but they require it the most. In national risings its place is supplied by natural qualities, which develop themselves there more rapidly.
2. Standing Armies opposed to standing Armies, can more easily dispense with it, than a standing Army opposed to a national insurrection, for in that case, the troops are more scattered, and the divisions left more to themselves. But where an Army can be kept concentrated, the genius of the General takes a greater place, and supplies what is wanting in the spirit of the Army. Therefore generally military virtue becomes more necessary the more the theatre of operations and other circumstances make the War complicated, and cause the forces to be scattered.

From these truths the only lesson to be derived is this, that if an Army is deficient in this quality, every endeavour should be made to simplify the operations of the War as much as possible, or to introduce double efficiency in the organization of the Army in some other respect, and not to expect from the mere name of a standing Army, that which only the veritable thing itself can give.

The military virtue of an Army is, therefore, one of the most important moral powers in War, and where it is wanting, we either see its place supplied by one of the others, such as the great superiority of generalship or popular enthusiasm, or we find the results not commensurate with the exertions made. How much that is great, this spirit, this sterling worth of an army, this refining of ore into the polished metal, has already done, we see in the history of the Macedonians under Alexander, the Roman legions under Caesar, the Spanish infantry under Alexander Farnese, the Swedes under Gustavus Adolphus and Charles XII, the Prussians under Frederick the Great, and the French under Buonaparte. We must purposely shut our eyes against all historical proof, if we do not admit, that the astonishing successes of these Generals and their greatness in situations of extreme difficulty, were only possible with Armies possessing this virtue.

This spirit can only be generated from two sources, and only by these two conjointly; the first is a succession of campaigns and great victories; the other is, an activity of the Army carried sometimes to the highest pitch. Only by these, does the soldier learn to know his powers. The more a General is in the habit of demanding from his troops, the surer he will be that his demands will be answered. The soldier is as proud of overcoming toil as he is of surmounting danger. Therefore it is only in the soil of incessant activity and exertion that the germ will thrive, but also only in the sunshine of victory. Once it becomes a *strong tree*, it will stand against the fiercest storms of misfortune and defeat, and even against the indolent inactivity of peace, at least for a time. It can therefore only be created in War, and under great Generals, but no doubt it may last at least for several generations, even under Generals of moderate capacity, and through considerable periods of peace.

With this generous and noble spirit of union in a line of veteran troops, covered with scars and thoroughly inured to War, we must not compare the self-esteem and vanity of a standing Army,[93] held together merely by the glue of service-regulations and a drill book; a certain plodding earnestness and strict discipline may keep up military virtue for a long time, but can never create it; these things therefore have a certain value, but must not be overrated. Order, smartness, good will, also a certain degree of pride and high feeling are qualities of an Army formed in time of peace which are to be prized but cannot stand alone. The whole retains the whole, and as with glass too quickly cooled, a single crack breaks the whole mass. Above all, the highest spirit in the world changes only too easily at the first check into depression, and one might say into a kind of rhodomontade of alarm, the French *sauve qui peut*. Such an Army can only achieve something through its leader, never by itself. It must be led with double caution, until by degrees, in victory and hardships, the strength grows into the full armour. Beware then of confusing the *spirit* of an Army with its temper.

CHAPTER VI

BOLDNESS

THE place and part which boldness takes in the dynamic system of powers, where it stands opposed to Foresight and prudence, has been stated in the chapter on the certainty of the result in order thereby to show, that theory has no right to restrict it by virtue of its legislative power.

But this noble impulse, with which the human soul raises itself above the most formidable dangers, is to be regarded as an active principle peculiarly belonging to War. In fact, in what branch of human activity should boldness have a right of citizenship if not in War?

From the transport-driver and the drummer up to the General, it is the noblest of virtues, the true steel which gives the weapon its edge and brilliancy.

Let us admit in fact it has in War even its own prerogatives. Over and above the result of the calculation of space, time, and quantity, we must allow a certain percentage which boldness derives from the weakness of others, whenever it gains the mastery. It is therefore, virtually, a creative power. This is not difficult to demonstrate philosophically. As often as boldness encounters hesitation, the probability of the result is of necessity in its favour, because the very state of hesitation implies a loss of equilibrium already. It is only when it encounters cautious foresight – which we may say is just as bold, at all events just as strong and powerful as itself – that it is at a disadvantage; such cases, however, rarely occur. Out of the whole multitude of prudent men in the world, the great majority are so from timidity.

Amongst large masses, boldness is a force, the special cultivation of which can never be to the detriment of other forces, because the great mass is bound to be a higher will by the framework and joints of the order of battle and of the service, and therefore is guided by an intelligent power which is extraneous. Boldness is therefore here only like a spring held down until its action is required.

The higher the rank the more necessary it is that boldness should be accompanied by a reflective mind, that it may not be a mere blind outburst of passion to no purpose; for with increase of rank it becomes always less a matter of self-sacrifice and more a matter of the preservation of others, and the good of the whole. Where regulations of the service, as a kind of second nature, prescribe for the masses, reflection must be the guide of the General, and in his case individual boldness in action may easily become a fault. Still, at the same time, it is a fine failing, and must not be looked at in the same light as any other. Happy the Army in which an untimely boldness frequently manifests itself; it is an exuberant growth which shows a rich soil. Even foolhardiness, that is boldness without an object, is not to be despised; in point of fact it is the same energy of feeling, only exercised as a kind of passion without any co-operation of the intelligent faculties. It is only when it strikes at the root of obedience, when it treats with contempt the orders of superior authority, that it must be repressed as a dangerous evil, not on its own account but on account of the act of disobedience, for there is nothing *in War* which is of *greater importance than obedience.*

The reader will readily agree with us that, supposing an equal degree of discernment to be forthcoming in a certain number of cases, a thousand times as many of them will end in disaster through over-anxiety as through boldness.

One would suppose it natural that the interposition of a reasonable object should stimulate boldness, and therefore lessen its intrinsic merit, and yet the reverse is the case in reality.

The intervention of lucid thought or the general supremacy of mind deprives the emotional forces of a great part of their power. On that account *boldness becomes of rarer occurrence the higher we ascend the scale of rank*, for whether the discernment and the understanding do or do not increase with these ranks still the Commanders, in their several stations as they rise, are pressed upon more and more severely by objective things, by relations and claims from without, so that they become the more perplexed the lower the degree of their individual intelligence. This so far as regards War is the chief foundation of the truth of the French proverb:

'Tel brille au second qui s'éclipse au premier.'

Almost all the Generals who are represented in history as merely having attained to mediocrity, and as wanting in decision when in supreme command, are men celebrated in their antecedent career for their boldness and decision.

In those motives to bold action which arise from the pressure of necessity we must make a distinction. Necessity has its degrees of intensity. If it lies near at hand, if the person acting is in the pursuit of his object driven into great dangers in order to escape others equally great, then we can only admire his resolution, which still has also its value. If a young man to show his skill in horsemanship leaps across a deep cleft, then he is bold; if he makes the same leap pursued by a troop of head-chopping Janissaries he is only resolute. But the farther off the necessity from the point of action, the greater the number of relations intervening which the mind has to traverse in order to realize them, by so much the less does necessity take from boldness in action. If Frederick the Great, in the year 1756, saw that War was inevitable, and that he could only escape destruction by being beforehand with his enemies, it became necessary for him to commence the War himself, but at the same time it was certainly very bold: for few men in his position would have made up their minds to do so.

Although Strategy is only the province of Generals-in-Chief or Commanders in the higher positions, still boldness in all the other branches of an Army is as little a matter of indifference to it as their other military virtues. With an Army belonging to a bold race, and in which the spirit of boldness has been always nourished, very different things may be undertaken than with one in which this virtue is unknown; for that reason we have considered it in connexion with an Army. But our subject is specially the boldness of the General, and yet we have not much to say about it after having described this military virtue in a general way to the best of our ability.

The higher we rise in a position of command, the more of the mind, understanding, and penetration predominate in activity, the more therefore is boldness, which is a property of the feelings kept in subjection, and for that reason we find it so rarely in the highest positions. But then, so much the more should it be admired. Boldness, directed by an overruling intelligence, is the stamp of the hero: this boldness does not consist in venturing directly against the nature of things, in a downright contempt of the laws of probability, but, if a choice is once made, in the rigorous adherence to that higher calculation which genius, the tact of judgement, has gone over with the speed of lightning. The more boldness lends wings to the mind and the discernment, so much the farther they will reach in their flight, so much the more comprehensive will be the view, the more exact the result, but certainly always only in the sense that with greater objects greater dangers are connected. The ordinary man, not to speak of the weak and irresolute, arrives at an exact result so far as such is possible without ocular demonstration, at most after diligent reflection in his chamber, at a distance from danger and responsibility. Let danger and responsibility draw close round him in every direction, then he loses the power of comprehensive vision, and if he retains this in any measure by the influence of others, still he will lose his power of *decision*, because in that point no one can help him.

We think then that it is impossible to imagine a distinguished General without boldness, that is to say, that no man can become one who is not born with this power of the soul, and we therefore look upon it as the first requisite for such a career. How much of this inborn power, developed and moderated through education and the circumstances of life, is left when the man has attained a high position, is the second question. The greater this power still is, the stronger will genius be on the wing, the higher will be its flight. The risks become always greater, but the purpose grows with them. Whether its lines proceed out of and get their direction from a distant necessity, or whether they converge to the keystone of a building which ambition has planned, whether Frederick or Alexander acts, is much the same as regards the critical view. If the one excites the imagination more because it is bolder, the other pleases the understanding most, because it has in it more absolute necessity.

We have still to advert to one very important circumstance.

The spirit of boldness can exist in an Army, either because it is in the people, or because it has been generated in a successful War conducted by able Generals. In the latter case it must of course be dispensed with at the commencement.

Now in our days there is hardly any other means of educating the spirit of a people in this respect, except by War, and that too under bold Generals. By it alone can that effeminacy of feeling be counteracted, that propensity to seek for the enjoyment of comfort, which cause degeneracy in a people rising in prosperity and immersed in an extremely busy commerce.

A Nation can hope to have a strong position in the political world only if its character and practice in actual War mutually support each other in constant reciprocal action.

CHAPTER VII

PERSEVERANCE

THE reader expects to hear of angles and lines, and finds, instead of these citizens of the scientific world, only people out of common life, such as he meets with every day in the street. And yet the author cannot make up his mind to become a hair's breadth more mathematical than the subject seems to him to require, and he is not alarmed at the surprise which the reader may show.

In War more than anywhere else in the world things happen differently to what we had expected, and look differently when near, to what they did at a distance. With what serenity the architect can watch his work gradually rising and growing into his plan. The doctor, although much more at the mercy of mysterious agencies and chances than the architect, still knows enough of the forms and effects of his means. In War, on the other hand, the Commander of an immense whole finds himself in a constant whirlpool of false and true information, of mistakes committed through fear, through negligence, through precipitation, of contraventions of his authority, either from mistaken or correct motives, from ill will, true or false sense of duty, indolence or exhaustion, of accidents which no mortal could have foreseen. In short, he is the victim of a hundred thousand impressions, of which the most have an intimidating, the fewest an encouraging tendency. By long experience in War, the tact is acquired of readily appreciating the value of these incidents; high courage and stability of character stand proof against them, as the rock resists the beating of the waves. He who would yield to these impressions would never carry out an undertaking, and on that account *perseverance* in the proposed object, as long as there is no decided reason against it, is a most necessary counterpoise. Further, there is hardly any celebrated enterprise in War which was not achieved by endless exertion, pains, and privations; and as here the weakness of the physical and moral man is ever disposed to yield, only an immense force of will, which manifests itself in perseverance admired by present and future generations, can conduct us to our goal.

CHAPTER VIII

SUPERIORITY OF NUMBERS

THIS is in tactics, as well as in Strategy, the most general principle of victory, and shall be examined by us first in its generality, for which we may be permitted the following exposition:

Strategy fixes the point where, the time when, and the numerical force with which the battle is to be fought. By this triple determination it has therefore a very essential influence on the issue of the combat. If tactics has fought the battle, if the result is over, let it be victory or defeat, Strategy makes such use of it as can be made in accordance with the great object of the War. This object is naturally often a very distant one, seldom does it lie quite close at hand. A series of other objects subordinate themselves to it as means. These objects, which are at the same time means to a higher purpose, may be practically of various kinds; even the ultimate aim of the whole War may be a different one in every case. We shall make ourselves acquainted with these things according as we come to know the separate objects which they come in contact with; and it is not our intention here to embrace the whole subject by a complete enumeration of them, even if that were possible. We therefore let the employment of the battle stand over for the present.

Even those things through which Strategy has an influence on the issue of the combat, inasmuch as it establishes the same, to a certain extent decrees them, are not so simple that they can be embraced in one single view. For as Strategy appoints time, place and force, it can do so in practice in many ways, each of which influences in a different manner the result of the combat as well as its consequences. Therefore we shall only get acquainted with this also by degrees, that is, through the subjects which more closely determine the application.

If we strip the combat of all modifications which it may undergo according to its immediate purpose and the circumstances from which it proceeds, lastly if we set aside the valour of the troops, because that is a given quantity, then there remains only the bare conception of the combat, that is a combat without form, in which we distinguish nothing but the number of the combatants.

This number will therefore determine victory. Now from the number of things above deducted to get to this point, it is shown that the superiority in numbers in a battle is only one of the factors employed to produce victory: that therefore so far from having with the superiority in number obtained all, or even only the principal thing, we have perhaps got very little by it, according as the other circumstances which cooperate happen to vary.

But this superiority has degrees, it may be imagined as twofold, threefold or fourfold, and every one sees, that by increasing this way, it must (at last) overpower everything else.

In such an aspect we grant, that the superiority in numbers is the most important factor in the result of a combat, only it must be sufficiently great to be a counterpoise to all the other cooperating circumstances. The direct result of this is, that the greatest possible number of troops should be brought into action at the decisive point.

Whether the troops thus brought are sufficient or not, we have then done in this respect all that our means allowed. This is the first principle in Strategy, therefore in general as now stated, it is just as well suited for Greeks and Persians, or for Englishmen and Mahrattas, as for French and Germans. But we shall take a glance at our relations in Europe, as respects War, in order to arrive at some more definite idea on this subject.

Here we find Armies much more alike in equipment, organization, and practical skill of every kind. There only remains a difference in the military virtue of Armies, and in the talent of Generals which may fluctuate with time from side to side. If we go through the military history of modern Europe, we find no example of a Marathon.

Frederick the Great beat 80,000 Austrians at Leuthen with about 30,000 men, and at Rosbach with 25,000 some 50,000 allies; these are however the only instances of victories gained against an enemy double, or more than double in numbers. Charles XII, in the battle of Narva, we cannot well quote, for the Russians were at that time hardly to be regarded as Europeans, also the principal circumstances, even of the battle, are too little known. Buonaparte had at Dresden 120,000 against 220,000, therefore not the double. At Kollin, Frederick the Great did not succeed, with 30,000 against 50,000 Austrians, neither did Buonaparte in the desperate battle of Leipsic, where he was 160,000 strong, against 280,000.

From this we may infer, that it is very difficult in the present state of Europe, for the most talented General to gain a victory over an enemy double his strength. Now if we see double numbers prove such a weight in the scale against the greatest Generals, we may be sure, that in ordinary cases, in small as well as great combats, an important superiority of numbers, but which need not be over two to one, will be sufficient to ensure the victory, however disadvantageous other circumstances may be. Certainly we may imagine a defile which even tenfold would not suffice to force, but in such a case it can be no question of a battle at all.

We think, therefore, that under our conditions, as well as in all similar ones, the superiority at the decisive point is a matter of capital importance, and that this subject, in the generality of cases, is decidedly the most important of all. The strength at the decisive point depends on the absolute strength of the Army, and on skill in making use of it.

The first rule is therefore to enter the field with an Army as strong as possible. This sounds very like a commonplace, but still it is really not so.

In order to show that for a long time the strength of forces was by no means regarded as a chief point, we need only observe that in most, and even in the most detailed histories of the Wars in the eighteenth century, the strength of the Armies is either not given at all, or only incidentally, and in no case is any special value laid upon it. Tempelhof in his history of the Seven Years'

War is the earliest writer who gives it regularly, but at the same time he does it only very superficially.

Even Massenbach, in his manifold critical observations on the Prussian campaigns of 1793–4 in the Vosges, talks a great deal about hills and valleys, roads and footpaths, but does not say a syllable about mutual strength.

Another proof lies in a wonderful notion which haunted the heads of many critical historians, according to which there was a certain size of an Army which was the best, a normal strength, beyond which the forces in excess were burdensome rather than serviceable.[94]

Lastly, there are a number of instances to be found, in which all the available forces were not really brought into the battle, or into the War, because the superiority of numbers was not considered to have that importance which in the nature of things belongs to it.

If we are thoroughly penetrated with the conviction that with a considerable superiority of numbers everything possible is to be effected, then it cannot fail that this clear conviction reacts on the preparations for the War, so as to make us appear in the field with as many troops as possible, and either to give us ourselves the superiority, or at least to guard against the enemy obtaining it. So much for what concerns the absolute force with which the War is to be conducted.

The measure of this absolute force is determined by the Government; and although with this determination the real action of War commences, and it forms an essential part of the Strategy of the War, still in most cases the General who is to command these forces in the War must regard their absolute strength as a given quantity, whether it be that he has had no voice in fixing it, or that circumstances prevented a sufficient expansion being given to it.

There remains nothing, therefore, where an absolute superiority is not attainable, but to produce a relative one at the decisive point, by making skilful use of what we have.

The calculation of space and time appears as the most essential thing to this end – and this has caused that subject to be regarded as one which embraces nearly the whole art of using military forces. Indeed, some have gone so far as to ascribe to great strategists and tacticians a mental organ peculiarly adapted to this point.

But the calculation of time and space, although it lies universally at the foundation of Strategy, and is to a certain extent its daily bread, is still neither the most difficult, nor the most decisive one.

If we take an unprejudiced glance at military history, we shall find that the instances in which mistakes in such a calculation have proved the cause of serious losses are very rare, at least in Strategy. But if the conception of a skilful combination of time and space is fully to account for every instance of a resolute and active Commander beating several separate opponents with one and the same army (Frederick the Great, Buonaparte), then we perplex ourselves unnecessarily with conventional language. For the sake of clearness and the profitable use of conceptions, it is necessary that things should always be called by their right names.

The right appreciation of their opponents (Daun, Schwartzenberg), the audacity to leave for a short space of time a small force only before them, energy in forced marches, boldness in sudden attacks, the intensified activity which great souls acquire in the moment of danger, these are the grounds of such victories; and what have these to do with the ability to make an exact calculation of two such simple things as time and space?

But even this ricocheting play of forces, 'when the victories at Rosbach and Montmirail give the impulse to victories at Leuthen and Montereau', to which great Generals on the defensive have often trusted, is still, if we would be clear and exact, only a rare occurrence in history.

Much more frequently the relative superiority – that is, the skilful assemblage of superior forces at the decisive point – has its foundation in the right appreciation of those points, in the judicious direction which by that means has been given to the forces from the very first, and in the resolution required to sacrifice the unimportant to the advantage of the important – that is, to keep the forces concentrated in an overpowering mass. In this, Frederick the Great and Buonaparte are particularly characteristic.

We think we have now allotted to the superiority in numbers the importance which belongs to it; it is to be regarded as the fundamental idea, always to be aimed at before all and as far as possible.

But to regard it on this account as a necessary condition of victory would be a complete misconception of our exposition; in the conclusion to be drawn from it there lies nothing more than the value which should attach to numerical strength in the combat. If that strength is made as great as possible, then the maxim is satisfied; a review of the total relations must then decide whether or not the combat is to be avoided for want of sufficient force.[95]

CHAPTER IX

THE SURPRISE

FROM the subject of the foregoing chapter, the general endeavour to attain a relative superiority, there follows another endeavour which must consequently be just as general in its nature: this is the *surprise* of the enemy. It lies more or less at the foundation of all undertakings, for without it the preponderance at the decisive point is not properly conceivable.

The surprise is, therefore, not only the means to the attainment of numerical superiority; but it is also to be regarded as a substantive principle in itself, on account of its moral effect. When it is successful in a high degree, confusion and broken courage in the enemy's ranks are the consequences; and of the degree to which these multiply a success, there are examples enough, great and small. We are not now speaking of the particular surprise which belongs to the attack, but of the endeavour by measures generally, and especially by the distribution of forces, to surprise the enemy, which can be imagined just as well in the defensive, and which in the tactical defence particularly is a chief point.

We say, surprise lies at the foundation of all undertakings

without exception, only in very different degrees according to the nature of the undertaking and other circumstances.

This difference, indeed, originates in the properties or peculiarities of the Army and its Commander, in those even of the Government.

Secrecy and rapidity are the two factors in this product; and these suppose in the Government and the Commander-in-Chief great energy, and on the part of the Army a high sense of military duty. With effeminacy and loose principles it is in vain to calculate upon a surprise. But so general, indeed so indispensable, as is this endeavour, and true as it is that it is never wholly unproductive of effect, still it is not the less true that it seldom succeeds to a *remarkable* degree, and this follows from the nature of the idea itself. We should form an erroneous conception if we believed that by this means chiefly there is much to be attained in War. In idea it promises a great deal; in the execution it generally sticks fast by the friction of the whole machine.

In tactics the surprise is much more at home, for the very natural reason that all times and spaces are on a smaller scale. It will, therefore, in Strategy be the more feasible in proportion as the measures lie nearer to the province of tactics, and more difficult the higher up they lie towards the province of policy.

The preparations for a War usually occupy several months; the assembly of an Army at its principal positions requires generally the formation of depots and magazines, and long marches, the object of which can be guessed soon enough.

It therefore rarely happens that one State surprises another by a War, or by the direction which it gives the mass of its forces. In the seventeenth and eighteenth centuries, when War turned very much upon sieges, it was a frequent aim, and quite a peculiar and important chapter in the Art of War, to invest a strong place unexpectedly, but even that only rarely succeeded.[96]

On the other hand, with things which can be done in a day or two, a surprise is much more conceivable, and, therefore, also it is often not difficult thus to gain a march upon the enemy, and thereby a position, a point of country, a road, etc. But it is evident that what surprise gains in this way in easy execution, it loses in the efficacy, as the greater the efficacy the greater always the difficulty of execution. Whoever thinks that with such surprises on a small scale, he may connect great results – as, for example, the gain of a battle, the capture of an important magazine – believes in something which it is certainly very possible to imagine, but for which there is no warrant in history; for there are upon the whole very few instances where anything great has resulted from such surprises; from which we may justly conclude that inherent difficulties lie in the way of their success.

Certainly, whoever would consult history on such points must not depend on sundry battle steeds of historical critics, on their wise dicta and self-complacent terminology, but look at facts with his own eyes. There is, for instance, a certain day in the campaign in Silesia, 1761, which, in this respect, has attained a kind of notoriety. It is 22 July, on which Frederick the Great gained on Laudon the march to Nossen, near Neisse, by which, as is said, the junction of the Austrian and Russian armies in Upper Silesia became impossible, and, therefore, a period of four weeks was gained by the King. Whoever reads over this occurrence carefully in the principal histories,[97] and considers it impartially, will, in the march of 22 July, never find this importance; and generally in the whole of the fashionable logic on this subject, he will see nothing but contradictions; but in the proceedings of Laudon, in this renowned period of manoeuvres, much that is unaccountable. How could one, with a thirst for truth, and clear conviction, accept such historical evidence?

When we promise ourselves great effects in a campaign from the principle of surprising, we think upon great activity, rapid resolutions, and forced marches, as the means of producing them; but that these things, even when forthcoming in a very high degree, will not always produce the desired effect, we see in examples given by two Generals, who may be allowed to have had the greatest talent in the use of these means, Frederick the Great and Buonaparte. The first when he left Dresden so suddenly in July 1760, and falling upon Lascy, then turned against Dresden, gained nothing by the whole of that intermezzo, but rather placed his affairs in a condition notably worse, as the fortress Glatz fell in the meantime.

In 1813, Buonaparte turned suddenly from Dresden twice

against Blücher, to say nothing of his incursion into Bohemia from Upper Lusatia, and both times without in the least attaining his object. They were blows in the air which only cost him time and force, and might have placed him in a dangerous position in Dresden.

Therefore, even in this field, a surprise does not necessarily meet with great success through the mere activity, energy, and resolution of the Commander; it must be favoured by other circumstances. But we by no means deny that there can be success; we only connect with it a necessity of favourable circumstances, which, certainly do not occur very frequently, and which the Commander can seldom bring about himself.

Just those two Generals afford each a striking illustration of this. We take first Buonaparte in his famous enterprise against Blücher's Army in February 1814, when it was separated from the Grand Army, and descending the Marne. It would not be easy to find a two days' march to surprise the enemy productive of greater results than this; Blücher's Army, extended over a distance of three days' march, was beaten in detail, and suffered a loss nearly equal to that of defeat in a great battle. This was completely the effect of a surprise, for if Blücher had thought of such a near possibility of an attack from Buonaparte[98] he would have organized his march quite differently. To this mistake of Blücher's the result is to be attributed. Buonaparte did not know all these circumstances, and so there was a piece of good fortune that mixed itself up in his favour.

It is the same with the battle of Liegnitz, 1760. Frederick the Great gained this fine victory through altering during the night a position which he had just before taken up. Laudon was through this completely surprised, and lost 70 pieces of artillery and 10,000 men. Although Frederick the Great had at this time adopted the principle of moving backwards and forwards in order to make a battle impossible, or at least to disconcert the enemy's plans, still the alteration of position on the night of the 14–15 was not made exactly with that intention, but as the King himself says, because the position of the 14th did not please him. Here, therefore, also chance was hard at work; without this happy conjunction of the attack and the change of position in the night, and the difficult nature of the country, the result would not have been the same.

Also in the higher and highest province of Strategy there are some instances of surprises fruitful in results. We shall only cite the brilliant marches of the Great Elector against the Swedes from Franconia to Pomerania and from the Mark (Brandenburg) to the Pregel in 1757, and the celebrated passage of the Alps by Buonaparte, 1800. In the latter case an Army gave up its whole theatre of war by a capitulation, and in 1757 another Army was very near giving up its theatre of war and itself as well. Lastly, as an instance of a War wholly unexpected, we may bring forward the invasion of Silesia by Frederick the Great. Great and powerful are here the results everywhere, but such events are not common in history if we do not confuse with them cases in which a State, for want of activity and energy (Saxony 1756, and Russia, 1812), has not completed its preparations in time.

Now there still remains an observation which concerns the essence of the thing. A surprise can only be effected by that party which gives the law to the other; and he who is in the right gives the law. If we surprise the adversary by a wrong measure, then instead of reaping good results, we may have to bear a sound blow in return; in any case the adversary need not trouble himself much about our surprise, he has in our mistake the means of turning off the evil. As the offensive includes in itself much more positive action than the defensive, so the surprise is certainly more in its place with the assailant, but by no means invariably, as we shall hereafter see. Mutual surprises by the offensive and defensive may therefore meet, and then that one will have the advantage who has hit the nail on the head the best.

So should it be, but practical life does not keep to this line so exactly, and that for a very simple reason. The moral effects which attend a surprise often convert the worst case into a good one for the side they favour, and do not allow the other to make any regular determination. We have here in view more than anywhere else not only the chief Commander, but each single one, because a surprise has the effect in particular of greatly loosening unity, so that the individuality of each separate leader easily comes to light.

Much depends here on the general relation in which the two parties stand to each other. If the one side through a general moral superiority can intimidate and outdo the other, then he can make use of the surprise with more success, and even reap good fruit where properly he should come to ruin.

CHAPTER X

STRATAGEM

STRATAGEM implies a concealed intention, and therefore is opposed to straightforward dealing, in the same way as wit is the opposite of direct proof. It has therefore nothing in common with means of persuasion, of self-interest, of force, but a great deal to do with deceit, because that likewise conceals its object. It is itself a deceit as well when it is done, but still it differs from what is commonly called deceit, in this respect that there is no direct breach of word. The deceiver by stratagem leaves it to the person himself whom he is deceiving to commit the errors of understanding which at last, flowing into *one* result, suddenly change the nature of things in his eyes. We may therefore say, as wit is a sleight of hand with ideas and conceptions, so stratagem is a sleight of hand with actions.

At first sight it appears as if Strategy had not improperly derived its name from stratagem; and that, with all the real and apparent changes which the whole character of War has undergone since the time of the Greeks, this term still points to its real nature.

If we leave to tactics the actual delivery of the blow, the battle itself, and look upon Strategy as the art of using this means with skill, then besides the forces of the character, such as burning ambition which always presses like a spring, a strong will which hardly bends, etc., etc., there seems no subjective quality so suited to guide and inspire strategic activity as stratagem. The general tendency to surprise, treated of in the foregoing chapter, points to this conclusion, for there is a degree of stratagem, be it ever so small, which lies at the foundation of every attempt to surprise.

But however much we feel a desire to see the actors in War outdo each other in hidden activity, readiness, and stratagem, still we must admit that these qualities show themselves but little in history, and have rarely been able to work their way to the surface from amongst the mass of relations and circumstances.

The explanation of this is obvious, and it is almost identical with the subject matter of the preceding chapter.

Strategy knows no other activity than the regulating of combat with the measures which relate to it. It has no concern, like ordinary life, with transactions which consist merely of words – that is, in expressions, declarations, etc. But these, which are very inexpensive, are chiefly the means with which the wily one takes in those he practises upon.[99]

That which there is like it in War, plans and orders given merely as make-believers, false reports sent on purpose to the enemy – is usually of so little effect in the strategic field that it is only resorted to in particular cases which offer of themselves, therefore cannot be regarded as spontaneous action which emanates from the leader.

But such measures as carrying out the arrangements for a battle, so far as to impose upon the enemy, require a considerable expenditure of time and power; of course, the greater the impression to be made, the greater the expenditure in these respects. And as this is usually not given for the purpose, very few demonstrations, so-called, in Strategy, effect the object for which they are designed. In fact, it is dangerous to detach large forces for any length of time merely for a trick, because there is always the risk of its being done in vain, and then these forces are wanted at the decisive point.

The chief actor in War is always thoroughly sensible of this sober truth, and therefore he has no desire to play at tricks of agility. The bitter earnestness of necessity presses so fully into direct action that there is no room for that game. In a word, the pieces on the strategical chess-board want that mobility which is the element of stratagem and subtility.

The conclusion which we draw, is that a correct and penetrating eye is a more necessary and more useful quality for a

General than craftiness, although that also does no harm if it does not exist at the expense of necessary qualities of the heart, which is only too often the case.

But the weaker the forces become which are under the command of Strategy, so much the more they become adapted for stratagem, so that to the quite feeble and little, for whom no prudence, no sagacity is any longer sufficient at the point where all art seems to forsake him, stratagem offers itself as a last resource. The more helpless his situation, the more everything presses towards one single, desperate blow, the more readily stratagem comes to the aid of his boldness. Let loose from all further calculations, freed from all concern for the future, boldness and stratagem intensify each other, and thus collect at one point an infinitesimal glimmering of hope into a single ray, which may likewise serve to kindle a flame.

CHAPTER XI

ASSEMBLY OF FORCES IN SPACE

THE best Strategy is *always to be very strong*, first generally then at the decisive point. Therefore, apart from the energy which creates the Army, a work which is not always done by the General, there is no more imperative and no simpler law for Strategy than to *keep the forces concentrated.* No portion is to be separated from the main body unless called away by some urgent necessity. On this maxim we stand firm, and look upon it as a guide to be depended upon. What are the reasonable grounds on which a detachment of forces may be made we shall learn by degrees. Then we shall also see that this principle cannot have the same general effects in every War, but that these are different according to the means and end.

It seems incredible, and yet it has happened a hundred times, that troops have been divided and separated merely through a mysterious feeling of conventional manner, without any clear perception of the reason.

If the concentration of the whole force is acknowledged as the norm, and every division and separation as an exception which must be justified, then not only will that folly be completely avoided, but also many an erroneous ground for separating troops will be barred admission.

CHAPTER XII

ASSEMBLY OF FORCES IN TIME

We have here to deal with a conception which in real life diffuses many kinds of illusory light. A clear definition and development of the idea is therefore necessary, and we hope to be allowed a short analysis.

War is the shock of two opposing forces in collision with each other, from which it follows as a matter of course that the stronger not only destroys the other, but carries it forward with it in its movement. This fundamentally admits of no successive action of powers, but makes the simultaneous application of all forces intended for the shock appear as a primordial law of War.

So it is in reality, but only so far as the struggle resembles also in practice a mechanical shock, but when it consists in a lasting mutual action of destructive forces, then we can certainly imagine a successive action of forces. This is the case in tactics, principally because firearms form the basis of all tactics, but also for other reasons as well. If in a fire combat 1,000 men are opposed to 500, then the gross loss is calculated from the amount of the enemy's force and our own; 1,000 men fire twice as many shots as 500, but more shots will take effect on the 1,000 than on the 500 because it is assumed that they stand in closer order than the other. If we were to suppose the number of hits to be double, then the losses on each side would be equal. From the 500 there would be for example 200 disabled, and out of the body of 1,000 likewise the same; now if the 500 had kept another body of equal number quite out of fire, then both sides would have 800 effective men; but of these, on the one side there would be 500 men quite fresh, fully supplied with ammunition, and in their full vigour; on the other side only 800 all alike shaken in their order, in want of sufficient ammunition and weakened in physical force. The assumption that the 1,000 men merely on account of their greater number would lose twice as many as 500 would have lost in their place, is certainly not correct; therefore the greater loss which the side suffers that has placed the half of its force in reserve, must be regarded as a disadvantage in that original formation; further it must be admitted, that in the generality of cases the 1,000 men would have the advantage at the first commencement of being able to drive their opponent out of his position and force him to a retrograde movement; now, whether these two advantages are a counterpoise to the disadvantage of finding ourselves with 800 men to a certain extent disorganized by the combat, opposed to an enemy who is not materially weaker in numbers and who has 500 quite fresh troops, is one that cannot be decided by pursuing an analysis further, we must here rely upon experience, and there will scarcely be an officer experienced in War who will not in the generality of cases assign the advantage to that side which has the fresh troops.

In this way it becomes evident how the employment of too many forces in combat may be disadvantageous; for whatever advantages the superiority may give in the first moment, we may have to pay dearly for in the next.

But this danger only endures as long as the disorder, the state of confusion and weakness lasts, in a word, up to the crisis which every combat brings with it even for the conqueror. Within the duration of this relaxed state of exhaustion, the appearance of a proportionate number of fresh troops is decisive.

But when this disordering effect of victory stops, and therefore only the moral superiority remains which every victory gives, then it is no longer possible for fresh troops to restore the combat, they would only be carried along in the general movement; a beaten Army cannot be brought back to victory a day after by means of a strong reserve. Here we find ourselves at the source of a highly material difference between tactics and strategy.

The tactical results, the results within the four corners of the battle, and before its close, lie for the most part within the limits of that period of disorder and weakness. But the strategic result, that is to say, the result of the total combat, of the victories realized, let them be small or great, lies completely (beyond) outside of that period. It is only when the results of partial combats have bound themselves together into an independent whole, that the strategic result appears, but then, the state of crisis is over, the forces have resumed their original form, and are now only weakened to the extent of those actually destroyed (placed *hors de combat*).

The consequence of this difference is, that tactics can make a continued use of forces, Strategy only a simultaneous one.

If I cannot, in tactics, decide all by the first success, if I have to fear the next moment, it follows of itself that I employ only so much of my force for the success of the first moment as appears sufficient for that object, and keep the rest beyond the reach of fire or conflict of any kind, in order to be able to oppose fresh troops to fresh, or with such to overcome those that are exhausted. But it is not so in Strategy. Partly, as we have just shown, it has not so much reason to fear a reaction after a success realized, because with that success the crisis stops; partly all the forces strategically employed are not necessarily weakened. Only so much of them as have been tactically in conflict with the enemy's force, that is, engaged in partial combat, are weakened by it; consequently, only so much as was unavoidably necessary, but by no means all which was strategically in conflict with the enemy, unless tactics has expended them unnecessarily. Corps which, on account of the general superiority in numbers, have either been little or not at all engaged, whose presence alone has assisted in the result, are after the decision the same as they were before, and for new enterprises as efficient as if they had been entirely inactive. How greatly such corps which thus constitute our excess may contribute to the total success is evident in itself; indeed, it is not difficult to see how they may even diminish considerably the loss of the forces engaged in tactical conflict on our side.

If, therefore, in Strategy the loss does not increase with the number of the troops employed, but is often diminished by it, and if, as a natural consequence, the decision in our favour is, by that means, the more certain, then it follows naturally that in Strategy we can never employ too many forces, and consequently also that they must be applied simultaneously to the immediate purpose.

But we must vindicate this proposition upon another ground. We have hitherto only spoken of the combat itself; it is the real activity in War, but men, time, and space, which appear as the elements of this activity, must, at the same time, be kept in view, and the results of their influence brought into consideration also.

Fatigue, exertion, and privation constitute in War a special principle of destruction, not essentially belonging to contest, but more or less inseparably bound up with it, and certainly one which especially belongs to Strategy. They no doubt exist in tactics as well, and perhaps there in the highest degree; but as the duration of the tactical acts is shorter, therefore the small effects of exertion and privation on them can come but little into consideration. But in Strategy on the other hand, where time and space are on a larger scale, their influence is not only always very considerable, but often quite decisive. It is not at all uncommon for a victorious Army to lose many more by sickness than on the field of battle.

If, therefore, we look at this sphere of destruction in Strategy in the same manner as we have considered that of fire and close combat in tactics, then we may well imagine that everything which comes within its vortex will, at the end of the campaign or of any other strategic period, be reduced to a state of weakness, which makes the arrival of a fresh force decisive. We might therefore conclude that there is a motive in the one case as well as the other to strive for the first success with as few forces as possible, in order to keep up this fresh force for the last.

In order to estimate exactly this conclusion, which, in many cases in practice, will have a great appearance of truth, we must direct our attention to the separate ideas which it contains. In the first place, we must not confuse the notion of reinforcement with that of fresh unused troops. There are few campaigns at the end of which an increase of force is not earnestly desired by the conqueror as well as the conquered, and indeed should appear decisive; but that is not the point here, for that increase of force could not be necessary if the force had been so much larger at the first. But it would be contrary to all experience to suppose that an Army coming fresh into the field is to be esteemed higher in point of moral value than an Army already in the field, just as a tactical reserve is more to be esteemed than a body of troops which has been already severely handled in the fight. Just as much as an unfortunate campaign lowers the courage and moral powers of an Army, a successful one raises these elements in their value. In the generality of cases, therefore, these influences are compensated, and then there remains over and above as clear gain the habituation to War. We should besides look more here to successful than to unsuccessful campaigns, because when the greater probability of the latter may be seen beforehand, without doubt forces are wanted, and, therefore, the reserving a portion for future use is out of the question.

The point being settled, then the question is, Do the losses which a force sustains through fatigues and privations increase in proportion to the size of the force, as is the case in a combat? And to that we answer 'No.'

The fatigues of War result in a great measure from the dangers with which every moment of the act of War is more or less impregnated. To encounter these dangers at all points, to proceed onwards with security in the execution of one's plans, gives employment to a multitude of agencies which make up the tactical and strategic service of the Army. This service is more difficult the weaker an Army is, and easier as its numerical superiority over that of the enemy increases. Who can doubt this? A campaign against a much weaker enemy will therefore cost smaller efforts than against one just as strong or stronger.

So much for the fatigues. It is somewhat different with the privations; they consist chiefly of two things, the want of food, and the want of shelter for the troops, either in quarters or in suitable camps. Both these wants will no doubt be greater in proportion as the number of men on one spot is greater. But does not the superiority in force afford also the best means of spreading out and finding more room, and therefore more means of subsistence and shelter?

If Buonaparte, in his invasion of Russia in 1812, concentrated his Army in great masses upon one single road in a manner never heard of before, and thus caused privations equally unparalleled, we must ascribe it to his maxim *that it is impossible to be too strong at the decisive point*. Whether in this instance he did not strain the principle too far is a question which would be out of place here; but it is certain that, if he had made a point of avoiding the distress which was by that means brought about, he had only to advance on a greater breadth of front. Room was not wanted for the purpose in Russia, and in very few cases can it be wanted. Therefore, from this no ground can be deduced to prove that the simultaneous employment of very superior forces must produce greater weakening. But now, supposing that in spite of the general relief afforded by setting apart a portion of the Army, wind and weather and the toils of War had produced a diminution even on the part which as a spare force had been reserved for later use, still we must take a comprehensive general view of the whole, and therefore ask, Will this diminution of force suffice to counterbalance the gain in forces, which we, through our superiority in numbers, may be able to make in more ways than one?

But there still remains a most important point to be noticed. In a partial combat, the force required to obtain a great result can be approximately estimated without much difficulty, and, consequently, we can form an idea of what is superfluous. In Strategy this may be said to be impossible, because the strategic result has no such well-defined object and no such circumscribed limits as the tactical. Thus what can be looked upon in tactics as an excess of power, must be regarded in Strategy as a means to give expansion to success, if opportunity offers for it; with the magnitude of the success the gain in force increases at the same time, and in this way the superiority of numbers may soon reach a point which the most careful economy of forces could never have attained.

By means of his enormous numerical superiority, Buonaparte was enabled to reach Moscow in 1812, and to take that central capital. Had he by means of this superiority succeeded in completely defeating the Russian Army, he would, in all probability, have concluded a peace in Moscow which in any other way was much less attainable. This example is used to explain the idea, not to prove it, which would require a circumstantial demonstration, for which this is not the place.

All these reflections bear merely upon the idea of a successive employment of forces, and not upon the conception of a reserve properly so called, which they, no doubt, come in contact with throughout, but which, as we shall see in the following chapter, is connected with some other considerations.

What we desire to establish here is, that if in tactics the military force through the mere duration of actual employment suffers a diminution of power, if time, therefore, appears as a factor in the result, this is not the case in Strategy in a material degree. The destructive effects which are also produced upon the forces in Strategy by time, are partly diminished through their mass, partly made good in other ways, and, therefore, in Strategy it cannot be an object to make time an ally on its own account by bringing troops successively into action.

We say on 'its own account', for the influence which time, on account of other circumstances which it brings about but which are different from itself can have, indeed must necessarily have, for one of the two parties, is quite another thing, is anything but indifferent or unimportant, and will be the subject of consideration hereafter.

The rule which we have been seeking to set forth is, therefore, that all forces which are available and destined for a strategic object should be *simultaneously* applied to it; and this application will be so much the more complete the more everything is compressed into one act and into one movement.

But still there is in Strategy a renewal of effort and a persistent action which, as a chief means towards the ultimate success, is more particularly not to be overlooked, it is the *continual development of new forces*. This is also the subject of another chapter, and we only refer to it here in order to prevent the reader from having something in view of which we have not been speaking.

We now turn to a subject very closely connected with our present considerations, which must be settled before full light can be thrown on the whole, we mean the *strategic reserve*.

CHAPTER XIII

STRATEGIC RESERVE

A RESERVE has two objects which are very distinct from each other, namely, first, the prolongation and renewal of the combat, and secondly, for use in case of unforeseen events. The first object implies the utility of a successive application of forces, and on that account cannot occur in Strategy. Cases in which a corps is sent to succour a point which is supposed to be about to fall are plainly to be placed in the category of the second object, as the resistance which has to be offered here could not have been sufficiently foreseen. But a corps which is destined expressly to prolong the combat, and with that object in view is placed in rear, would be only a corps placed out of reach of fire, but under the command and at the disposition of the General Commanding in the action, and accordingly would be a tactical and not a strategic reserve.

But the necessity for a force ready for unforeseen events may also take place in Strategy, and consequently there may also be a strategic reserve, but only where unforeseen events are imaginable. In tactics, where the enemy's measures are generally first ascertained by direct sight, and where they may be concealed by every wood, every fold of undulating ground, we must naturally always be alive, more or less, to the possibility of unforeseen events, in order to strengthen, subsequently, those points which appear too weak, and, in fact, to modify generally the disposition of our troops, so as to make it correspond better to that of the enemy.

Such cases must also happen in Strategy, because the strategic act is directly linked to the tactical. In Strategy also many a measure is first adopted in consequence of what is actually seen, or in consequence of uncertain reports arriving from day to day, or even from hour to hour, and lastly, from the actual results of the combats; it is, therefore, an essential condition of strategic command that, according to the degree of uncertainty, forces must be kept in reserve against future contingencies.

In the defensive generally, but particularly in the defence of certain obstacles of ground, like rivers, hills, etc., such contingencies, as is well known, happen constantly.

But this uncertainty diminishes in proportion as the strategic activity has less of the tactical character, and ceases almost altogether in those regions where it borders on politics.

The direction in which the enemy leads his columns to the combat can be perceived by actual sight only; where he intends to pass a river is learnt from a few preparations which are made shortly before; the line by which he proposes to invade our country is usually announced by all the newspapers before a pistol shot has been fired. The greater the nature of the measure the less it will take the enemy by surprise. Time and space are so considerable, the circumstances out of which the action proceeds so public and little susceptible of alteration, that the coming event is either made known in good time, or can be discovered with reasonable certainty.

On the other hand the use of a reserve in this province of Strategy, even if one were available, will always be less efficacious the more the measure has a tendency towards being one of a general nature.

We have seen that the decision of a partial combat is nothing in itself, but that all partial combats only find their complete solution in the decision of the total combat.

But even this decision of the total combat has only a relative meaning of many different gradations, according as the force over which the victory has been gained forms a more or less great and important part of the whole. The lost battle of a corps may be repaired by the victory of the Army. Even the lost battle of an Army may not only be counterbalanced by the gain of a more important one, but converted into a fortunate event (the two days of Kulm, 29 and 30 August 1813[100]). No one can doubt this; but it is just as clear that the weight of each victory (the successful issue of each total combat) is so much the more substantial the more important the part conquered, and that therefore the possibility of repairing the loss by subsequent events diminishes in the same proportion. In another place we shall have to examine this more in detail; it suffices for the present to have drawn attention to the indubitable existence of this progression.

If we now add lastly to these two considerations the third, which is, that if the persistent use of forces in tactics always shifts the great result to the end of the whole act, the law of the simultaneous use of the forces in Strategy, on the contrary, lets the principal result (which need not be the final one) take place almost always at the commencement of the great (or whole) act, then in these three results we have grounds sufficient to find strategic reserves always more superfluous, always more useless, always more dangerous, the more general their destination.

The point where the idea of a strategic reserve begins to become inconsistent is not difficult to determine: it lies in the *supreme decision*. Employment must be given to all the forces within the space of the supreme decision, and every reserve (active force available) which is only intended for use after that decision is opposed to common sense.

If, therefore, tactics has in its reserves the means of not only meeting unforeseen dispositions on the part of the enemy, but also of repairing that which never can be foreseen, the result of the combat, should that be unfortunate; Strategy on the other hand must, at least as far as relates to the capital result, renounce the use of these means. As a rule, it can only repair the losses sustained at one point by advantages gained at another, in a few cases by moving troops from one point to another; the idea of preparing for such reverses by placing forces in reserve beforehand, can never be entertained in Strategy.

We have pointed out as an absurdity the idea of a strategic reserve which is not to cooperate in the capital result, and as it is so beyond a doubt, we should not have been led into such an analysis as we have made in these two chapters, were it not that, in the disguise of other ideas, it looks like something better, and frequently makes its appearance. One person sees in it the acme of strategic sagacity and foresight; another rejects it, and with it the idea of any reserve, consequently even of a tactical one. This confusion of ideas is transferred to real life, and if we would see a memorable instance of it we have only to call to mind that Prussia in 1806 left a reserve of 20,000 men cantoned in the Mark, under Prince Eugene of Wurtemberg, which could not possibly reach the Saale in time to be of any use, and that another force of 25,000 men belonging to this power remained in East and South Prussia, destined only to be put on a war-footing afterwards as a reserve.

After these examples we cannot be accused of having been fighting with windmills.

CHAPTER XIV

ECONOMY OF FORCES

THE road of reason, as we have said, seldom allows itself to be reduced to a mathematical line by principles and opinions. There remains always a certain margin. But it is the same in all the practical arts of life. For the lines of beauty there are no abscissae and ordinates; circles and ellipses are not described by means of their algebraical formulae. The actor in War therefore soon finds he must trust himself to the delicate tact of judgement which, founded on natural quickness of perception, and educated by reflection, almost unconsciously seizes upon the right; he soon finds that at one time he must simplify the law (by reducing it) to some prominent characteristic points which form his rules; that at another the adopted method must become the staff on which he leans.

As one of these simplified characteristic points as a mental appliance, we look upon the principle of watching continually over the cooperation of all forces, or in other words, of keeping constantly in view that no part of them should ever be idle. Whoever has forces where the enemy does not give them sufficient employment, whoever has part of his forces on the march – that is, allows them to lie dead – while the enemy's are fighting, he is a bad manager of his forces. In this sense there is a waste of forces, which is even worse than their employment to no purpose. If there must be action, then the first point is that all parts act, because the most purposeless activity still keeps employed and destroys a portion of the enemy's force, whilst troops completely inactive are for the moment quite neutralized. Unmistakably this idea is bound up with the principles contained in the last three chapters, it is the same truth, but seen from a somewhat more comprehensive point of view and condensed into a single conception.

CHAPTER XV

GEOMETRICAL ELEMENT

THE length to which the geometrical element or form in the disposition of military force in War can become a predominant principle, we see in the art of fortification, where geometry looks after the great and the little. Also in tactics it plays a great part. It is the basis of elementary tactics, or of the theory of moving troops; but in field fortification, as well as in the theory of positions, and of their attack, its angles and lines rule like law-givers who have to decide the contest. Many things here were at one time misapplied, and others were mere fribbles; still, however, in the tactics of the present day, in which in every combat the aim is to surround the enemy, the geometrical element has attained anew a great importance in a very simple, but constantly recurring application. Nevertheless, in tactics, where all is more movable, where the moral forces, individual traits, and chance are more influential than in a war of sieges, the geometrical element can never attain to the same degree of supremacy as in the latter. But less still is its influence in Strategy; certainly here, also, form in the disposition of troops, the shape of countries and states is of great importance; but the geometrical element is not decisive, as in fortification, and not nearly so important as in tactics. The manner in which this influence exhibits itself, can only be shown by degrees at those places where it makes its appearance, and deserves notice. Here we wish more to direct attention to the difference which there is between tactics and Strategy in relation to it.

In tactics time and space quickly dwindle to their absolute minimum. If a body of troops is attacked in flank and rear by the enemy, it soon gets to a point where retreat no longer remains; such a position is very close to an absolute impossibility of continuing the fight; it must therefore extricate itself from it, or avoid getting into it. This gives to all combinations aiming at this from the first commencement a great efficiency, which chiefly consists in the disquietude which it causes the enemy as to consequences. This is why the geometrical disposition of the forces is such an important factor in the tactical product.

In Strategy this is only faintly reflected, on account of the greater space and time. We do not fire from one theatre of war upon another;[101] and often weeks and months must pass before a strategic movement designed to surround the enemy can be executed. Further, the distances are so great that the probability of hitting the right point at last, even with the best arrangements, is but small.

In Strategy therefore the scope for such combinations, that is for those resting on the geometrical element, is much smaller, and for the same reason the effect of an advantage once actually gained at any point is much greater. Such advantage has time to bring all its effects to maturity before it is disturbed, or quite neutralized therein, by any counteracting apprehensions. We therefore do not hesitate to regard as an established truth, that in Strategy more depends on the number and the magnitude of the victorious combats, than on the form of the great lines by which they are connected.

A view just the reverse has been a favourite theme of modern theory, because a greater importance was supposed to be thus given to Strategy, and, as the higher functions of the mind were seen in Strategy, it was thought by that means to ennoble War, and, as it was said – through a new substitution of ideas – to make it more scientific.[102] We hold it to be one of the principal uses of a complete theory openly to expose such vagaries, and as the geometrical element is the fundamental idea from which theory usually proceeds, therefore we have expressly brought out this point in strong relief.

CHAPTER XVI

ON THE SUSPENSION OF THE ACT IN WAR

IF one considers War as an act of mutual destruction, we must of necessity imagine both parties as making some progress; but at the same time, as regards the existing moment, we must almost as necessarily suppose the one party in a state of expectation, and only the other actually advancing, for circumstances can never be actually the same on both sides, or continue so. In time a change must ensue, from which it follows that the present moment is more favourable to one side than the other. Now if we suppose that both commanders have a full knowledge of this circumstance, then the one has a motive for action, which at the same time is a motive for the other to wait; therefore, according to this it cannot be for the interest of both at the same time to advance, nor can waiting be for the interest of both at the same time. This opposition of interest as regards the object is not deduced here from the principle of general polarity, and therefore is not in opposition to the argument in the fifth chapter of the second book; it depends on the fact that here in reality the same thing is at once an incentive or motive to both commanders, namely the probability of improving or impairing their position by future action.

But even if we suppose the possibility of a perfect equality of circumstances in this respect, or if we take into account that through imperfect knowledge of their mutual position such an equality may appear to the two Commanders to subsist, still the difference of political objects does away with this possibility of suspension. One of the parties must of necessity be assumed politically to be the aggressor, because no War could take place from defensive intentions on both sides. But the aggressor has the positive object, the defender merely a negative one. To the first then belongs the positive action, for it is only by that means that he can attain the positive object; therefore, in cases where both parties are in precisely similar circumstances, the aggressor is called upon to act by virtue of his positive object.

Therefore, from this point of view, a suspension in the act of Warfare, strictly speaking, is in contradiction with the nature of the thing; because two Armies, being two incompatible elements, should destroy one another unremittingly, just as fire and water can never put themselves in equilibrium, but act and react upon one another, until one quite disappears. What would be said of two wrestlers who remained clasped round each other for hours without making a movement. Action in War, therefore, like that of a clock which is wound up, should go on running down in regular motion. But wild as is the nature of War it still wears the chains of human weakness, and the contradiction we see here, viz. that man seeks and creates dangers which he fears at the same time will astonish no one.

If we cast a glance at military history in general, we find so much the opposite of an incessant advance towards the aim, that *standing still* and *doing nothing* is quite plainly the *normal condition* of an Army in the midst of War, *acting*, the *exception*. This must almost raise a doubt as to the correctness of our conception. But if military history leads to this conclusion when viewed in the mass the latest series of campaigns redeems our position. The War of the French Revolution shows too plainly its reality, and only proves too clearly its necessity. In these operations, and especially in the campaigns of Buonaparte, the conduct of War attained to that unlimited degree of energy which we have represented as the natural law of the element. This degree is therefore possible, and if it is possible then it is necessary.

How could any one in fact justify in the eyes of reason the expenditure of forces in War, if acting was not the object? The baker only heats his oven if he has bread to put into it; the horse is only yoked to the carriage if we mean to drive; why then make the enormous effort of a War if we look for nothing else by it but like efforts on the part of the enemy?

So much in justification of the general principle; now as to its modifications, as far as they lie in the nature of the thing and are independent of special cases.

There are three causes to be noticed here, which appear as

innate counterpoises and prevent the over-rapid or uncontrollable movement of the wheel-work.

The first, which produces a constant tendency to delay, and is thereby a retarding principle, is the natural timidity and want of resolution in the human mind, a kind of inertia in the moral world, but which is produced not by attractive, but by repellent forces, that is to say, by dread of danger and responsibility.

In the burning element of War, ordinary natures appear to become heavier; the impulsion given must therefore be stronger and more frequently repeated if the motion is to be a continuous one. The mere idea of the object for which arms have been taken up is seldom sufficient to overcome this resistant force, and if a warlike enterprising spirit is not at the head, who feels himself in War in his natural element, as much as a fish in the ocean, or if there is not the pressure from above of some great responsibility, then standing still will be the order of the day, and progress will be the exception.

The second cause is the imperfection of human perception and judgement, which is greater in War than anywhere, because a person hardly knows exactly his own position from one moment to another, and can only conjecture on slight grounds that of the enemy, which is purposely concealed; this often gives rise to the case of both parties looking upon one and the same object as advantageous for them, while in reality the interest of one must preponderate; thus then each may think he acts wisely by waiting another moment, as we have already said in the fifth chapter of the second book.

The third cause which catches hold, like a ratchet wheel in machinery, from time to time producing a complete standstill, is the greater strength of the defensive form. A may feel too weak to attack B, from which it does not follow that B is strong enough for an attack on A. The addition of strength, which the defensive gives is not merely lost by assuming the offensive, but also passes to the enemy just as, figuratively expressed, the difference of $a + b$ and $a - b$ is equal to $2b$. Therefore it may so happen that both parties, at one and the same time, not only feel themselves too weak to attack, but also are so in reality.

Thus even in the midst of the act of War itself, anxious

sagacity and the apprehension of too great danger find vantage ground, by means of which they can exert their power, and tame the elementary impetuosity of War.

However, at the same time these causes without an exaggeration of their effect, would hardly explain the long states of inactivity which took place in military operations, in former times, in Wars undertaken about interests of no great importance, and in which inactivity consumed nine-tenths of the time that the troops remained under arms. This feature in these Wars, is to be traced principally to the influence which the demands of the one party, and the condition, and feeling of the other, exercised over the conduct of the operations, as has been already observed in the chapter on the essence and object of War.

These things may obtain such a preponderating influence as to make of War a half-and-half affair. A War is often nothing more than an armed neutrality, or a menacing attitude to support negotiations or an attempt to gain some small advantage by small exertions, and then to wait the tide of circumstances, or a disagreeable treaty obligation, which is fulfilled in the most niggardly way possible.

In all these cases in which the impulse given by interest is slight, and the principle of hostility feeble, in which there is no desire to do much, and also not much to dread from the enemy; in short, where no powerful motives press and drive, cabinets will not risk much in the game; hence this tame mode of carrying on War, in which the hostile spirit of real War is laid in irons.

The more War becomes in this manner devitalized so much the more its theory becomes destitute of the necessary firm pivots and buttresses for its reasoning; the necessary is constantly diminishing, the accidental constantly increasing.

Nevertheless in this kind of Warfare, there is also a certain shrewdness, indeed, its action is perhaps more diversified, and more extensive than in the other. Hazard played with rouleaux of gold seems changed into a game of commerce with groschen. And on this field, where the conduct of War spins out the time with a number of small flourishes, with skirmishes at outposts, half in earnest half in jest, with long dispositions which end in nothing, with positions and marches, which afterwards are designated as skilful only because their infinitesimally small causes are lost, and common sense can make nothing of them, here on this very field many theorists find the real Art of War at home: in these feints, parades, half and quarter thrusts of former Wars, they find the aim of all theory, the supremacy of mind over matter, and modern Wars appear to them mere savage fisticuffs, from which nothing is to be learnt, and which must be regarded as mere retrograde steps towards barbarism. This opinion is as frivolous as the objects to which it relates. Where great forces and great passions are wanting, it is certainly easier for a practised dexterity to show its game; but is then the command of great forces, not in itself a higher exercise of the intelligent faculties? Is then that kind of conventional sword-exercise not comprised in and belonging to the other mode of conducting War? Does it not bear the same relation to it as the motions upon a ship to the motion of the ship itself? Truly it can take place only under the tacit condition that the adversary does no better. And can we tell, how long he may choose to respect those conditions? Has not then the French Revolution fallen upon us in the midst of the fancied security of our old system of War, and driven us from Chalons to Moscow? And did not Frederick the Great in like manner surprise the Austrians reposing in their ancient habits of War, and make their monarchy tremble? Woe to the cabinet which, with a shilly-shally policy, and a routine-ridden military system, meets with an adversary who, like the rude element, knows no other law than that of his intrinsic force. Every deficiency in energy and exertion is then a weight in the scales in favour of the enemy; it is not so easy then to change from the fencing posture into that of an athlete, and a slight blow is often sufficient to knock down the whole.

The result of all the causes now adduced is, that the hostile action of a campaign does not progress by a continuous, but by an intermittent movement, and that, therefore, between the separate bloody acts, there is a period of watching, during which both parties fall into the defensive, and also that usually a higher object causes the principle of aggression to predominate on one side, and thus leaves it in general in an advancing position, by which then its proceedings become modified in some degree.

CHAPTER XVII

ON THE CHARACTER OF MODERN WAR

THE attention which must be paid to the character of War as it is now made, has a great influence upon all plans, especially on strategic ones.

Since all methods formerly usual were upset by Buonaparte's luck and boldness, and first-rate Powers almost wiped out at a blow; since the Spaniards by their stubborn resistance have shown what the general arming of a nation and insurgent measures on a great scale can effect, in spite of weakness and porousness of individual parts; since Russia, by the campaign of 1812 has taught us, first, that an Empire of great dimensions is not to be conquered (which might have been easily known before), secondly, that the probability of final success does not in all cases diminish in the same measure as battles, capitals, and provinces are lost (which was formerly an incontrovertible principle with all diplomatists, and therefore made them always ready to enter at once into some bad temporary peace), but that a nation is often strongest in the heart of its country, if the enemy's offensive power has exhausted itself, and with what enormous force the defensive then springs over to the offensive; further, since Prussia (1813) has shown that sudden efforts may add to an Army sixfold by means of the militia, and that this militia is just as fit for service abroad as in its own country; since all these events have shown what an enormous factor the heart and sentiments of a Nation may be in the product of its political and military strength, in fine, since governments have found out all these additional aids, it is not to be expected that they will let them lie idle in future Wars, whether it be that danger threatens their own existence, or that restless ambition drives them on.

That a War which is waged with the whole weight of the national power on each side must be organized differently in principle to those where everything is calculated according to the relations of standing Armies to each other, it is easy to perceive. Standing Armies once resembled fleets, the land force the sea force in their relations to the remainder of the State, and from that the Art of War on shore had in it something of naval tactics, which it has now quite lost.

CHAPTER XVIII

TENSION AND REST

The dynamic law of war

WE have seen in the sixteenth chapter of this book (page 290), how, in most campaigns, much more time used to be spent in standing still and inaction than in activity. Now, although, as observed in the preceding chapter we see quite a different character in the present form of War, still it is certain that real action will always be interrupted more or less by long pauses; and this leads to the necessity of our examining more closely the nature of these two phases of War.

If there is a suspension of action in War, that is, if neither party wills something positive, there is rest, and consequently equilibrium, but certainly an equilibrium in the largest signification, in which not only the moral and physical war-forces, but all relations and interests, come into calculation. As soon as ever one of the two parties proposes to himself a new positive object, and commences active steps towards it, even if it is only by preparations, and as soon as the adversary opposes this, there is a tension of powers; this lasts until the decision takes place – that is, until one party either gives up his object or the other has conceded it to him.

This decision – the foundation of which lies always in the combat-combinations which are made on each side – is followed by a movement in one or other direction.

When this movement has exhausted itself, either in the difficulties which had to be mastered, in overcoming its own internal friction, or through new resistant forces prepared by the acts of the enemy, then either a state of rest takes place or a new tension with a decision, and then a new movement, in most cases in the opposite direction.

This speculative distinction between equilibrium, tension, and motion is more essential for practical action than may at first sight appear.

In a state of rest and of equilibrium a varied kind of activity may prevail on one side that results from opportunity, and does not aim at a great alteration. Such an activity may contain important combats – even pitched battles – but yet it is still of quite a different nature, and on that account generally different in its effects.

If a state of tension exists, the effects of the decision are always greater partly because a greater force of will and a greater pressure of circumstances manifest themselves therein; partly because everything has been prepared and arranged for a great movement. The decision in such cases resembles the effect of a mine well closed and tamped, whilst an event in itself perhaps just as great, in a state of rest, is more or less like a mass of powder puffed away in the open air.

At the same time, as a matter of course, the state of tension must be imagined in different degrees of intensity, and it may therefore approach gradually by many steps towards the state of rest, so that at the last there is a very slight difference between them.

Now the real use which we derive from these reflections is the conclusion that every measure which is taken during a state of tension is more important and more prolific in results than the same measure could be in a state of equilibrium, and that this importance increases immensely in the highest degrees of tension.

The cannonade of Valmy, 20 September 1792, decided more than the battle of Hochkirch, 14 October 1758.

In a tract of country which the enemy abandons to us because he cannot defend it, we can settle ourselves differently from what we should do if the retreat of the enemy was only made with the view to a decision under more favourable circumstances. Again, a strategic attack in course of execution, a faulty position, a single false march, may be decisive in its consequence;

whilst in a state of equilibrium such errors must be of a very glaring kind, even to excite the activity of the enemy in a general way.

Most bygone Wars, as we have already said, consisted, so far as regards the greater part of the time, in this state of equilibrium or at least in such short tensions with long intervals between them, and weak in their effects, that the events to which they gave rise were seldom great successes, often they were theatrical exhibitions, got up in honour of a royal birthday (Hochkirch), often a mere satisfying of the honour of the arms (Kunersdorf), or the personal vanity of the commander (Freiberg).

That a Commander should thoroughly understand these states, that he should have the tact to act in the spirit of them, we hold to be a great requisite, and we have had experience in the campaign of 1806 how far it is sometimes wanting. In that tremendous tension, when everything pressed on towards a supreme decision, and that alone with all its consequences should have occupied the whole soul of the Commander, measures were proposed and even partly carried out (such as the reconnaissance towards Franconia), which at the most might have given a kind of gentle play of oscillation within a state of equilibrium. Over these blundering schemes and views, absorbing the activity of the Army, the really necessary means, which could alone save, were lost sight of.

But this speculative distinction which we have made is also necessary for our further progress in the construction of our theory, because all that we have to say on the relation of attack and defence, and on the completion of this double-sided act, concerns the state of the crisis in which the forces are placed during the tension and motion, and because all the activity which can take place during the condition of equilibrium can only be regarded and treated as a corollary; for that crisis is the real War and this state of equilibrium only its reflection.

BOOK FOUR

THE COMBAT

CHAPTER I

INTRODUCTORY

HAVING in the foregoing book examined the subjects which may be regarded as the efficient elements of War, we shall now turn our attention to the combat as the real activity in Warfare, which, by its physical and moral effects, embraces sometimes more simply, sometimes in a more complex manner, the object of the whole campaign. In this activity and in its effects these elements must, therefore, reappear.

The formation of the combat is tactical in its nature; we only glance at it here in a general way in order to get acquainted with it in its aspect as a whole. In practice the minor or more immediate objects give every combat a characteristic form; these minor objects we shall not discuss until hereafter. But these peculiarities are in comparison to the general characteristics of a combat mostly only insignificant, so that most combats are very like one another, and, therefore, in order to avoid repeating that which is general at every stage, we are compelled to look into it here, before taking up the subject of its more special application.

In the first place, therefore, we shall give in the next chapter, in a few words, the characteristics of the modern battle in its tactical course, because that lies at the foundation of our conceptions of what the battle really is.

CHAPTER II

CHARACTER OF THE MODERN BATTLE

ACCORDING to the notion we have formed of tactics and strategy, it follows, as a matter of course, that if the nature of the former is changed, that change must have an influence on the latter. If tactical facts in one case are entirely different from those in another, then the strategic must be so also, if they are to continue consistent and reasonable. It is therefore important to characterize a general action in its modern form before we advance with the study of its employment in strategy.

What do we do now usually in a great battle? We place ourselves quietly in great masses arranged contiguous to and behind one another. We deploy relatively only a small portion of the whole, and let it wring itself out in a fire-combat which lasts for several hours, only interrupted now and again, and removed hither and thither by separate small shocks from charges with the bayonet and cavalry attacks. When this line has gradually exhausted part of its warlike ardour in this manner and there remains nothing more than the cinders, it is withdrawn[103] and replaced by another.

In this manner the battle on a modified principle burns slowly away like wet powder, and if the veil of night commands it to stop, because neither party can any longer see, and neither chooses to run the risk of blind chance, then an account is taken by each side respectively of the masses remaining, which can be called still effective, that is, which have not yet quite collapsed like extinct volcanoes; account is taken of the ground gained or lost, and of how stands the security of the rear; these results with the special impressions as to bravery and cowardice, ability and stupidity, which are thought to have been observed in ourselves and in the enemy are collected into one single total impression, out of which there springs the resolution to quit the field or to renew the combat on the morrow.

This description, which is not intended as a finished picture of a modern battle, but only to give its general tone, suits for the offensive and defensive, and the special traits which are given, by the object proposed, the country, etc., etc., may be introduced into it, without materially altering the conception.

But modern battles are not so by accident; they are so because the parties find themselves nearly on a level as regards military organization and the knowledge of the Art of War, and because the warlike element inflamed by great national interests has broken through artificial limits and now flows in its natural channel. Under these two conditions, battles will always preserve this character.

This general idea of the modern battle will be useful to us in the sequel in more places than one, if we want to estimate the value of the particular coefficients of strength, country, etc., etc. It is only for general, great, and decisive combats, and such as come near to them that this description stands good; inferior ones have changed their character also in the same direction but less than great ones. The proof of this belongs to tactics; we shall, however, have an opportunity hereafter of making this subject plainer by giving a few particulars.

CHAPTER III

THE COMBAT IN GENERAL

THE Combat is the real warlike activity, everything else is only its auxiliary; let us therefore take an attentive look at its nature.

Combat means fighting, and in this the destruction or conquest of the enemy is the object, and the enemy, in the particular combat, is the armed force which stands opposed to us.

This is the simple idea; we shall return to it, but before we can do that we must insert a series of others.

If we suppose the State and its military force as a unit, then the most natural idea is to imagine the War also as one great combat, and in the simple relations of savage nations it is also not much otherwise. But our Wars are made up of a number of great and small simultaneous or consecutive combats, and this severance of the activity into so many separate actions is owing to the great multiplicity of the relations out of which War arises with us.

In point of fact, the ultimate object of our Wars, the political one, is not always quite a simple one; and even were it so, still the action is bound up with such a number of conditions and considerations to be taken into account, that the object can no longer be attained by one single great act but only through a number of greater or smaller acts which are bound up into a whole; each of these separate acts is therefore a part of a whole, and has consequently a special object by which it is bound to this whole.

We have already said that every strategic act can be referred to the idea of a combat, because it is an employment of the military force, and at the root of that there always lies the idea of fighting. We may therefore reduce every military activity in the province of Strategy to the unit of single combats, and occupy ourselves with the object of these only; we shall get acquainted with these special objects by degrees as we come to speak of the causes which produce them; here we content ourselves with saying that every combat, great or small, has its own peculiar object in subordination to the main object. If this is the case then, the destruction and conquest of the enemy is only to be regarded as the means of gaining this object; as it unquestionably is.

But this result is true only in its form, and important only on account of the connexion which the ideas have between themselves, and we have only sought it out to get rid of it at once.

What is overcoming the enemy? Invariably the destruction of his military force, whether it be by death, or wounds, or any means; whether it be completely or only to such a degree that he can no longer continue the contest; therefore as long as we set aside all special objects of combats, we may look upon the complete or partial destruction of the enemy as the only object of all combats.

Now we maintain that in the majority of cases, and especially in great battles, the special object by which the battle is individualized and bound up with the great whole is only a weak modification of that general object, or an ancillary object bound up with it, important enough to individualize the battle, but always insignificant in comparison with that general object; so that if that ancillary object alone should be obtained, only an unimportant part of the purpose of the combat is fulfilled. If this assertion is correct, then we see that the idea, according to which the destruction of the enemy's force is only the means, and something else always the object, can only be true in form, but, that it would lead to false conclusions if we did not recollect that this destruction of the enemy's force is comprised in that object, and that this object is only a weak modification of it.

Forgetfulness of this led to completely false views before the Wars of the last period, and created tendencies as well as fragments of systems, in which theory thought it raised itself so much the more above handicraft, the less it supposed itself to stand in need of the use of the real instrument, that is the destruction of the enemy's force.

Certainly such a system could not have arisen unless supported by other false suppositions, and unless in place of the destruction of the enemy, other things had been substituted to which an efficacy was ascribed which did not rightly belong to them. We shall attack these falsehoods whenever occasion requires, but we could not treat of the combat without claiming for it the real importance and value which belong to it, and giving warning against the errors to which merely formal truth might lead.

But now how shall we manage to show that in most cases, and in those of most importance, the destruction of the enemy's Army is the chief thing? How shall we manage to combat that extremely subtle idea, which supposes it possible, through the use of a special artificial form, to effect by a small direct destruction of the enemy's forces a much greater destruction indirectly, or by means of small but extremely well-directed blows to produce such paralysation of the enemy's forces, such a command over the enemy's will, that this mode of proceeding is to be viewed as a great shortening of the road? Undoubtedly a victory at one point may be of more value than at another. Undoubtedly there is a scientific arrangement of battles amongst themselves, even in Strategy, which is in fact nothing but the Art of thus arranging them. To deny that is not our intention, but we assert that the direct destruction of the enemy's forces is everywhere predominant; we contend here for the overruling importance of this destructive principle and nothing else.

We must, however, call to mind that we are now engaged with Strategy, not with tactics, therefore we do not speak of the means which the former may have of destroying at a small expense a large body of the enemy's forces, but that under direct destruction we understand the tactical results, and that, therefore, our assertion is that only great tactical results can lead to great strategical ones, or, as we have already once before more distinctly expressed it, *the tactical successes* are of paramount importance in the conduct of War.

The proof of this assertion seems to us simple enough, it lies in the time which every complicated (artificial) combination requires. The question whether a simple attack, or one more carefully prepared, i.e. more artificial, will produce greater effects, may undoubtedly be decided in favour of the latter as long as the enemy is assumed to remain quite passive. But every carefully combined attack requires time for its preparation, and if a counterstroke by the enemy intervenes, our whole design may be upset. Now if the enemy should decide upon some simple attack, which can be executed in a shorter time, then he gains the initiative, and destroys the effect of the great plan. Therefore, together with the expediency of a complicated attack we must consider all the dangers which we run during its preparation, and should only adopt it if there is no reason to fear that the enemy will disconcert our scheme. Whenever this is the case we must ourselves choose the simpler, i.e. quicker way, and lower our views in this sense as far as the character, the relations of the enemy, and other circumstances may render necessary. If we quit the weak impressions of abstract ideas and descend to the region of practical life, then it is evident that a bold, courageous, resolute enemy will not let us have time for wide-reaching skilful combinations, and it is just against such a one we should require skill the most. By this it appears to us that the advantage of simple and direct results over those that are complicated is conclusively shown.

Our opinion is not on that account that the simple blow is the best, but that we must not lift the arm too far for the time given to strike, and that this condition will always lead more to direct conflict the more warlike our opponent is. Therefore, far from making it our aim to gain upon the enemy by complicated plans, we must rather seek to be beforehand with him by greater simplicity in our designs.

If we seek for the lowest foundation-stones of these converse propositions we find that in the one it is ability, in the other, courage. Now, there is something very attractive in the notion that a moderate degree of courage joined to great ability will produce greater effects than moderate ability with great courage. But unless we suppose these elements in a disproportionate relation, not logical, we have no right to assign to ability this advantage over courage in a field which is called danger, and which must be regarded as the true domain of courage.

After this abstract view we shall only add that experience, very far from leading to a different conclusion, is rather the sole cause which has impelled us in this direction, and given rise to such reflections.

Whoever reads history with a mind free from prejudice cannot fail to arrive at a conviction that of all military virtues, energy in the conduct of operations has always contributed the most to the glory and success of arms.

How we make good our principle of regarding the destruction of the enemy's force as the principal object, not only in the War as a whole but also in each separate combat, and how that principle suits all the forms and conditions necessarily demanded by the relations out of which War springs, the sequel will show. For the present all that we desire is to uphold its general importance, and with this result we return again to the combat.

CHAPTER IV

THE COMBAT IN GENERAL

(CONTINUATION)

IN the last chapter we showed the destruction of the enemy as the true object of the combat, and we have sought to prove by a special consideration of the point, that this is true in the majority of cases, and in respect to the most important battles, because the destruction of the enemy's Army is always the preponderating object in War. The other objects which may be mixed up with this destruction of the enemy's force, and may have more or less influence, we shall describe generally in the next chapter, and become better acquainted with by degrees afterwards; here we divest the combat of them entirely, and look upon the destruction of the enemy as the complete and sufficient object of any combat.

What are we now to understand by destruction of the enemy's Army? A diminution of it relatively greater than that on our own side. If we have a great superiority in numbers over the enemy, then naturally the same absolute amount of loss on both sides is for us a smaller one than for him, and consequently may be regarded in itself as an advantage. As we are here considering the combat as divested of all (other) objects, we must also exclude from our consideration the case in which the combat is used only indirectly for a greater destruction of the enemy's force; consequently also, only that direct gain which has been made in the mutual process of destruction, is to be regarded as the object, for this is an absolute gain, which runs through the whole campaign, and at the end of it will always appear as pure profit. But every other kind of victory over our opponent will either have its motive in other objects, which we have completely excluded here, or it will only yield a temporary relative advantage. An example will make this plain.

If by a skilful disposition we have reduced our opponent to such a dilemma, that he cannot continue the combat without danger, and after some resistance he retires, then we may say, that we have conquered him at that point; but if in this victory we have expended just as many forces as the enemy, then in closing the account of the campaign, there is no gain remaining from this victory, if such a result can be called a victory. Therefore overcoming the enemy, that is, placing him in such a position that he must give up the fight, counts for nothing in itself, and for that reason cannot come under the definition of object. There remains, therefore, as we have said, nothing over except the direct gain which we have made in the process of destruction; but to this belong not only the losses which have taken place in the course of the combat, but also those which, after the withdrawal of the conquered part, take place as direct consequences of the same.

Now is known by experience, that the losses in physical forces in the course of a battle seldom present a great difference between victor and vanquished respectively, often none at all, sometimes even one bearing an inverse relation to the result, and that the most decisive losses on the side of the vanquished only commence with the retreat, that is, those which the conqueror does not share with him. The weak remains of battalions already in disorder are cut down by cavalry, exhausted men strew the ground, disabled guns and broken caissons are abandoned, others in the bad state of the roads cannot be removed quickly enough, and are captured by the enemy's troops, during the night numbers lose their way, and fall defenceless into the enemy's hands, and thus the victory mostly gains bodily substance after it is already decided. Here would be a paradox, if it did not solve itself in the following manner.

The loss in physical force is not the only one which the two sides suffer in the course of the combat; the moral forces also are shaken, broken, and go to ruin. It is not only the loss in men, horses and guns, but in order, courage, confidence, cohesion and plan, which come into consideration when it is a question whether the fight can be still continued or not. It is principally the moral forces which decide here, and in all cases in which the conqueror has lost as heavily as the conquered, it is these alone.

The comparative relation of the physical losses is difficult to estimate in a battle, but not so the relation of the moral ones. Two things principally make it known. The one is the loss of the ground on which the fight has taken place, the other the superiority of the enemy's reserve. The more our reserves have diminished as compared with those of the enemy, the more force we have used to maintain the equilibrium; in this at once, an evident proof of the moral superiority of the enemy is given which seldom fails to stir up in the soul of the Commander a certain bitterness of feeling, and a sort of contempt for his own troops. But the principal thing is, that men who have been engaged for a long continuance of time are more or less like burnt-out cinders; their ammunition is consumed; they have melted away to a certain extent; physical and moral energies are exhausted, perhaps their courage is broken as well. Such a force, irrespective of the diminution in its number, if viewed as an organic whole, is very different from what it was before the combat; and thus it is that the loss of moral force may be measured by the reserves that have been used as if it were on a foot-rule.

Lost ground and want of fresh reserves, are, therefore, usually the principal causes which determine a retreat; but at the same time we by no means exclude or desire to throw in the shade other reasons, which may lie in the interdependence of parts of the Army, in the general plan, etc.

Every combat is therefore the bloody and destructive measuring of the strength of forces, physical and moral; whoever at the close has the greatest amount of both left is the conqueror.

In the combat the loss of moral force is the chief cause of the decision; after that is given, this loss continues to increase until it reaches its culminating-point at the close of the whole act. This then is the opportunity the victor should seize to reap his harvest by the utmost possible restrictions of his enemy's forces, the real object of engaging in the combat. On the beaten side, the loss of all order and control often makes the prolongation of resistance by individual units, by the further punishment they are certain to suffer, more injurious than useful to the whole. The spirit of the mass is broken; the original excitement about losing or winning, through which danger was forgotten, is spent, and to the majority danger now appears no longer an appeal to their courage, but rather the endurance of a cruel punishment. Thus the instrument in the first moment of the enemy's victory is weakened and blunted, and therefore no longer fit to repay danger by danger.

This period, however, passes; the moral forces of the conquered will recover by degrees, order will be restored, courage will revive, and in the majority of cases there remains only a small part of the superiority obtained, often none at all. In some cases, even, although rarely, the spirit of revenge and intensified hostility may bring about an opposite result. On the other hand, whatever is gained in killed, wounded, prisoners, and guns captured can never disappear from the account.

The losses in a battle consist more in killed and wounded; those after the battle, more in artillery taken and prisoners. The first the conqueror shares with the conquered, more or less, but the second not; and for that reason they usually only take place on one side of the conflict, at least, they are considerably in excess on one side.

Artillery and prisoners are therefore at all times regarded as the true trophies of victory, as well as its measure, because through these things its extent is declared beyond a doubt. Even the degree of moral superiority may be better judged of by them than by any other relation, especially if the number of killed and wounded is compared therewith; and here arises a new power increasing the moral effects.

We have said that the moral forces, beaten to the ground in battle and in the immediately succeeding movements, recover themselves gradually, and often bear no traces of injury; this is the case with small divisions of the whole, less frequently with large divisions; it may, however, also be the case with the main Army, but seldom or never in the State or Government to which the Army belongs. These estimate the situation more impartially and from a more elevated point of view, and recognize in the number of trophies taken by the enemy, and their relation to the number of killed and wounded, only too easily and well, the measure of their own weakness and inefficiency.

In point of fact, the lost balance of moral power must not be treated lightly because it has no absolute value, and because it does not of necessity appear in all cases in the amount of the results at the final close; it may become of such excessive weight as to bring down everything with an irresistible force. On that account it may often become a great aim of the operations of which we shall speak elsewhere. Here we have still to examine some of its fundamental relations.

The moral effect of a victory increases, not merely in proportion to the extent of the forces engaged, but in a progressive ratio – that is to say, not only in extent, but also in its intensity. In a beaten detachment order is easily restored. As a single frozen limb is easily revived by the rest of the body, so the courage of a defeated detachment is easily raised again by the courage of the rest of the Army as soon as it rejoins it. If, therefore, the effects of a small victory are not completely done away with, still they are partly lost to the enemy. This is not the case if the Army itself sustains a great defeat; then one with the other fall together. A great fire attains quite a different heat from several small ones.

Another relation which determines the moral value of a victory is the numerical relation of the forces which have been in conflict with each other. To beat many with few is not only a double success, but shows also a greater, especially a more general superiority, which the conquered must always be fearful of encountering again. At the same time this influence is in reality hardly observable in such a case. In the moment of real action, the notions of the actual strength of the enemy are generally so uncertain, the estimate of our own commonly so incorrect, that the party superior in numbers either does not admit the disproportion, or is very far from admitting the full truth, owing to which, he evades almost entirely the moral disadvantages which would spring from it. It is only hereafter in history that the truth, long suppressed through ignorance, vanity, or a wise discretion, makes its appearance, and then it certainly casts a lustre on the Army and its Leader, but it can then do nothing more by its moral influence for events long past.

If prisoners and captured guns are those things by which the victory principally gains substance, its true crystallizations, then the plan of the battle should have those things specially in view; the destruction of the enemy by death and wounds appears here merely as a means to an end.

How far this may influence the dispositions in the battle is not an affair of Strategy, but the decision to fight the battle is in intimate connexion with it, as is shown by the direction given to our forces, and their general grouping, whether we threaten the enemy's flank or rear, or he threatens ours. On this point, the number of prisoners and captured guns depends very much, and it is a point which, in many cases, tactics alone cannot satisfy, particularly if the strategic relations are too much in opposition to it.

The risk of having to fight on two sides, and the still more dangerous position of having no line of retreat left open, paralyse the movements and the power of resistance; further, in case of defeat, they increase the loss, often raising it to its extreme point, that is, to destruction. Therefore, the rear being endangered makes defeat more probable, and, at the same time, more decisive.

From this arises, in the whole conduct of the War, and especially in great and small combats, a perfect instinct to secure our own line of retreat and to seize that of the enemy; this follows from the conception of victory, which, as we have seen, is something beyond mere slaughter.

In this effort we see, therefore, the first immediate purpose in the combat, and one which is quite universal. No combat is imaginable in which this effort, either in its double or single form, does not go hand in hand with the plain and simple stroke of force. Even the smallest troop will not throw itself upon its enemy without thinking of its line of retreat, and, in most cases, it will have an eye upon that of the enemy also.

We should have to digress to show how often this instinct is prevented from going the direct road, how often it must yield to the difficulties arising from more important considerations: we shall, therefore, rest contented with affirming it to be a general natural law of the combat.

It is, therefore, active; presses everywhere with its natural weight, and so becomes the pivot on which almost all tactical and strategic manoeuvres turn.

If we now take a look at the conception of victory as a whole, we find in it three elements:

1. The greater loss of the enemy in physical power.
2. In moral power.
3. His open avowal of this by the relinquishment of his intentions.

The returns made up on each side of losses in killed and wounded, are never exact, seldom truthful, and in most cases, full of intentional misrepresentations. Even the statement of the number of trophies is seldom to be quite depended on; consequently, when it is not considerable it may also cast a doubt even on the reality of the victory. On the loss in moral forces there is no realiable measure, except in the trophies: therefore, in many cases, the giving up the contest is the only real evidence of the victory. It is, therefore, to be regarded as a confession of inferiority – as the lowering of the flag, by which, in this particular instance, right and superiority are conceded to the enemy, and this degree of humiliation and disgrace, which, however, must be distinguished from all the other moral consequences of the loss of equilibrium, is an essential part of the victory. It is this part alone which acts upon the public opinion outside the Army, upon the people and the Government in both belligerent States, and upon all others in any way concerned.

But renouncement of the general object is not quite identical with quitting the field of battle, even when the battle has been very obstinate and long kept up; no one says of advanced posts, when they retire after an obstinate combat, that they have given up their object; even in combats aimed at the destruction of the enemy's Army, the retreat from the battlefield is not always to be regarded as a relinquishment of this aim, as for instance, in retreats planned beforehand, in which the ground is disputed foot by foot; all this belongs to that part of our subject where we shall speak of the separate object of the combat; here we only wish to draw attention to the fact that in most cases the giving up of the object is very difficult to distinguish from the retirement from the battlefield, and that the impression produced by the latter, both in and out of the Army, is not to be treated lightly.

For Generals and Armies whose reputation is not made, this is in itself one of the difficulties in many operations, justified by circumstances when a succession of combats, each ending in retreat, may appear as a succession of defeats, without being so in reality, and when that appearance may exercise a very depressing influence. It is impossible for the retreating General by making known his real intentions to prevent the moral effect spreading to the public and his troops, for to do that with effect he must disclose his plans completely, which of course would run counter to his principal interests to too great a degree.

In order to draw attention to the special importance of this conception of victory we shall only refer to the battle of Soor, the trophies from which were not important (a few thousand prisoners and twenty guns), and where Frederick proclaimed his victory by remaining for five days after on the field of battle, although his retreat into Silesia had been previously determined on, and was a measure natural to his whole situation. According to his own account, he thought he would hasten a peace by the moral effect of his victory. Now although a couple of other successes were likewise required, namely, the battle of Katholisch Hennersdorf, in Lusatia, and the battle of Kesseldorf, before this peace took place, still we cannot say that the moral effect of the battle of Soor was *nil*.

If it is chiefly the moral force which is shaken by defeat, and if the number of trophies reaped by the enemy mounts up to an unusual height, then the lost combat becomes a rout, but this is not the necessary consequence of every victory. A rout only sets in when the moral force of the defeated is very severely shaken; then there often ensues a complete incapability of further resistance, and the whole action consists of giving way, that is of flight.

Jena and Belle Alliance were routs, but not so Borodino.

Although without pedantry we can here give no single line of separation, because the difference between the things is one of degrees, yet still the retention of the conception is essential as a central point to give clearness to our theoretical ideas and it is a want in our terminology that for a victory over the enemy tantamount to a rout, and a conquest of the enemy only tantamount to a simple victory, there is only one and the same word to use.

CHAPTER V

ON THE SIGNIFICATION OF THE COMBAT

HAVING in the preceding chapter examined the combat in its absolute form, as the miniature picture of the whole War, we now turn to the relations which it bears to the other parts of the great whole. First we inquire what is more precisely the signification of a combat.

As War is nothing else but a mutual process of destruction, then the most natural answer in conception, and perhaps also in reality, appears to be that all the powers of each party unite in one great volume and all results in one great shock of these masses. There is certainly much truth in this idea, and it seems to be very advisable that we should adhere to it and should on that account look upon small combats at first only as necessary loss, like the shavings from a carpenter's plane. Still, however, the thing cannot be settled so easily.

That a multiplication of combats should arise from a fractioning of forces is a matter of course, and the more immediate objects of separate combats will therefore come before us in the subject of a fractioning of forces; but these objects, and together with them, the whole mass of combats may in a general way be brought under certain classes, and the knowledge of these classes will contribute to make our observations more intelligible.

Destruction of the enemy's military forces is in reality the object of all combats; but other objects may be joined thereto, and these other objects may be at the same time predominant; we must therefore draw a distinction between those in which the destruction of the enemy's forces is the principal object, and those in which it is more the means. The destruction of the enemy's force, the possession of a place or the possession of some object may be the general motive for a combat, and it may be either one of these alone or several together, in which case however usually one is the principal motive. Now the two principal forms of War, the offensive and defensive, of which we shall shortly speak, do not modify the first of these motives but they certainly do modify the other two, and therefore if we arrange them in a scheme they would appear thus:

Offensive.	*Defensive.*
1. Destruction of enemy's force.	1. Destruction of enemy's force.
2. Conquest of a place.	2. Defence of a place.
3. Conquest of some object.	3. Defence of some object.

These motives, however, do not seem to embrace completely the whole of the subject, if we recollect that there are reconnaissances and demonstrations, in which plainly none of these three points is the object of the combat. In reality we must, therefore, on this account be allowed a fourth class. Strictly speaking, in reconnaissances in which we wish the enemy to show himself, in alarms by which we wish to wear him out, in demonstrations by which we wish to prevent his leaving some point or to draw him off to another, the objects are all such as can only be attained indirectly and *under the pretext of one of the three objects specified in the table*, usually of the second; for the enemy whose aim is to reconnoitre must draw up his force as if he really intended to attack and defeat us, or drive us off, etc. etc., But this pretended object is not the real one, and our present question is only as to the latter; therefore, we must to the above three objects of the offensive further add a fourth, which is to lead the enemy to make a false conclusion. That offensive means only are conceivable in connexion with this object, lies in the nature of the thing.

On the other hand we must observe that the defence of a place may be of two kinds, either absolute, if as a general question the point is not to be given up, or relative if it is only required for a certain time. The latter happens perpetually in the combats of advanced posts and rear guards.

That the nature of these different intentions of a combat must have an essential influence on the dispositions which are its preliminaries, is a thing clear in itself. We act differently if our object is merely to drive an enemy's post out of its place from what we should if our object was to beat him completely;

differently, if we mean to defend a place to the last extremity from what we should do if our design is only to detain the enemy for a certain time. In the first case we trouble ourselves little about the line of retreat, in the latter it is the principal point, etc.

But these reflections belong properly to tactics, and are only introduced here by way of example for the sake of greater clearness. What Strategy has to say on the different objects of the combat will appear in the chapters which touch upon these objects. Here we have only a few general observations to make, first, that the importance of the object decreases nearly in the order as they stand above, therefore, that the first of these objects must always predominate in the great battle; lastly, that the two last in a defensive battle are in reality such as yield no fruit, they are, that is to say, purely negative, and can, therefore, only be serviceable, indirectly, by facilitating something else which is positive. *It is, therefore, a bad sign of the strategic situation if battles of this kind become too frequent.*

CHAPTER VI

DURATION OF THE COMBAT

If we consider the combat no longer in itself but in relation to the other forces of war, then its duration acquires a special importance.

This duration is to be regarded to a certain extent as a second subordinate success. For the conqueror the combat can never be finished too quickly, for the vanquished it can never last too long. A speedy victory indicates a higher power of victory, a tardy decision is, on the side of the defeated, some compensation for the loss.

This is in general true, but it acquires a practical importance in its application to those combats, the object of which is a relative defence.

Here the whole success often lies in the mere duration. This is the reason why we have included it amongst the strategic elements.

The duration of a combat is necessarily bound up with its essential relations. These relations are, absolute magnitude of force, relation of force and (of the different) arms mutually, and nature of the country. Twenty thousand men do not wear themselves out upon one another as quickly as two thousand: we cannot resist an enemy double or three times our strength as long as one of the same strength; a cavalry combat is decided sooner than an infantry combat; and a combat between infantry only, quicker than if there is artillery as well; in hills and forests we cannot advance as quickly as on a level country; all this is clear enough.

From this it follows, therefore, that strength, relation of the three arms, and position, must be considered if the combat is to fulfil an object by its duration; but to set up this rule was of less importance to us in our present considerations than to connect with it at once the chief results which experience gives us on the subject.

Even the resistance of an ordinary Division of 8,000 to 10,000 men of all arms even opposed to an enemy considerably superior in numbers, will last several hours, if the advantages of country are not too preponderating, and if the enemy is only a little, or not at all, superior in numbers, the combat will last half a day. A Corps of three or four Divisions will prolong it to double the time; an Army of 80,000 or 100,000 to three or four times. Therefore the masses may be left to themselves for that length of time, and no separate combat takes place if within that time other forces can be brought up, whose cooperation mingles then at once into one stream with the results of the combat which has taken place.[104]

These calculations are the result of experience; but it is important to us at the same time to characterize more particularly the moment of the decision, and consequently the termination.

CHAPTER VII

DECISION OF THE COMBAT

No battle is decided in a single moment, although in every battle there arise moments of crisis, on which the result depends. The loss of a battle is, therefore, a gradual falling of the scale. But there is in every combat a point of time when it may be regarded as decided, in such a way that the renewal of the fight would be a new battle, not a continuation of the old one. To have a clear notion on this point of time, is very important, in order to be able to decide whether, with the prompt assistance of reinforcements, the combat can again be resumed with advantage.

Often in combats which are beyond restoration new forces are sacrificed in vain; often through neglect the decision has not been seized when it might easily have been secured. Here are two examples, which could not be more to the point:

When the Prince of Hohenlohe, in 1806, at Jena, with 35,000 men opposed to from 60,000 to 70,000, under Buonaparte, had accepted battle, and lost it – but lost it in such a way that the 35,000 might be regarded as dissolved – General Rüchel undertook to renew the fight with about 12,000; the consequence was that in a moment his force was scattered in like manner.

On the other hand, on the same day at Auerstadt, the Prussians maintained a combat with 25,000, against Davoust, who had 28,000, until midday, without success, it is true, but still without the force being reduced to a state of dissolution without even greater loss than the enemy, who was very deficient in cavalry; but they neglected to use the reserve of 18,000, under General Kalkreuth, to restore the battle which, under these circumstances, it would have been impossible to lose.

Each combat is a whole in which the partial combats combine themselves into one total result. In this total result lies the decision of the combat. This success need not be exactly a victory such as we have denoted in the sixth chapter, for often the preparations for that have not been made, often there is no opportunity if the enemy gives way too soon, and in most cases the decision, even when the resistance has been obstinate, takes place before such a degree of success is attained as would completely satisfy the idea of a victory.

We therefore ask, Which is commonly the moment of the decision, that is to say, that moment when a fresh, effective, of course not disproportionate, force, can no longer turn a disadvantageous battle?

If we pass over false attacks, which in accordance with their nature are properly without decision, then

1. If the possession of a movable object was the object of the combat, the loss of the same is always the decision.
2. If the possession of ground was the object of the combat, then the decision generally lies in its loss. Still not always, only if this ground is of peculiar strength, ground which is easy to pass over, however important it may be in other respects, can be re-taken without much danger.
3. But in all other cases, when these two circumstances have not already decided the combat, therefore, particularly in case the destruction of the enemy's force is the principal object, the decision is reacted at that moment when the conqueror ceases to feel himself in a state of disintegration, that is, of unserviceableness to a certain extent, when therefore, there is no further advantage in using the successive efforts spoken of in the twelfth chapter of the third book. On this ground we have given the strategic unity of the battle its place here.

A battle, therefore, in which the assailant has not lost his condition of order and perfect efficiency at all, or, at least, only in a small part of his force, whilst the opposing forces are, more or less, disorganized throughout, is also not to be retrieved; and just as little if the enemy has recovered his efficiency.

The smaller, therefore, that part of a force is which has really been engaged, the greater that portion which as reserve has contributed to the result only by its presence, so much the less will any new force of the enemy wrest again the victory from our hands, and that Commander who carries out to the furthest with his Army the principle of conducting the combat with the greatest economy of forces, and making the most of the moral effect of strong reserves, goes the surest way to victory. We must allow that the French, in modern times, especially when led by Buonaparte, have shown a thorough mastery in this.

Further, the moment when the crisis-stage of the combat ceases with the conqueror, and his original state of order is restored, takes place sooner the smaller the unit he controls. A picket of cavalry pursuing an enemy at full gallop will in a few minutes resume its proper order, and the crisis ceases: a whole regiment of cavalry requires a longer time; it lasts still longer with infantry, if extended in single lines of skirmishers, and longer again with Divisions of all arms, when it happens by chance that one part has taken one direction and another part another direction, and the combat has therefore caused a loss of the order of formation, which usually becomes still worse from no part knowing exactly where the other is. Thus, therefore, the point of time when the conqueror has collected the instruments he has been using, and which are mixed up and partly out of order, the moment when he has in some measure rearranged them and put them in their proper places, and thus brought the battle-workshop into a little order, this moment, we say, is always later, the greater the total force.

Again, this moment comes later if night overtakes the conqueror in the crisis, and, lastly, it comes later still if the country is broken and thickly wooded. But with regard to these two points, we must observe that night is also a great means of protection, and it is only seldom that circumstances favour the expectation of a successful result from a night attack, as on 10 March 1814, at Laon, where York against Marmont gives us an example completely in place here. In the same way a wooded and broken country will afford protection against a reaction to those who are engaged in the long crisis of victory. Both, therefore, the night as well as the wooded and broken country are obstacles which make the renewal of the same battle more difficult instead of facilitating it.

Hitherto, we have considered assistance arriving for the losing side as a mere increase of force, therefore, as a reinforcement coming up directly from the rear, which is the most usual case. But the case is quite different if these fresh forces come upon the enemy in flank or rear.

On the effect of flank or rear attacks so far as they belong to Strategy, we shall speak in another place: such a one as we have here in view, intended for the restoration of the combat, belongs chiefly to tactics, and is only mentioned because we are here speaking of tactical results, our ideas, therefore, must trench upon the province of tactics.

By directing a force against the enemy's flank and rear its efficacy may be much intensified; but this is so far from being a necessary result always that the efficacy may, on the other hand, be just as much weakened. The circumstances under which the combat has taken place decide upon this part of the plan as well as upon every other, without our being able to enter thereupon here. But, at the same time, there are in it two things of importance for our subject: first, *flank and rear attacks have, as a rule, a more favourable effect on the consequences of the decision than upon the decision itself.* Now as concerns the retrieving a battle, the first thing to be arrived at above all is a favourable decision and not magnitude of success. In this view one would therefore think that a force which comes to re-establish our combat is of less assistance if it falls upon the enemy in flank and rear, therefore separated from us, than if it joins itself to us directly; certainly, cases are not wanting where it is so, but we must say that the majority are on the other side, and they are so on account of the second point which is here important to us.

This second point *is the moral effect of the surprise, which, as a rule, a reinforcement coming up to re-establish a combat has generally in its favour.* Now the effect of a surprise is always heightened if it takes place in the flank or rear, and an enemy completely engaged in the crisis of victory in his extended and scattered order, is less in a state to counteract it. Who does not feel that an attack in flank or rear, which at the commencement of the battle, when the forces are concentrated and prepared for such an event would be of little importance, gains quite another weight in the last moment of the combat.

We must, therefore, at once admit that in most cases a reinforcement coming up on the flank or rear of the enemy will be more efficacious, will be like the same weight at the end of a longer lever, and therefore that under these circumstances, we may undertake to restore the battle with the same force which employed in a direct attack would be quite insufficient. Here results almost defy calculation, because the moral forces gain completely the ascendancy. This is therefore the right field for boldness and daring.

The eye must, therefore, be directed on all these objects, all these moments of cooperating forces must be taken into consideration, when we have to decide in doubtful cases whether or not it is still possible to restore a combat which has taken an unfavourable turn.

If the combat is to be regarded as not yet ended, then the new contest which is opened by the arrival of assistance fuses into the former; therefore they flow together into one common result, and the first disadvantage vanishes completely out of the calculation. But this is not the case if the combat was already decided; then there are two results separate from each other. Now if the assistance which arrives is only of a relative strength, that is, if it is not in itself alone a match for the enemy, then a favourable result is hardly to be expected from this second combat: but if it is so strong that it can undertake the second combat without regard to the first, then it may be able by a favourable issue to compensate or even overbalance the first combat, but never to make it disappear altogether from the account.

At the battle of Kunersdorf, Frederick the Great at the first onset carried the left of the Russian position, and took seventy pieces of artillery; at the end of the battle both were lost again, and the whole result of the first combat was wiped out of the account. Had it been possible to stop at the first success, and to put off the second part of the battle to the coming day, then, even if the King had lost it, the advantages of the first would always have been a set off to the second.

But when a battle proceeding disadvantageously is arrested and turned before its conclusion, its minus result on our side not only disappears from the account, but also becomes the foundation of a greater victory. If, for instance, we picture to ourselves exactly the tactical course of the battle, we may easily see that until it is finally concluded all successes in partial combats are only decisions in suspense, which by the capital decision may not only be destroyed, but changed into the opposite. The more our forces have suffered, the more the enemy will have expended on his side; the greater, therefore, will be the crisis for the enemy, and the more the superiority of our fresh troops will tell. If now the total result turns in our favour, if we wrest from the enemy the field of battle and recover all the trophies again, then all the forces which he has sacrificed in obtaining them become sheer gain for us, and our former defeat becomes a stepping-stone to a greater triumph. The most brilliant feats which with victory the enemy would have so highly prized that the loss of forces which they cost would have been disregarded, leave nothing now behind but regret at the sacrifice entailed. Such is the alteration which the magic of victory and the curse of defeat produces in the specific weight of the same elements.

Therefore, even if we are decidedly superior in strength, and are able to repay the enemy his victory by a greater still, it is always better to forestall the conclusion of a disadvantageous combat, if it is of proportionate importance, so as to turn its course rather than to deliver a second battle.

Field-Marshal Daun attempted in the year 1760 to come to the assistance of General Laudon at Leignitz, whilst the battle lasted; but when he failed, he did not attack the King next day, although he did not want for means to do so.

For these reasons serious combats of advance guards which precede a battle are to be looked upon only as necessary evils, and when not necessary they are to be avoided.[105]

We have still another conclusion to examine.

If on a regular pitched battle, the decision has gone against one, this does not constitute a motive for determining on a new one. The determination for this new one must proceed from other relations. This conclusion, however, is opposed by a moral force, which we must take into account: it is the feeling of rage and revenge. From the oldest Field-Marshal to the youngest drummer-boy this feeling is general, and, therefore, troops are never in better spirits for fighting than when they have to wipe out a stain. This is, however, only on the supposition that the beaten portion is not too great in proportion to the whole, because otherwise the above feeling is lost in that of powerlessness.

There is therefore a very natural tendency to use this moral force to repair the disaster on the spot, and on that account chiefly to seek another battle if other circumstances permit. It then lies in the nature of the case that this second battle must be an offensive one.

In the catalogue of battles of second-rate importance there are many examples to be found of such retaliatory battles; but great battles have generally too many other determining causes to be brought on by this weaker motive.

Such a feeling must undoubtedly have led the noble Blücher with his third Corps to the field of battle on 14 February 1814, when the other two had been beaten three days before at Montmirail. Had he known that he would have come upon Buonaparte in person, then, naturally, preponderating reasons would have determined him to put off his revenge to another day: but he hoped to revenge himself on Marmont, and instead of gaining the reward of his desire for honourable satisfaction, he suffered the penalty of his erroneous calculation.

On the duration of the combat and the moment of its decision depend the distances from each other at which those masses should be placed which are intended to fight *in conjunction with* each other. This disposition would be a tactical arrangement in so far as it relates to one and the same battle; it can, however, only be regarded as such, provided the position of the troops is so compact that two separate combats cannot be imagined, and consequently that the space which the whole occupies can be regarded strategically as a mere point. But in War, cases frequently occur where even those forces intended to fight *in unison* must be so far separated from each other that while their union for one common combat certainly remains the principal object, still the occurrence of separate combats remains possible. Such a disposition is therefore strategic.

Dispositions of this kind are: marches in separate masses and columns, the formation of advance guards, and flanking columns, also the grouping of reserves intended to serve as supports for more than one strategic point; the concentration of several Corps from widely extended cantonments, etc., etc. We can see that the necessity for these arrangements may constantly arise, and may consider them something like the small change in the strategic economy, whilst the capital battles, and all that rank with them are the gold and silver pieces.

CHAPTER VIII

MUTUAL UNDERSTANDING AS TO A BATTLE

No battle can take place unless by mutual consent; and in this idea, which constitutes the whole basis of a duel, is the root of a certain phraseology used by historical writers, which leads to many indefinite and false conceptions.

According to the view of the writers to whom we refer, it has frequently happened that one Commander has offered battle to the other, and the latter has not accepted it.

But the battle is a very modified duel, and its foundation is not merely in the mutual wish to fight, that is in consent, but in the objects which are bound up with the battle: these belong always to a greater whole, and that so much the more, as even the whole war considered as a 'combat-unit' has political objects and conditions which belong to a higher standpoint. The mere desire to conquer each other therefore falls into quite a subordinate relation, or rather it ceases completely to be anything of itself, and only becomes the nerve which conveys the impulse of action from the higher will.

Amongst the ancients, and then again during the early period of standing Armies, the expression that we had offered battle to the enemy in vain, had more sense in it than it has now. By the ancients everything was constituted with a view to measuring each other's strength in the open field free from anything in the nature of a hindrance,[106] and the whole Art of war consisted in the organization, and formation of the Army, that is in the order of battle.

Now as their Armies regularly entrenched themselves in their camps, therefore the position in a camp was regarded as something unassailable, and a battle did not become possible until the enemy left his camp, and placed himself in a practicable country, as it were entered the lists.

If therefore we hear about Hannibal having offered battle to Fabius in vain, that tells us nothing more as regards the latter than that a battle was not part of his plan, and in itself neither proves the physical nor moral superiority of Hannibal; but with respect to him the expression is still correct enough in the sense that Hannibal really wished a battle.

In the early period of modern Armies, the relations were similar in great combats and battles. That is to say, great masses were brought into action, and managed throughout it by means of an order of battle, which like a great helpless whole required a more or less level plain and was neither suited to attack, nor yet to defence in a broken, close or even mountainous country. The defender therefore had here also to some extent the means of avoiding battle. These relations although gradually becoming modified, continued until the first Silesian War, and it was not until the Seven Years' War that attacks on an enemy posted in a difficult country gradually became feasible, and of ordinary occurrence: ground did not certainly cease to be a principle of strength to those making use of its aid, but it was no longer a charmed circle, which shut out the natural forces of War.

During the past thirty years War has perfected itself much more in this respect, and there is no longer anything which stands in the way of a General who is in earnest about a decision by means of battle; he can seek out his enemy, and attack him: if he does not do so he cannot take credit for having wished to fight, and the expression he offered a battle which his opponent did not accept, therefore now means nothing more than that he did not find circumstances advantageous enough for a battle, an admission which the above expression does not suit, but which it only strives to throw a veil over.

It is true the defensive side can no longer refuse a battle, yet he may still avoid it by giving up his position, and the role with which that position was connected: this is however half a victory for the offensive side, and an acknowledgement of his superiority for the present.

This idea in connexion with the cartel of defiance can therefore no longer be made use of in order by such rhodomontade to qualify the inaction of him whose part it is to advance, that is, the offensive. The defender who as long as he does not give way, must have the credit of willing the battle, may certainly say, he has offered it if he is not attacked, if that is not understood of itself.

But on the other hand, he who now wishes to, and can retreat cannot easily be forced to give battle. Now as the advantages to the aggressor from this retreat are often not sufficient, and a substantial victory is a matter of urgent necessity for him, in that way the few means which there are to compel such an opponent also to give battle are often sought for and applied with particular skill.

The principal means for this are – first *surrounding* the enemy so as to make his retreat impossible, or at least so difficult that it is better for him to accept battle; and, secondly, *surprising* him. This last way, for which there was a motive formerly in the extreme difficulty of all movements, has become in modern times very inefficacious. From the pliability and manoeuvring capabilities of troops in the present day, one does not hesitate to commence a retreat even in sight of the enemy, and only some special obstacles in the nature of the country can cause serious difficulties in the operation.

As an example of this kind the battle of Neresheim may be given, fought by the Archduke Charles with Moreau in the Rauhe Alp, 11 August 1796, merely with a view to facilitate his retreat, although we freely confess we have never been able quite to understand the argument of the renowned general and author himself in this case.

The battle of Rosbach is another example, if we suppose the commander of the allied army had not really the intention of attacking Frederick the Great.

Of the battle of Soor, the King himself says that it was only fought because a retreat in the presence of the enemy appeared to him a critical operation; at the same time the King has also given other reasons for the battle.

On the whole, regular night surprises excepted, such cases will always be of rare occurrence, and those in which an enemy is compelled to fight by being practically surrounded, will happen mostly to single corps only, like Mortier's at Dürrenstein 1809, and Vandamme at Kulm, 1813.

CHAPTER IX

THE BATTLE

Its Decision

WHAT is a battle? A conflict of the main body, but not an unimportant one about a secondary object, not a mere attempt which is given up when we see betimes that our object is hardly within our reach: it is a conflict waged with all our forces for the attainment of a decisive victory.

Minor objects may also be mixed up with the principal object, and it will take many different tones of colour from the circumstances out of which it originates, for a battle belongs also to a greater whole of which it is only a part, but because the essence of War is conflict, and the battle is the conflict of the main Armies, it is always to be regarded as the real centre of gravity of the War, and therefore its distinguishing character is, that unlike all other encounters, it is arranged for, and undertaken with the sole purpose of obtaining a decisive victory.

This has an influence on the *manner of its decision*, on the *effect of the victory contained in it*, and determines *the value which theory is to assign to it as a means to an end.* On that account we make it the subject of our special consideration, and at this stage before we enter upon the special ends which may be bound up with it, but which do not essentially alter its character if it really deserves to be termed a battle.

If a battle takes place principally on its own account, the

elements of its decision must be contained in itself; in other words, victory must be striven for as long as a possibility or hope remains. It must not, therefore, be given up on account of secondary circumstances, but only and alone in the event of the forces appearing completely insufficient.

Now how is that precise moment to be described?

If a certain artificial formation and cohesion of an Army is the principal condition under which the bravery of the troops can gain a victory, as was the case during a great part of the period of the modern Art of War, *then the breaking up of this formation* is the decision. A beaten wing which is put out of joint decides the fate of all that was connected with it. If as was the case at another time the essence of the defence consists in an intimate alliance of the Army with the ground on which it fights and its obstacles, so that Army and position are only one, then the *conquest* of *an essential point* in this position is the decision. It is said the key of that position is lost, it cannot therefore be defended any further; the battle cannot be continued. In both cases the beaten Armies are very much like the broken strings of an instrument which cannot do their work.

That geometrical as well as this geographical principle which had a tendency to place an Army in a state of crystallizing tension which did not allow of the available powers being made use of up to the last man, have at least so far lost their influence that they no longer predominate. Armies are still led into battle in a certain order, but that order is no longer of decisive importance; obstacles of ground are also still turned to account to strengthen a position, but they are no longer the only support.

We attempted in the second chapter of this book to take a general view of the nature of the modern battle. According to our conception of it, the order of battle is only a disposition of the forces suitable to the convenient use of them, and the course of the battle a mutual slow wearing away of these forces upon one another, to see which will have soonest exhausted his adversary.

The resolution therefore to give up the fight arises, in a battle more than in any other combat, from the relation of the fresh reserves remaining available; for only these still retain all their moral vigour, and the cinders of the battered, knocked-about battalions, already burnt out in the destroying element, must not be placed on a level with them; also lost ground as we have elsewhere said, is a standard of lost moral force; it therefore comes also into account, but more as a sign of loss suffered than for the loss itself, and the number of fresh reserves is always the chief point to be looked at by both Commanders.

In general, an action inclines in one direction from the very commencement, but in a manner little observable. This direction is also frequently given in a very decided manner by the arrangements which have been made previously, and then it shows a want of discernment in that General who commences battle under these unfavourable circumstances without being aware of them. Even when this does not occur it lies in the nature of things that the course of a battle resembles rather a slow disturbance of equilibrium which commences soon, but as we have said almost imperceptibly at first, and then with each moment of time becomes stronger and more visible, than an oscillating to and fro, as those who are misled by mendacious descriptions usually suppose.

But whether it happens that the balance is for a long time little disturbed, or that even after it has been lost on one side it rights itself again, and is then lost on the other side, it is certain at all events that in most instances the defeated General foresees his fate long before he retreats, and that cases in which some critical event acts with unexpected force upon the course of the whole have their existence mostly in the colouring with which every one depicts his lost battle.

We can only here appeal to the decision of unprejudiced men of experience, who will, we are sure, assent to what we have said, and answer for us to such of our readers as do not know War from their own experience. To develop the necessity of this course from the nature of the thing would lead us too far into the province of tactics, to which this branch of the subject belongs; we are here only concerned with its results.

If we say that the defeated General foresees the unfavourable result usually some time before he makes up his mind to give up the battle, we admit that there are also instances to the contrary, because otherwise we should maintain a proposition contradictory in itself. If at the moment of each decisive tendency of a battle it should be considered as lost, then also no further forces should be used to give it a turn, and consequently this decisive tendency could not precede the retreat by any length of time. Certainly there are instances of battles which after having taken a decided turn to one side have still ended in favour of the other; but they are rare, not usual; these exceptional cases, however, are reckoned upon by every General against whom fortune declares itself, and he must reckon upon them as long as there remains a possibility of a turn of fortune. He hopes by stronger efforts, by raising the remaining moral forces, by surpassing himself, or also by some fortunate chance that the next moment will bring a change, and pursues this as far as his courage and his judgement can agree. We shall have something more to say on this subject, but before that we must show what are the signs of the scales turning.

The result of the whole combat consists in the sum total of the results of all partial combats; but these results of separate combats are settled by different considerations.

First by the pure moral power in the mind of the leading officers. If a General of Division has seen his battalions forced to succumb, it will have an influence on his demeanour and his reports, and these again will have an influence on the measures of the Commander-in-Chief; therefore even those unsuccessful partial combats which to all appearance are retrieved, are not lost in their results, and the impressions from them sum themselves up in the mind of the Commander without much trouble, and even against his will.

Secondly, by the quicker melting away of our troops, which can be easily estimated in the slow and relatively little tumultuary course of our battles.

Thirdly, by lost ground.

All these things serve for the eye of the General as a compass to tell the course of the battle in which he is embarked. If whole batteries have been lost and none of the enemy's taken; if battalions have been overthrown by the enemy's cavalry, whilst those of the enemy everywhere present impenetrable masses;

if the line of fire from his order of battle wavers involuntarily from one point to another; if fruitless efforts have been made to gain certain points, and the assaulting battalions each time been scattered by well-directed volleys of grape and case; if our artillery begins to reply feebly to that of the enemy – if the battalions under fire diminish unusually fast, because with the wounded crowds of unwounded men go to the rear; if single Divisions have been cut off and made prisoners through the disruption of the plan of the battle; if the line of retreat begins to be endangered: the Commander may tell very well in which direction he is going with his battle. The longer this direction continues, the more decided it becomes, so much the more difficult will be the turning, so much the nearer the moment when he must give up the battle. We shall now make some observations on this moment.

We have already said more than once that the final decision is ruled mostly by the relative number of the fresh reserves remaining at the last; that Commander who sees his adversary is decidedly superior to him in this respect makes up his mind to retreat. It is the characteristic of modern battles that all mischances and losses which take place in the course of the same can be retrieved by fresh forces, because the arrangement of the modern order of battle, and the way in which troops are brought into action, allow of their use almost generally, and in each position. So long, therefore, as that Commander against whom the issue seems to declare itself still retains a superiority in reserve force, he will not give up the day. But from the moment that his reserves begin to become weaker than his enemy's, the decision may be regarded as settled, and what he now does depends partly on special circumstances, partly on the degree of courage and perseverance which he personally possesses, and which may degenerate into foolish obstinacy. How a Commander can attain to the power of estimating correctly the still remaining reserves on both sides is an affair of skilful practical genius, which does not in any way belong to this place; we keep ourselves to the result as it forms itself in his mind. But this conclusion is still not the moment of decision properly, for a motive which only arises gradually does not answer to that, but is only a general motive towards resolution, and the resolution itself requires still some special immediate causes. Of these there are two chief ones which constantly recur, that is, the danger of retreat, and the arrival of night.

If the retreat with every new step which the battle takes in its course becomes constantly in greater danger, and if the reserves are so much diminished that they are no longer adequate to get breathing room, then there is nothing left but to submit to fate, and by a well-conducted retreat to save what, by a longer delay ending in flight and disaster, would be lost.

But night as a rule puts an end to all battles, because a night combat holds out no hope of advantage except under particular circumstances; and as night is better suited for a retreat than the day, so, therefore, the Commander who must look at the retreat as a thing inevitable, or as most probable, will prefer to make use of the night for his purpose.

That there are, besides the above two usual and chief causes, yet many others also, which are less or more individual and not to be overlooked, is a matter of course; for the more a battle tends towards a complete upset of equilibrium the more sensible is the influence of each partial result in hastening the turn. Thus the loss of a battery, a successful charge of a couple of regiments of cavalry, may call into life the resolution to retreat already ripening.

As a conclusion to this subject, we must dwell for a moment on the point at which the courage of the Commander engages in a sort of conflict with his reason.

If, on the one hand the overbearing pride of a victorious conqueror, if the inflexible will of a naturally obstinate spirit, if the strenuous resistance of noble feelings will not yield the battlefield, where they must leave their honour, yet on the other hand, reason counsels not to give up everything, not to risk the last upon the game, but to retain as much over as is necessary for an orderly retreat. However highly we must esteem courage and firmness in War, and however little prospect there is of victory to him who cannot resolve to seek it by the exertion of all his power, still there is a point beyond which perseverance can only be termed desperate folly, and therefore can meet with no approbation from any critic. In the most celebrated of all battles, that of Belle-Alliance, Buonaparte used his last reserve in an effort to retrieve a battle which was past being retrieved. He spent his last farthing, and then, as a beggar, abandoned both the battlefield and his crown.

CHAPTER X

EFFECTS OF VICTORY

According to the point from which our view is taken, we may feel as much astonished at the extraordinary results of some great battles as at the want of results in others. We shall dwell for a moment on the nature of the effect of a great victory.

Three things may easily be distinguished here: the effect upon the instrument itself, that is, upon the Generals and their Armies; the effect upon the States interested in the War; and the particular result of these effects as manifested in the subsequent course of the campaign.

If we only think of the trifling difference which there usually is between victor and vanquished in killed, wounded, prisoners, and artillery lost on the field of battle itself, the consequences which are developed out of this insignificant point seem often quite incomprehensible, and yet, usually, everything only happens quite naturally.

We have already said in the seventh chapter that the magnitude of a victory increases not merely in the same measure as the vanquished forces increase in number, but in a higher ratio. The moral effects resulting from the issue of a great battle are greater on the side of the conquered than on that of the conqueror: they lead to greater losses in physical force, which then in turn react on the moral element, and so they go on mutually supporting and intensifying each other. On this moral effect we must therefore lay special weight. It takes an opposite direction on the one side from that on the other; as it undermines the energies of the conquered so it elevates the powers and energy of the conqueror. But its chief effect is upon the vanquished, because here it is the direct cause of fresh losses, and besides it is homogeneous in nature with danger, with the fatigues, the hardships, and generally with all those embarrassing circumstances by which War is surrounded, therefore enters into league with them and increases by their help, whilst with the conqueror all these things are like weights which give a higher swing to his courage. It is therefore found, that the vanquished sinks much further below the original line of equilibrium than the conqueror raises himself above it; on this account, if we speak of the effects of victory we allude more particularly to those which manifest themselves in the vanquished army. If this effect is more powerful in an important combat than in a smaller one, so again it is much more powerful in a great battle than in a minor one. The great battle takes place for the sake of itself, for the sake of the victory which it is to give, and which is sought for with the utmost effort. Here on this spot, in this very hour, to conquer the enemy is the purpose in which the plan of the War with all its threads converges, in which all distant hopes, all dim glimmerings of the future meet, fate steps in before us to give an answer to the bold question. This is the state of mental tension not only of the Commander but of his whole Army down to the lowest waggon-driver, no doubt in decreasing strength but also in decreasing importance.

According to the nature of the thing, a great battle has never at any time been an unprepared, unexpected, blind routine service, but a grand act, which, partly of itself and partly from the aim of the Commander, stands out from amongst the mass of ordinary efforts, sufficiently to raise the tension of all minds to a higher degree. But the higher this tension with respect to the issue, the more powerful must be the effect of that issue.

Again, the moral effect of victory in our battles is greater than it was in the earlier ones of modern military history. If the former are as we have depicted them, a real struggle of forces to the utmost, then the sum total of all these forces, of the physical as well as the moral, must decide more than certain special dispositions or mere chance.

A single fault committed may be repaired next time; from

good fortune and chance we can hope for more favour on another occasion; but the sum total of moral and physical powers cannot be so quickly altered, and, therefore, what the award of a victory has decided appears of much greater importance for all futurity. Very probably, of all concerned in battles, whether in or out of the Army, very few have given a thought to this difference, but the course of the battle itself impresses on the minds of all present in it such a conviction, and the relation of this course in public documents, however much it may be coloured by twisting particular circumstances, shows also, more or less, to the world at large that the causes were more of a general than of a particular nature.

He who has not been present at the loss of a great battle will have difficulty in forming for himself a living or quite true idea of it, and the abstract notions of this or that small untoward affair will never come up to the perfect conception of a lost battle. Let us stop a moment at the picture.

The first thing which overpowers the imagination – and we may indeed say, also the understanding – is the diminution of the masses; then the loss of ground, which takes place always, more or less, and, therefore, on the side of the assailant also, if he is not fortunate; then the rupture of the original formation, the jumbling together of troops, the risks of retreat, which, with few exceptions may always be seen sometimes in a less sometimes in a greater degree; next the retreat, the most part of which commences at night, or, at least, goes on throughout the night. On this first march we must at once leave behind a number of men completely worn out and scattered about, often just the bravest, who have been foremost in the fight who held out the longest: the feeling of being conquered, which only seized the superior officers on the battlefield, now spreads through all ranks, even down to the common soldiers, aggravated by the horrible idea of being obliged to leave in the enemy's hands so many brave comrades, who but a moment since were of such value to us in the battle, and aggravated by a rising distrust of the chief Commander, to whom, more or less, every subordinate attributes as a fault the fruitless efforts he has made; and this feeling of being conquered is no ideal picture over which one might become master; it is an evident truth that the enemy is superior to us; a truth of which the causes might have been so latent before that they were not to be discovered, but which, in the issue, comes out clear and palpable, or which was also, perhaps, before suspected, but which in the want of any certainty, we had to oppose by the hope of chance, reliance on good fortune, Providence or a bold attitude. Now, all this has proved insufficient, and the bitter truth meets us harsh and imperious.

All these feelings are widely different from a panic, which in an Army fortified by military virtue never, and in any other, only exceptionally, follows the loss of a battle. They must arise even in the best of Armies, and although long habituation to War and victory together with great confidence in a Commander may modify them a little here and there, they are never entirely wanting in the first moment. They are not the pure consequences of lost trophies; these are usually lost at a later period, and the loss of them does not become generally known so quickly; they will therefore not fail to appear even when the scale turns in the slowest and most gradual manner and they constitute that effect of a victory upon which we can always count in every case.

We have already said that the number of trophies intensifies this effect.

It is evident that an Army in this condition, looked at as an instrument, is weakened! How can we expect that when reduced to such a degree that, as we said before, it finds new enemies in all the ordinary difficulties of making War, it will be able to recover by fresh efforts what has been lost! Before the battle there was a real or assumed equilibrium between the two sides; this is lost, and, therefore, some external assistance is requisite to restore it; every new effort without such external support can only lead to fresh losses.

Thus, therefore, the most moderate victory of the chief Army must tend to cause a constant sinking of the scale on the opponent's side, until new external circumstances bring about a change. If these are not near, if the conqueror is an eager opponent, who, thirsting for glory, pursues great aims, then a first-rate Commander, and in the beaten Army a true military spirit, hardened by many campaigns are required, in order to stop the swollen stream of prosperity from bursting all bounds, and to moderate its course by small but reiterated acts of resistance, until the force of victory has spent itself at the goal of its career.

And now as to the effect of defeat beyond the Army, upon the Nation and Government! It is the sudden collapse of hopes stretched to the utmost, the downfall of all self-reliance. In place of these extinct forces, fear, with its destructive properties of expansion, rushes into the vacuum left, and completes the prostration. It is a real shock upon the nerves, which one of the two athletes receives from the electric spark of victory. And that effect, however different in its degrees, is never completely wanting. Instead of every one hastening with a spirit of determination to aid in repairing the disaster, every one fears that his efforts will only be in vain, and stops, hesitating with himself, when he should rush forward; or in despondency he lets his arm drop, leaving everything to fate.

The consequence which this effect of victory brings forth in the course of the War itself depends in part on the character and talent of the victorious General, but more on the circumstances from which the victory proceeds, and to which it leads. Without boldness and an enterprising spirit on the part of the leader, the most brilliant victory will lead to no great success, and its force exhausts itself all the sooner on circumstances, if these offer a strong and stubborn opposition to it. How very differently from Daun, Frederick the Great would have used the victory at Kollin; and what different consequences France, in place of Prussia, might have given a battle of Leuthen!

The conditions which allow us to expect great results from a great victory we shall learn when we come to the subjects with which they are connected; then it will be possible to explain the disproportion which appears at first sight between the magnitude of a victory and its results, and which is only too readily attributed to a want of energy on the part of the conqueror. Here, where we have to do with the great battle in itself, we shall merely say that the effects now depicted never fail to attend a victory, that they mount up with the intensive strength of the victory – mount up more the more the whole strength of the Army has been concentrated in it, the more the whole military power of the Nation is contained in that Army, and the State in that military power.

But then the question may be asked, Can theory accept this effect of victory as absolutely necessary? – must it not rather endeavour to find out counteracting means capable of neutralizing these effects? It seems quite natural to answer this question in the affirmative; but heaven defend us from taking that wrong course of most theories, out of which is begotten a mutually devouring *Pro et Contra.*

Certainly that effect is perfectly necessary, for it has its foundation in the nature of things, and it exists, even if we find means to struggle against it; just as the motion of a cannon ball is always in the direction of the terrestrial, although when fired from east to west part of the general velocity is destroyed by this opposite motion.

All War supposes human weakness, and against that it is directed.[107]

Therefore, if hereafter in another place we examine what is to be done after the loss of a great battle, if we bring under review the resources which still remain, even in the most desperate cases, if we should express a belief in the possibility of retrieving all, even in such a case; it must not be supposed we mean thereby that the effects of such a defeat can by degrees be completely wiped out, for the forces and means used to repair the disaster might have been applied to the realization of some positive object; and this applies both to the moral and physical forces.

Another question is, whether, through the loss of a great battle, forces are not perhaps roused into existence, which otherwise would never have come to life. This case is certainly conceivable, and it is what has actually occurred with many Nations. But to produce this intensified reaction is beyond the province of military art, which can only take account of it where it might be assumed as a possibility.

If there are cases in which the fruits of a victory appear rather of a destructive nature in consequence of the reaction of the forces which it had the effect of rousing into activity – cases which certainly are very exceptional – then it must the more surely be granted, that there is a difference in the effects which one and the same victory may produce according to the character of the people or state, which has been conquered.

CHAPTER XI

THE USE OF THE BATTLE

WHATEVER form the conduct of War may take in particular cases, and whatever we may have to admit in the sequel as necessary respecting it: we have only to refer to the conception of War to be convinced of what follows:

1. The destruction of the enemy's military force, is the leading principle of War, and for the whole chapter of positive action the direct way to the object.
2. This destruction of the enemy's force, must be principally effected by means of battle.
3. Only great and general battles can produce great results.
4. The results will be greatest when combats unite themselves in one great battle.
5. It is only in a great battle that the General-in-Chief commands in person, and it is in the nature of things, that he should place more confidence in himself than in his subordinates.

From these truths a double law follows, the parts of which mutually support each other; namely, that the destruction of the enemy's military force is to be sought for principally by great battles, and their results; and that the chief object of great battles must be the destruction of the enemy's military force.

No doubt the annihilation-principle is to be found more or less in other means – granted there are instances in which through favourable circumstances in a minor combat, the destruction of the enemy's forces has been disproportionately great (Maxen), and on the other hand in a battle, the taking or holding a single post may be predominant in importance as an object – but as a general rule it remains a paramount truth, that battles are only fought with a view to the destruction of the enemy's Army, and that this destruction can only be effected by their means.

The battle may therefore be regarded as War concentrated, as the centre of effort of the whole War or campaign. As the sun's rays unite in the focus of the concave mirror in a perfect image, and in the fulness of their heat; to the forces and circumstances of War, unite in a focus in the great battle for one concentrated utmost effort.

The very assemblage of forces in one great whole, which takes place more or less in all Wars indicates an intention to strike a decisive blow with this whole, either voluntarily as assailant, or constrained by the opposite party as defender. When this great blow does not follow, then some modifying, and retarding motives have attached themselves to the original motive of hostility, and have weakened, altered or completely checked the movement. But also, even in this condition of mutual inaction which has been the keynote in so many Wars, the idea of a possible battle serves always for both parties as a point of direction, a distant focus in the construction of their plans. The more War is War in earnest, the more it is a venting of animosity and hostility, a mutual struggle to overpower, so much the more will all activities join deadly contest, and also the more prominent in importance becomes the battle.

In general, when the object aimed at is of a great and positive nature, one therefore in which the interests of the enemy are deeply concerned, the battle offers itself as the most natural means; it is, therefore, also the best as we shall show more plainly hereafter: and, as a rule, when it is evaded from aversion to the great decision, punishment follows.

The positive object belongs to the offensive, and therefore the battle is also more particularly his means. But without examining the conception of offensive and defensive more minutely here, we must still observe that, even for the defender in most cases, there is no other effectual means with which to meet the exigencies of his situation, to solve the problem presented to him.

The battle is the bloodiest way of solution. True, it is not merely reciprocal slaughter, and its effect is more a killing of the enemy's courage than of the enemy's soldiers, as we shall see more plainly in the next chapter – but still blood is always its price, and slaughter its character as well as name; from this the humanity in the General's mind recoils with horror.

But the soul of the man trembles still more at the thought of the decision to be given with one single blow. *In one point* of space and time all action is here pressed together, and at such a moment there is stirred up within us a dim feeling as if in this narrow space all our forces could not develop themselves and come into activity, as if we had already gained much by mere time, although this time owes us nothing at all. This is all mere illusion, but even as illusion it is something, and the same weakness which seizes upon the man in every other momentous decision may well be felt more powerfully by the General, when he must stake interest of such enormous weight upon one venture.

Thus, then, Statesmen and Generals have at all times endeavoured to avoid the decisive battle, seeking either to attain their aim without it, or dropping that aim unperceived. Writers on history and theory have then busied themselves to discover in some other feature in these campaigns not only an equivalent for the decision by battle which has been avoided, but even a higher art. In this way, in the present age, it came very near to this, that a battle in the economy of War was looked upon as an evil, rendered necessary through some error committed, as a morbid paroxysm to which a regular prudent system of War would never lead: only those Generals were to deserve laurels who knew how to carry on War without spilling blood, and the theory of War – a real business for Brahmins – was to be specially directed to teaching this.

Contemporary history has destroyed this illusion,[108] but no one can guarantee that it will not sooner or later reproduce itself, and lead those at the head of affairs to perversities which please man's weakness, and therefore have the greater affinity for his nature. Perhaps, by-and-by, Buonaparte's campaigns and battles will be looked upon as mere acts of barbarism and stupidity, and we shall once more turn with satisfaction and confidence to the dress-sword of obsolete and musty institutions and forms. If theory gives a caution against this, then it renders a real service to those who listen to its warning voice. *May we succeed in lending a hand to those who in our dear native land are called upon to speak with authority on these matters, that we may be their guide into this field of inquiry, and excite them to make a candid examination of the subject.*[109]

Not only the conception of War but experience also leads us to look for a great decision only in a great battle. From time immemorial, only great victories have led to great successes on the offensive side in the absolute form, on the defensive side in a manner more or less satisfactory. Even Buonaparte would not have seen the day of Ulm, unique in its kind, if he had shrunk from shedding blood; it is rather to be regarded as only a second crop from the victorious events in his preceding campaigns. It is not only bold, rash, and presumptuous Generals who have sought to complete their work by the great venture of a decisive battle, but also fortunate ones as well; and we may rest satisfied with the answer which they have thus given to this vast question.

Let us not hear of Generals who conquer without bloodshed. If a bloody slaughter is a horrible sight, then that is a ground for paying more respect to War, but not for making the sword we wear blunter and blunter by degrees from feelings of humanity, until some one steps in with one that is sharp and lops off the arm from our body.

We look upon a great battle as a principal decision, but certainly not as the only one necessary for a War or a campaign. Instances of a great battle deciding a whole campaign, have been frequent only in modern times, those which have decided a whole War, belong to the class of rare exceptions.

A decision which is brought about by a great battle depends naturally not on the battle itself, that is on the mass of combatants engaged in it, and on the intensity of the victory, but also on a number of other relations between the military forces opposed to each other, and between the States to which these forces belong. But at the same time that the principal mass of the force available is brought to the great duel, a great decision is also brought on, the extent of which may perhaps be foreseen in many respects, though not in all, and which although not the only one, still is the *first* decision, and as such, has an influence on those which succeed. Therefore a deliberately planned great battle, according to its relations, is more or less, but always in some degree, to be regarded as the leading means and central point of the whole system. The more a General takes the field in the true spirit of War as well as of every contest, with the feeling and the idea, that is the conviction, that he must and will conquer, the more he will strive to throw every weight into the scale in the first battle, hope and strive to win everything by it. Buonaparte hardly ever entered upon a War without thinking of conquering his enemy at once in the first battle,[110] and Frederick the Great, although in a more limited sphere, and with interests of less magnitude at stake, thought the same when, at the head of a small Army, he sought to disengage his rear from the Russians or the Federal Imperial Army.

The decision which is given by the great battle, depends, we have said, partly on the battle itself, that is on the number of troops engaged, and partly on the magnitude of the success.

How the General may increase its importance in respect to the first point is evident in itself and we shall merely observe that according to the importance of the great battle, the number of cases which are decided along with it increases, and that therefore Generals who, confident in themselves have been lovers of great decisions, have always managed to make use of the greater part of their troops in it without neglecting on that account essential points elsewhere.

As regards the consequences or speaking more correctly the effectiveness of a victory, that depends chiefly on four points:

1. On the tactical form adopted as the order of battle.
2. On the nature of the country.
3. On the relative proportions of the three arms.
4. On the relative strength of the two Armies.

A battle with parallel fronts and without any action against a flank will seldom yield as great success as one in which the defeated Army has been turned, or compelled to change front more or less. In a broken or hilly country the successes are likewise smaller, because the power of the blow is everywhere less.

If the cavalry of the vanquished is equal or superior to that of the victor, then the effects of the pursuit are diminished, and by that great part of the results of victory are lost.

Finally it is easy to understand that if superior numbers are on the side of the conqueror, and he uses his advantage in that respect to turn the flank of his adversary, or compel him to change front, greater results will follow than if the conqueror had been weaker in numbers than the vanquished. The battle of Leuthen may certainly be quoted as a practical refutation of this principle, but we beg permission for once to say what we otherwise do not like, *no rule without an exception.*

In all these ways, therefore, the Commander has the means of giving his battle a decisive character; certainly he thus exposes himself to an increased amount of danger, but his whole line of action is subject to that dynamic law of the moral world.

There is then nothing in War which can be put in comparison with the great battle in point of importance, *and the acme of strategic ability is displayed in the provision of means for this great event, in the skilful determination of place and time, and direction of troops, and in the good use made of success.*

But it does not follow from the importance of these things that they must be of a very complicated and recondite nature; all is here rather simple, the art of combination by no means great; but there is great need of quickness in judging of circumstances, need of energy, steady resolution, a youthful spirit of enterprise – heroic qualities, to which we shall often have to refer. There is, therefore, but little wanted here of that which can be taught by books and there is much that, if it can be taught at all, must come to the General through some other medium than printer's type.

The impulse towards a great battle, the voluntary, sure progress to it, must proceed from a feeling of innate power and a clear sense of the necessity; in other words, it must proceed from inborn courage and from perceptions sharpened by contact with the higher interests of life.

Great examples are the best teachers, but it is certainly a misfortune if a cloud of theoretical prejudices comes between, for even the sunbeam is refracted and tinted by the clouds. To destroy such prejudices, which many a time rise and spread themselves like a miasma, is an imperative duty of theory, for the misbegotten offspring of human reason can also be in turn destroyed by pure reason.

CHAPTER XII

STRATEGIC MEANS OF UTILIZING VICTORY

THE more difficult part, viz. that of perfectly preparing the victory, is a silent service of which the merit belongs to Strategy and yet for which it is hardly sufficiently commended. It appears brilliant and full of renown by turning to good account a victory gained.

What may be the special object of a battle, how it is connected with the whole system of a War, whither the career of victory may lead according to the nature of circumstances, where its culminating-point lies – all these are things which we shall not enter upon until hereafter. But under any conceivable circumstances the fact holds good, that without a pursuit no victory can have a great effect, and that, however short the career of victory may be, it must always lead beyond the first steps in pursuit; and in order to avoid the frequent repetition of this, we shall now dwell for a moment on this necessary supplement of victory in general.

The pursuit of a beaten Army commences at the moment that Army, giving up the combat, leaves its position; all previous movements in one direction and another belong not to that but to the progress of the battle itself. Usually victory at the moment here described, even if it is certain, is still as yet small and weak in its proportions, and would not rank as an event of any great positive advantage if not completed by a pursuit on the first day. Then it is mostly, as we have before said, that the trophies which give substance to the victory begin to be gathered up. Of this pursuit we shall speak in the next place.

Usually both sides come into action with their physical powers considerably deteriorated, for the movements immediately preceding have generally the character of very urgent circumstances. The efforts which the forging out of a great combat costs, complete the exhaustion; from this it follows that the victorious party is very little less disorganized and out of his original formation than the vanquished, and therefore requires time to reform, to collect stragglers, and issue fresh ammunition to those who are without. All these things place the conqueror himself in the state of crisis of which we have already spoken. If now the defeated force is only a detached portion of the enemy's Army, or if it has otherwise to expect a considerable reinforcement, then the conqueror may easily run into the obvious danger of having to pay dear for his victory, and this consideration, in such a case, very soon puts an end to pursuit, or at least restricts it materially. Even when a strong accession of force by the enemy is not to be feared, the conqueror finds in the above circumstances a powerful check to the vivacity of his pursuit. There is no reason to fear that the victory will be snatched away, but adverse combats are still possible, and may diminish the advantages which up to the present have been gained. Moreover, at this moment the whole weight of all that is sensuous in an Army, its wants and weaknesses, are dependent on the will of the Commander. All the thousands under his command require rest and refreshment, and long to see a stop put to toil and danger for the present; only a few, forming an exception, can see and feel beyond the present moment; it is only amongst this little number that there is sufficient mental vigour to think, after what is absolutely necessary at the moment has been done, upon those results which at such a moment only appear to the rest as mere embellishments of victory – as a luxury of triumph. But all these thousands have a voice in the council of the General, for through the various steps of the military hierarchy these interests of the sensuous creature have their sure conductor into the heart of the Commander. He himself, through mental and bodily fatigue, is more or less weakened in his natural activity, and thus it happens then that, mostly from these causes, purely incidental to human nature, less is done than might have been done, and that generally what is done is to be ascribed entirely to the *thirst for glory*, the *energy*, indeed also the *hard-heartedness* of the General-in-Chief. It is only thus we can explain the hesitating manner in which many Generals follow up a victory which superior numbers have given them. The first pursuit of the enemy we limit in general to the extent of the first day, including the night following the victory. At the end of that period the necessity of rest ourselves prescribes a halt in any case.

This first pursuit has different natural degrees.

The first is, if cavalry alone are employed; in that case it amounts usually more to alarming and watching than to pressing the enemy in reality, because the smallest obstacle of ground is generally sufficient to check the pursuit. Useful as cavalry may be against single bodies of broken demoralized troops, still when opposed to the bulk of the beaten Army it becomes again only the auxiliary arm, because the troops in retreat can employ fresh reserves to cover the movement, and, therefore, at the next trifling obstacle of ground, by combining all arms they can make a stand with success. The only exception to this is in the case of an army in actual flight in a complete state of dissolution.

The second degree is, if the pursuit is made by a strong advance-guard composed of all arms, the greater part consisting naturally of cavalry. Such a pursuit generally drives the enemy as far as the nearest strong position for his rear-guard, or the next position affording space for his Army. Neither can usually be found at once, and, therefore, the pursuit can be carried further; generally, however, it does not extend beyond the distance of one or at most a couple of leagues, because otherwise the advance-guard would not feel itself sufficiently supported.

The third and most vigorous degree is when the victorious Army itself continues to advance as far as its physical powers can endure. In this case the beaten Army will generally quit such ordinary positions as a country usually offers on the mere show of an attack, or of an intention to turn its flank; and the rear-guard will be still less likely to engage in an obstinate resistance.

In all three cases the night, if it sets in before the conclusion of the whole act, usually puts an end to it, and the few instances in which this has not taken place, and the pursuit has been continued throughout the night, must be regarded as pursuits in an exceptionally vigorous form.

If we reflect that in fighting by night everything must be, more or less, abandoned to chance, and that at the conclusion of a battle the regular cohesion and order of things in an army must inevitably be disturbed, we may easily conceive the reluctance of both Generals to carrying on their business under such disadvantageous conditions. If a complete dissolution of the vanquished Army, or a rare superiority of the victorious Army in military virtue does not ensure success, everything would in a manner be given up to fate, which can never be for the interest of anyone, even of the most foolhardy General. As a rule, therefore, night puts an end to pursuit, even when the battle has only been decided shortly before darkness sets in. This allows the conquered either time for rest and to rally immediately, or, if he retreats during the night it gives him a march in advance. After this break the conquered is decidedly in a better condition; much of that which had been thrown into confusion has been brought again into order, ammunition has been renewed, the whole has been put into a fresh formation. Whatever further encounter now takes place with the enemy is a new battle not a continuation of the old, and although it may be far from promising absolute success, still it is a fresh combat, and not merely a gathering up of the debris by the victor.

When, therefore, the conqueror can continue the pursuit itself throughout the night, if only with a strong advance-guard composed of all arms of the service, the effect of the victory is immensely increased, of this the battles of Leuthen and La Belle Alliance are examples.

The whole action of this pursuit is mainly tactical, and we only dwell upon it here in order to make plain the difference which through it may be produced in the effect of a victory.

This first pursuit, as far as the nearest stopping-point, belongs as a right to every conqueror, and is hardly in any way connected with his further plans and combinations. These may considerably diminish the positive results of a victory gained with the main body of the Army, but they cannot make this first use of it impossible; at least cases of that kind, if conceivable at all, must be so uncommon that they should have no appreciable influence on theory. And here certainly we must say that the example afforded by modern Wars opens up quite a new field for energy. In preceding Wars, resting on a narrower basis, and altogether more circumscribed in their scope, there were many unnecessary conventional restrictions in various ways, but particularly in this point. *The conception, Honour of Victory* seemed to Generals so much by far the chief thing that they thought the less of the complete destruction of the enemy's military force, as in point of fact that destruction of force appeared to them only as one of the many means in War, not by any means as the principal, much less as the only means; so that they the more readily put the sword in its sheath the moment the enemy had lowered his. Nothing seemed more natural to them than to stop the combat as soon as the decision was obtained, and to regard all further carnage as unnecessary cruelty. Even if this false philosophy did not determine their resolutions entirely, still it was a point of view by which representations of the exhaustion of all powers, and physical impossibility of continuing the struggle, obtained readier evidence and greater weight. Certainly the sparing one's own instrument of victory is a vital question if we only possess this one, and foresee that soon the time may arrive when it will not be sufficient for all that remains to be done, for every continuation of the offensive must lead ultimately to complete exhaustion. But this calculation was still so far false, as the further loss of forces by a continuance of the pursuit could bear no proportion to that which the enemy must suffer. That view, therefore, again could only exist because the military forces were not considered the vital factor. And so we find that in former Wars real heroes only – such as Charles XII, Marlborough, Eugene, Frederick the Great – added a vigorous pursuit to their victories when they were decisive enough and that other Generals usually contented themselves with the possession of the field of battle. In modern times the greater energy infused into the conduct of Wars through the greater importance of the circumstances from which they have proceeded has thrown down these conventional barriers; the pursuit has become an all-important business for the conqueror; trophies have on that account multiplied in extent, and if there are cases also in modern Warfare in which this has not been the case, still they belong to the list of exceptions, and are to be accounted for by peculiar circumstances.

At Gorschen and Bautzen nothing but the superiority of the allied cavalry prevented a complete rout, at Gross Beeren and Dennewitz the ill-will of Bernadotte, the Crown Prince of Sweden; at Laon the enfeebled personal condition of Blücher, who was then seventy years of age and at the moment confined to a dark room owing to an injury to his eyes.

But Borodino is also an illustration to the point here, and we cannot resist saying a few more words about it, partly because we do not consider the circumstances are explained simply by attaching blame to Buonaparte, partly because it might appear as if this, and with it a great number of similar cases, belonged to that class which we have designated as so extremely rare, cases in which the general relations seize and fetter the General at the very beginning of the battle. French authors in particular, and great admirers of Buonaparte (Vaudancourt, Chambray, Ségur), have blamed him decidedly because he did not drive the Russian Army completely off the field, and use his last reserves to scatter it, because then what was only a lost battle would have been a complete rout. We should be obliged to diverge too far to describe circumstantially the mutual situation of the two Armies; but this much is evident, that when Buonaparte passed the Niemen with his Army the same corps which afterwards fought at Borodino numbered 300,000 men, of whom now only 120,000 remained, he might therefore well be apprehensive that he would not have enough left to march upon Moscow, the point on which everything seemed to depend. The victory which he had just gained gave him nearly a certainty of taking that capital, for that the Russians would be in a condition to fight a second battle within eight days seemed in the highest degree improbable; and in Moscow he hoped to find peace. No doubt the complete dispersion of the Russian Army would have made this peace much more certain; but still the first consideration was to get to Moscow, that is, to get there with a force with which he should appear dictator over the capital, and through that over the Empire and the Government. The force which he brought with him to Moscow was no longer sufficient for that, as shown in the sequel, but it would have been still less so if, in scattering the Russian Army, he had scattered his own at the same time. Buonaparte was thoroughly alive to all this, and in our eyes he stands completely justified. But on that account this case is still not to be reckoned amongst those in which, through the general relations, the General is interdicted from following up his victory, for there never was in his case any question of mere pursuit. The victory was decided at four o'clock in the afternoon, but the Russians still occupied the greater part of the field of battle; they were not yet disposed to give up the ground, and if the attack had been renewed, they would still have offered a most determined resistance, which would have undoubtedly ended in their complete defeat, but would have cost the conqueror much further bloodshed. We must therefore reckon the Battle of Borodino as amongst battles, like Bautzen, left unfinished. At Bautzen the vanquished preferred to quit the field sooner; at Borodino the conqueror preferred to content himself with a half victory, not because the decision appeared doubtful, but because he was not rich enough to pay for the whole.

Returning now to our subject, the deduction from our reflections in relation to the first stage of pursuit is, that the energy thrown into it chiefly determines the value of the victory; that this pursuit is a second act of the victory, in many cases more important also than the first, and that strategy, whilst here approaching tactics to receive from it the harvest of success, exercises the first act of her authority by demanding this completion of the victory.

But further, the effects of victory are very seldom found to stop with this first pursuit; now first begins the real career to which victory lent velocity. This course is conditioned as we have already said, by other relations of which it is not yet time to speak. But we must here mention, what there is of a general character in the pursuit in order to avoid repetition when the subject occurs again.

In the further stages of pursuit, again, we can distinguish three degrees: the simple pursuit, a hard pursuit, and a parallel march to intercept.

The simple *following* or *pursuing* causes the enemy to continue his retreat, until he thinks he can risk another battle. It will therefore in its effect suffice to exhaust the advantages gained, and besides that, all that the enemy cannot carry with him, sick, wounded, and disabled from fatigue, quantities of baggage, and carriages of all kinds, will fall into our hands, but this mere following does not tend to heighten the disorder in the enemy's Army, an effect which is produced by the two following causes.

If, for instance, instead of contenting ourselves with taking up every day the camp the enemy has just vacated, occupying just as much of the country as he chooses to abandon, we make our arrangements so as every day to encroach further, and accordingly with our advance-guard organized for the purpose, attack his rear-guard every time it attempts to halt, then such a course will hasten his retreat, and consequently tend to increase his disorganization. This it will principally effect by the character of continuous flight, which his retreat will thus assume. Nothing has such a depressing influence on the soldier, as the sound of the enemy's cannon afresh at the moment when, after a forced march he seeks some rest; if this excitement is continued from day to day for some time, it may lead to a complete rout. There lies in it a constant admission of being obliged to obey the law of the enemy, and of being unfit for any resistance, and the consciousness of this cannot do otherwise than weaken the moral of an Army in a high degree. The effect of pressing the enemy in this way attains a maximum when it drives the enemy to make night marches. If the conqueror scares away the discomfited opponent at sunset from a camp which has just been taken up either for the main body of the Army, or for the rear-guard, the conquered must either make a night march, or alter his position in the night, retiring further away, which is much the same thing; the victorious party can on the other hand pass the night in quiet.

The arrangement of marches, and the choice of positions depend in this case also upon so many other things, especially on the supply of the Army, on strong natural obstacles in the country, on large towns, etc., etc., that it would be ridiculous pedantry to attempt to show by a geometrical analysis how the pursuer, being able to impose his laws on the retreating enemy, can compel him to march at night while he takes his rest. But nevertheless it is true and practicable that marches in pursuit may be so planned as to have this tendency, and that the efficacy of the pursuit is very much enhanced thereby. If this is seldom attended to in the execution, it is because such a procedure is more difficult for the pursuing Army, than a regular adherence to ordinary marches in the daytime. To start in good time in the morning, to encamp at midday, to occupy the rest of the day in providing for the ordinary wants of the Army, and to use the night for repose, is a much more convenient method than to regulate one's movements exactly according to those of the enemy, therefore to determine nothing till the last moment, to start on the march, sometimes in the morning, sometimes in the evening, to be always for several hours in the presence of the enemy, and exchanging cannon shots with him, and keeping up skirmishing fire, to plan manoeuvres to turn him, in short, to make the whole outlay of tactical means which such a course renders necessary. All that naturally bears with a heavy weight on the pursuing Army, and in War, where there are so many burdens to be borne, men are always inclined to strip off those which do not seem absolutely necessary. These observations are true, whether applied to a whole Army or as in the more usual case, to a strong advance-guard. For the reasons just mentioned, this second method of pursuit, this continued pressing of the enemy pursued is rather a rare occurrence; even Buonaparte in his Russian campaign, 1812, practised it but little, for the reasons here apparent, that the difficulties and hardships of this campaign, already threatened his Army with destruction before it could reach its object; on the other hand, the French in their other campaigns have distinguished themselves by their energy in this point also.

Lastly, the third and most effectual form of pursuit is, the parallel march to the immediate object of the retreat.

Every defeated Army will naturally have behind it, at a greater or less distance, some point, the attainment of which is the first purpose in view, whether it be that failing in this its further retreat might be compromised, as in the case of a defile, or that it is important for the point itself to reach it before the enemy, as in the case of a great city, magazines, etc., or, lastly, that the Army at this point will gain new powers of defence, such as a strong position, or junction with other corps.

Now if the conqueror directs his march on this point by a lateral road, it is evident how that may quicken the retreat of the beaten Army in a destructive manner, convert it into hurry, perhaps into flight.[111] The conquered has only three ways to counteract this: the first is to throw himself in front of the enemy, in order by an unexpected attack to gain that probability of success which is lost to him in general from his position; this plainly supposes an enterprising bold General, and an excellent Army, beaten but not utterly defeated; therefore, it can only be employed by a beaten Army in very few cases.

The second way is hastening the retreat; but this is just what the conqueror wants, and it easily leads to immoderate efforts on the part of the troops, by which enormous losses are sustained, in stragglers, broken guns, and carriages of all kinds.

The third way is to make a detour, and get round the nearest point of interception, to march with more ease at a greater distance from the enemy, and thus to render the haste required less damaging. This last way is the worst of all, it generally turns out like a new debt contracted by an insolvent debtor, and leads to greater embarrassment. There are cases in which this course is advisable; others where there is nothing else left; also instances in which it has been successful; but upon the whole it is certainly true that its adoption is usually influenced less by a clear persuasion of its being the surest way of attaining the aim than by another inadmissible motive – this motive is the dread of encountering the enemy. Woe to the Commander who gives in to this! However much the moral of his Army may have deteriorated, and however well founded may be his apprehensions of being at a disadvantage in any conflict with the enemy, the evil will only be made worse by too anxiously avoiding every possible risk of collision. Buonaparte in 1813 would never have brought over the Rhine with him the 30,000 or 40,000 men who remained after the battle of Hanau,[112] if he had avoided that battle and tried to pass the Rhine at Mannheim or Coblenz. It is just by means of small combats carefully prepared and executed, and in which the defeated army being on the defensive, has always the assistance of the ground – it is just by these that the moral strength of the Army can first be resuscitated.

The beneficial effect of the smallest successes is incredible; but with most Generals the adoption of this plan implies great self-command. The other way, that of evading all encounter, appears at first so much easier, that there is a natural preference for its adoption. It is therefore usually just this system of evasion which best promotes the view of the pursuer, and often ends with the complete downfall of the pursued; we must, however, recollect here that we are speaking of a whole Army, not of a single Division, which, having been cut off, is seeking to join the main Army by making a detour; in such a case circumstances are different, and success is not uncommon. But there is one condition requisite to the success of this race of two Corps for an object, which is that a Division of the pursuing army should follow by the same road which the pursued has taken, in order to pick up stragglers, and keep up the impression which the presence of the enemy never fails to make. Blücher neglected this in his, in other respects unexceptionable, pursuit after La Belle Alliance.

Such marches tell upon the pursuer as well as the pursued, and they are not advisable if the enemy's Army rallies itself upon another considerable one; if it has a distinguished General at its head, and if its destruction is not already well prepared. But when this means can be adopted, it acts also like a great mechanical power. The losses of the beaten Army from sickness and fatigue are on such a disproportionate scale, the spirit of the Army is so weakened and lowered by the constant solicitude about impending ruin, that at last anything like a well organized stand is out of the question; every day thousands of prisoners fall into the enemy's hands without striking a blow. In such a season of complete good fortune, the conqueror need not hesitate about dividing his forces in order to draw into the vortex of destruction everything within reach of his Army, to cut off detachments, to take fortresses unprepared for defence, to occupy large towns, etc., etc. He may do anything until a new state of things arises, and the more he ventures in this way the longer will it be before that change will take place.

There is no want of examples of brilliant results from grand decisive victories, and of great and vigorous pursuits in the wars of Buonaparte. We need only quote Jena 1806, Ratisbonne 1809, Leipsic 1813, and Belle-Alliance 1815.

CHAPTER XIII

RETREAT AFTER A LOST BATTLE

In a lost battle the power of an Army is broken, the moral to a greater degree than the physical. A second battle unless fresh favourable circumstances come into play, would lead to a complete defeat, perhaps, to destruction. This is a military axiom. According to the usual course the retreat is continued up to that point where the equilibrium of forces is restored, either by reinforcements, or by the protection of strong fortresses, or by great defensive positions afforded by the country, or by a separation of the enemy's force. The magnitude of the losses sustained, the extent of the defeat, but still more the character of the enemy, will bring nearer or put off the instant of this equilibrium. How many instances may be found of a beaten Army rallied again at a short distance, without its circumstances having altered in any way since the battle. The cause of this may be traced to the moral weakness of the adversary, or to the preponderance gained in the battle not having been sufficient to make a lasting impression.

To profit by this weakness or mistake of the enemy, not to yield one inch breadth more than the pressure of circumstances demands, but above all things, in order to keep up the moral forces to as advantageous a point as possible, a slow retreat, offering incessant resistance, and bold courageous counterstrokes, whenever the enemy seeks to gain any excessive advantages, are absolutely necessary. Retreats of great Generals and of Armies inured to War have always resembled the retreat of a wounded lion, and such is, undoubtedly, also the best theory.

It is true that at the moment of quitting a dangerous position we have often seen trifling formalities observed which caused a waste of time, and were, therefore, attended with danger, whilst in such cases everything depends on getting out of the place speedily. Practised Generals reckon this maxim a very important one. But such cases must not be confounded with a general retreat after a lost battle. Whoever then thinks by a few rapid marches to gain a start, and more easily to recover a firm standing, commits a great error. The first movements should be as small as possible, and it is a maxim in general not to suffer ourselves to be dictated to by the enemy. This maxim cannot be followed without bloody fighting with the enemy at our heels, but the gain is worth the sacrifice; without it we get into an accelerated pace which soon turns into a headlong rush, and costs merely in stragglers more men than rear-guard combats, and besides that extinguishes the last remnants of the spirit of resistance.

A strong rear-guard composed of picked troops, commanded by the bravest General, and supported by the whole Army at critical moments, a careful utilization of ground, strong ambuscades wherever the boldness of the enemy's advance-guard, and the ground, afford opportunity; in short, the preparation and the system of regular small battles – these are the means of following this principle.

The difficulties of a retreat are naturally greater or less according as the battle has been fought under more or less favourable circumstances, and according as it has been more or less obstinately contested. The battle of Jena and La Belle-Alliance show how impossible anything like a regular retreat may become, if the last man is used up against a powerful enemy.

Now and again it has been suggested[113] to divide for the purpose of retreating, therefore to retreat in separate divisions or even eccentrically. Such a separation as is made merely for convenience, and along with which concentrated action continues possible and is kept in view, is not what we now refer to; any other kind is extremely dangerous, contrary to the nature of the thing, and therefore a great error. Every lost battle is a principle of weakness and disorganization; and the first and immediate desideratum is to concentrate, and in concentration to recover order, courage, and confidence. The idea of harassing the enemy by separate corps on both flanks at the moment when he is following up his victory, is a perfect anomaly; a faint-hearted pedant might be overawed by his enemy in that manner, and for such a case it may answer; but where we are not sure of this failing in our opponent it is better let alone. If the strategic relations after a battle require that we should cover ourselves right and left by detachments, so much must be done, as from circumstances is unavoidable, but this fractioning must always be regarded as an evil, and we are seldom in a state to commence it the day after the battle itself.

If Frederick the Great after the battle of Kollin, and the raising of the siege of Prague retreated in three columns that was done not out of choice, but because the position of his forces, and the necessity of covering Saxony, left him no alternative, Buonaparte after the battle of Brienne, sent Marmont back to the Aube, whilst he himself passed the Seine, and turned towards Troyes; but that this did not end in disaster, was solely owing to the circumstances that the Allies, instead of pursuing divided their forces in like manner, turning with the one part (Blücher) towards the Marne, while with the other (Schwartzenberg), from fear of being too weak, they advanced with exaggerated caution.

BOOK FIVE

PLAN OF WAR

CHAPTER I

INTRODUCTION

IN the chapter on the essence and object of War, we sketched, in a certain measure, its general conception, and pointed out its relations to surrounding circumstances, in order to commence with a sound fundamental idea. We there cast a glance at the manifold difficulties which the mind encounters in the consideration of this subject, whilst we postponed the closer examination of them, and stopped at the conclusion, that the overthrow of the enemy, consequently the destruction of his combatant force, is the chief object of the whole of the action of War. This put us in a position to show in the following chapter, that the means which the act of War employs is the combat alone. In this manner we think we have obtained at the outset a correct point of view.

Having now gone through singly all the principal relations and forms which appear in military action, but are extraneous to, or outside of, the combat, in order that we might fix more distinctly their value, partly through the nature of the thing, partly from the lessons of experience which military history affords, purify them from, and root out, those vague ambiguous ideas which are generally mixed up with them, and also to put prominently forward the real object of the act of War, the destruction of the enemy's combatant force as the primary object universally belonging to it; we now return to War as a whole, as we propose to speak of the Plan of War, and of campaigns; and that obliges us to revert to the ideas in our first book.

In these chapters, which are to deal with the whole question, is contained Strategy, properly speaking, in its most comprehensive and important features. We enter this innermost part of its domain, where all other threads meet, not without a degree of diffidence, which, indeed, is amply justified.

If, on the one hand, we see how extremely simple the operations of War appear; if we hear and read how the greatest Generals speak of it, just in the plainest and briefest manner, how the government and management of this ponderous machine, with its hundred thousand limbs, is made no more of in their lips than if they were only speaking of their own persons, so that the whole tremendous act of War is individualized into a kind of duel; if we find the motives also of their action brought into connexion sometimes with a few simple ideas, sometimes with some excitement of feeling; if we see the easy, sure, we might almost say light, manner in which they treat the subject – and now see, on the other hand, the immense number of circumstances which present themselves for the consideration of the mind; the long, often indefinite distances to which the threads of the subject run out and the number of combinations which lie before us; if we reflect that it is the duty of theory to embrace all this systematically, that is with clearness and fullness, and always to refer the action to the necessity of a sufficient cause, then comes upon us an overpowering dread of being dragged down to a pedantic dogmatism, to crawl about in the lower regions of heavy abstruse conceptions, where we shall never meet any great captain, with his natural *coup d'œil.* If the result of an attempt at theory is to be of this kind, it would have been as well, or rather, it would have been better, not to have made the attempt; it could only bring down on theory the contempt of genius, and the attempt itself would soon be forgotten. And on the other hand, this facile *coup d'œil* of the General, this simple art of forming notions, this personification of the whole action of War, is so entirely and completely the soul of the right method of conducting War, that in no other but this broad way is it possible to conceive that freedom of the mind which is indispensable if it is to dominate events, not to be overpowered by them.

With some fear we proceed again; we can only do so by pursuing the way which we have prescribed for ourselves from the first. Theory ought to throw a clear light on the mass of objects, that the mind may the easier find its bearings; theory ought to pull up the weeds which error has sown broadcast; it should show the relations of things to each other, separate the important from the trifling. Where ideas resolve themselves spontaneously into such a core of Truth as is called Principle, when they of themselves keep such a line as forms a rule, Theory should indicate the same.

Whatever the mind seizes, the rays of light which are awakened in it by this exploration amongst the fundamental notions of things, *that is the assistance which Theory affords the mind.* Theory can give no formulas with which to solve problems; it cannot confine the mind's course to the narrow line of necessity by Principle set up on both sides. It lets the mind take a look at the mass of objects and their relations, and then allows it to go free to the higher regions of action, there to act according to the measure of its natural forces, with the energy of the whole of those forces combined, and to grasp the *True* and the *Right*, as one single clear idea, which, shooting forth from under the united pressure of all these forces, would seem to be rather a product of feeling than of reflection.[114]

CHAPTER II

ABSOLUTE AND REAL WAR

THE Plan of the War comprehends the whole Military Act; through it that Act becomes a whole, which must have one final determinate object, in which all particular objects must become absorbed. No War is commenced, or, at least, no War should be commenced, if people acted wisely, without first seeking a reply to the question, What is to be attained by and in the same? The first is the final object; the other is the intermediate aim. By this chief consideration the whole course of the War is prescribed, the extent of the means and the measure of energy are determined; its influence manifests itself down to the smallest organ of action.

We said in the first chapter, that the overthrow of the enemy is the natural end of the act of War; and that if we would keep within the strictly philosophical limits of the idea, there can be no other in reality.

As this idea must apply to both the belligerent parties, it must follow, that there can be no suspension in the Military Act, and peace cannot take place until one or other of the parties concerned is overthrown.

In the chapter on the suspension of the Belligerent Act, we have shown how the simple principle of hostility applied to its embodiment, man, and all circumstances out of which it makes a War, is subject to checks and modifications from causes which are inherent in the apparatus of War.

But this modification is not nearly sufficient to carry us from the original conception of War to the concrete form in which it almost everywhere appears. Most Wars appear only as an angry feeling on both sides, under the influence of which, each side takes up arms to protect himself, and to put his adversary in fear, and – when opportunity offers, to strike a blow. They are, therefore, not like mutually destructive elements brought into collision, but like tensions of two elements still apart which discharge themselves in small partial shocks.

But what is now the non-conducting medium which hinders the complete discharge? Why is the philosophical conception not satisfied? That medium consists in the number of interests, forces, and circumstances of various kinds, in the existence of the State, which are affected by the War, and through the infinite ramifications of which the logical consequence cannot be carried out as it would on the simple threads of a few conclusions; in this labyrinth it sticks fast, and man, who in great things as well as in small, usually acts more on the impulse of ideas and feelings, than according to strictly logical conclusions, is hardly conscious of his confusion, unsteadiness of purpose, and inconsistency.

But if the intelligence by which the War is decreed could even go over all these things relating to the War, without for a moment losing sight of its aim, still all the other intelligences in the State which are concerned may not be able to do the same; thus an opposition arises, and with that comes the necessity for a force capable of overcoming the inertia of the whole mass – a force which is seldom forthcoming to the full.

This inconsistency takes place on one or other of the two sides, or it may be on both sides, and becomes the cause of the

War being something quite different to what it should be, according to the conception of it – a half-and-half production, a thing without a perfect inner cohesion.

This is how we find it almost everywhere, and we might doubt whether our notion of its absolute character or nature was founded in reality, if we had not seen real warfare make its appearance in this absolute completeness just in our own times. After a short introduction performed by the French Revolution, the impetuous Buonaparte quickly brought it to this point. Under him it was carried on without slackening for a moment until the enemy was prostrated, and the counter stroke followed almost with as little remission. Is it not natural and necessary that this phenomenon should lead us back to the original conception of War with all its rigorous deductions?

Shall we now rest satisfied with this idea, and judge of all Wars according to it, however much they may differ from it – deduce from it all the requirements of theory?

We must decide upon this point, for we can say nothing trustworthy on the Plan of War until we have made up our minds whether War should only be of this kind, or whether it may be of another kind.

If we give an affirmative to the first, then our Theory will be, in all respects, nearer to the necessary, it will be a clearer and more settled thing. But what should we say then of all Wars since those of Alexander up to the time of Buonaparte, if we except some campaigns of the Romans? We should have to reject them in a lump, and yet we cannot, perhaps, do so without being ashamed of our presumption. But an additional evil is, that we must say to ourselves, that in the next ten years there may perhaps be a War of that same kind again, in spite of our Theory; and that this Theory, with a rigorous logic, is still quite powerless against the force of circumstances. We must, therefore, decide to construe War as it is to be, and not from pure conception, but by allowing room for everything of a foreign nature which mixes up with it and fastens itself upon it – all the natural inertia and friction of its parts, the whole of the inconsistency, the vagueness and hesitation (or timidity) of the human mind: we shall have to grasp the idea that War, and the form which we give it, proceeds from ideas, feelings, and circumstances which dominate for the moment; indeed, if we would be perfectly candid we must admit that this has even been the case where it has taken its absolute character, that is, under Buonaparte.

If we must do so, if we must grant that War originates and takes its form not from a final adjustment of the innumerable relations with which it is connected, but from some amongst them which happen to predominate, then it follows, as a matter of course, that it rests upon a play of possibilities, probabilities, good fortune and bad, in which rigorous logical deduction often gets lost, and in which it is in general a useless, inconvenient instrument for the head; then it also follows that War may be a thing which is sometimes War in a greater, sometimes in a lesser degree.

All this, theory must admit, but it is its duty to give the foremost place to the absolute form of War, and to use that form as a general point of direction, that whoever wishes to learn something from theory, may accustom himself never to lose sight of it, to regard it as the natural measure of all his hopes and fears, in order to approach it *where he can, or where he must.*

That a leading idea, which lies at the root of our thoughts and actions, gives them a certain tone and character, even when the immediately determining grounds come from totally different regions, is just as certain as that the painter can give this or that tone to his picture by the colours with which he lays on his ground.

Theory is indebted to the last Wars for being able to do this effectually now. Without these warning examples of the destructive force of the element set free, she might have talked herself hoarse to no purpose; no one would have believed possible what all have now lived to see realized.

Would Prussia have ventured to penetrate into France in the year 1798 with 70,000 men, if she had foreseen that the reaction in case of failure would be so strong as to overthrow the old balance of power in Europe?

Would Prussia, in 1806, have made War with 100,000 against France, if she had supposed that the first pistol shot would be a spark in the heart of the mine, which would blow it into the air?

CHAPTER III

(A) INTERDEPENDENCE OF THE PARTS IN WAR

ACCORDING as we have in view the absolute form of War, or one of the real forms deviating more or less from it, so likewise different notions of its result will arise.

In the absolute form, where everything is the effect of its natural and necessary cause, one thing follows another in rapid succession; there is, if we may use the expression, no neutral space; there is – on account of the manifold reactionary effects which War contains in itself,[115] on account of the connexion in which, strictly speaking, the whole series of combats[116] follow one after another, on account of the culminating point which every victory has, beyond which losses and defeats commence – on account of all these natural relations of War there is, I say, only *one result*, to wit, the *final result*. Until it takes place nothing is decided, nothing won, nothing lost. Here we may say indeed: the end crowns the work. In this view, therefore, War is an indivisible whole, the parts of which (the subordinate results) have no value except in their relation to this whole. The conquest of Moscow, and of half Russia in 1812, was of no value to Buonaparte unless it obtained for him the peace which he desired. But it was only a part of his Plan of campaign; to complete that Plan, one part was still wanted, the destruction of the Russian Army, if we suppose this, added to the other success, then the peace was as certain as it is possible for things of this kind to be. This second part Buonaparte missed at the right time, and he could never afterwards attain it, and so the whole of the first part was not only useless, but fatal to him.

To this view of the relative connexion of results in War, which may be regarded as extreme, stands opposed another extreme, according to which War is composed of single independent results, in which, as in any number of games played, the preceding has no influence on the next following; everything here, therefore, depends only on the sum total of the results, and we can lay up each single one like a counter at play.[117]

Just as the first kind of view derives its truth from the nature of things, so we find that of the second in history. There are cases without number in which a small moderate advantage might have been gained without any very onerous condition being attached to it. The more the element of War is modified the more common these cases become; but as little as the first of the views now imagined was ever completely realized in any War, just as little is there any War in which the last suits in all respects, and the first can be dispensed with.

If we keep to the first of these supposed views, we must perceive the necessity of every War being looked upon as a whole from the very commencement, and that at the very first step forwards, the Commander should have in his eye the object to which every line must converge.

If we admit the second view, then subordinate advantages may be pursued on their own account, and the rest left to subsequent events.

As neither of these forms of conception is entirely without result, therefore theory cannot dispense with either. But it makes this difference in the use of them, that it requires the first to be laid as a fundamental idea at the root of everything, and that the latter shall only be used as a modification which is justified by circumstances.

If Frederick the Great in the years 1742, 1744, 1757, and 1758, thrust out from Silesia and Saxony a fresh offensive point into the Austrian Empire, which he knew very well could not lead to a new and durable conquest like that of Silesia and Saxony, it was done not with a view to the overthrow of the Austrian Empire, but from a lesser motive, namely, to gain time and strength; and it was optional with him to pursue that subordinate object without being afraid that he should thereby risk his whole existence.[118] But if Prussia in 1806, and Austria in 1805, 1809, proposed to themselves a still more moderate object, that of driving the French over the Rhine, they would not have acted in a reasonable manner if they had not first scanned in their minds the whole series of events which, either in the case of success or of the reverse, would probably follow the first step, and lead up to peace. This was quite indispensable, as well to enable them to determine with themselves how far victory might be followed up without danger, and how and where they would be in a condition to arrest the course of victory on the enemy's side.

An attentive consideration of history shows wherein the difference of the two cases consists. At the time of the Silesian War in the eighteenth century, War was still a mere Cabinet affair, in which the people only took part as a blind instrument; at the beginning of the nineteenth century the people on each side weighed in the scale. The Commanders opposed to Frederick the Great were men who acted on commission, and just on that account men in whom caution was a predominant characteristic; the opponent of the Austrians and Prussians may be described in a few words as the very God of War himself.

Must not these different circumstances give rise to quite different considerations? Should they not in the years 1805, 1806 and 1809 have pointed to the extremity of disaster as a very close possibility, nay, even a very great probability, and should they not at the same time have led to widely different plans and measures from any merely aimed at the conquest of a couple of fortresses or a paltry province?

They did not do so in a degree commensurate with their importance, although both Austria and Prussia judging by their armaments, felt that storms were brewing in the political atmosphere. They could not do so because those relations at that time were not yet so plainly developed as they have since been from history. It is just those very campaigns of 1805, 1806, 1809, and following ones, which have made it easier for us to form a conception of modern absolute War in its destroying energy.

Theory demands, therefore, that at the commencement of every War its character and main outline shall be defined according to what the political conditions and relations lead us to anticipate as probable. The more that, according to this probability, its character approaches the form of absolute War; the more its outline embraces the mass of the belligerent States and draws them into the vortex – so much the more complete will be the relation of events to one another and the whole, but so much the more necessary will it also be not to take the first step without thinking what may be the last.

(B) OF THE MAGNITUDE OF THE OBJECT OF THE WAR, AND THE EFFORTS TO BE MADE

The compulsion which we must use towards our enemy will be regulated by the proportions of our own and his political demands. In so far as these are mutually known they will give the measure of the mutual efforts; but they are not always quite so evident, and this may be a first ground of a difference in the means adopted by each.

The situation and relations of the States are not like each other; this may become a second cause.

The strength of will, the character and capabilities of the Governments are as little like; this is a third cause.

These three elements cause an uncertainty in the calculation of the amount of resistance to be expected, consequently an uncertainty as to the amount of means to be applied and the object to be chosen.

As in War the want of sufficient exertion may result not only in failure but in positive harm, therefore, the two sides respectively seek to outstrip each other, which produces a reciprocal action.

This might lead to the utmost extremity of exertion, if it were possible to define such a point. But then regard for the amount of the political demands would be lost, the means would lose all relation to the end, and in most cases this aim at an extreme effort would be wrecked by the opposing weight of forces within itself.

In this manner, he who undertakes War is brought back again

into a middle course, in which he acts to a certain extent upon the principle of only applying so much force and aiming at such an object in War as is just sufficient for the attainment of its political object.[119] To make this principle practicable he must renounce every absolute necessity of a result, and throw out of the calculation remote contingencies.

Here, therefore, the action of the mind leaves the province of science, strictly speaking, of logic and mathematics, and becomes in the widest sense of the term an *Art*, that is, skill in discriminating, by the tact of judgement among an infinite multitude of objects and relations, that which is the most important and decisive. This tact of judgement consists unquestionably more or less in some intuitive comparison of things and relations by which the remote and unimportant are more quickly set aside, and the more immediate and important are sooner discovered than they could be by strictly logical deduction.

In order to ascertain the real scale of the means which we must put forth for War, we must think over the political object both on our own side and on the enemy's side; we must consider the power and position of the enemy's State as well as of our own, the character of his Government and of his people, and the capacities of both, and all that again on our own side, and the political connexions of other States, and the effect which the War will produce on those States. That the determination of these diverse circumstances and their diverse connexions with each other is an immense problem, that it is the true flash of genius which discovers here in a moment what is right, and that it would be quite out of the question to become master of the complexity merely by a methodical study, it is easy to conceive.[120]

In this sense Buonaparte was quite right when he said that it would be a problem in algebra before which a Newton might stand aghast.

If the diversity and magnitude of the circumstances and the uncertainty as to the right measure augment in a high degree the difficulty of obtaining a right result, we must not overlook the fact that although the incomparable *importance* of the matter does not increase the complexity and difficulty of the problem, still it very much increases the merit of its solution. In men of an ordinary stamp freedom and activity of mind are depressed, not increased, by the sense of danger and responsibility; but where these things give wings to strengthen the judgement, there undoubtedly must be unusual greatness of soul.

First of all, therefore, we must admit that the judgement on an approaching War, on the end to which it should be directed, and on the means which are required, can only be formed after a full consideration of the whole of the circumstances in connexion with it: with which therefore must also be combined the most individual traits of the moment; next, that this decision, like all in military life, cannot be purely objective, but must be determined by the mental and moral qualities of Princes, Statesmen, and Generals, whether they are united in the person of one man or not.

The subject becomes general and more fit to be treated of in the abstract if we look at the general relations in which States have been placed by circumstances at different times. We must allow ourselves here a passing glance at history.

Half-civilized Tartars, the republics of ancient times, the feudal lords and commercial cities of the Middle Ages, kings of the eighteenth century, and, lastly, princes and people of the nineteenth century, all carry on War in their own way, carry it on differently, with different means, and for a different object.

The Tartars seek new abodes. They march out as a nation with their wives and children, they are, therefore, greater than any other Army in point of numbers, and their object is to make the enemy submit or expel him altogether. By these means they would soon overthrow everything before them if a high degree of civilization could be made compatible with such a condition.

The old republics, with the exception of Rome, were of small extent; still smaller their Armies, for they excluded the great mass of the populace; they were too numerous and lay too close together not to find an obstacle to great enterprises in the natural equilibrium in which small separate parts always place themselves according to the general law of nature: therefore their Wars were confined to devastating the open country and taking some towns in order to ensure to themselves in these a certain degree of influence for the future.

Rome alone forms an exception, but not until the later period of its history. For a long time, by means of small bands, it carried on the usual warfare with its neighbours for booty and alliances. It became great more through the alliances which it formed, and through which neighbouring peoples by degrees became amalgamated with it into one whole, than through actual conquests. It was only after having spread itself in this manner all over Southern Italy, that it began to advance as a really conquering power. Carthage fell, Spain and Gaul were conquered, Greece subdued, and its dominion extended to Egypt and Asia. At this period its military power was immense, without its efforts being in the same proportion. These forces were kept up by its riches; it no longer resembled the ancient republics, nor itself as it had been; it stands alone.

Just as peculiar in their way are the Wars of Alexander. With a small Army, but distinguished for its intrinsic perfection, he overthrew the decayed fabric of the Asiatic States; without rest, and regardless of risks, he traverses the breadth of Asia, and penetrates into India. No republics could do this. Only a King, in a certain measure his own condottiere, could get through so much so quickly.

The great and small monarchies of the Middle Ages carried on their Wars with feudal levies. Everything was then restricted to a short period of time; whatever could not be done in that time was held to be impracticable. The feudal force itself was raised through an organization of vassaldom; the bond which held it together was partly legal obligation, partly a voluntary contract; the whole formed a real confederation. The armament and tactics were based on the right of might, on single combat, and therefore little suited to large bodies. In fact, at no period has the union of States been so weak, and the individual citizen so independent. All this influenced the character of the Wars at that period in the most distinct manner. They were comparatively rapidly carried out, there was little time spent idly in camps, but the object was generally only punishing, not subduing the enemy. They carried off his cattle, burnt his towns, and then returned home again.

The great commercial towns and small republics brought

forward the condottieri. That was an expensive, and therefore, as far as visible strength, a very limited military force; as for its intensive strength, it was of still less value in that respect; so far from their showing anything like extreme energy or impetuosity in the field, their combats were generally only sham-fights. In a word, hatred and enmity no longer roused a State to personal activity, but had become articles of trade; War lost a great part of its danger, altered completely its nature, and nothing we can say of the character it then assumed would be applicable to it in its reality.

The feudal system condensed itself by degrees into a decided territorial supremacy; the ties binding the State together became closer; obligations which concerned the person were made the subject of composition; by degrees gold became the substitute in most cases, and the feudal levies were turned into mercenaries. The condottieri formed the connecting-link in the change, and were therefore, for a time, the instrument of the more powerful States; but this had not lasted long when the soldier, hired for a limited term, was turned into a *standing mercenary*, and the military force of States now became an Army, having its base in the public treasury.

It is only natural that the slow advance to this stage caused a diversified interweaving of all three kinds of military force. Under Henry IV we find the feudal contingents, condottieri, and standing Army all employed together. The condottieri carried on their existence up to the period of the Thirty Years' War, indeed there are some slight traces of them even in the eighteenth century.

The other relations of the States of Europe at these different periods were quite as peculiar as their military forces. Upon the whole this part of the world had split up into a mass of petty States, partly republics in a state of internal dissension, partly small monarchies in which the power of the government was very limited and insecure. A State in either of these cases could not be considered as a real unity; it was rather an agglomeration of loosely connected forces. Neither, therefore, could such a State be considered an intelligent being, acting in accordance with simple logical rules.

It is from this point of view we must look at the foreign politics and Wars of the Middle Ages. Let us only think of the continual expeditions of the Emperors of Germany into Italy for five centuries, without any substantial conquest of that country resulting from them, or even having been so much as in view. It is easy to look upon this as a fault repeated over and over again – as a false view which had its root in the nature of the times, but it is more in accordance with reason to regard it as the consequence of a hundred important causes which we can partially realize in idea, but the vital energy of which it is impossible for us to understand so vividly as those who were brought into actual conflict with them. As long as the great States which have risen out of this chaos required time to consolidate and organize themselves, their whole power and energy is chiefly directed to that point; their foreign Wars are few, and those that took place bear the stamp of a State unity not yet well cemented.

The Wars between France and England are the first that appear, and yet at that time France is not to be considered as really a monarchy, but as an agglomeration of dukedoms and countships; England, although bearing more the semblance of a unity, still fought with the feudal organization, and was hampered by serious domestic troubles.

Under Louis XI, France made its greatest step towards internal unity; under Charles VIII it appears in Italy as a power bent on conquest; and under Louis XIV it had brought its political state and its standing Army to the highest perfection.

Spain attains to unity under Ferdinand the Catholic; through accidental marriage connexions, under Charles V, suddenly arose the great Spanish monarchy, composed of Spain, Burgundy, Germany, and Italy united. What this colossus wanted in unity and internal political cohesion, it made up for by gold, and its standing Army came for the first time into collision with the standing Army of France. After Charles's abdication, the great Spanish colossus split into two parts, Spain and Austria. The latter, strengthened by the acquisition of Bohemia and Hungary, now appears on the scene as a great power, towing the German Confederation like a small vessel behind her.

The end of the seventeenth century, the time of Louis XIV, is to be regarded as the point in history at which the standing military power, such as it existed in the eighteenth century, reached the zenith. That military force was based on enlistment and money. States had organized themselves into complete unities, and the Governments, by commuting the personal obligations of their subjects into a money payment, had concentrated their whole power in their treasuries. Through the rapid strides in social improvements, and a more enlightened system of government, this power had become very great in comparison to what it had been. France appeared in the field with a standing Army of a couple of hundred thousand men, and the other powers in proportion.

The other relations of States had likewise altered. Europe was divided into a dozen kingdoms and two republics; it was now conceivable that two of these powers might fight with each other without ten times as many others being mixed up in the quarrel, as would certainly have been the case formerly. The possible combinations in political relations were still manifold, but they could be discerned and determined from time to time according to probability.

Internal relations had almost everywhere settled down into a pure monarchical form; the rights and influence of privileged bodies or estates had gradually died away, and the Cabinet had become a complete unity, acting for the State in all its external relations. The time had therefore come when a suitable instrument and a despotic will could give War a form in accordance with the theoretical conception.

And at this epoch appeared three new Alexanders – Gustavus Adolphus, Charles XII, and Frederick the Great, whose aim was, by small but highly disciplined Armies, to raise little States to the rank of great monarchies, and to throw down everything that opposed them. Had they only had to deal with Asiatic States they would have more closely resembled Alexander in the parts they acted. In any case, we may look upon them as the precursors of Buonaparte as respects that which may be risked in War.

But what War gained on the one side in force and consistency was lost again on the other side.

Armies were supported out of the treasury, which the Sovereign regarded partly as his private purse, or at least as a resource belonging to the Government, and not to the people. Relations with other States, except with respect to a few commercial subjects, mostly concerned only the interests of the treasury or of the Government, not those of the people; at least ideas tended everywhere in that way. The Cabinets, therefore, looked upon themselves as the owners and administrators of large estates, which they were continually seeking to increase without the tenants on these estates being particularly interested in this improvement. The people, therefore, who in the Tartar invasions were everything in War, who, in the old republics, and in the Middle Ages (if we restrict the idea to those possessing the rights of citizens), were of great consequence, were in the eighteenth century absolutely nothing directly, having only still an indirect influence on the War, through their virtues and faults.

In this manner, in proportion as the Government separated itself from the people, and regarded itself as the State, War became more exclusively a business of the Government, which it carried on by means of the money in its coffers and the idle vagabonds it could pick up in its own and neighbouring countries. The consequence of this was, that the means which the Government could command had tolerably well-defined limits, which could be mutually estimated, both as to their extent and duration; this robbed War of its most dangerous feature: namely, the effort towards the extreme, and the hidden series of possibilities connected therewith.

The financial means, the contents of the treasury, the state of credit of the enemy, were approximately known as well as the size of his Army. Any large increase of these at the outbreak of a War was impossible. Inasmuch as the limits of the enemy's power could thus be judged of, a State felt tolerably secure from complete subjugation, and as the State was conscious at the same time of the limits of its own means, it saw itself restricted to a moderate aim. Protected from an extreme, there was no necessity to venture on an extreme. Necessity no longer giving an impulse in that direction, that impulse could only now be given by courage and ambition. But these found a powerful counterpoise in the political relations. Even Kings in command were obliged to use the instrument of War with caution. If the Army was dispersed, no new one could be got, and except the Army there was nothing. This imposed as a necessity great prudence in all undertakings. It was only when a decided advantage seemed to present itself that they made use of the costly instrument; to bring about such an opportunity was a General's art; but until it was brought about they floated to a certain degree in an absolute vacuum, there was no ground of action, and all forces, that is, all designs, seemed to rest. The original motive of the aggressor faded away in prudence and circumspection.

Thus War, in reality, became a regular game in which Time and Chance shuffled the cards; but in its signification it was only diplomacy somewhat intensified, a more vigorous way of negotiating, in which battles and sieges were substituted for diplomatic notes. To obtain some moderate advantage in order to make use of it in negotiations for peace was the aim even of the most ambitious.

This restricted, shrivelled-up form of War proceeded, as we have said, from the narrow basis on which it was supported. But that excellent Generals and Kings, like Gustavus Adolphus, Charles XII, and Frederick the Great, at the head of Armies just as excellent, could not gain more prominence in the general mass of phenomena – that even these men were obliged to be contented to remain at the ordinary level of moderate results, is to be attributed to the balance of power in Europe. Now that States had become greater, and their centres further apart from each other, what had formerly been done through direct perfectly natural interests, proximity, contact, family connexions, personal friendship, to prevent any one single State among the number from becoming suddenly great was effected by a higher cultivation of the art of diplomacy. Political interests, attractions and repulsions developed into a very refined system, so that a cannon shot could not be fired in Europe without all the Cabinets having some interest in the occurrence.

A new Alexander must therefore try the use of a good pen as well as his good sword; and yet he never went very far with his conquests.

But although Louis XIV had in view to overthrow the balance of power in Europe, and at the end of the seventeenth century had already got to such a point as to trouble himself little about the general feeling of animosity, he carried on War just as it had heretofore been conducted; for while his Army was certainly that of the greatest and richest monarch in Europe, in its nature it was just like others.

Plundering and devastating the enemy's country, which play such an important part with Tartars, with ancient nations, and even in the Middle Ages, were no longer in accordance with the spirit of the age. They were justly looked upon as unnecessary barbarity, which might easily induce reprisals, and which did more injury to the enemy's subjects than the enemy's Government, therefore, produced no effect beyond throwing the Nation back many stages in all that relates to peaceful arts and civilization. War, therefore, confined itself more and more, both as regards means and end, to the Army itself. The Army, with its fortresses and some prepared positions, constituted a State in a State, within which the element of War slowly consumed itself. All Europe rejoiced at its taking this direction, and held it to be the necessary consequence of the spirit of progress. Although there lay in this an error, inasmuch as the progress of the human mind can never lead to what is absurd, can never make five out of twice two, as we have already said and must again repeat, still upon the whole this change had a beneficial effect for the people; only it is not to be denied that it had a tendency to make War still more an affair of the State, and to separate it still more from the interests of the people. The plan of a War on the part of the State assuming the offensive in those times consisted generally in the conquest of one or other of the enemy's provinces; the plan of the defender was to prevent this; the particular plan of campaign was to take one or other of the enemy's fortresses, or to prevent one of our own from being taken; it was only when a battle became unavoidable for this purpose that it was sought for and fought. Whoever fought a battle without this unavoidable necessity, from mere innate desire of gaining a victory, was reckoned a General with too much daring. Generally the campaign passed over with one siege, or, if it was a very active one, with two sieges, and winter quarters, which were regarded as a necessity, and during which the faulty arrangements of the one could never be taken advantage of by the other and in which the mutual relations of the two parties almost entirely ceased, formed a distinct limit to the activity which was considered to belong to one campaign.

If the forces opposed were too much on an equality, or if the aggressor was decidedly the weaker of the two, then neither battle nor siege took place, and the whole of the operations of the campaign pivoted on the maintenance of certain positions and magazines, and the regular exhaustion of particular districts of country.

As long as War was universally conducted in this manner, and the natural limits of its force were so close and obvious, so far from anything absurd being perceived in it, all was considered to be in the most regular order; and criticism, which in the eighteenth century began to turn its attention to the field of art in War, addressed itself to details without troubling itself much about the beginning and the end. Thus there was eminence and perfection of every kind, and even Field-Marshal Daun – to whom it was chiefly owing that Frederick the Great completely attained his object, and that Maria Theresa completely failed in hers – could still pass for a great General. Only now and again a more penetrating judgement made its appearance, that is, sound common sense acknowledged that with superior numbers something positive should be attained or War is badly conducted, whatever art may be displayed.

Thus matters stood when the French Revolution broke out; Austria and Prussia tried their diplomatic Art of War; this very soon proved insufficient. Whilst, according to the usual way of seeing things, all hopes were placed on a very limited military force in 1793, such a force as no one had any conception of made its appearance. War had again suddenly become an affair of the people, and that of a people numbering thirty millions, every one of whom regarded himself as a citizen of the State. Without entering here into the details of circumstances with which this great phenomenon was attended, we shall confine ourselves to the results which interest us at present. By this participation of the people in the War instead of a Cabinet and an Army, a whole Nation with its natural weight came into the scale. Henceforward, the means available – the efforts which might be called forth – had no longer any definite limits; the energy with which the War itself might be conducted had no longer any counterpoise, and consequently the danger for the adversary had risen to the extreme.

If the whole War of the Revolution passed over without all this making itself felt in its full force and becoming quite evident, if the Generals of the Revolution did not persistently press on to the final extreme, and did not overthrow the monarchies in Europe; if the German Armies now and again had the opportunity of resisting with success, and checking for a time the torrent of victory – the cause lay in reality in that technical incompleteness with which the French had to contend, which showed itself first amongst the common soldiers, then in the Generals, lastly, at the time of the Directory, in the Government itself.

After all this was perfected by the hand of Buonaparte, this military power, based on the strength of the whole nation, marched over Europe, smashing everything in pieces so surely and certainly, that where it only encountered the old-fashioned Armies the result was not doubtful for a moment. A reaction, however, awoke in due time. In Spain, the War became of itself an affair of the people. In Austria, in the year 1809, the Government commenced extraordinary efforts, by means of Reserves and Landwehr, which were nearer to the true object, and far surpassed in degree what this State had hitherto conceived possible. In Russia, in 1812, the example of Spain and Austria was taken as a pattern, the enormous dimensions of that Empire on the one hand allowed the preparations, although too long deferred, still to produce effect; and, on the other hand, intensified the effect produced. The result was brilliant. In Germany, Prussia rose up the first, made the War a National Cause, and without either money or credit and with a population reduced one-half, took the field with an Army twice as strong as that of 1806. The rest of Germany followed the example of Prussia sooner or later, and Austria, although less energetic than in

1809, still came forward with more than its usual strength. Thus it was that Germany and Russia, in the years 1813 and 1814, including all who took an active part in, or were absorbed in these two campaigns, appeared against France with about a million of men.

Under these circumstances, the energy thrown into the conduct of the War was quite different; and, although not quite on a level with that of the French, although at some points timidity was still to be observed, the course of the campaigns, upon the whole, may be said to have been in the new, not in the old, style. In eight months the theatre of War was removed from the Oder to the Seine. Proud Paris had to bow its head for the first time; and the redoubtable Buonaparte lay fettered on the ground.

Therefore, since the time of Buonaparte, War, through being first on one side, then again on the other, an affair of the whole Nation, has assumed quite a new nature, or rather it has approached much nearer to its real nature, to its absolute perfection. The means then called forth had no visible limit, the limit losing itself in the energy and enthusiasm of the Government and its subjects. By the extent of the means and the wide field of possible results, as well as by the powerful excitement of feeling which prevailed, energy in the conduct of War was immensely increased; the object of its action was the downfall of the foe; and not until the enemy lay powerless on the ground was it supposed to be possible to stop or to come to any understanding with respect to the mutual objects of the contest.

Thus, therefore, the element of War, freed from all conventional restrictions, broke loose, with all its natural force. The cause was the participation of the people in this great *affair of State*, and this participation arose partly from the effects of the French Revolution on the internal affairs of countries, partly from the threatening attitude of the French towards all Nations.

Now, whether this will be the case always in future, whether all Wars hereafter in Europe will be carried on with the whole power of the States, and, consequently, will only take place on account of great interests closely affecting the people, or whether a separation of the interests of the Government from those of the people will again gradually arise, would be a difficult point to settle; least of all shall we take it upon ourselves to settle it. But every one will agree with us, that bounds, which to a certain extent existed only in an unconsciousness of what is possible, when once thrown down, are not easily built up again; and that, at least, whenever great interests are in dispute, mutual hostility will discharge itself in the same manner as it has done in our times.

We here bring our historical survey to a close, for it was not our design to give at a gallop some of the principles on which War has been carried on in each age, but only to show how each period has had its own peculiar forms of War, its own restrictive conditions, and its own prejudices. Each period would, therefore, also keep its own theory of War, even if everywhere, in early times as well as in later, the task had been undertaken of working out a theory on philosophical principles. The events in each age must, therefore, be judged of in connexion with the peculiarities of the time, and only he who, less through an anxious study of minute details than through an accurate glance at the whole, can transfer himself into each particular age, is fit to understand and appreciate its Generals.

But this conduct of War, conditioned by the peculiar relations of States and of the military force employed, must still always contain in itself something more general, or rather something quite general, with which, above everything, theory is concerned.

The latest period of past time, in which War reached its absolute strength, contains most of what is of general application and necessary. But it is just as improbable that Wars henceforth will all have this grand character as that the wide barriers which have been opened to them will ever be completely closed again. Therefore, by a theory which only dwells upon this absolute War, all cases in which external influences alter the nature of War would be excluded or condemned as false. This cannot be the object of theory, which ought to be the science of War, not under ideal but under real circumstances. Theory, therefore, whilst casting a searching, discriminating and classifying glance at objects, should always have in view the manifold diversity of causes from which War may proceed, and should, therefore, so trace out its great features as to leave room for what is required by the exigencies of time and the moment.

Accordingly, we must add that the object which every one who undertakes War proposes to himself, and the means which he calls forth, are determined entirely according to the particular details of his position; on that very account they will also bear in themselves the character of the time and of the *general* relations; lastly, *that they are always subject to the general conclusions to be deduced from the nature of War.*

CHAPTER IV

ENDS IN WAR MORE PRECISELY DEFINED

Overthrow of the enemy

THE aim of War in conception must always be the overthrow of the enemy; this is the fundamental idea from which we set out.

Now, what is this overthrow? It does not always imply as necessary the complete conquest of the enemy's country. If the Germans had reached Paris in 1792, there – in all human probability – the War with the Revolutionary party would have been brought to an end at once for a season; it was not at all necessary at that time to beat their Armies beforehand, for those Armies were not yet to be looked upon as potent powers in themselves singly. On the other hand, in 1814, the Allies would not have gained everything by taking Paris if Buonaparte had still remained at the head of a considerable Army; but as his Army had nearly melted away, therefore, both in the years 1814 and 1815, the taking of Paris decided all. If Buonaparte in the year 1812, either before or after taking Moscow, had been able to give the Russian Army of 120,000 on the Kaluga road a complete defeat, such as he gave the Austrians in 1805, and the Prussian Army, 1806, then the possession of that capital would most probably have brought about a peace, although an enormous tract of country still remained to be conquered. In the year 1805 it was the battle of Austerlitz that was decisive; and, therefore, the previous possession of Vienna and two-thirds of the Austrian States was not of sufficient weight to gain for Buonaparte a peace; but, on the other hand also, after that battle of Austerlitz, the integrity of Hungary, still intact, was not of sufficient weight to prevent the conclusion of peace. In the Russian campaign, the complete defeat of the Russian Army was the last blow required: the Emperor Alexander had no other Army at hand, and, therefore, peace was the certain consequence of victory. If the Russian Army had been on the Danube along with the Austrian in 1805, and had shared in its defeat, then probably the conquest of Vienna would not have been necessary, and peace would have been concluded in Linz.

In other cases the complete conquest of a country has not been sufficient, as in the year 1807, in Prussia, when the blow levelled against the Russian auxiliary Army, in the doubtful battle of Eylau, was not decisive enough, and the undoubted victory of Friedland was required as a finishing blow, like the victory of Austerlitz eighteen months before.

We see that here, also, the result cannot be determined from general grounds; the individual causes, which no one knows who is not on the spot, and many of a moral nature which are never heard of, even the smallest traits and accidents, which only appear in history as anecdotes, are often decisive. All that theory can here say is as follows: That the great point is to keep the overruling relations of both parties in view. Out of them a certain centre of gravity, a centre of power and movement, will form itself, on which everything depends; and against this centre of gravity of the enemy, the concentrated blow of all the forces must be directed.

The little always depends on the great, the unimportant on the important, and the accidental on the essential. This must guide our view.

Alexander had his centre of gravity in his Army, so had Gustavus Adolphus, Charles XII, and Frederick the Great, and the career of any one of them would soon have been brought to a close by the destruction of his fighting force: in States torn by internal dissensions, this centre generally lies in the capital; in small States dependent on greater ones, it lies generally in the Army of these Allies; in a confederacy, it lies in the unity of interests; in a national insurrection, in the person of the chief leader, and in public opinion; against these points the blow must be directed. If the enemy by this loses his balance, no time must be allowed for him to recover it; the blow must be persistently repeated in the same direction, or, in other words, the conqueror must always direct his blows upon the mass, but not against a fraction of the enemy. It is not by conquering one of the enemy's provinces, with little trouble and superior numbers, and preferring the more secure possession of this unimportant conquest to great results, but by seeking out constantly the heart of the hostile power, and staking everything in order to gain all, that we can effectually strike the enemy to the ground.

But whatever may be the central point of the enemy's power against which we are to direct our operations, still the conquest and destruction of his Army is the surest commencement, and in all cases the most essential.

Hence we think that, according to the majority of ascertained facts, the following circumstances chiefly bring about the overthrow of the enemy:

(1). Dispersion of his Army if it forms, in some degree, a potential force.
(2). Capture of the enemy's capital city, if it is both the centre of the power of the State and the seat of political assemblies and factions.
(3). An effectual blow against the principal Ally, if he is more powerful than the enemy himself.

We have always hitherto supposed the enemy in War as a unity, which is allowable for considerations of a very general nature. But having said that the subjugation of the enemy lies in the overcoming his resistance, concentrated in the centre of gravity, we must lay aside this supposition and introduce the case in which we have to deal with more than one opponent.

If two or more States combine against a third, that combination constitutes, in a political aspect, only *one* War, at the same time this political union has also its degrees.

The question is whether each State in the coalition possesses an independent interest in, and an independent force with which to prosecute, the War; or whether there is one amongst them on whose interests and forces those of the others lean for support. The more that the last is the case, the easier it is to look upon the different enemies as one alone, and the more readily we can simplify our principal enterprise, to one great blow; and as long as this is in any way possible, it is the most thorough and complete means of success.

We may, therefore, establish it as a principle, that if we can conquer all our enemies by conquering one of them, the defeat of that one must be the aim of the War, because in that one we hit the common centre of gravity of the whole War.

There are very few cases in which this kind of conception is not admissible, and where this reduction of several centres of gravity to one cannot be made. But if this cannot be done, then indeed there is no alternative but to look upon the War as two or more separate Wars, each of which has its own aim. As this case supposes the substantive independence of several enemies, consequently a great superiority of the whole, therefore in this case the overthrow of the enemy cannot, in general, come into question.

We now turn more particularly to the question, When is such an object possible and advisable?

In the first place, our forces must be sufficient –

1. To gain a decisive victory over those of the enemy.
2. To make the expenditure of force which may be necessary to follow up the victory to a point at which it will no longer be possible for the enemy to regain his balance.

Next, we must feel sure that in our political situation such a result will not excite against us new enemies, who may compel us on the spot to set free our first enemy.

France, in the year 1806, was able completely to conquer Prussia, although in doing so it brought down upon itself the whole military power of Russia, because it was in a condition to cope with the Russians in Prussia.

France might have done the same in Spain in 1808 as far as regards England, but not as regards Austria. It was compelled to weaken itself materially in Spain in 1809, and must have quite given up the contest in that country if it had not had otherwise great superiority, both physically and morally, over Austria.

These three cases should therefore be carefully studied, that we may not lose in the last, the cause which we have gained in the former ones, and be condemned in costs.

In estimating the strength of forces, and that which may be effected by them, the idea very often suggests itself to look upon time by a dynamic analogy as a factor of forces, and to assume accordingly that half efforts, or half the number of forces would accomplish in two years what could only be effected in one year by the whole force united. This view, which lies at the bottom of military schemes, sometimes clearly, sometimes less plainly, is completely wrong.

An operation in War, like everything else upon earth, requires its time; as a matter of course we cannot walk from Wilna to Moscow in eight days; but there is no trace to be found in War of any reciprocal action between time and force, such as takes place in dynamics.

Time is necessary to both belligerents, and the only question is: Which of the two, judging by his position, has most reason to expect *special advantages* from time? Now (exclusive of peculiarities in the situation on one side or the other) the *vanquished* has plainly the most reason, at the same time certainly not by dynamic, but by psychological laws. Envy, jealousy, anxiety for self as well as now and again magnanimity, are the natural intercessors for the unfortunate; they raise up for him on the one hand friends, and on the other hand weaken and dissolve the coalition amongst his enemies. Therefore, by delay something advantageous is more likely to happen for the conquered than for the conqueror. Further, we must recollect that to make right use of a first victory, as we have already shown, a great expenditure of force is necessary; this is not a mere outlay once for all, but has to be kept up like housekeeping, on a great scale; the forces which have been sufficient to give us possession of a province are not always sufficient to meet this additional outlay; by degrees the strain upon our resources becomes greater, until at last it becomes insupportable; time, therefore, of itself may bring about a change.

Could the contributions which Buonaparte levied from the

Russians and Poles, in money and in other ways, in 1812, have procured the hundreds of thousands of men that he must have sent to Moscow in order to retain his position there?

But if the conquered provinces are sufficiently important, if there are in them points which are essential to the well-being of those parts which are not conquered, so that the evil, like a cancer, is perpetually of itself gnawing further into the system, then it is possible that the conqueror, although nothing further is done, may gain more than he loses. Now in this state of circumstances, if no help comes from without, then time may complete the work thus commenced; what still remains unconquered will, perhaps, fall of itself. Thus time may also become a factor of his forces, but this can only take place if a return blow from the conquered is no longer possible, a change of fortune in his favour no longer conceivable, when, therefore, this factor of his forces is no longer of any value to the conqueror; for he has accomplished the chief object, the danger of the culminating point is past, in short, the enemy is already subdued.

Our object in the above reasoning has been to show clearly that no conquest can be finished too soon, that spreading it over a *greater space of time* than is absolutely necessary for its completion, instead of *facilitating* it, makes it more *difficult*. If this assertion is true, it is further true also that if we are strong enough to effect a certain conquest, we must also be strong enough to do it in one march without intermediate stations. Of course we do not mean by this without short halts, in order to concentrate the forces, and make other indispensable arrangements.

By this view, which makes the character of a speedy and persistent effort towards a decision essential to offensive War, we think we have completely set aside all grounds for *that* theory which, in place of the irresistible continued following up of victory, would substitute a slow methodical system as being more sure and prudent. But even for those who have readily followed us so far, our assertion has, perhaps, after all so much the appearance of a paradox – is at first sight so much opposed and offensive to an opinion which, like an old prejudice, has taken deep root, and has been repeated a thousand times in books – that we considered it advisable to examine more closely the foundation of those plausible arguments which may be advanced.

It is certainly easier to reach an object near us than one at a distance, but when the nearest one does not suit our purpose it does not follow that dividing the work, that a resting-point, will enable us to get over the second half of the road easier. A small jump is easier than a large one, but no one on that account, wishing to cross a wide ditch, would jump half of it first.

If we look closely into the foundation of the conception of the so-called methodical offensive War, we shall find it generally consists of the following things:

1. Conquest of those fortresses belonging to the enemy which we meet with.
2. Laying in the necessary supplies.
3. Fortifying important points, as *magazines*, *bridges*, *positions*, etc.
4. Resting the troops in quarters during winter, or when they require to be recruited in health and refreshed.
5. Waiting for the reinforcements of the ensuing year.

If for the attainment of all these objects we make a formal division in the course of the offensive action, a resting-point in the movement, it is supposed that we gain a new base and renewed force, as if our own State was following up in the rear of the Army, and that the latter laid in renewed vigour for every fresh campaign.

All these praiseworthy motives may make the offensive War more convenient, but they do not make its results surer, and are generally only make-believes to cover certain counteracting forces, such as the feelings of the Commander or irresolution in the Cabinet. We shall try to roll them up from the left flank.

1. The waiting for reinforcements suits the enemy just as well, and is, we may say, more to his advantage. Besides, it lies in the nature of the thing that a State can place in line nearly as many combatant forces in one year as in two; for all the actual increase

of combatant force in the second year is but trifling in relation to the whole.

2. The enemy rests himself at the same time that we do.

3. The fortification of towns and positions is not the work of the Army, and therefore no ground for any delay.

4. According to the present system of subsisting Armies, magazines are more necessary when the troops are in cantonments than when they are advancing. As long as we advance with success, we continually fall into possession of some of the enemy's provision depots, which assist us when the country itself is poor.

5. The taking of the enemy's fortresses cannot be regarded as a suspension of the attack: it is an intensified progress, and therefore the seeming suspension which is caused thereby is not properly a case such as we allude to, it is neither a suspension nor a modifying of the use of force. But whether a regular siege, blockade, or a mere observation of one or other is most to the purpose is a question which can only be decided according to particular circumstances. We can only say this in general, that in answering this question another must be clearly decided, which is, whether the risk will not be too great if, while only blockading, we at the same time make a further advance. Where this is not the case, and when there is ample room to extend our forces, it is better to postpone the formal siege till the termination of the whole offensive movement. We must therefore take care not to be led into the error of neglecting the essential, through the idea of immediately making secure that which is conquered.

No doubt it seems as if, by thus advancing, we at once hazard the loss of what has been already gained. Our opinion, however, is that no division of action, no resting-point, no intermediate stations are in accordance with the nature of offensive War, and that when the same are unavoidable, they are to be regarded as an evil which makes the result not more certain, but, on the contrary, more uncertain; and further, that, strictly speaking, if from weakness or any cause we have been obliged to stop, a second spring at the object we have in view is, as a rule, impossible; but if such a second spring is possible, then the stoppage at the intermediate station was unnecessary, and that when an object at the very commencement is beyond our strength, it will always remain so.

We say this appears to be the general truth, by which we only wish to cut aside the idea that time of itself can do something for the advantage of the assailant. But as the political relations may change from year to year, therefore, on that account alone, many cases may happen which are exceptions to this general truth.

It may appear, perhaps, as if we had left our general point of view, and had nothing in our eye except offensive War; but it is not so by any means. Certainly, he who can set before himself the complete overthrow of the enemy as his object will not easily be reduced to take refuge in the defensive, the immediate object of which is only to keep possession; but as we stand by the declaration throughout, that a defensive without any positive principle is a contradiction in strategy as well as in tactics, and therefore always come back to the fact that every defensive, according to its strength, will seek to change to the attack as soon as it has exhausted the advantages of the defensive, so, therefore, however great or small the defence may be, we still also include in it contingently the overthrow of the enemy as an object which this attack may have, and which is to be considered as the proper object of the defensive, and we say that there may be cases in which the assailant, notwithstanding he has in view such a great object, may still prefer at first to make use of the defensive form. That this idea is founded in reality is easily shown by the campaign of 1812. The Emperor Alexander in engaging in the War did not perhaps think of ruining his enemy completely, as was done in the sequel; but is there anything which makes such an idea impossible? And yet, if so, would it not still remain very natural that the Russians began the War on the defensive?

CHAPTER V

ENDS IN WAR MORE PRECISELY DEFINED (CONTINUED)

Limited object

IN the preceding chapter we have said that, under the expression 'overthrow of the enemy', we understand the real absolute aim of the 'act of War'; now we shall see what remains to be done when the conditions under which this object might be attained do not exist.

These conditions presuppose a great physical or moral superiority, or a great spirit of enterprise, an innate propensity to extreme hazards. Now where all this is not forthcoming, the aim in the act of War can only be of two kinds; either the conquest of some small or moderate portion of the enemy's country, or the defence of our own until better times; this last is the usual case in defensive War.

Whether the one or the other of these aims is of the right kind can always be settled by calling to mind the expression used in reference to the last. *The waiting till more favourable times* implies that we have reason to expect such times hereafter, and this waiting for, that is, defensive War, is always based on this prospect; on the other hand, offensive War, that is, the taking advantage of the present moment, is always commanded when the future holds out a better prospect, not to ourselves, but to our adversary.

The third case, which is probably the most common, is when neither party has anything definite to look for from the future when therefore it furnishes no motive for decision. In this case the offensive War is plainly imperative upon him who is politically the aggressor, that is, who has the positive motive; for he has taken up arms with that object, and every moment of time which is lost without any good reason is so much lost time *for him.*

We have here decided for offensive or defensive War on grounds which have nothing to do with the relative forces of the combatants respectively, and yet it may appear that it would be nearer right to make the choice of the offensive or defensive chiefly dependent on the mutual relations of combatants in point of military strength; our opinion is, that in doing so we should just leave the right road. The logical correctness of our simple argument no one will dispute; we shall now see whether in the concrete case it leads to the contrary.

Let us suppose a small State which is involved in a contest with a very superior power, and foresees that with each year its position will become worse: should it not, if War is inevitable, make use of the time when its situation is furthest from the worst? Then it must attack, not because the attack *in itself* ensures any advantages – it will rather increase the disparity of forces – but because this State is under the necessity of either bringing the matter completely to an issue before the worst time arrives, or of gaining at least in the meantime some advantages which it may hereafter turn to account. This theory cannot appear absurd. But if this small State is quite certain that the enemy will advance against it, then, certainly, it can and may make use of the defensive against its enemy to procure a first advantage; there is then at any rate no danger of losing time.

If, again, we suppose a small State engaged in War with a greater, and that the future has no influence on their decisions, still, if the small State is politically the assailant, we demand of it also that it should go forward to its object.

If it has had the audacity to propose to itself a positive end in the face of superior numbers, then it must also act, that is, attack the foe, if the latter does not save it the trouble. Waiting would be an absurdity; unless at the moment of execution it has altered its political resolution, a case which very frequently occurs, and contributes in no small degree to give Wars an indefinite character.

These considerations on the limited object apply to its connexion both with offensive War and defensive War; we shall consider both in separate chapters. But we shall first turn our attention to another phase.

Hitherto we have deduced the modifications in the object of War solely from intrinsic reasons. The nature of the political view (or design) we have only taken into consideration in so far as it is or is not directed at something positive. Everything else in the political design is in reality something extraneous to War; but in the second chapter of the first book (End and Means in War) we have already admitted that the nature of the political object, the extent of our own or the enemy's demand, and our whole political relation practically have a most decisive influence on the conduct of the War, and we shall therefore devote the following chapter to that subject specially.

CHAPTER VI

(A) INFLUENCE OF THE POLITICAL OBJECT ON THE MILITARY OBJECT

WE never find that a State joining in the cause of another State takes it up with the same earnestness as its own. An auxiliary Army of moderate strength is sent; if it is not successful, then the Ally looks upon the affair as in a manner ended, and tries to get out of it on the cheapest terms possible.

In European politics it has been usual for States to pledge themselves to mutual assistance by an alliance offensive and defensive, not so far that the one takes part in the interests and quarrels of the other, but only so far as to promise one another beforehand the assistance of a fixed, generally very moderate, contingent of troops, without regard to the object of the War or the scale on which it is about to be carried on by the principals. In a treaty of alliance of this kind the Ally does not look upon himself as engaged with the enemy in a War properly speaking, which should necessarily begin with a declaration of War and end with a treaty of peace. Still, this idea also is nowhere fixed with any distinctness, and usage varies one way and another.

The thing would have a kind of consistency, and it would be less embarrassing to the theory of War if this promised contingent of ten, twenty, or thirty thousand men was handed over entirely to the State engaged in War, so that it could be used as required; it might then be regarded as a subsidized force. But the usual practice is widely different. Generally the auxiliary force has its own Commander, who depends only on his own Government, and to whom it prescribes an object such as best suits the shilly-shally measures it has in view.

But even if two States go to War with a third, they do not always both look in like measure upon this common enemy as one that they must destroy or be destroyed by themselves. The business is often settled like a commercial transaction; each, according to the amount of the risk he incurs or the advantage to be expected, takes shares in the concern to the extent of 30,000 or 40,000 men, and acts as if he could not lose more than the amount of his investment.

Not only is this the point of view taken when a State comes to the assistance of another in a cause in which it has, in a manner, little concern, but even when both have a common and very considerable interest at stake nothing can be done except under diplomatic reservation, and the contracting parties usually only agree to furnish a small stipulated contingent, in order to employ the rest of the forces according to the special ends to which policy may happen to lead them.

This way of regarding Wars entered into by reason of alliances was quite general, and was only obliged to give place to the natural way in quite modern times, when the extremity of danger drove men's minds into the natural direction (as in the Wars *against* Buonáparte), and when the most boundless power compelled them to it (as *under* Buonaparte). It was an abnormal thing, an anomaly, for War and Peace are ideas which in their foundation can have no gradations; nevertheless it was no mere diplomatic offspring which the reason could look down upon, but deeply rooted in the natural limitedness and weakness of human nature.

Lastly, even in Wars carried on without Allies, the political cause of a War has a great influence on the method in which it is conducted.

If we only require from the enemy a small sacrifice, then we content ourselves with aiming at a small equivalent by the War, and we expect to attain that by moderate efforts. The enemy reasons in very much the same way. Now, if one or the other finds that he has erred in his reckoning – that in place of being slightly superior to the enemy, as he supposed, he is, if anything, rather weaker, still, at that moment, money and all other means, as well as sufficient moral impulse for greater exertions, are very often deficient: in such a case he just does what is called 'the best he can'; hopes better things in the future, although he has not the slightest foundation for such hope, and the War in the meantime drags itself feebly along, like a body worn out with sickness.

Thus it comes to pass that the reciprocal action, the rivalry, the violence and impetuosity of War lose themselves in the stagnation of weak motives, and that both parties move with a certain kind of security in very circumscribed spheres.

If this influence of the political object is once permitted, as it then must be, there is no longer any limit, and we must be pleased to come down to such warfare as consists in a *mere threatening of the enemy* and in *negotiating*.

That the theory of War, if it is to be and to continue a philosophical study, finds itself here in a difficulty is clear.[121] All that is essentially inherent in the conception of War seems to fly from it, and it is in danger of being left without any point of support. But the natural outlet soon shows itself. According as a modifying principle gains influence over the act of War, or rather, the weaker the motives to action become, the more the action will glide into a passive resistance, the less eventful it will become, and the less it will require guiding principles. All military art then changes itself into mere prudence, the principal object of which will be to prevent the trembling balance from suddenly turning to our disadvantage, and the half War from changing into a complete one.

(B) WAR AS AN INSTRUMENT OF POLICY

HAVING made the requisite examination on both sides of that state of antagonism in which the nature of War stands with relation to other interests of men individually and of the bond of society, in order not to neglect any of the opposing elements – an antagonism which is founded in our own nature, and which, therefore, no philosophy can unravel – we shall now look for that unity into which, in practical life, these antagonistic elements combine themselves by partly neutralizing each other. We should have brought forward this unity at the very commencement if it had not been necessary to bring out this contradiction very plainly, and also to look at the different elements separately. Now, this unity is *the conception that War is only a part of political intercourse, therefore by no means an independent thing in itself.*

We know, certainly, that War is only called forth through the political intercourse of Governments and Nations; but in general it is supposed that such intercourse is broken off by War, and that a totally different state of things ensues, subject to no laws but its own.

We maintain, on the contrary, that War is nothing but a continuation of political intercourse, with a mixture of other means. We say mixed with other means in order thereby to maintain at the same time that this political intercourse does not cease by the War itself, is not changed into something quite different, but that, in its essence, it continues to exist, whatever may be the form of the means which it uses, and that the chief lines on which the events of the War progress, and to which they are attached, are only the general features of policy which run all through the War until peace takes place. And how can we conceive it to be otherwise? Does the cessation of diplomatic notes stop the political relations between different Nations and Governments? Is not War merely another kind of writing and language for political thoughts? It has certainly a grammar of its own, but its logic is not peculiar to itself.

Accordingly, War can never be separated from political intercourse, and if, in the consideration of the matter, this is done in any way, all the threads of the different relations are, to a certain extent, broken, and we have before us a senseless thing without an object.

This kind of idea would be indispensable even if War was perfect War, the perfectly unbridled element of hostility, for all the circumstances on which it rests, and which determine its leading features, viz. our own power, the enemy's power, Allies on both sides, the characteristics of the people and their Governments respectively, etc., as enumerated in the first chapter of the first book – are they not of a political nature, and are they not so intimately connected with the whole political intercourse that it is impossible to separate them? But this view is doubly indispensable if we reflect that real War is no such consistent effort tending to an extreme, as it should be according to the abstract idea, but a half-and-half thing, a contradiction in itself;[122] that, as such, it cannot follow its own laws, but must be looked upon as a part of another whole – and this whole is policy.

Policy in making use of War avoids all those rigorous conclusions which proceed from its nature; it troubles itself little about final possibilities, confining its attention to immediate probabilities. If such uncertainty in the whole action ensues therefrom, if it thereby becomes a sort of game, the policy of each Cabinet places its confidence in the belief that in this game it will surpass its neighbour in skill and sharp-sightedness.

Thus policy makes out of the all-overpowering element of War a mere instrument, changes the tremendous battle-sword, which should be lifted with both hands and the whole power of the body to strike once for all, into a light handy weapon, which is even sometimes nothing more than a rapier to exchange thrusts and feints and parries.

Thus the contradictions in which man, naturally timid, becomes involved by War may be solved, if we choose to accept this as a solution.

If War belongs to policy, it will naturally take its character from thence. If policy is grand and powerful, so also will be the War, and this may be carried to the point at which War attains to *its absolute form*.

In this way of viewing the subject, therefore, we need not shut out of sight the absolute form of War, we rather keep it continually in view in the background.

Only through this kind of view War recovers unity; only by it can we see all Wars as things of *one* kind; and it is only through it that the judgement can obtain the true and perfect basis and point of view from which great plans may be traced out and determined upon.

It is true the political element does not sink deep into the details of War. Vedettes are not planted, patrols do not make their rounds from political considerations; but small as is its influence in this respect, it is great in the formation of a plan for a whole War, or a campaign, and often even for a battle.

For this reason we were in no hurry to establish this view at the commencement. While engaged with particulars, it would have given us little help, and, on the other hand, would have distracted our attention to a certain extent; in the plan of a War or campaign it is indispensable.

There is, upon the whole, nothing more important in life than to find out the right point of view from which things should be looked at and judged of, and then to keep to that point; for we can only apprehend the mass of events in their unity from *one* standpoint; and it is only the keeping to one point of view that guards us from inconsistency.

If, therefore, in drawing up a plan of a War, it is not allowable to have a two-fold or three-fold point of view, from which things may be looked at, now with the eye of a soldier, then with that of an administrator, and then again with that of a politician, etc., then the next question is, whether *policy* is necessarily paramount and everything else subordinate to it.

That policy unites in itself, and reconciles all the interests of internal administrations, even those of humanity, and whatever else are rational subjects of consideration is presupposed, for it is nothing in itself, except a mere representative and exponent of all these interests towards other States. That policy may take a false direction, and may promote unfairly the ambitious ends, the private interests, the vanity of rulers, does not concern us here; for, under no circumstances can the Art of War be regarded as its preceptor, and we can only look at policy here as the representative of the interests generally of the whole community.

The only question, therefore, is whether in framing plans for a War the political point of view should give way to the purely military (if such a point is conceivable), that is to say, should disappear altogether, or subordinate itself to it, or whether the political is to remain the ruling point of view and the military to be considered subordinate to it.

That the political point of view should end completely when War begins is only conceivable in contests which are Wars of life and death, from pure hatred: as Wars are in reality, they are, as we before said, only the expressions or manifestations of policy itself. The subordination of the political point of view to the military would be contrary to common sense, for policy has declared the War; it is the intelligent faculty, War only the instrument, and not the reverse. The subordination of the military point of view to the political is, therefore, the only thing which is possible.

If we reflect on the nature of real War, and call to mind what has been said in the third chapter of this book, *that every War should be viewed above all things according to the probability of its character, and its leading features as they are to be deduced from the political forces and proportions*, and that often – indeed we may safely affirm, in our days, *almost* always – War is to be regarded as an organic whole, from which the single branches are not to be separated, in which therefore every individual activity flows into the whole, and also has its origin in the idea of this whole, then it becomes certain and palpable to us that the superior standpoint for the conduct of the War, from which its leading lines must proceed, can be no other than that of policy.

From this point of view the plans come, as it were, out of a cast; the apprehension of them and the judgement upon them become easier and more natural, our convictions respecting them gain in force, motives are more satisfying and history more intelligible.

At all events from this point of view there is no longer in the nature of things a necessary conflict between the political and military interests, and where it appears it is therefore to be regarded as imperfect knowledge only. That policy makes demands on the War which it cannot respond to, would be contrary to the supposition that it knows the instrument which it is going to use, therefore, contrary to a natural and indispensable supposition. But if policy judges correctly of the march of military events, it is entirely its affair to determine what are the events and what the direction of events most favourable to the ultimate and great end of the War.

In one word, the Art of War in its highest point of view is policy, but, no doubt, a policy which fights battles instead of writing notes.

According to this view, to leave a great military enterprise or the plan for one, to *a purely military judgement and decision* is a distinction which cannot be allowed, and is even prejudicial; indeed, it is an irrational proceeding to consult professional soldiers on the plan of a War, that they may give a *purely military opinion* upon what the Cabinet ought to do; but still more absurd is the demand of Theorists that a statement of the available means of War should be laid before the General, that he may draw out a purely military plan for the War or for a campaign in accordance with those means. Experience in general also teaches us that notwithstanding the multifarious branches and scientific character of military art in the present day, still the leading outlines of a War are always determined by the Cabinet, that is, if we would use technical language, by a political not a military organ.

This is perfectly natural. None of the principal plans which are required for a War can be made without an insight into the political relations; and, in reality, when people speak, as they often do, of the prejudicial influence of policy on the conduct of a War, they say in reality something very different to what they intend. It is not this influence but the policy itself which should be found fault with. If policy is right, that is, if it succeeds in hitting the object, then it can only act with advantage on the War. If this influence of policy causes a divergence from the object, the cause is only to be looked for in a mistaken policy.

It is only when policy promises itself a wrong effect from certain military means and measures, an effect opposed to their nature, that it can exercise a prejudicial effect on War by the course it prescribes. Just as a person in a language with which he is not conversant sometimes says what he does not intend, so policy, when intending right, may often order things which do not tally with its own views.

This has happened times without end, and it shows that a certain knowledge of the nature of War is essential to the management of political intercourse.

But before going further, we must guard ourselves against a false interpretation of which this is very susceptible. We are far from holding the opinion that a War Minister smothered in official papers, a scientific engineer, or even a soldier who has been well tried in the field, would, any of them, necessarily make the best Minister of State where the Sovereign does not act for himself; or, in other words, we do not mean to say that this acquaintance with the nature of War is the principal qualification for a War Minister; elevation, superiority of mind, strength of character, these are the principal qualifications which he must possess; a knowledge of War may be supplied in one way or the other. France was never worse advised in its military and political affairs than by the two brothers Belleisle and the Duke of Choiseul, although all three were good soldiers.

If War is to harmonize entirely with the political views and policy, to accommodate itself to the means available for War, there is only one alternative to be recommended when the statesman and soldier are not combined in one person, which is, to make the Commander-in-Chief a member of the Cabinet, that he may take part in its councils and decisions on important occasions. But then, again, this is only possible when the Cabinet, that is, the Government itself, is near the theatre of War, so that things can be settled without a serious waste of time.

This is what the Emperor of Austria did in 1809, and the allied Sovereigns in 1813, 1814, 1815, and the arrangement proved completely satisfactory.

The influence of any military man except the General-in-Chief in the Cabinet is extremely dangerous; it very seldom leads to able vigorous action. The example of France in 1793, 1794, 1795, when Carnot, while residing in Paris, managed the conduct of the War, is to be avoided, as a system of terror is not at the command of any but a revolutionary government.

We shall now conclude with some reflections derived from history.

In the last decade of the past century, when that remarkable change in the Art of War in Europe took place by which the best Armies found that a part of their method of War had become utterly unserviceable, and events were brought about of a magnitude far beyond what any one had any previous conception of, it certainly appeared that a false calculation of everything was to be laid to the charge of the Art of War. It was plain that while confined by habit within a narrow circle of conceptions, she had been surprised by the force of a new state of relations, lying, no doubt, outside that circle, but still not outside the nature of things.

Those observers who took the most comprehensive view ascribed the circumstance to the general influence which policy had exercised for centuries on the Art of War, and undoubtedly to its very great disadvantage, and by which it had sunk into a half-measure, often into mere sham-fighting. They were right as to fact, but they were wrong in attributing it to something accidental, or which might have been avoided.

Others thought that everything was to be explained by the momentary influence of the particular policy of Austria, Prussia, England, etc., with regard to their own interests respectively.

But is it true that the real surprise by which men's minds were seized was confined to the conduct of War, and did not rather relate to policy itself? That is: Did the ill success proceed from the influence of policy on the War, or from a wrong policy itself?

The prodigious effects of the French Revolution abroad were evidently brought about much less through new methods and views introduced by the French in the conduct of War than through the changes which it wrought in state-craft and civil administration, in the character of Governments, in the condition of the people, etc. That other Governments took a mistaken view of all these things; that they endeavoured, with their ordinary means, to hold their own against forces of a novel kind and overwhelming in strength – all that was a blunder in policy.

Would it have been possible to perceive and mend this error by a scheme for the War from a purely military point of view?

Impossible. For if there had been a philosophical strategist, who merely from the nature of the hostile elements had foreseen all the consequences, and prophesied remote possibilities, still it would have been practically impossible to have turned such wisdom to account.

If policy had risen to a just appreciation of the forces which had sprung up in France, and of the new relations in the political state of Europe, it might have foreseen the consequences which must follow in respect to the great features of War, and it was only in this way that it could arrive at a correct view of the extent of the means required as well as of the best use to make of those means.

We may therefore say, that the twenty years' victories of the Revolution are chiefly to be ascribed to the erroneous policy of the Governments by which it was opposed.

It is true these errors first displayed themselves in the War, and the events of the War completely disappointed the expectations which policy entertained. But this did not take place because policy neglected to consult its military advisers. That Art of War in which the politician of the day could believe, namely, that derived from the reality of War at that time, that which belonged to the policy of the day, that familiar instrument which policy had hitherto used – *that* Art of War, I say, was naturally involved in the error of policy, and therefore could not teach it anything better. It is true that War itself underwent important alterations both in its nature and forms, which brought it nearer to its absolute form; but these changes were not brought about because the French Government had, to a certain extent, delivered itself from the leading-strings of policy; they arose from an altered policy, produced by the French Revolution, not only in France, but over the rest of Europe as well. This policy had called forth other means and other powers, by which it became possible to conduct War with a degree of energy which could not have been thought of otherwise.

Therefore, the actual changes in the Art of War are a consequence of alterations in policy; and, so far from being an argument for the possible separation of the two, they are, on the contrary, very strong evidence of the intimacy of their connexion.

Therefore, once more: War is an instrument of policy; it must necessarily bear its character, it must measure with its scale: the conduct of War, in its great features, is therefore policy itself, which takes up the sword in place of the pen, but does not on that account cease to think according to its own laws.

CONCLUDING REMARKS BY ANATOL RAPOPORT

A pamphlet entitled *Clausewitz, Jomini, Schlieffen*, published in 1951 at West Point (The United States Military Academy) concludes with these words: 'Clausewitz's influence is not dead. The philosophy of *On War* is the philosophy of Bismarck's Blood and Iron and the philosophy of *Mein Kampf*'. Peter Paret, in his bibliographical survey on Clausewitz, comments:

> Besides being bad history, this confuses recognition that war is an arm of national policy with eagerness to engage in it. In the fall of 1964 the Department of Military Art and Engineering at West Point issued a new edition of the pamphlet with a much improved section on Clausewitz by Colonel John R. Elting.

The possible reasons for the 'rehabilitation' of Clausewitz in the United States were discussed in the Introduction. It is not clear, however, why it is 'bad history' to trace a line from Clausewitz to Bismarck to Hitler. On the contrary, in the light of the military history of Prussia and Germany from 1815 to 1945, the line seems clear and revealing. As for confusing the recognition that war is an arm of national policy with eagerness to engage in it, the point would have been well taken if it were a matter of distinguishing between well-defined categories. That this is the case in the present instance is by no means certain. Clausewitz may not have influenced statesmen to be 'eager' to engage in war (although this, too, is debatable); but he has certainly influenced them (indeed, he exhorted them) to be ready and willing to go to war if the prize was worth it. A clear distinction among readiness, willingness, and eagerness can hardly be made on objective grounds.

Clausewitz taught that states should not engage in wars without a reason. He also held it to be self-evident that states should go to war if they deemed it necessary to do so. However, if war is held to be evil (which hardly anyone today disputes), then the instrumentality of war does not by itself absolve the war-maker. If it did, we should also absolve the kidnapper who does not kill his victim unless the circumstances demand it, the embezzler who does not really want money but only the things that money can buy, and the rapist who excuses his brutality on the grounds that the object of his desire would not yield.

The real confusion is perpetrated by the apologists of *Realpolitik*. A favourite stance with the exponents of that school of thought is a plea for the recognition of war as an arm of national policy. However, 'recognition' has two meanings, namely, (1) 'awareness of', and (2) 'extension of legitimacy to'. Clausewitz's great achievement was in having made people *aware* of the way war can be used as an arm of national policy. In his day the question of the legitimacy of war did not arise. In our day this question is forced upon us. The disciples of Clausewitz in effect plead for 'recognizing' war as an arm of national policy in the sense of accepting its legitimacy. And since war in the nuclear age has become a political absurdity, a vast amount of discussion is devoted to theorizing about 'limited' wars, controlled escalation, the game of threats, self-terminating 'nuclear exchanges' and the like. All this investment of intellectual effort seems to be motivated to a considerable degree by a determination to preserve the struggle for power as the theoretical bedrock of political reality.

Here we have another source of confusion, namely between the nature of political reality and of physical reality. Physical reality can, at least to a first approximation, be taken 'to be what it is'. Hence to recognize it means to be aware of it, and it is futile to question its legitimacy. Physical laws are neither made nor abrogated by men. Political reality, however, includes what men think it is. Hence the 'freezing' of the struggle for power as the theoretical basis of political reality *makes* the political philosophy of war a 'realistic' philosophy. The rest follows. For if war is perceived as a normal stage in the relations among states, then it behoves each state to become proficient in the 'art of war'. As all states become proficient in the art of war, the advantages that might have accrued to one state from such proficiency are effectively cancelled by the proficiency of other states! The net result is only a burgeoning destructiveness of wars. Granting for a moment that the modern disciples of Clausewitz recognize the prohibitive costliness of offensive wars (among comparable states), they have not answered satisfactorily the question of what *political* objectives are served by the continual state of readiness for war, if it is too costly for every one concerned to undertake war. Deterrence (the usual rationale for this state) was not in Clausewitz's lexicon of political objectives. Preparation for war, in Clausewitz's estimation, had only one objective – war. Since history has vindicated this view, Clausewitz has earned the title of 'realist'. Note, however, that Clausewitz's view is in almost direct opposition to those who see in perpetual readiness and willingness (but not 'eagerness') to wage war a pre-condition for ensuring peace.

The only wars today which can be said to be fought for political objectives are the wars of counter-insurgency. Here the argument can indeed be made that the prize is worth the price, since the devastation takes place far away from the territory of the war-waging state and the shock of the fantastic costs is absorbed by the fantastic wealth of the (now only) state which has committed its national policy to waging counter-insurgency warfare. However, counter-insurgency warfare cannot go on forever. Either such wars will trap the United States in a spiral of uncontrollably mounting destruction, or the mounting costs (both material and psychic) will finally overcome the acquiescence of its people to any military adventure their government deems necessary to undertake. Eventually a great deal more political weight will have to be given to one factor which Clausewitz knew well, but which many of his current disciples have forgotten, namely, the essential ingredient of what Clausewitz called the People's War. It is the autonomous motivations of people on the spot, the efforts and sacrifices of the local populations resisting a foreign invader. Ironically, the very aspect of war which gave the main impetus to the train of Clausewitz's thought may be the very aspect which will put an end to the only wars (of counter-insurgency) which can still be rationalized as a continuation of policy by other means. It is becoming clear that war is not a continuation of policy but a failure of policy.

In my opinion, the conclusion is inescapable that the political philosophy of war is bankrupt. It continues only as a vestige. Just as the monarchs clung to the doctrine of the Divine Right of Kings after it had lost its support among those who gave any thought to such matters; just as chattel slavery hung on after its economic basis had collapsed, so the idea that the struggle for power is the prime mover of politics persists in an age when the renunciation of the struggle has become a prerequisite of survival.

NOTES

1. Later, however, Clausewitz's theory becomes frankly prescriptive. Having fathomed the 'nature of war', Clausewitz pleads for freeing war from the fetters in which timid leaders had kept it until the coming of Napoleon. The following passage is especially revealing:

> Let us not hear of Generals who conquer without bloodshed. If a bloody slaughter is a horrible sight, then that is a ground for paying more respect to War, but not for making the sword we wear blunter and blunter by degrees from feelings of humanity, until some one steps in with one that is sharp and lops off the arm from our body. (p. 345).

2. cf. Alfred Vagts, *A History of Militarism*, Part I, Chapter 2.

3. R. R. Palmer writes: 'Desertion was the nightmare of all eighteenth century commanders, especially in disorganized Germany, where men of the same language could be found on both sides in every war. In 1744 Frederick the Great had to stop his advance to Bohemia because his army began to melt away.' (In E. E. Earle [ed.], *Makers of Modern Strategy*, Chapter 3.)

The bright conspicuous uniforms of the period are partly explained by the desertion problem. It was more important to prevent the men from leaving the field of battle (by making them highly visible) than to make them less conspicuous targets. Palmer (*op. cit.*) cites Frederick the Great: '. . . therefore (since honour has no effect on them), they must fear their officers more than any danger.' And again: 'If a soldier during an action looks about as if to flee, or so much as sets a foot outside the line, the non-commissioned officer standing behind him will run him through with his bayonet . . .'

4. When Napoleon later tried to make his peace with the old world of dynasties, aristocracy, and legitimate succession by marrying a Hapsburg princess, the memory of his earlier deeds spoke louder than his belated gestures. Neither the princes nor the peoples saw him as a traditional legitimate ruler. He remained for them a symbol – frightening or tempting – of the titanic possibilities of the new epoch.

5. B. M. Shaposnikov, *Mozg Armii* (The Brain of the Army), cited in R. L. Garthoff, *Soviet Military Doctrine*, p. 11.

6. Dated 18 September 1806. In a letter written on 12 October, two days before the Battle of Jena (disastrous to the Prussians), we read: 'The day after tomorrow . . . there will be a great battle, for which the entire Army is longing. I myself look forward to this day with joy as I would to my own wedding day.' (In Karl Schwartz, *Leben des Generals Carl von Clausewitz*, p. 219; p. 226; my translation – A.R.)

7. See Note 73.

8. Alfred Vagts, *A History of Militarism*, Part I, Chapter 5.

9. Walter Goerlitz, *History of the German General Staff*, Chapter 2.

10. Alfred Vagts, *A History of Militarism*, p. 30, also Chapter 6.

11. Introduction to the New and Revised Edition of J. J. Graham's translation of Clausewitz's *Vom Kriege*.

12. Niccoló Machiavelli, *The Florentine History*, p. 235.

13. N. Machiavelli, *The Art of War*.

14. Introduction to *The Makers of Modern Strategy*.

15. The reference is to *The Proud Tower* by Barbara W. Tuchman, a book which vividly describes the last decades of monarchical Europe.

16. Some advocates of imperial expansion (before 1914) shared this interpretation of imperialism, among others Cecil Rhodes. (cf. W. L. Langer, *The Diplomacy of Imperialism*, Vol. I, Chapter 3.)

17. Lenin did allow for the existence of a small well paid 'workers' aristocracy' who gained from empire and war in contrast to the rest of the workers. He also cited Engels on the possible emergence of whole 'nations of bourgeois', for example Britain pitted against the peoples of the colonies. (cf. letter from Engels to Kautsky, 12 December 1882, quoted by Lenin in his *Imperialism*, p. 89.)

18. Quoted in E. M. Earle (ed.), *Makers of Modern Strategy*, p. 341.

19. V. I. Lenin, *Materialism and Empiriocriticism*.

20. V. D. Sokolovsky (ed.), *Military Strategy*, p. 17.

21. An extensive collection of Lenin's comments on Clausewitz appears in *Leninsky Sbornik* (The Lenin Collection), Vol. XII, pp. 389–452. Raymond L. Garthoff in his *Soviet Military Doctrine* summarizes Clausewitz's influence on Soviet military thought between the two world wars.

It should be borne in mind, however, that the concept of war as an evil by-product of specific obsolete social systems is an integral part of the Soviet philosophy of war. The flyleaf quotations in B. Ts. Urlanis's large study *Wars and the European Populations* read: 'The end of wars, peace among nations, the cessation of robbery and coercion, just this is our ideal ...' (Lenin); 'Wars have been doubtless the greatest misfortune of humanity throughout its history' (Khrushchev).

We point this out not with a view of contrasting Soviet diplo-military policy with that of other great powers (since similar pronouncements have been made by states actively engaged in war), but merely with the view of emphasizing a trend in Soviet official thought (which every publication on a subject as important as war must reflect). This trend is essentially inimical to the Clausewitzian philosophy of war.

Further evidence is found in the Soviet official-ideological distinction between 'just' and 'unjust' wars (always emphasized in connexion with a categorical rejection of pacifism). Urlanis notes (pp. 8–9) that it is possible for one side to fight a 'just' war while the other is fighting an 'unjust' one; and it is possible for both sides to fight an 'unjust' war; but it is not possible for both sides to fight a 'just' war. The concept of 'just' and 'unjust' wars does not appear in Clausewitz. Implicity, however, Clausewitz views all national wars as 'just' (on both sides), since in his view nationhood is the highest form of social organization and a nation asserts its very essence through war. The image of war as a way of 'resolving' conflicts among nations with its implied attitude, 'may the most deserving win' does not occur in the Soviet philosophy of war.

22. It is not unlikely, of course, that as the Soviet Union becomes more accustomed to its role of a super-power (in which the military necessarily plays an important political role), Clausewitzian patterns will become more pronounced in her foreign policy. Evidence of this trend can perhaps be discerned in the Soviet Middle East policy.

23. Such time-course charting theories are called dynamic. A

static theory investigates equilibrium states in which a system can remain until it is disturbed.

24. Lewis F. Richardson, *Arms and Insecurity*, Chapters 2, 3.

25. L. F. Richardson, *Statistics of Deadly Quarrels*; Quincy Wright, *A Study of War*.

26. cf. K. W. Deutsch and J. David Singer, 'Multipolar Power Systems and International Stability'; R. J. Rummel, 'Some Dimensions in the Foreign Relations of Nations'; R. Tanter, 'Dimensions of Conflict within and between Nations, 1958–1960'.

27. cf. Walter Goerlitz, *History of the German General Staff*, Chapters IV and VI.

28. See, for example, 'Summary of the Instructions to His Royal Highness the Crown Prince', included as an appendix in the New Revised Edition of J. J. Graham's translation of Clausewitz's *Vom Kriege*.

29. John S. Pustay writes:

> It is obviously imperative that the United States ... design and employ appropriate doctrine and instrumentalities to aid in the prevention of insurgency warfare in developing areas. Because such action will be too late for some nations, it is equally obligatory that similar steps be taken to facilitate and orient American assistance to states already involved in combating the Communist operation. (*Counter-insurgency Warfare*, p. 11.)

30. A clear exposition of traditional American philosophy of war is given by Robert W. Tucker in *The Just War*.

31. This awareness was well expressed in the title of Albert Wohlstetter's article, 'The Delicate Balance of Terror'. The year 1958 marks the end of the Americans' conviction of their own military omnipotence, as evidenced in a large output of strategic literature calling for a realistic assessment of the distribution of power in world affairs. See, as examples, H. A. Kissinger, *Nuclear Weapons and Foreign Policy*: also A. Wolfers *et al.*, *Developments in Military Technology and their Impact on United States Strategy and Foreign Policy*.

32. cf. H. Kahn, 'The Nature and Feasibility of War and Deterrence'; T. C. Schelling, *Arms and Influence*, esp. Chapter 2, 'The Art of Commitment'.

33. cf. T. C. Schelling, 'Strategy, Tactics, and Non-Zero-Sum Theory', in A. Mensch, *Theory of Games*, p. 476.

34. cf. R. E. Osgood, *Limited War. The Challenge to American Strategy*; K. Knorr, and T. Read (eds.), *Limited Strategic War.*

35. The idea parallels that of Clausewitz: the magnitude of military effort is proportional to that of the political objective to be achieved and to the resistance to be encountered (p. 374 ff.)

36. The keynote of the new theme was sounded clearly in H. A. Kissinger's *Nuclear Weapons and Foreign Policy.*

37. The authors who go beyond purely military considerations also emphasize the 'moral' asymmetry of the present world, thereby departing from the stance of objectivity. Raymond Aron, for example, in comparing the political aims of the Communist and non-Communist worlds, insists that the goal pursued by the Communists is to 'destroy' the West, while the aim of the West is only to make the Communists relinquish this goal. (*Peace and War*, p. 672 ff.)

J. S. Pustay views revolutions in underdeveloped countries as a progressive disease infesting the world. He described them as

> a cellular development of resistance against an incumbent political regime ... which expands from the initial stage of subversion-infiltration [Phase 1] through the initial stages of overt resistance by small armed bands [Phase 2] and insurrection [Phase 3] to final fruition in civil war [Phase 4] (*Counter-insurgency Warfare*, p. 5).

Consequently one deals with such processes best by arresting them at the start: 'The sooner a Communist insurgency can be recognized and the earlier the countĕr-insurgency operations can begin in earnest, the greater will be the chance of success for the incumbent régime.' (p. 78). See also the section entitled: 'A Proposal for a U.S. Counter-insurgency Support Establishment', pp. 171 ff.

It should be noted that by an 'incumbent' regime, Pustay does not necessarily mean the one in power. For example, he cites the successful suppressions of Arbenz's government in Guatemala and of Mossadegh's government in Iran as victories for the 'incumbent régime'. Apparently in Pustay's view an 'incumbent régime' is any group (whether a regime or not, whether in power or not) which opposes social change unacceptable to the United States. An 'insurgent' group is one which attempts to promote such change (regardless of its power or of its legitimacy status).

38. Quoted by Carl Oglesby in *The Nation*, 5 June 1967, p. 720.

39. Some writers on politics go to even greater lengths to emphasize the complexity of their subject. Perhaps it is their purpose to discourage any attempt to apply rational methods of inquiry to politics. Bernard Crick, for example, writes:

politics is a bold prudence, a diverse unity, an armed conciliation, a natural artifice, or creative compromise and a serious game on which free civilization depends; it is a reforming conserver, a sceptical believer and a pluralistic moralist; it has a lively sobriety, a complex simplicity, an untidy elegance, a rough civility and an everlasting immediacy . . . (In *Defence of Politics*, p. 156).

40. See also Raymond Aron's introduction to Kahn's *Thinking About the Unthinkable*.

41. This distinction is emphasized even more strongly by Schelling in the following passage:

Recall the trouble we had persuading Mossadegh [premier of Iran] in the early 1950's that he might do his country irreparable damage if he did not become more reasonable with respect to his country and the Anglo-Iranian Oil Company. Threats did not get through to him very well. He wore pajamas, and, according to reports, he wept. And when British or American diplomats tried to explain what would happen to his country if he continued to be obstinate, . . . it was apparently uncertain whether he even comprehended what was being said to him. It must have been a little like trying to persuade a new puppy that you will beat him to death if he wets the floor. (*Arms and Influence*, p. 38.)

One senses a note of exasperation with some one who refuses to play a 'man's game'. Shortly after these attempts at persuasion failed, Mossadegh's government was overthrown by a coup credited to the United States Central Intelligence Agency.

42. H. Kahn, *On Escalation*, pp. 185–6.

43. A. Rapoport, *Strategy and Conscience*.

44. A research organization, working largely on problems contracted by United States military agencies.

45. D. G. Brennan, review of *Strategy and Conscience*.

46. cf. Irving Horowitz, *The War Game*.

47. R. E. Osgood, *Limited War. The Challenge to American Strategy*, p. ix.

48. This situation can be formulated as a two-person game in which each player has two options. If the disutility of being killed while the other lives is larger than the disutility of mutual destruction, the game is known as 'Prisoner's Dilemma'. In

the contrary case (assuming, for example, that the combatant who disengages alone loses the bout but is spared), the game is known as 'Chicken'. This designation refers to the game played by two drivers, rushing to a head-on collision. If one swerves while the other holds to his course, the swerver loses (is 'chicken'). See Notes 57, 65.

49. T. C. Schelling, 'The Strategy of Conflict: Prospectus for a Reorientation of Game Theory'.

50. cf. J. B. Phelps *et al.*, *Accidental War: Some Dangers in the 1960's;* J. D. Singer, *Deterrence, Arms Control, and Disarmament*, Chapter 4.

The installation of the 'hot line', a direct channel of communication between Washington and Moscow, is a safety device sometimes cited by the strategic community as evidence of their understanding of the problem.

51. Practically all *serious* military applications of game theory are made in the context of the zero-sum game. For example, in *Theory of Games: Techniques and Applications* (the proceedings of a conference sponsored by NATO), wherever an actual model of a conflict situation is depicted, specific enough to allow the calculation of optimal strategies or 'strategy mixes', it is almost invariably a two-person zero-sum model. This is not surprising since only such games suggest an unambiguously rational 'solution'. By way of exception, the so-called Inspector–Evader game has been cast in a non-zero-sum model. (cf. M. Maschler, 'A price leadership method for solving the inspector's non-constant-sum game'.) However, as Maschler himself notes, this game is characterized by a basic asymmetry: the Inspector can announce his strategy in advance, while the Evader cannot. Kahn and Schelling often assume (unjustifiably, in my opinion) this asymmetry to be present in certain situations which amount to games of Chicken. (See Note 48.)

52. In Karl Schwartz, *Leben des Generals Carl von Clausewitz*, p. 211. (My translation. – A.R.)

53. Marshal V. D. Sokolovsky of the U.S.S.R. writes:

In forming alliances, bourgeois diplomacy is, as a rule, guided by the principle of selfish advantage. . . . [T]hese alliances, allegedly formed for mutual defense . . . have always led to war. . . . For this reason, the Soviet Union, true to its peaceful policy, decisively rejects the formation of military alliances. It was only the creation by imperialist countries of aggressive military blocs which threaten the socialist countries that forced the Soviet Union to unite with other socialist countries in a military alliance . . . (*Military Strategy*, pp. 21–2).

Oskar Morgenstern of the United States describes the style of United States global operations thus: 'We work through "legal channels" and thereby stimulate about as much interest and appreciation among the people of other countries as a hearing of an antitrust case in an appellate court could generate with the general public in the United States.' He describes the Soviet style thus: 'Russia, on the other hand, infiltrates and undermines – whenever possible.' (O. Morgenstern, *The Question of National Defense*, p. 278.)

54. O. Morgenstern apparently agrees with this view. He writes:

> It is the phenomenal complexity of war which itself has begun to pose scientific problems of the first magnitude – new problems moreover, problems that do not arise in the ordinary humdrum life . . .
>
> In ancient times it was the adventure of the warrior, his wanderings through foreign lands, which pulled so many toward warfare. Now the same kind of fascination lies in the work the great experimental stations do all over the world – always connected with some potential or actual warlike applications.

From these observations Morgenstern draws a broad philosophical and sociological conclusion:

> 'War is the father of all things' [a quotation from Heraclitus] is once more true in a singularly perverted sense: war preparations are necessary in order to justify the deepest human desire for knowledge. Society will not support research and enormously expensive experimentation on other grounds. Society does not accept the desire for knowledge as legitimate unless it is somehow tied to war. (*The Question of National Defense*, pp. 294–305.)

The Neo-Clausewitzians' view of man and society is typically a projection of the power wielders' obsessions. They tend to obscure, dismiss, or ignore whatever role nurturing, cooperative, creative, or humane impulses may have played or may still play in human history.

55. The dismissal of international law as being of no consequence in the relations of one state to another is one of the fundamental tenets of the Clausewitzian view. It has been largely retained by the Neo-Clausewitzians.

56. The reference is to the wars of 1813–15 in which Napoleon

was finally crushed and from which Clausewitz drew the conclusion that the era of 'cabinet' wars was replaced by the era of national wars.

57. Formulated as a two-person game, the 'rational' choice between two options, arming or disarming, is clearly arming. For if he (the potential enemy) is disarmed, then clearly it is to my advantage to remain armed (so that I can dictate to him); if he remains armed, I must also remain armed (else he will dictate to me). The paradox that it may be of advantage to *both* parties to disarm ('Prisoner's Dilemma', cf. Note 48) never occurred to Clausewitz but is recognized in certain contexts by the Clausewitzians. (cf. Schelling, 'The Strategy of Conflict: Prospectus for a Reorientation of Game Theory'.)

58. Here is the germ of the idea of de-escalation (cf. C. E. Osgood, *Alternative to War or Surrender*). It is not developed further. Clausewitz sees the 'logic of conflict' as a one way street.

59. Here Clausewitz admits a rational basis for a limited war. Still, in his view, the limitation of military objectives depends entirely on the political objectives; that is, war effort is to be commensurate with what is demanded from the enemy and what can be achieved. In our day the threat of a nuclear holocaust puts a limitation on what can be demanded. In other words, military capabilities place limits on political objectives not because the capabilities are insufficient but because they are excessive. The Neo-Clausewitzians' preoccupation with limited war stems from this circumstance.

60. Clausewitz conceived conflict only as a 'zero-sum game', in which whatever benefits one side necessarily hurts the other.

61. Although the conception of international relations as a game of strategy is entirely consistent with Clausewitz's view, here he does not use the word 'game' in the game-theoretical sense. The emphasis is on the role of chance (not an essential element in games of strategy) and on the psychological characteristics of the participants (e.g. attitudes toward risk-taking). Risk-taking propensities assume considerable importance in the paradigms of international conflict proposed by the Neo-Clausewitzians; but this factor properly belongs to psychological, not game-theoretical analysis. Strategic competence is of no help in the analysis of situations where risk-taking propensity is an important determinant of outcomes.

62. Clausewitz constantly emphasizes the human element as a factor in war, whose decisive role in the Revolutionary and Napoleonic wars he clearly recognized. As war became progressively mechanized, morale appeared less important (except in specific critical situations). In our day the emphasis on morale is directly related to the degree in which war is seen in ideological or eschatological terms. Thus Mao Tze-Tung, de-emphasizing technology, lifts morale to the role of practically the sole decisive factor in war (cf. Mao Tze-Tung, *Strategic Problems of China's Revolutionary War; On Protracted War*).

63. Elsewhere (*Fights, Games, and Debates*) I have named three elements (or modes) of conflict. Clausewitz's 'animosity' and 'reason' clearly correspond to the first two. Nothing in Clausewitz's analysis corresponds to 'debate', since Clausewitz conceived conflict not as a search for truth or justice but only as a struggle of wills. The idea of conflict resolution is entirely foreign to his way of thinking.

64. Note the misleading analogy. If the forces are equal, each is expected to get about half of what he hoped for. It would be disastrous to apply this logic to what the Neo-Clausewitzians call a 'nuclear exchange'.

65. cf. the notion of 'resolve', as it is treated by the Neo-Clausewitzians. Herman Kahn, for example, in describing the game of Chicken (cf. Note 48), writes:

> The 'skillful' player may get into the car quite drunk, throwing whisky bottles out of the window to make it clear to everybody just how drunk he is. He wears very dark glasses so that he cannot see much, if anything. As soon as the car reaches high speed, he takes the steering wheel and throws it out of the window. If his opponent is watching, he has won.

Kahn recognizes also the danger involved in relying on 'resolve'. He goes on to say, 'If his opponent is not watching, he has a problem; likewise if both players try this strategy.' Nevertheless, he concludes, '. . . under current conditions, we may have to be willing to play the international version of this game whether we like it or not.' (*On Escalation*, p. 11.)

66. Clausewitz thought of combat as taking place on a 'field of battle', visible to the Commander, whose personal presence is felt by the troops. Large modern battles are not fought under these conditions. Whatever courage is displayed by the troops

is more a reflection of loyalty to comrades than to the Commander. (cf. Stouffer *et al.*, *The American Soldier*, Vol. 2, Chapter 3.)

67. These time magnitudes are obviously entirely obsolete.

68. This is not inconsistent with Clausewitz's basic principle of the primacy of political authority over the military. The General must *know* state policy, but he does not direct it.

69. Compare the simplicity of the greatest scientific theories with the difficulty of applying them to predict the behaviour of complex systems.

70. The War of 1870 furnishes a marked illustration. Von Moltke and von Goeben, not to mention many others, had both seen service in this manner, the former in Turkey and Syria, the latter in Spain. – F.N.M.

As noted in the Foreword (cf. p. 19), the employment of foreign generals was a normal practice in the eighteenth century. The loyalty of a soldier was then to his profession, not to his land of birth. As war became national this practice was largely discontinued.

71. In the nuclear age, threats have assumed (at least in the minds of the strategists) a strategic importance equal to or surpassing that of actual combat. The crucial feature of nuclear threats is that they generally become worthless if they have to be carried out. This aspect of war was unknown in Clausewitz's day. (cf. Wohlstetter, *The Delicate Balance of Terror*.)

72. One of the advantages enjoyed by Napoleon was a result of reducing the maintenance component of the field army to a minimum. His armies took what they could from the countryside through which they marched. W. Rüstow (*Geschichte der Infanterie*) estimated that at the peak of the Napoleonic wars the baggage accompanying the French infantry per man was at most one-eighth that of the Prussian infantry.

73. Clausewitz's first published article, 'Bemerkungen über die reine und angewandte Strategie des Herrn v. Bülow, oder Kritik der dahin enthaltenden Ansichten', was a devastating criticism of eighteenth-century tactics. The repeated references which Clausewitz makes to formalistic, pedantic conceptions of strategy and tactics are especially interesting. Clausewitz was an adjutant on the staff of General Phull, a Prussian, who was in 1812 in the service of the Russian tsar. This Phull was made an object of ridicule in Tolstoy's novel *War and Peace*. A model of a

perfect pedant, Phull (in Tolstoy's portrayal) was utterly convinced of the efficacy of his 'geometrically demonstrable' tactics and treated all evidence to the contrary as proof that his manoeuvres were not properly executed. Clausewitz may have been as exasperated as Tolstoy by Phull's total inability to consider the unforeseen and the role of the human element in war. However, Tolstoy went much farther than Clausewitz by denying that men (*least of all* leaders) could by the exercise of either will or reason influence the course of large-scale human events.

74. Compare the contemporary calculations of 'post-nuclear recovery' (e.g. H. Kahn, *On Thermonuclear War*, pp. 74–95).

75. In our day the interdependence of a fruitful theory and concrete experience is taken for granted. In Clausewitz's time, especially in Germany, where 'professorial philosophy' enjoyed enormous prestige, this interdependence had to be repeatedly pointed out.

76. A perceptive remark concerning the interdependence of cognition and judgement. We get to know something only if we have selected it as in some way relevant, hence have exercised judgement. Similarly, we make judgements on the basis of what we think we know.

77. The Condottieri were professional mercenary soldiers of which many European armies were composed in the fourteenth–sixteenth centuries; also the entrepreneurs who raised such armies. See Clausewitz's further remarks on this subject, pp. 378.

78. The analogy has become much closer since Clausewitz's time. Now that the first business of the State is regarded as the development of the facilities for trade, war between great nations is only a question of time. No Hague Conference can avert it. – F.N.M.

This was presumably written in 1908, the year which L. F. Richardson took as the beginning of the arms race that preceded the First World War (cf. p. 43).

79. The 'oblique order of battle' was the formula with which General Phull, as portrayed by Tolstoy in *War and Peace*, was obsessed (see Note 73).

80. An example of a theory which includes the 'peculiar method' of the French Revolutionary armies can be given. A soldier who believes that he has something to fight for need not

be visible to his commander at all times (unlike the soldier who is kept from deserting because he fears his sergeant more than the enemy). Consequently the tactics of the French Revolutionary armies did not require closely packed columns and allowed the use of *tirailleurs*.

81. Compare Clausewitz, *Hinterlassene Werke*, 2nd edition, Vol. IV, p. 276 ff. – F.N.M.

82. Here Clausewitz shows by concrete example the labyrinth of calculations involved in diplo-military strategic decisions – the epitome of Clausewitzian wisdom. His purpose is to show that the rationality of a decision is relative to the depth of the analysis pursued (or the remoteness of the goal envisaged). However, all of the goals are of the same kind: strategic advantages in the pursuit of power. There is no goal beyond power. Recall O'Brien's remark in Orwell's *Nineteen Eighty-Four* (p. 269), 'The object of power is power.'

83. Compare *Hinterlassene Werke*, 2nd edition, Vol. IV, p. 107 ff. – F.N.M.

84. Compare *Hinterlassene Werke*, 2nd edition, Vol. VII, p. 193 ff. – F.N.M.

85. This corresponds to the notion of expected utility in modern decision theory, i.e. the utility of an outcome multiplied by the probability of its occurrence. (cf. J. D. Singer, *Deterrence, Arms Control, and Disarmament*, Chapter 2.) The problem always remains, however, of assigning numerical utilities to outcomes and of estimating probabilities of events. In this connexion, see the editor's *Strategy and Conscience*, Chapter 3.

86. 'Frage an das Schicksal', a familiar quotation from Schiller. (*Translator's note.*)

87. Contemporary theoreticians of nuclear war sometimes mention 'psychological effects' in passing, but since data are so far completely lacking, these references are extremely speculative. Two examples will suffice to establish their flavour.

> Now just imagine yourself in the post-war situation. Everybody will have been subjected to extreme anxiety, unfamiliar environment, strange foods, minimum toilet facilities, inadequate shelters, and the like. Under these conditions some high percentage of the population is going to be nauseated, and nausea is very catching. If one man vomits, everybody vomits. Almost everyone is likely to think he has received too much radiation. Morale may be so affected that many

survivors may refuse to participate in constructive activities, but would content themselves with sitting down and waiting to die – some may even become violent and destructive.

However, this situation would be quite different if radiation meters were distributed. Assume now that a man gets sick from a cause other than radiation. Not believing this, his morale begins to drop. You look at his meter and say, 'You have received only ten roentgens, why are you vomiting? Pull yourself together and work.' (H. Kahn, *On Thermonuclear War*, p. 86.)

A key question is whether the mass of public thoughout the nation will be capable of that measure of understanding and discipline necessary to permit the government to conduct and suffer limited [nuclear] reprisals. (C. C. Abt and Ithiel de Sola Pool in K. Knorr and T. Read [eds.], *Limited Strategic War*, pp. 199–200.)

88. Clausewitz thinks like a scientist. An event can corroborate a hypothesis but can never prove it. True, in the next paragraph Clausewitz alludes to a *proof* of a theory by several converging lines of evidence. We would rather say that the *credibility* of a theory is thereby established for practical purposes.

89. It seems strange that Clausewitz does not mention the Battles of Crécy (1346) and Agincourt (1415).

90. This paragraph refers to the works of Lloyd, Bülow, indeed to all the eighteenth-century writers, from whose influence we in England are not yet free. – F.N.M. See Note 113. – A.R.

91. The whole of this chapter is directed against the theories of the Austrian Staff in 1814. It may be taken as the foundation of modern teaching of the Prussian General Staff. See especially von Kämmer. – F.N.M.

92. Written shortly after the Great Napoleonic Campaigns. – F.N.M.

93. Clausewitz is, of course, thinking of the long-service standing armies of his own youth. – F.N.M.

94. Tempelhof and Montalembert are the first we recollect as examples – the first in a passage of his first part, page 148; the other in his correspondence to the plan of operations of the Russians in 1759. (Clausewitz's note.)

The reference to Tempelhof is to *Geschichte des Siebenjähigen Krieges*, a translation of a work by Lloyd (see Note 113). The reference to Montalembert (according to W. Hahlweg, editor of the Sixteenth Edition of *Vom Kriege*, Bonn, 1952) is to the correspondence of the Marquis de Montalembert, published in London in 1777. – A.R.

95. Owing to our freedom from invasion, and to the conditions which arise in our Colonial Wars, we have not yet, in England, arrived at a correct appreciation of the value of superior numbers in War, and still adhere to the idea of an Army just 'big enough', which Clausewitz has so unsparingly ridiculed. – F.N.M.

96. Railways, steamships, and telegraphs have, however, enormously modified the relative importance and practicability of surprise. – F.N.M.

Presumably by 'modified' Col. Maude means enhanced. The airplane, the submarine, and especially the intercontinental ballistic missile have elevated the element of surprise to a major strategic factor (at least in the minds of the devotees of 'pre-emptive strikes'). – A.R.

97. Tempelhof, The Veteran, Frederick the Great (Clausewitz's note).

Compare also (Clausewitz) *Hinterlassene Werke*, Vol. X, p. 158. – F.N.M.

According to W. Hahlweg, the reference to The Veteran concerns a work published under that pen name, dealing with the relations between Austria and Prussia, published in Breslau, 1781–91.

98. Blücher believed his march to be covered by Pahlen's Cossacks but these had been withdrawn without warning to him by the Grand Army Headquarters under Schwartzenberg. – F.N.M.

99. As already noted, this is no longer true. Threat and counter-threat, bluff and counter-bluff are now integral factors of diplo-military strategy.

100. Refers to the destruction of Vandamme's column, which had been sent unsupported to intercept the retreat of the Austrians and Prussians from Dresden – but was forgotten by Napoleon. – F.N.M.

101. Now we can. – A.R.

102. Similarly those games of chess become immortalized where ingenious combination play triumphs over superior forces. Clausewitz seems to dismiss this romantic view of military strategy. For him war is 'noble' enough, but it is a rather prosaic business, based on sober principles. As a chess player Clausewitz would probably rely on sound positional rather than on brilliant combinatorial play.

103. The relief of the fighting line played a great part in the battles of the Smooth-Bore era; it was necessitated by the fouling of the muskets, physical fatigue of the men and consumption of ammunition, and was recognized as both necessary and advisable by Napoleon himself. – F.N.M.

104. Under the then existing conditions of armament understood. This point is of supreme importance, as practically the whole conduct of a great battle depends on a correct solution of this question – viz. How long can a given command prolong its resistance? If this is incorrectly answered in practice – the whole manoeuvre depending on it may collapse – e.g. Kuropatkin at Liav-Yang, September 1904. – F.N.M.

105. This, however, was not Napoleon's view. A vigorous attack on his advance guard he held to be necessary always, to fix the enemy's attention and 'paralyse his independent will-power'. It was the failure to make this point which in August 1870 led von Moltke repeatedly into the very jaws of defeat, from which only the lethargy of Bazaine on the one hand and the initiative of his subordinates, notably of von Alversleben, rescued him. This is the essence of the new Strategic Doctrine of the French General Staff. See the works of Bonnal, Foch, etc. – F.N.M.

106. Note the custom of sending mutual challenges, fix time and place for action, and 'enhazelug' the battlefield in Anglo-Saxon times. – F.N.M.

107. The political philosophy of war in a nutshell.

108. On the Continent only, it still preserves full vitality in the minds of British politicians and pressmen. – F.N.M.

109. This prayer was abundantly granted – *vide* the German victories of 1870. – F.N.M.

110. This was Molte's essential idea in his preparation for the war of 1870. See his secret memorandum issued to G.O.C.s on 7 May 1870, pointing to a battle on the Upper Saar as his primary purpose. – F.N.M.

111. This point is exceptionally well treated by Bernhardi in his *Cavalry in Future Wars*. London: Murray, 1906. – F.N.M.

However admirably its role in future wars was discussed by General Bernhardi, the cavalry can hardly be said to have had a future in 1906. – A.R.

112. At Hanau (30 October 1813) the Bavarians, some 50,000 strong, threw themselves across the line of Napoleon's retreat

from Leipsic. By a masterly use of its artillery the French tore the Bavarians asunder and marched over their bodies. – F.N.M.

113. Lloyd, Bülow (Clausewitz's note).

The Lloyd to whom Clausewitz refers (1720–83) is the author of a history of the Seven Years' War, translated into German and annotated by Georg Friedrich Tempelhof. Hahlweg (editor of the Sixteenth German Edition) identifies him as Humphrey Evans Lloyd and as a 'Russian General'. According to the *Great Soviet Encyclopedia*, which refers to him as Henry Lloyd, he was born in England and served in the Russian Army. Alfred Vagts in his *History of Militarism* calls him William Lloyd (son of an English divine) and states that he was a military adventurer who served the French, the Austrians, the Prussians, the British (as a political agent), and the Russians. (Perhaps this explains the variety of his Christian names.)

Both Lloyd's career and his outlook (he conceived of war as a fine art and theorized about the possibility of leading a continual war without battles) represent the epitome of the eighteenth-century outlook.

Dietrich Heinrich Bülow (1757–1807) was the leading military authority in pre-Clausewitzian Prussia (see Note 73). In his later years, however, he became a worshipper of Napoleon and a convert to the cause of enlisting nationalism in warfare.

114. In the exact sciences, theory is used precisely in the sense rejected by Clausewitz, namely, in the sense of a collection of theorems deduced rigorously from postulates formulated in 'if so, . . . then so' terms, i.e. as formulas. Clausewitz here uses 'theory' in the sense often used in the social sciences, namely, as a synthesis of concepts which illuminate the subject matter without necessarily enabling us to make specific predictions or to control specific situations.

115. cf. Book I, Chapter 1. (Clausewitz's note.)

116. cf. Book I, Chapter 2. (Clausewitz's note.)

117. If we substitute 'series of wars' for 'series of combats' the political model approaches the messianic–eschatological model of war (cf. p. 15 ff.). From this point of view nothing is decided by the outcome of a single *war*. Only the end result of a series of wars determines the success or failure of an undertaking, in this case of a career of conquest, since the acquisition of territory or of power necessitates further acquisitions to safeguard what has been acquired. Seen in this way, the 'victorious' wars of

Napoleon, the German victories of 1864, 1866, and 1870, and the triumphs of Japan over China (1895) and over Russia (1905) were only episodes presaging the eventual defeat of France, Germany, and Japan. If, then, we extend Clausewitz's dictum that only the outcome of the final *battle* counts in a war to an equally reasonable dictum that only the outcome of the final *war* counts in the career of a war-waging state, we must conclude on the basis of historical experience that military prowess is more likely to lead to defeat than to victory.

118. Had Frederick the Great gained the Battle of Kollin, and taken prisoners the chief Austrian Army with its two field-Marshals in Prague, it would have been such a tremendous blow that he might then have entertained the idea of marching to Vienna to make the Austrian Court tremble, and gain a peace directly. This, in these times, unparalleled result, which would have been quite like what we have seen in our day, only still more wonderful and brilliant from the contest being between a little David and a great Goliath, might very probably have taken place after the gain of this one battle; but that does not contradict the assertion above maintained, for it only refers to what the King originally looked forward to from his offensive. The surrounding and taking prisoners the enemy's Army was an event which was beyond all calculation, and which the King never thought of, at least not until the Austrians laid themselves open to it by the unskilful position in which they placed themselves at Prague. (Clausewitz's note.)

119. See Note 59. Note, however, the reservation in the next sentence.

120. Evidently this was not the case in the United States involvement in South-east Asia.

121. The Neo-Clausewitzians see no difficulty here. They view the continuum between war and peace as a natural consequence of the perpetual struggle for power. Clausewitz also repeatedly refers to this continuum (as he will in a moment), but he finds it difficult to reconcile it with the 'philosophical' study of war, probably because the philosophical mode of thought in which he was immersed was traditionally concerned with singling out clearly distinguishable categories to which the status of reality was assigned.

122. Again the 'half-and-half' nature of war is seen by Clausewitz as a 'contradiction'.

REFERENCES

Abt, C. C., and de Sola Pool, Ithiel. 'The Constraint of Public Attitudes', in K. Knorr and T. Read (eds.), *Limited Strategic War*. New York: Frederick A. Praeger, 1962, Ch. 7, pp. 199–240; also London: Pall Mall Press, 1962.

Aron, Raymond. *Peace and War. A Theory of International Relations*. Translated from the French by Richard Howard and Annette Baker Fox. Garden City, N.Y.: Doubleday, 1966; also London: Weidenfeld & Nicolson, 1967.

Bacon, Francis. *Novum Organum*. Oxford: The Clarendon Press. 1889.

Bernhardi, Friedrich Adam Julius. *Cavalry in Future Wars*. Translated by Charles Sydney Goldman. London: John Murray, 1906.

Brennan, D. G. Review of A. Rapoport's *Strategy and Conscience*, *Bulletin of Atomic Scientists*, Vol. 21, No. 10, 1965, pp. 25–30.

Clausewitz, Carl von. 'Bemerkungen über die reine und angewandte Strategie des Herrn v. Bülow, oder Kritik der darin enthaltenden Ansichten', *Neue Bellona*, Vol. 9, No. 3, 1805.

Clausewitz, Carl von. *Hinterlassene Werke des Generals von Clausewitz über Krieg und Kriegsführung*. Berlin: 1832–37.

Clausewitz, Carl von. *On War*. Translated by Colonel J. J. Graham, new and revised edition with an Introduction and Notes by Colonel F. N. Maude (8th impression). London: Routledge, 1966; also New York: Barnes & Noble, 1966.

Clausewitz, Carl von. *Vom Kriege* (16th edition). (Edited and annotated by Werner Hahlweg.) Bonn: Fred. Dümmlers Verlag, 1952.

Crick, Bernard. *In Defence of Politics*. 1962. Chicago: University of Chicago Press, 1962; also London: Weidenfeld & Nicolson, 1962; also Penguin Books, 1964.

Deutsch, Karl W. and Singer, J. David. 'Multipolar Power Systems and International Stability', *World Politics*, Vol. 16, No. 3, 1964, 390–406.

Earle, Edward Mead (ed.). *Makers of Modern Strategy. Military Thought from Machiavelli to Hitler*. Princeton: Princeton University Press, 1943.

Garthoff, Raymond L. *Soviet Military Doctrine*. Glencoe, Ill.: Free Press, 1953.

Goerlitz, Walter. *History of the German General Staff 1657–1945*. Translated by Brian Battershaw. New York: Frederick A. Praeger, 1953.

Hitler, Adolf. *Mein Kampf*. New York: Stackpole Sons, 1939.

Hobbes, Thomas. *Leviathan* (2nd edition). London and New York: G. Routledge & Sons, 1886.

Horowitz, Irvine L. *The War Game. Studies in the New Civilian Militarism*. New York: Ballantine Books, 1963.

Hume, David. *Enquiry Concerning Human Understanding*. Chicago: The Open Court Publishing Co., 1927; also Oxford University Press, n.e., 1966.

Kahn, Herman. *On Escalation. Metaphors and Scenarios*. New York, Washington: Frederick A. Praeger, 1965; also London: Pall Mall Press, 1965.

Kahn, Herman. *On Thermonuclear War*. Princeton: Princeton University Press, 1960; also Oxford University Press, 1960.

Kahn, Herman. 'The Nature and Feasibility of War and Deterrence', in Davis B. Bobrow (ed.), *Components of Defense Policy*. Chicago: Rand McNally & Company, 1965.

Kahn, Herman. *Thinking about the Unthinkable*. New York: Horizon Press, 1962; also London: Weidenfeld & Nicolson, 1963.

Kissinger, Henry A. *Nuclear Weapons and Foreign Policy*. New York: Harper, 1957; also Oxford University Press, 1957.

Knorr, Klaus and Read, Thornton (eds.). *Limited Strategic War*. New York: Frederick A. Praeger, 1962; also London: Pall Mall Press, 1962.

Langer, William L. *The Diplomacy of Imperialism. 1890–1902*. New York and London: A. A. Knopf, 1935.

Lenin, Nikolai (V. I.). *Imperialism*. New York: The Vanguard Press, 1929.

Lenin, V. I. *Materialism and Empirio-criticism. Critical Comments on a Reactionary Philosophy*. New York: International Publishers, 1927.

Leninsky Sbornik (a serial publication). Moscow-Leningrad: Institut Lenina, 1924——.

Lloyd, Henry. *Geschichte des Siebenjährigen Krieges*. Translated from English and annotated by G. F. Tempelhof. Berlin: J. F. Unger, 1783–1801.

Machiavelli, Niccoló. *The Art of War*. Indianapolis: Bobbs-Merrill, 1965.

Machiavelli, Niccoló. *The Florentine History*. Translated from the Italian by Ninian Hill Thomson. London: Constable & Co., 1906.

Machiavelli, Niccoló. *The Prince*. Translated by George Bull. Harmondsworth and Baltimore: Penguin Books, 1961.

Mao Tze-Tung. *On Protracted War*. Peking: Foreign Language Press, 1954.

Mao Tze-Tung. *Strategic Problems of China's Revolutionary War*. Peking: Foreign Language Press, 1954.

Marx, Karl. *Capital*. New York: The Modern Library, 1936.

Maschler, Michael. 'A Price Leadership Method for Solving the Inspector's Non-constant-sum Game', *Naval Research Logistics Quarterly*, Vol. 13, 1966, pp. 11–33.

Mensch, A. (ed.). *Theory of Games, Techniques and Applications* (The proceedings of a conference under the aegis of the NATO Scientific Affairs Committee at Toulon, 29 June–3 July 1964). London: The English Universities Press, 1966.

Montalembert, Marc-René. *Correspondance de Mr le Marquis de Montalembert*. London, 1777.

Morgenstern, Oskar. *The Question of National Defense*. New York: Random House, 1959.

Oglesby, Carl. 'Vietnam: This is Guernica', *Nation*, 204, p. 720, 5 June 1967.

Orwell, George. *Nineteen Eighty-Four*. London: Secker & Warburg, 1959; also Penguin Books, 1954.

Osgood, Charles E. *Alternative to War or Surrender*. Urbana: University of Illinois Press, 1962.

Osgood, Robert E. *Limited War. The Challenge to American Strategy*. Chicago: The University of Chicago Press, 1957.

Paret, Peter. 'Clausewitz. A bibliographical Survey', *World Politics*, Vol. 17, No. 2, 1965, pp. 272–85.

Phelps, John B., *et al. Accidental War. Some Dangers in the 1960's*. Columbus: Mershon National Security Program, June 1960.

Pustay, John S. *Counter-insurgency Warfare*. New York: The Free Press of Glencoe and London: Collier-Macmillan, 1965.

Rapaport, Anatol. *Fights, Games, and Debates*. Ann Arbor: University of Michigan Press, 1960.

Rapoport, Anatol, *Strategy and Conscience*. New York, Evanston, and London: Harper & Row, 1964.

Richardson, Lewis F. *Arms and Insecurity*. Pittsburgh: Boxwood Press, and Chicago: Quadrangle Books, 1960; also London: Stevens, 1960.

Richardson, Lewis F. *Statistics of Deadly Quarrels*. Pittsburgh: Boxwood Press, and Chicago: Quadrangle Books, 1960; also London: Stevens, 1960.

Rummel, R. J. 'Some Dimensions in the Foreign Relations of Nations', *Journal of Peace Research*, 1966 3, pp. 201–24.

Rüstow, Wilhelm. *Geschichte der Infanterie*. Nordhausen: F. Foerstemann, 1864.

Schelling, Thomas C. *Arms and Influence*. New Haven and London: Yale University Press, 1966.

Schelling, Thomas C. 'The Strategy of Conflict: Prospectus for a Reorientation of Game Theory', *The Journal of Conflict Resolution*, Vol. 2, No. 3, 1958, pp. 203–64.

Schelling, Thomas C. 'Strategy, Tactics and Non-Zero-Sum Theory', in A. Mensch (ed.), *Theory of Games, Techniques and Applications*. London: English Universities Press, 1966.

Schwarts, Karl. *Leben des Generals Carl von Clausewitz und der Frau Maria von Clausewitz*. Berlin: Fred. Dümmlers Verlag, 1878.

Shaposhnikov, Boris M. *Mozg Armii*. Moscow–Leningrad: Gosizdat, 1929.

Singer, J. David. *Deterrence, Arms Control, and Disarmament*. Columbus: Ohio State University Press, 1962.

Smith, Adam. *The Wealth of Nations*. London: J. M. Dent & Sons, and New York: E. P. Dutton & Co., 1934–7.

Sokolovsky, Vasilii D. (ed.). *Military Strategy. Soviet Doctrine and Concepts*. New York and London: Frederick A. Praeger, 1963.

Stouffer, Samuel A., *et al. The American Soldier: Adjustment During Army Life*. New York: John Wiley & Sons, and London: Oxford University Press, 1949.

Tanter, Raymond. 'Dimensions of Conflict within and between Nations, 1958–1960', *Journal of Conflict Resolution*, Vol. 10, No. 1, 1966, pp. 41–64.

Tolstoy, Leo. *War and Peace*. New York: Grosset & Dunlap, 1956; also Penguin, 1957.

Tuchman, Barbara W. *The Proud Tower. A Portrait of the World Before the War, 1890–1914*. New York: The Macmillan Company, 1966; also London: Hamish Hamilton, 1966.

Tucker, Robert W. *The Just War. Exposition of American Con-*

cept. Baltimore: The Johns Hopkins Press, 1960; also Oxford University Press, 1961.

Urlanis, B. Ts. *Voinyi Narodoselenie Evropy* (Wars and the European Populations). Moscow: Izdatelstvo Sotsialno-ekonomicheskoi Literatury, 1960.

Vagts, Alfred. *A History of Militarism*, revised edition. New York: Meridian Books, 1959; also London: Hollis & Co., 1960.

Von Neumann, John, and Morgenstern, Oskar. *Theory of Games and Economic Behavior* (2nd edition). Princeton: Princeton University Press, 1947; also Oxford University Press, 1947.

Wohlstetter, Albert. 'The Delicate Balance of Terror', *Foreign Affairs*, Vol. 37, No. 2, 1958.

Wolfers, Arnold, *et al. Developments in Military Technology and their Impact on United States Strategy and Foreign Policy*. Washington: Washington Center of Foreign Policy Research (prepared for U.S. Senate Foreign Relations Committee), 1959.

Wright, Quincy. *A Study of War*. Chicago: University of Chicago Press, 1942 (2nd edition, 1965).

GLOSSARY OF MILITARY LEADERS, AUTHORS, AND ENGAGEMENTS

Alexander, the Great, King of Macedonia 356–323 B.C. Conqueror of Greece and of the Persian Empire; usually named one of history's greatest military leaders.

Alexander I, 1777–1825. Emperor of Russia. Waged war against Napoleon in the Campaign of 1805, in which the Russians and the Austrians were defeated; concluded peace in 1807 (Tilsit), which lasted until Napoleon's invasion of Russia in 1812. After the Napoleonic wars Alexander became one of the founders of the Holy Alliance (with Austria and Prussia) aimed at suppressing revolution in Europe.

Alvensleben, Karl Gebhard, 1778–1831. Prussian soldier; participated in French Revolutionary Wars (campaigns of 1792, 1794) under the Duke of Brunswick; in the Battle of Jena (1806); in the Battle of Bautzen (1813).

Arcis (N.E. France). Site of engagement in the Campaign of 1814, one of several reverses suffered by Napoleon in that campaign.

Arjuna. Mythical Hindu leader; a hero of the *Mahabharata* (an epic).

Auerstädt (Saxony). Site of battle in the Campaign of 1806, shortly after the Battle of Jena; defeat of the Prussians by the French (14 October). The Battle of Jena was fought on the same day.

Augustus, Prince (1696–1763). Augustus III, King of Poland and Elector of Saxony; supported Austria in the Silesian Wars and again in the Seven Years' War.

Austerlitz (Moravia). Battle in the Campaign of 1805 (2 December); Napoleon's decisive victory over the Russians and the Austrians.

Auvray, Louis Marie, 1762–1833. French soldier, Marshal of France; served with Napoleon.

Bassano, Duke of (Hugues-Bernard-Maret), 1763–1839. French diplomat and statesman; supported Napoleon and accompanied him on his campaigns; made Duke in 1809.

Bautzen (Saxony). Site of battle in the Campaign of 1813;

Russians and Prussians defeated by Napoleon (20 May). Also called Gross Gorchen.

Belle Alliance (see Waterloo).

Bazaine, Achille-François, 1811–88. French soldier, Marshal of France; commander of the army corps in Lorraine in the War of 1870; capitulated on 28 October, denounced as traitor by Gambetta.

Belleisle, Charles-Louis-Auguste-Fouquet, Count, then Duke, 1684–1761. French soldier in the service of Louis XV; Marshal of France; led an unsuccessful campaign against Piedmont in 1746; made Minister of War in 1750.

Belleisle, Louis-Charles-Armand-Fouquet, 1693–1746; brother of the above; killed in the campaign against Piedmont in 1746.

Benedek, Ludwig August, Ritter von, 1804–81. Commander of the Auatrian army in the Battle of Königgrätz (Sadowa), decisively defeated by the Prussians.

Bernadotte, Jean, later Charles XIV, King of Sweden, 1763–1844. French soldier, made Marshal of France in 1804; held political posts under Napoleon; invited to become Crown Prince of Sweden in 1810 (adopted as son of childless Charles XIII); became king in 1818.

Bernhardi, Friedrich von, 1849–1930. German soldier and military writer, noted as the author of *Deutschland und der nächste Krieg* (Germany and the Next War, 1912), in which he vigorously defended war as an institution. This work was often quoted as evidence of Germany's aggressive intention in the First World War.

Blücher, Gebhard Leberecht von, 1742–1819. Prussian soldier; field-marshal; one of the most prominent military leaders in the Napoleonic wars.

Bonnal (probably Edmond Bonnal de Gange, 1839–1915). French military writer, author of *Les Royalistes contre l'armée, 1815–20.*

Borodino (near Moscow). Most famous battle of the Campaign of 1812, where the Russians, after a long retreat, made a stand in defence of Moscow. The Russians retreated but were not routed. The French lost 25,000, the Russians 38,000.

Brienne (France). Site of engagement in the Campaign of 1814 (29 January). Napoleon tried unsuccessfully to prevent the juncture of Blücher's and Schwartzenberg's forces.

Brandt, Heinrich, 1789–1868. Prussian soldier; served under Napoleon (in the Grand Army of the Dukedom of Warsaw,

1807–13); rejoined the Prussian army in 1813; author of military works, e.g., *Grundzüge der Taktik der drei Waffen* (Foundations of Tactics of the Three Arms, 1833), widely translated.

Bunzelwitz (Silesia). The site of Frederick the Great's entrenched camp in the Seven Years' War (1761).

Bülow (see Note 113).

Buonaparte (Napoleon Bonaparte), 1769–1821. French soldier (of Corsican origin), later Emperor of France and conqueror of most of Europe. Hostile writers often referred to him as Buonaparte to emphasize his non-French origin. (He himself spelled it so until 1796.)

Caesar, Caius Julius (100–44 B.C.) Roman soldier and statesman, and military writer; conqueror of Gaul; usually named as one of history's most outstanding military leaders.

Campo Formio (N.E. Italy). Site of temporary peace treaty between France and Austria (17 October 1797) advantageous to France.

Carnot, Lazare-Nicolas-Marguerite, 1753–1823. French scientist, soldier, and politician, especially prominent in the early period of the French Revolutionary Wars, author of treatises on military topics; father of Nicolas-Léonard-Sadi Carnot who is generally credited with the first formulation of the Second Law of Thermodynamics.

Chambray, Georges, Marquis, 1783–1850 (?). French soldier and historian; participated in the Campaigns of 1806, 1807, 1809; captured by the Russians in 1812; returned to France after the fall of Napoleon and continued in military service; author of *Histoire de l'expédition de Russie* and *La philosophie de la guerre* (1827).

Champ Aubert (N. France). An engagement in the Campaign of 1814 (one of three on three consecutive days) in which Napoleon, already fighting a losing war, scored a success against the British under York.

Charles, Archduke, 1771–1847. Austrian soldier, son of Emperor Leopold II, field-marshal; fought against France since 1793; faced Napoleon in Bavaria in 1809 and was defeated; wounded in the Battle of Wagram.

Charles V, 1500–58. Emperor of the Holy Roman Empire; succeeded Ferdinand the Catholic as King of Spain; chosen emperor in 1519; established Spanish rule over the Netherlands.

Charles VIII, 1470–98. King of France, son of Louis XI; invaded Italy in 1494. This invasion is sometimes mentioned as the beginning of the European 'national state' system.

Charles XII, King of Sweden, 1682–1718. Waged wars against Denmark, Poland, and Russia; suffered severe defeat by the Russians at Poltava (1709).

Choiseul, Etienne-François, Duke, 1719–85. French statesman and soldier; Minister of Foreign Affairs, then, succeeding Belleisle, Minister of War to Louis XV.

Condé, Louis II de Bourbon, Prince (surnamed the Great), 1621–86. French soldier; fought in many wars waged by Louis XIV. The fact that some historians see fit to deny that Condé's stature compares with that of Alexander, Frederick II, Napoleon, etc., indicates that he was a very prominent figure in military history.

Daun, Leopold Joseph, Graf, 1705–66. Austrian soldier; commander-in-chief in the Seven Years' War; won some successes against Frederick the Great; heavily defeated by the Prussians in 1760 and severely wounded.

Davout, Louis-Nicolas, 1770–1823. French soldier; Marshal of France; distinguished in the Battle of Austerlitz (1805) and at Auerstädt (1806); held various political posts under Napoleon.

Diebitsch (Diebitsch-Zabalkansky), Johann Karl Friedrich Anton, Count, 1785–1831. Soldier of German descent in Russian service; participated in the Campaign of 1805; wounded in the Battle of Austerlitz; fought in the Battles of Dresden and Leipzig (1813).

Dresden (Saxony). Site of Napoleon's last major victory (27 August 1813), where the Austrians and the Russians were routed. Napoleon, however, did not exploit the success, having succumbed to a lethargic mood, which came over him with increasing frequency in the last years of his career.

Dürrenstein (near Krems, Austria). Site of action in the Campaign of 1805 (11 November), erroneously dated 1809 in this volume.

Étoges (N. France). Site of an engagement in the Campaign of 1814, in which Napoleon, already fighting a losing war, scored a surprise success against the Prussians under Blücher (February).

Eugène (François Eugène), Prince of Savoy-Carignan, 1663–1736. Outstanding military leader of French origin in the service of Emperor Leopold I of Austria. He had been denied a commission by Louis XIV. Fought against France. It is said that Louis XIV, having realized his earlier mistake, offered Eugène a Marshal's baton, the governship of Champagne, and a pension of 20,000 pistoles ($80,000), but that Eugène declined to return to the service of his land of birth.

Fabius (Quintus Fabius Maximus), died in 203 B.C., Roman soldier, noted for his cautious tactics against Hannibal (surnamed Cuncator – 'the Delayer').

Farnese, Alexander, 1546–92. Military leader of Spanish origin in the service of Austria; noted for his aggressive tactics. It is said that as a young man he would roam the streets of Madrid, provoking passers-by to sword fights.

Ferdinand II, The Catholic, 1452–1516. King of United Spain (with Isabella); expelled the Moors from the Iberian Peninsula in 1492; admired by Machiavelli; laid the groundwork for Spain's imperial power.

Feuquières, Antoine Manassés de Pas, Marquis, 1648–1711. French soldier, served with Marshal Luxemburg in various campaigns in the late seventeenth century; author of *Mémoirs sur la guerre* (1711). (English translation, *Memoirs of the Marquis de Feuquières*, London, 1737.)

Foch, Ferdinand, 1851–1929. French soldier, Marshal of France, supreme commander of Allied forces on the Western Front at the end of the First World War; a zealous student of German military thought and an admirer of Clausewitz.

Francis II, 1768–1835. Emperor of Austria at the time of Austria's defeats by Napoleon in 1805 and 1809.

Frederick II, the Great, King of Prussia, 1712–86. Outstanding military figure; waged several wars, notably the Silesian Wars against Austria (1740–46); a principal in the Seven Years' War (1756–63). The militarization of Prussia is often traced to his career. Clausewitz sometimes refers to Frederick as simply the King.

Freiberg (Saxony). Site of the Prussians' victory over Austria in the Seven Years' War (29 October 1762), which led to the armistice (24 November).

French Revolutionary Wars. The general designation of the continental wars in the period between the French Revolution and the interlude of 1801–3. The principal campaigns were in the Low Countries, in Germany, and in Italy, where Napoleon won his first spectacular victories.

Friedland (E. Germany). Battle in the Campaign of 1807, noted chiefly for the first display of Napoleon's novel artillery tactics; Russians defeated; peace concluded between Napoleon and Emperor Alexander of Russia shortly afterwards (at Tilsit) which lasted until Napoleon's invasion of Russia in 1812.

Glatz (Silesia). Prussian stronghold captured by the Austrians under Laudon in the Seven Years' War (26 July 1760).

Gneisenau, August Wilhelm Anton Neidhardt, Graf, 1760–1831. Prussian soldier, field-marshal; served as first general field officer under von Scharnhorst (Chief of Staff); made Chief of General Staff in 1813; Chief of Staff under Blücher in 1815.

Grawert, Johann Andreas Rudolf von, 1746–1817. Prussian soldier; participated in the Battle of Jena and in the Campaign of 1812 against Russia (when Prussia was allied with Napoleon).

Gustavus Adolphus, King of Sweden, 1594–1632. Noted military figure; led several campaigns in Livonia against Poland and in the Thirty Years' War; killed in battle.

Gross Gorchen (see Bautzen).

Hanau (see Note 112).

Hannibal, 247–183 or 182 B.C. Carthaginian military leader, invaded Italy in 218 B.C. during the Second Punic War.

Hennersdorf (Bohemia). Site of engagement in the Second Silesian War (23 November 1745); Austrians defeated by Prussians.

Henry IV, King of France, 1553–1610. Participated in religious wars in France; at first a Protestant, later converted to Catholicism.

Hoche, Lazare, 1768–97. French soldier, distinguished in the Revolutionary Wars; Minister of War for a short period in 1797.

Hochkirch (Saxony). Battle in the Seven Years' War (14 October 1758). Austrians under Daun defeated Frederick of Prussia with a superior force (90,000 *vs.* 37,000). The victory was costly, however, and did not interfere with Frederick's retreat into Silesia.

Hohenlohe, Ingelfinger Friedrich Ludwig, Prince, 1746–1818. Prussian soldier; fought in the Campaign of the Rhine in 1794; noted for the crushing defeat at Jena, where his army was virtually destroyed by Napoleon (14 October 1806). Hohenlohe surrendered the remainder of his forces and spent two years as a prisoner in France.

Hollabrünn (Lower Austria). Site of an action in the Campaign of 1805 (16 November).

Jena (Thuringia). Perhaps the most decisive battle of the Napoleonic Wars (14 October 1806). Prussian army of 120,000 men was completely routed and its commander taken prisoner. This defeat led to a reorganization of the Prussian army and the eventual build-up of the vast Prussian military machine.

Kalkreuth (Kalckreuth), Friedrich Adolf, 1736–1818. Prussian soldier; fought against France since 1792; unsuccessfully defended Dantzig in 1807; vigorous opponent of Prussian army reforms of 1808–14.

Kaluga Road. On his retreat from Moscow Napoleon attempted to take this road instead of the Smolensk Road on which he came, since that route had been devastated. He was prevented from doing so. Forced upon the Smolensk Road, his army was subjected to privations which contributed to its dissolution.

Kesseldorf (Saxony). Site of a victory by the Prussians under Leopold von Anhalt over the Saxons in the Second Silesian War (15 December 1745).

Kiesewetter, Johann Christoph, 1666–1744. German philosopher, author of a glossary of military terms and expressions with historical annotations. In an anecdote, related by Col. F. N. Maude, the translator of this work, Clausewitz is described by Brandt as an adherent of Kiesewetter 'who had indoctrinated him in the philosophy of Kant'. This does not seem likely since Kant was only twenty years old when Kiesewetter died.

Kolin (Bohemia). Battle in the Seven Years' War (18 June 1757). Austrians under Daun defeated the Prussians and lifted the siege of Prague.

Königgrätz (Bohemia). Battle in the War of 1866 (Seven Weeks' War) in which the Prussians scored a decisive victory over the Austrians (3 July); also known as the Battle of Sadowa.

Kruger, Stephanus Johannes Paulus, 1825–1904. President of the South African Republic and leader of the Boers in the events leading up to the Boer War between the Boers and the British.

Kulm (Bohemia). Battle in the Campaign of 1813 (29–30 August); the French defeated by the Austrians, Prussians, and Russians.

Kunersdorf (E. Germany). Site of a major defeat of Frederick of Prussia by the Austrians and the Russians in the Seven Years' War (12 August 1759).

Kouropatkin, Alexei Nikolaevich, 1848–1925. Russian Commander-in-Chief in the Russo-Japanese War (1904–5).

Laon (N. France). Battle in the Campaign of 1814. Napoleon, defeated by the Allies, was left with only 30,000 men and henceforth had to abandon all plans of offensive operations.

Le Bou, Gustave, 1841–1931, French sociologist, student of mass psychology; author of *La Psychologie des foules* (Psychology of Mobs, 1895).

Liao-Yang (Manchuria). Battle in the Russo–Japanese War; Russians defeated by the Japanese (25 August–2 September 1904).

Laudon, Gideon Ernst, 1716–90. Austrian soldier; fought in the Silesian Wars and in the Seven Years' War; defeated the Prussians at Kunersdorf.

Lascy, Joseph Franz Moritz, Count, 1725–1801. Austrian soldier; fought against Frederick the Great in the Seven Years' War; scored successes in 1756 and 1758.

Liegnitz. Town in Silesia, site of a battle in the Seven Years' War. Frederick the Great defeated the Austrians under Laudon, 15 August 1760.

Leipzig (Saxony). Battle in the Campaign of 1813, also known as the Battle of Nations. Napoleon suffered a major defeat, which initiated the disintegration of his power (18 October 1813).

Leuthen (Silesia). The greatest of Frederick's victories in the Seven Years' War. With 43,000 men he attacked 72,000 under Charles of Lorraine and utterly routed the latter. Frederick lost 6,000 men; Charles 22,000. Breslau fell to the Prussians.

Lichtenberg, Georg Christoph, 1742–99. German satirist.

Liegnitz (Silesia). Action in the Seven Years' War, in which an attempted encirclement of Prussian forces by the Austrians and the Russians was frustrated by Frederick the Great (15 August 1760).

Lloyd (see Note 113).

Louis XI, 1423–83. King of France, sometimes mentioned as the founder of diplomatic art as an end in itself.

Louis XIV, 1638–1715. King of France; waged lengthy wars of conquest that eventually exhausted France and prepared the crisis of absolute monarchy.

Louis, Prince. Probably Louis Ferdinand (?–1806), nephew of Frederick the Great.

Luxemburg, François-Henri de Montmorency-Bouteville, Duke, 1628–95. French soldier, Marshal of France; served under

Condé; defeated the Prince of Orange and ravaged Holland in 1673; also defeated William III of England in 1691.

MacDonald, Jacques-Étienne-Joseph-Alexandre, 1765–1840. French soldier; Marshal of France; fought in the Revolutionary Wars, then under Napoleon; distinguished in the Battle of Wagram; remained faithful to Napoleon after many deserted him following his defeats.

Mantua (Lombardy). City besieged by Napoleon in 1796. Several attempts by the Austrians to lift the siege were repulsed; Mantua surrendered 2 February 1797.

Marathon. Battle in the Graeco–Persian War. Athenians under Miltiades defeated the Persians 490 B.C. It is sometimes cited as a foremost example of a decisive battle.

Maria Theresia, 1717–80. Empress of Austria. The Silesian Wars and the Seven Years' War were fought during her reign.

Marlborough, John Churchill, Duke, 1650–1722. English soldier, noted for his victories over the French in the War of the Spanish Succession.

Marmont, Auguste-Frédéric-Louis Viesse de, 1774–1852. French soldier, Marshal of France; served in the Revolutionary Wars and under Napoleon; defected in 1814.

Massenbach, Christian von, 1768–1827. German tactician and historian; served with Hohenlohe during the Napoleonic Wars; in 1817 convicted of disclosing state secrets (in his historical writings) and sentenced to fourteen years' imprisonment; pardoned in 1826.

Mélas, Michel, 1730–1806. German soldier; participated in Seven Years' War; served as commander of Austrian forces under Suvorov (Russian general in command of combined Austro–Russian forces in 1799).

Moltke, Helmuth Karl Bernhard, 1800–91. Chief of Prussian, then German General Staff; organizer of the victorious wars against Austria (1866) and France (1870).

Moltke, Helmuth Johannes Ludwig von, 1848–1916. Chief of Germany's General Staff at the beginning of the First World War; inherited from his predecessor Schlieffen the master plan for a war on two fronts *vs.* France and Russia; relieved of duty in September 1914, when the offensive against France was stopped.

Montalembert, Marc-René, Marquis, 1714–1800. French military engineer and writer, inventor of a new system of field fortifications; emigrated at the start of the Revolution but returned and was made general in 1792; worked with Lazare Carnot.

Montereau (N. France). An engagement in the Campaign of 1814 in which Napoleon suddenly struck at the pursuing Allies and scored a success (18 February).

Montmirail (N. France). An engagement in the Campaign of 1814, in which Napoleon scored a surprise success against the Allies (February); see also Étoges and Champ Aubert.

Moreau, Jean-Victor-Marie, 1763–1813. French soldier; participated in the Revolutionary Wars; noted for his victory over the Austrians in the Battle of Hohenlinden; opposed Napoleon after 1800 and was exiled; joined anti-Bonaparte forces in 1813; mortally wounded in the Battle of Dresden.

Mormant (N. France). Site of an engagement in the Campaign of 1814, one of several in which Napoleon scored successes against the pursuing Allies.

Napoleonic Wars. The general designation of the continental wars in the period between the 'peace' of 1801–3 and 1815, when Napoleon waged wars against different combinations of states (some of which at times sided with him). The principal successful campaigns were those of 1805 against Austria (aided by Russia); 1806–7 against Prussia (aided by Russia); and 1809 against Austria. The campaign of 1812, the invasion of Russia, resulted in the loss of Napoleon's entire army. In the campaigns of 1813 and 1814 Napoleon passed to the defensive and was finally defeated. His last attempt in 1815 ended at Waterloo.

Narva (Estonia). Scene of defeat of the Russians under Peter the Great by the Swedes under Charles XII (30 November 1700)

Neresheim (Württemberg). Site of engagement in French Revolutionary Wars (11 August 1796).

Pahlen, Pavel Petrovich, ?–1836. Russian soldier, distinguished in the campaigns of 1812, 1813, and 1814.

Pandav, *ca* tenth century B.C., leader of one of two feuding families in India, a hero of *Mahabharata* (an epic).

Phul (see Note 73).

Punic Wars. A series of wars in the third and second centuries B.C. between Rome and Carthage, ending in the complete destruction of the latter.

Puységur, Jacques-François, 1656–1743. French soldier, Marshal of France in the service of Louis XIV.

Ratisbon (Regensburg, Bavaria). Battle in the Campaign of 1809 (23 April). The Austrians were defeated and the French sacked the city.

Rivoli (Rivoli Veronese, N. Italy). Site of engagement in Napoleon's Italian Campaign, 14 January 1797; Austrians defeated.

Rossbach (Thuringia). Battle in the Seven Years' War (5 November 1757). Prussians under Seydlitz (21,000) defeated French and Austrians (41,000); Allies lost 7,000 men, the Prussians 550.

Rüchel, Ernst Friedrich Wilhelm Philipp, 1754–1823. Prussian soldier; fought in the Revolutionary Wars against France since 1792; served under Hohenlohe, for whom he had little respect; committed his troops too late in the Battle of Jena; launched rash attacks to redeem his mistake, wounded and taken prisoner.

Saalfeld (Thuringia). Sight of a defeat of the Prussians under the Duke of Brunswick by the French (10 October 1806), a few days before the Battle of Jena.

Scharnhorst, Gerhard Johann David von, 1755–1813. Prussian soldier; 'father' of the German General Staff; active in the Prussian Army Reform Commission, created after the defeat of Prussia at Jena; received a wound in the Battle of Lutzen (1813) from which he did not recover.

Schwartzenberg, Karl Philipp, Prince, 1771–1820. Austrian soldier and diplomat; was made general at the age of twenty-five; won a victory against the French in 1805 and managed to disengage after the defeat of Ulm; Vice President of the Supreme War Council (1805–8); distinguished in the Battle of Wagram.

Sedan (N. France). Site of decisive defeat of the French by the Prussians (1 September 1870), leading to the capitulation of Napoleon III and the dissolution of his empire.

Seven Years' War, 1756–63. Principal antagonists: Austria *vs* Prussia, Russia on Austria's side until 1762; also France and Sweden; Britain allied with Prussia. Coincided with the war between England and France in America, known as the French and Indian War. In 1762, upon the death of Empress Elizabeth of Russia, Peter III, an admirer of Frederick the Great, concluded peace and later aided Frederick until he (Peter) himself was deposed by his wife (Catherine II), who, however, did not resume the war. Frederick was saved from defeat by Russia's switch.

Ségur, Louis-Phillippe, Count, 1753–1830. French historian, a favourite of Napoleon, who conferred upon him several honours but never invested him with political power.

Silesian Wars, 1740–42 and 1744–5. Wars waged by Frederick the Great against Austria for the possession of Silesia, which he gained. These wars were part of a wider war (War of the Austrian Succession) in which France and England also participated.

Soor (Bohemia). Site of Frederick's victory over the Austrians in the Second Silesian War (30 September 1745), opening the road to Dresden.

St Privat-Gravelotte. Battle in the Franco–Prussian War (18 August 1870). The French attempted to break through Prussian lines and failed. Thereupon Metz was besieged, and the Germans advanced on Chalon Segan.

Tauentzien, Bogislaw Friedrich Emanuel, Graf, 1760–1824. Prussian soldier; participated in the Battle of Jena; in 1813 commanded a corps and captured some cities from the retreating French.

Tauroggen. Town in Lithuania, seat of a convention at which the Prussian Auxiliary Corps was declared 'neutral' in the Campaign of 1812.

Tempelhof (see Notes 94 and 97).

Thirty Years' War. General name given to a series of religious wars (1618–48) which resulted in the devastation of Germany.

Ulm (Württemberg). Site of the Austrians' entrenched camp in the Campaign of 1805 (under General Mack) and of their crushing defeat by Napoleon (October).

Valmy (N. France). Battle in the French Revolutionary Wars (20 September 1792). The cannonade cost the Prussians and the French only 200 casualties; nevertheless the Prussians abandoned their plan to attack, and withdrew. This battle is cited by Delbruck (*Geschichte der Kriegskunst*) as the first confrontation between the 'Frederickian' and the 'Neo-French' (i.e., French Revolutionary) tactics.

Veteran (see Note 97).

Von der Goltz, probably Rüdiger, Count, 1865–1946. Prussian general; commanded the Baltic Division in the First World War; in cooperation with Mannerheim of Finland crushed the Bolshevik revolution in the Baltic countries; during the Weimar Republic headed an extreme right wing political organization.

Vandamme, Dominique-René, Count, 1770–1830. French soldier; served in the Revolutionary and Napoleonic Wars, distinguished in the Battle of Austerlitz; compelled to surrender at Kulm in the Campaign of 1813; rejoined Napoleon in 1815 and fought at Waterloo.

Vaudancourt (Vaudoncourt), Frédéric-François-Guillaume, 1772–1845. French soldier; served under Moreau, later mostly in administrative and organization positions until 1809 when he returned to line duty; taken prisoner by the Russians in 1812; offered position in Russian service in 1814, which he refused; rejoined Napoleon in the Hundred Days; condemned to death by the restored Monarchy; fled into exile.

Vitry (N. France). Blücher's base of operations in February 1814.

Wagram (near Vienna). Battle in the Campaign of 1809; French defeated Austrians (5–6 July) but suffered heavy casualties.

Wallenstein, Albrecht Wenzel Eusebius von, 1583–1634. German soldier and statesman, prominent in the Thirty Years' War, in the service of the Emperor; was subsequently accused of treason and murdered. The murderers were rewarded by the Emperor.

War of Austrian Succession, 1740–48 (see Silesian Wars).

Wars of Liberation. The Campaigns of 1813 and 1814 were so called by the Prussians, who arose against Napoleon after his reverses in the Campaign of 1812.

War of Spanish Succession, 1701–14. Dynastic war between France (allied with Savoy, Bavaria, Cologne) and Austria (allied with Prussia and England).

War of 1870. Prussia decisively defeated France. Thereafter the German Empire was established under Prussian leadership.

Waterloo (also called Belle Alliance). Napoleon's last battle, in which he was defeated by a mixed force of English, Belgians, and Dutch commanded by Wellington, and Prussians commanded by Blücher (18 June 1815).

Wellington, Arthur Wellesley, Duke, 1769–1852. British soldier; fought against France in the Revolutionary Wars under York and in the Napoleonic Wars in Spain and Portugal (1811–12); most celebrated by the final victory over Napoleon at Waterloo (18 June 1815).

Wittgenstein, Ludwig Adolf Peter, 1769–1843. Russian soldier of German descent; participated in the Battle of Austerlitz and Friedland; commanded the right wing of the Russian army in the Campaign of 1812; took command of Russian army after Kutuzov's death; severely wounded in 1814.

Württemberg. Crown Prince of (later William I, King of Württemberg). Was temporarily allied with Napoleon but joined the Allies against him in 1813.

York, Frederick Augustus, Duke, 1763–1827. Second son of George III; commanded English contingent of Coburg's army in the French Revolutionary Wars, made field-marshal in 1795 and commander-in-chief in 1798.

INDEX

References to G are to be found in the glossary on p. 439.